The Defeat of the German U-Boats

Studies in Maritime History
William N. Still, Jr., General Editor

The Defeat of the German U-Boats
The Battle of the Atlantic

David Syrett

UNIVERSITY OF SOUTH CAROLINA PRESS

Copyright © 1994 University of South Carolina

Published in Columbia, South Carolina, by the
University of South Carolina Press

Manufactured in the United States of America

Library of Congress Cataloging-in-Publication Data

Syrett, David.
     The defeat of the German U-boats : Battle of the Atlantic /
David Syrett.
          p.   cm.
     Includes bibliographical references and index.
     ISBN 0–87249–984–7 (alk. paper)
     1. World War, 1939–1945 — Naval operations — Submarine.   2. World
War, 1939–1945 — Campaigns — Atlantic Ocean.   3. Anti-submarine
warfare — History.   4. World War, 1939–1945 — Naval operations,
British.   5. World War, 1939–1945 — Naval operations, American.
6. World War, 1939–1945 — Naval operations, German.   I. Title.
D780.S96   1994
940.54'516'09163 — dc20   93–44333

For Eleni

CONTENTS

PREFACE

The Battle of the Atlantic began on 1 September 1939 and lasted until V-E Day 1945. It was the longest, largest, and most complex naval battle in history. During the course of this huge sprawling conflict, hundreds of Allied ships and scores of German U-boats were sunk, and thousands of Allied and German sailors were either killed, wounded, or posted as missing. The Battle of the Atlantic began in the maritime approaches to Great Britain, with U-boats operating alone against independently sailing merchant ships. As the resources became available, the Allies combated the U-boats by instituting a system of convoys.

The Germans countered the Allied convoys by shifting the area of U-boat operations to regions where Allied merchant shipping still sailed independently. Thus, when the first Allied convoys were used along the east coast of the United Kingdom, German U-boat operations were simply moved west into the eastern Atlantic. With the extension of the convoy system into the Atlantic and the entry of the United States into the war, U-boat operations were undertaken off the east coast of North America and in the West Indies. Thousands of tons of independently sailing Allied merchant ships were sunk in these campaigns. But, as the U-boats shifted their areas of operation, the Allies relentlessly expanded their system of convoys until, by the end of 1942, most Allied merchant ships in the North Atlantic were sailing under convoy.

It was at this time that the Germans began sustained attacks against Allied convoys proceeding back and forth across the North Atlantic—with U-boats operating in groups known as wolf packs. They chose this area because the North Atlantic convoy route was not only the weak link in the Allied system of convoys, but also the most important of those routes, the route that would have a decisive effect on the Allied conduct of the war. At the beginning of 1943, Allied convoys running between North America and Great Britain were especially vulnerable to attack by U-boats because a great part of their voyage had to be made without air cover, and the Germans judged Allied escort forces in the mid-Atlantic to be seriously deficient. The results of a successful 1943 U-boat campaign in the North Atlantic would be strategically important beyond calculation. If the U-boats were successful there, Britain would be neutralized; there would be no more aid to Russia; the Allied offensive in the Mediterranean could not be sustained; and there would be no invasion of northwest Europe in 1944.

The German U-boats' offensive in the North Atlantic reached the height of its success in March of 1943, when they sunk 108 ships consisting of 627,377 tons at a cost of only fourteen U-boats lost. But the tide then began to turn. In April the U-boats worldwide sank only fifty-six Allied ships of 327,943 tons, losing fifteen U-boats to all causes. Then, in May, the U-boats sunk only fifty Allied ships of 264,852 tons and lost forty U-boats in the process.[1] Indeed, at the end of May 1943, the unequal equation of rare U-boat victories over ships in Allied convoys versus heavy losses suffered at the hands of Allied escorts persuaded the Germans to break off U-boat operations in the North Atlantic.

Following their strategy of shifting the weight of attack to apparent weak spots in the Allied convoy defenses, the Germans then moved their operations to the central Atlantic, where Allied convoys ran between the United States and the Mediterranean. There they were defeated again in the summer of 1943 by American hunter-killer groups built around escort aircraft carriers. In September and October 1943 the German wolf packs returned to the convoy routes in the North Atlantic. Roundly defeated again in that theater, the wolf packs sought their prey in one last group of convoy routes. In November, even though they were on the verge of total defeat, the wolf packs attempted to attack Allied convoys proceeding between Gibraltar and Great Britain.

Vanquished again in the Gibraltar-Britain sea lanes, the Germans gave up wolf pack operations against Allied convoys in the mid-Atlantic and withdrew eastward. For the rest of the war, they waged what amounted to a maritime guerrilla war in European seas. The wolf packs' humiliation was one of the decisive defeats for the Germans in World War II, for it ended their bid to cut Allied maritime supply lines running across the North Atlantic.

This book is a study of how and why the U-boats were defeated in the North Atlantic during the period April to December 1943. It focuses on combat between Allied convoys and groups of German U-boats in order to show how both the Allies and the Germans used tactics, intelligence, electronic devices, and weapon systems to fight the battle. Victory or defeat in the Battle of the Atlantic depended greatly on each side's ability to decrypt the other's command radio communications and to determine the location of seaborne radio transmitters by means of D/F, or direction finding equipment. Each side then had to use the resulting information correctly to deploy U-boats to attack convoys or to route convoys away from concentrations of submarines. Once contact between a convoy and the U-boats occurred, victory or defeat depended in a large part on the ability of one side or the other to use or to counter tactical electronic devices such as HF/DF (high frequency direction finders) or radar. However, the fruits of communications intelligence and electronic devices were useless if either side lacked or misused weapon systems such as ships and aircraft in a convoy battle. It is almost axiomatic to say that the Allies had the material advantage over the Germans in World War II, but victory in the Battle of the Atlantic did not go automatically to the side which had the advantage of material weight. The Allies won the Battle of the Atlantic in 1943 because they could, and did, correctly deploy and use the material and intelligence resources available to them. The Germans discovered that they had increasing difficulties in locating Allied convoys to attack and that when a U-boat made contact with a convoy it was increasingly difficult if not impossible to attack the Allied ships successfully. In their attempts to intercept and attack Allied convoys, the Germans also suffered prohibitive losses of U-boats from Allied air and surface escorts. A less determined and disciplined force than the U-boat service would have ended wolf pack operations far sooner. Only after months of ineffectual and costly attempts to intercept and attack Allied convoys in the North Atlantic did the Germans finally end the wolf pack campaign against Allied convoys at the beginning of December 1943.

Because the narrative thrust of this study follows the sound of the guns, readers should be warned that there are a number of aspects of the Battle of the Atlantic which are not considered in the pages that follow. For example, this book will not examine why and how each side obtained various weapon systems and electronic devices used in the battle. Nor will there be a discussion of the mechanics of code breaking. While the allocation of resources such as aircraft will be noted, the decision-making processes involved will not be explained. Problems of high command and grand strategy will be touched upon lightly for the most part. And, in general, tactical procedures and policies, weapon systems, intelligence procedures and sources, and the like will be described and explained only as they affected the battle during April to December 1943—without much attention to the history of their development. Even with these omissions, the tale of that battle of sea and air, of guns and cryptology, is one of the most fascinating epochs in modern military history and technological development.

I must begin my acknowledgments by expressing gratitude to the staffs of a number of libraries and archives in Great Britain and the United States without whose assistance this book would not have been possible. In Great Britain I wish to thank the staffs of the Public Record Office, the National Maritime Museum, and the Institute of Historical Research of the University of London; and, in the United States, the staffs of the National Archives, the Naval Historical Center, and the Rosenthal Library of Queens College, CUNY. I wish also to thank Dr. Mary-Jo Kline of New York, Mr. R. M. Coppock of the Ministry of Defense in London who answered a number of my questions, and Dr. W. A. B. Douglas, director of the Directorate of History, National Defense Headquarters, Ottawa, Canada who has assisted in this project from the beginning. The research for this book was supported in part by the City University of New York PSC-CUNY Research Award Program.

Even with this distinguished list of advisers, I know that I will be guilty of inadvertent errors. Of course, I am wholly responsible for any sins of omission and commission.

ABBREVIATIONS

ASV	Air to surface vessel radar
BdU	*Befehlshaber der Unterseeboote*
COMINCH	Commander in chief, US fleet
D/F	Direction finding
GAF	German Air Force
GUS	Gibraltar to United States convoy
HF/DF	High frequency direction finder
HX	Fast eastbound North Atlantic convoy
KMS	Great Britain to Gibraltar convoy
MKS	Gibraltar to Great Britain convoy
NA	National Archives, Washington, D.C.
NA, SRGN	Individual translations of German U-boat radio messages
NA, SRH	Special research histories
NA, SRMN	Discrete records of historical cryptologic impact: US Navy
NHC	Naval Historical Center, Washington, D.C.
PRO	Public Record Office, London, England
PRO, ADM	Admiralty records
PRO, AIR	Air Ministry records
PRO, DEFE	Intercepted German radio messages
PRO, PREM	Prime Minister's papers
OD	Operations division, German Naval staff
ON	Fast westbound North Atlantic convoy
ONS	Slow westbound North Atlantic convoy

ORP	Polish Navy ship
RAF	Royal Air Force
RCAF	Royal Canadian Air Force
RN	Royal Navy
RNR	Royal Navy Reserve
RNVR	Royal Navy Volunteer Reserve
SC	Slow eastbound North Atlantic convoy
SL/MKS	Combined Sierra Leone/Gibraltar to Great Britain convoy
TG	Task group
UGS	United States to Gibraltar convoy
USN	United States Navy
USNR	United States Naval Reserve
VLR	Very long range

The Defeat of the German U-Boats

Chapter 1

Prerequisites

Allied leaders meeting at Casablanca in January of 1943 resolved that the defeat of the U-boats in the North Atlantic must "remain a first charge on the resources of the United Nations."[1] Elimination of the U-boats in the North Atlantic was an absolute prerequisite to Allied victory. In the first forty months of World War II, the U-boats sank 2,177 merchant ships totaling 11,045,284 tons, while the number of merchant ships lost to all other causes was negligible in comparison. During the period September 1939 to the end of 1942, aircraft sank 2,300,465 tons amounting to 809 merchant ships; mines sank 1,108,216 tons consisting of 442 ships; warships sank 390,607 tons representing 103 merchant ships; merchant raiders sank 787,569 tons representing 128 merchant ships; E-boats sank 177,995 tons representing 75 merchant ships; unknown or other causes sank 956,126 tons representing 600 merchant ships. And in the first three months of 1943, U-boats sank a further 208 merchant ships totaling 1,189,833 tons, while during the same period the Germans lost only forty U-boats.[2] In a single monumental convoy battle fought over convoys HX 229 and SC 122, twenty-one Allied merchant ships were sunk at the cost to the Germans of only one U-boat destroyed.[3]

This huge loss of shipping to U-boats in the North Atlantic compounded and increased the shortage of merchant shipping confronting the Allies in the first quarter of 1943. Owing to this shortage, the Allies found it almost impossible to provide the required vessels to maintain essential civilian programs such as imports of food and raw material into Great Britain, while at the same time provide the ships required to support military operations.[4] The Allies were confronted with a worldwide shipping crisis which profoundly affected the conduct of the war. The Allies had to have a victory over the U-boats in

1

1943 if they were to be able to go on the offensive in Western Europe in 1944.[5]

The conduct of the Battle of the Atlantic by both the Allies and the Germans was in some respects determined by decisions made before or at the beginning of the war. Weapon systems which are the products of advanced technology take time to develop for deployment in combat. The ships, aircraft, and electronic devices employed by the Allies and Germans during the convoy battles of 1943 were conceived in most cases long before their use in battle.

The German navy was not prepared to fight the Battle of the Atlantic at the beginning of the war. Under the terms of the Z-Plan, adopted on 27 January 1939, it was the intention of the Germans to build a balanced fleet of surface ships capable of confronting the Royal Navy in 1948. But the Z-Plan was overtaken by events with the beginning of World War II, and the Germans began the war with a small surface fleet and fifty-seven U-boats.[6] Immediately after the beginning of the war, it was decided to build twenty-nine U-boats a month. But a lack of interest on Hitler's part and a general shortage of materials retarded this program. It took as much as two years from laying down the keel through commissioning and training to make a U-boat operational.[7] As a result, the German U-boat fleet increased very slowly during the first years of the war. By January 1942 there were only 91 operational U-boats and 158 others either undergoing trials or being used for training. However, a year later, in January 1943, there were 240 operational U-boats and 185 U-boats engaged in trials and training duties.[8] And on 4 April 1943 the Allies estimated that there were ninety-five U-boat operating in the Atlantic.[9]

The German U-boat fleet between June 1935 and May 1945 totaled 1,162 vessels of which the most numerous were the Type VII U-boats. The Germans constructed 705 Type VII U-boats which formed the backbone of the U-boat fleet in 1943. There were seven different variants of the Type VII U-boat; the most numerous were the 661 units of the Type VIIC.[10] All the variants of the Type VII U-boats were essentially the same. A Type VIIC/41 for example, displaced 759 tons surfaced and 860 tons submerged. This U-boat was 67.2 meters long with a beam of 6.2 meters. These U-boats were powered by two diesel engines of 1,400 BHP each and two electric engines of 750 HP each which could propel the vessel at 17 knots on the surface and, for a very short time, at a top speed of 6 knots when submerged. This was a surface speed faster than some Allied escorts. The type VIIC/41 had a range of 6,500 nautical miles at 12 knots on the surface and 80 nautical miles submerged. The Type VIIC/41 U-boats could crash dive in twenty-five to thirty seconds, and were rated to a depth of 309 feet—which at times was greatly exceeded. U-boats of the Type VIIC/41 had four torpedo tubs in the bow and one in the stern and could carry a total of fourteen torpedoes. These vessels were equipped with one 8.8 centimeter deck gun mounted forward of the conning tower and one 2 centimeter gun. After 1942, with the increased threat of aircraft, the number of small caliber guns for antiaircraft defense on each U-boat was increased.[11] The Type VIIC/41 U-boats, like all the other German U-boats, were tough and could withstand considerable pounding and punishment.

The U-boats in service in 1943 were splendid examples of German ship building—reliant, resilient, and robust. But they were also refined examples of the weapon systems with which the Germans had fought the Allies in World War I with serious limitations. That is, the German U-boats in service in 1943 were nothing more than ocean-going torpedo boats which were capable of submerging and moving around underwater at slow speeds for limited periods of time. This was a serious flaw as submersion was the only effective weapon available for the U-boats to combat aircraft. And, as a final handicap, the vast majority of the U-boats at sea in 1943, especially the Type VII vessels, did not have the range to conduct prolonged operations, even in the North Atlantic, without being refueled at sea.

The U-boats' technological limitations might have been somewhat mitigated or blunted if the Germans had been able to mount modern electronic devices on these vessels. German hydrophones were perhaps the best in the world, but the U-boats were not equipped with sonar.[12] The Germans never developed and deployed an effective search radar for U-boats.[13] The reason for this was that most of the German navy's radar development efforts went into radar fire control for the guns of major surface ships and not into the development of search radars which were common at the time to Allied navies. Further, a great deal of the German electronic research and development effort was expended on producing radar warning devices to counter Allied airborne radar.[14] In the last half of 1942 the Germans produced and fitted on the U-boats a radar detector known as *Metox*—officially FuMB 1—which could detect Allied airborne radar operating on a wave length of 1.4 meters. But in 1943 the Allies began to deploy microwave airborne radar. At the same time the Germans concluded that the *Metox* detectors gave off radiation which they wrongly thought could be used to detect U-boats at sea. The result of these developments was that during the summer of 1943 there was a rush within the German navy to develop a radar detector which could pick up 9.7 centimeter radar signals from Allied aircraft and which at the same time did not give off radiation. The Germans were not wholly successful in producing a detector of Allied airborne microwave radar. Instead, they became obsessed with the possibly that the Allies were locating U-boats by means of infrared radiation,[15] and they wasted huge amounts of time on problems of infrared detection of U-boats, which was a blind alley, and thereby were possibly the victims of an Allied deception ploy.[16]

During 1943 the Germans also attacked the problem of Allied airborne radar by attempting to produce an antiradar coating for U-boats which would reduce or destroy the signature of Allied radars. At the same time the Germans also produced a radar decoy, known as *aphrodite,* which went into service in September 1943. *Aphrodite* was a hydrogen-filled balloon supporting strips of aluminum foil to be launched from a surfaced U-boat to divert and decoy Allied airborne radar. Antiradar coating was never made practical, and *aphrodite* was found difficult to deploy and did not really fool the Allies.[17] One result of the concentration of research and development efforts on the detecting or decoying of Allied airborne radar was the almost total lack of effort expended by the German Navy on measures to counter the search radars on Allied surface escorts which were critical to the defense of Allied convoys in the North Atlantic. By 1943 the German navy's electronic warfare capabilities, specifically in terms of electronic sensors such as radar and radar counter measures, were inadequate to offset Allied advances in this technology.

Grand Admiral Karl Doenitz, former commander of the U-boat service and commander in chief of the German Navy since 30 January 1943, was the driving force behind German U-boat warfare in World War II. Doenitz, who had been a U-boat commander in World War I, came to the conclusion that the German U-boats had been defeated in that conflict by the Allied strategy of convoys. During the interwar years, Doenitz gave considerable thought to the problem of how to use U-boats to overcome convoys.[18] Doenitz thought the next war in the North Atlantic would be in many respects a repeat of the German U-boat offensive in World War I. Strategically, the objective would be to cut off European supply lines to North America by means of U-boat operations.[19] In World War I the German U-boats had operated singly against Allied merchant ships, and the Germans had been defeated when the Allies instituted the system of convoys.[20] In the peacetime years that followed, Doenitz worked out the strategy and tactics for U-boats to overcome an Allied strategy of convoys.

The histories of previous maritime wars showed that a strategy based on a system of convoys was the best way to protect merchant shipping from attack in a *guerre de course* with the least expenditure of effort. This was the lesson of the great maritime wars of the seventeenth and eighteenth centuries as well as World War I, when, Winston Churchill later argued, Allied losses to U-boats would have been drastically reduced if Allied shipping had sailed in convoys instead of independently, even if they were unescorted by warships.[21] The tactical and strategic concept of convoy was simple. If, for example, eighty merchant ships were sailing independently, then an enemy had eighty different points of attack—while the defender had eighty different points to defend. If, however, there were eighty merchant ships grouped together into a convoy, it was much more difficult for an enemy to locate and intercept them than if the eighty ships were scattered across the ocean at random. A convoy gave the defender only one place to defend—the convoy itself—and the attacker only one place to attack. An enemy attacking a convoy was open to counterattack by the convoy escort. Therefore, to mount a successful attack on the convoy the enemy would first find the convoy and then either overpower or elude the convoy's escort. Locating and then attacking a convoy in the face of an armed escort was a much more difficult problem than attacking a number of merchant ships sailing independently. Further, convoys did not stop, and if an attacker fell behind a convoy, then it must catch up if the attack was to be renewed. If the convoy's escort deterred the enemy from attacking the merchant ships under escort, then the ultimate objective of the convoy had been achieved, which was the ability to pass merchant ships across bodies of water free from attack without fighting battles.[22]

Convoys were also economical. Operational experience showed that the larger the number of merchant ships in a convoy, then proportionately fewer warships were required in the escort.[23] This was also borne out in operational experience.[24] As a result, Allied convoys in 1943 were increased in size. At the beginning of the year, the average size of a transatlantic convoy was about forty ships, but in the early summer of 1943 Americans began sailing from the United States to Gibraltar with convoys consisting of ninety or more ships.[25]

Doenitz intended to overcome convoys by instituting mass attacks on them by wolf packs of U-boats. These tactics called for a number of U-boats to be stationed in a patrol line across the path of an oncoming convoy. When a convoy was sighted by one U-boat, the other U-boats of the group would be summoned by radio to converge on the convoy. And when the required number of U-boats had gained contact with a convoy, they would undertake a mass night attack, using their relatively high surface speed and low silhouettes to elude the escorts to get inside the radar screen before attacking the merchant ships with torpedoes. Before the war, these tactics were successfully tried and practiced by the German U-boats.[26]

In contrast to Allied escort groups, command and control of the U-boats in a wolf pack was exercised from a single shore-based headquarters because Doenitz thought that a commander in a U-boat at sea would not have the required communications and staff support.[27] The requirements of commanding and controlling scores of U-boats at sea from a headquarters ashore resulted in the German navy developing one of the most complex and sophisticated radio communication systems in the world by 1943. This system of centralized shore-based command and control also resulted in literally thousands of orders, reports, and the like being sent by radio back and forth between U-boats at sea and the *Befehlshaber der Unterseeboote,* or BdU, ashore.[28] While the Germans must have realized that this form of command and control by radio made the German U-boat service vulnerable to an allied intelligence attack, they discounted the degree of hazard.[29]

One of the major problems confronting the U-boats in the Atlantic was locating Allied convoys. The German navy from time to time during the course of the war attempted to get the German Air Force (GAF) to provide long-range reconnaissance flights over the North Atlantic to procure intelligence about the movement of Allied shipping, but the GAF was incapable and unwilling to provide the necessary flights.[30] As a result, the U-boat service had to rely for the most part on cryptographic intelligence for information on the movements of Allied convoys. The Germans had been reading various British codes since the 1930s. In December 1941 the B-Dienst, the code-breaking section of German naval intelligence, began to read the British Naval Cipher No. 3, which was used by the Americans, British, and Canadians to send each other information about the arrangements for convoys and routes for stragglers. From Naval Cipher No. 3, the B-Dienst obtained decrypts which gave the BdU information about ten to twenty hours in advance of Allied convoy movements.[31] The B-Dienst's period of greatest success was from January to June 1943, and after the war the US Navy estimated that it "was quite possible the Allied failure to prevent the Germans from decrypting their convoy cipher was accountable for the loss of 100 ships." This run of cryptographic success lasted until June 1943, when the Allies changed their ciphers.[32]

In 1939 the Royal Navy was much stronger than the German Navy, but the British were, nevertheless, unprepared to fight the Battle of the Atlantic and to deal with attacks on merchant shipping by the U-boats. Part of the problem was that the "ten year rule" (which required that each year all defense planning, construction, and spending be based upon the assumption that Britain would not have to fight a major war for the next ten years) and a general shortage of money led the Royal Navy in the interwar years to put most of its resources into building and maintaining the capital ships required to form a balanced battle fleet, while giving the problems of trade protection little in terms of resources or planning. Also, at the beginning of the war, the Royal Navy believed that the U-boat problem was manageable if not totally solved because the number of German submarines was relatively small and the British had developed asdic, later known as sonar.[33] To compound these errors in judgment, relations between the RAF and the Royal Navy were at best strained, and the maritime arm of the RAF—Coastal Command—began the war with unsuitable aircraft for hunting U-boats, no airborne depth charges, and aircrews untrained in anti-U-boat operations.[34]

On declaring war against Germany, Britain could protect its trade with only a few sloops, World War I destroyers, and antique aircraft. When the fighting began in September 1939, convoys were instituted to protect only merchant shipping along Britain's east coast, and for the most part the Royal Navy hoped to defend such vessels with offensive patrols and hunter-killer groups in the maritime approaches to Britain. One reason for this policy was the failure of many navy officers and others to understand the importance of trade protection. They looked upon convoys as a secondary or "defensive," believing that the true role of warships was offensive actions in which they sought out and destroyed the enemy on the high seas with hunter-killer groups.[35] However, this strategy was quickly shown to be inadequate in the first months of the war, as the German U-boats sank 114 merchant ships totaling 421,156 tons. Twelve of these ships were in convoy, five were stragglers from convoys, and the other ninety-seven ships were sailing independently.[36]

Even in 1939, there were a number of British officials including Winston Churchill, the First Lord of the Admiralty, who knew from the experience of World War I that convoys were the most effective means to protect shipping from attack, but such knowledge was of little help by itself without sufficient escort vessels and aircraft available to set up an all-embracing system of convoy. It was not until 27 May 1941 that the first convoy was provided with an anti-U-boat escort for the entire length of its voyage from North America to Great Britain. In July of 1940, for example, merchant ships sailing from Britain to North America were escorted only as far as 17° west, at which point they then sailed independently to North America. The failure to provide escorts for the entire Atlantic crossing cost the British many merchant ships, but the simple fact was that at the beginning of the war the Royal Navy did not have the ships required to provide escorts for convoys. Further, naval operation in Norway, Italy's entrance into the war, and the threat of invasion in 1940 cut deeply into the resources of the Royal Navy.

It was not until the summer of 1941 that new construction and US aid gave the Royal Navy and the Royal Canadian Navy a sufficient number of escorts to begin even an effective system of convoys in the

Atlantic.[37] That construction program, in turn, reflected long-range peacetime planning. In the years just before the beginning of the war, the Admiralty had anticipated the need to increase the number of ships in the Royal Navy that could be used as escorts. In 1937 the Admiralty designed an ocean escort sloop known as the Black Swan class to be built to naval specifications. The first such sloop was laid down on 20 June 1938. Although the Black Swan sloops were excellent escorts, heavily armed and capable of 20 knots, only thirty-seven were launched because of their high cost and the length of construction time. Moreover, even before war came in September 1939, it was determined that escort vessels would be needed in such large numbers that there was neither the time nor the money to build the required number to naval specifications. Thus the majority of escorts designed and built by the British and Canadians during World War II were constructed in civilian yards according to more flexible "classification society" rules and merchant shipbuilding practices, with standards set forth by Lloyd's of London. This policy saved time and money and made the maximum use of shipbuilding capacity in Britain and Canada. The first and perhaps most well known of these war-built escorts was the Flower class corvette. These ships were constructed to serve as escorts in coastal waters and were a modified version of the whale catcher, *Southern Pride*, which was built by Smith's Dock Company Ltd. of South Bank on Tees. In the summer of 1939 the Royal Navy ordered sixty Flower class corvettes and after the beginning of the war the Canadian government ordered sixty-four Flower class corvettes built in Canada for the Royal Canadian Navy. By the end of the war, 214 Flower class corvettes had been constructed in Britain and Canada at the cost of about £90,000 per ship. These corvettes were 190 feet long with a beam of 33 feet 1 inch, capable of 16 knots, and at the beginning armed only with depth charges, one 4-inch gun, and several machine guns. The Flower class corvettes were designed for use in coastal waters and, although very good sea boats, they offered cramped and dreadful working and living conditions for their crews in heavy seas. Nonetheless, they became the mainstay of the British and Canadian ocean escort groups during the years 1940 to 1942.[38]

These British and Canadian escort craft were supplemented by American-built ships as early as September 1940, when the United

States transferred fifty "flushed decked" World War I destroyers to the British. Seven of these destroyers were manned by the Royal Canadian Navy. Those that entered the Royal Navy were known as Town class destroyers because they were usually named for towns common to both the United States and Britain. These destroyers were 314 feet long with a beam of 31 feet and could go more than 30 knots. When they were turned over to the British, most had a main armament of four 4-inch guns and twelve torpedo tubes. Like all destroyers, these ships were not really suitable to service as escorts in the North Atlantic because they were too fast and too heavily armed, with long hulls and narrow beams that gave them too great a turning radius. Nevertheless, the great shortage of ships forced the Royal Navy to employ them as convoy escorts. The British modified these American destroyers for escort duty by removing some of the 4-inch guns and torpedo tubes and replacing them with smaller weapons, such as 20mm Oerlikons; increasing the space for depth charge storage; and fitting new depth charge throwers. To increase these ships' stability, the foremast and three after-funnels were short-ened, while the after-mast was removed.[39]

At the beginning of the war the Admiralty assigned a number of "V and W" class destroyers to escort duties.[40] These ships made poor escorts for, like the Town class destroyers, they were too fast, had too many guns, operated with a very long turning radius, and had little endurance. In the years 1941 to 1943, twenty-one of these de-stroyers were converted into long-range escorts. Most of their heavy guns were replaced by weapons such as 20mm Oerlikons, and in most cases the torpedo tubes were also removed. To increase each ship's range, its No. 1 boiler and funnel were removed, and this space was used for additional fuel bunkers and for accommodation of the ship's crew. In the course of the war, the British also modified other fleet destroyers, such as HMS *Duncan* and HMS *Hesperus*, to serve as escorts.[41] And in 1943, with the suspension of convoys to Russia, a number of fleet destroyers were reassigned from the home fleet to convoy work in the North Atlantic.[42] A number of American and Canadian fleet destroyers also saw service in the North Atlantic dur-ing 1943.

As the war went on and the U-boat campaign in the Atlantic inten-sified, the British built and commissioned River class frigates. These were specifically designed with the endurance to escort convoys and to fight U-boats. River class frigates were much larger and more complex than Flower class corvettes with a length of 283 feet and breadth of 36 feet 6 inches. Capable of a speed of 20 knots, fitted with depth charges and a hedgehog, (a mortar like weapon which throws bombs forward of the ship that explode on contact with the U-boat) and armed with two 4-inch guns plus a number of 20mm Oerlikons, the River class frigates proved to be very suitable as escorts in the North Atlantic. Fifty-seven of these frigates were built during the war, and the first came into service in 1942.[43]

As the war went on, Allied convoys and their escorts were equipped with increasingly sophisticated electronic equipment which enabled the Allies at first to blunt and then to overcome the German wolf packs. At the beginning of 1941, Allied escorts were fitted as fast as possible with radar sets capable of locating surfaced U-boats.[44] As more and more escorts were equipped with radar, night surface attacks on convoys by U-boats became increasingly difficult—in fact, to the point of impossibility. As early as the night of 17 March 1941, the Germans were given a lesson of what was to come when the U-100, after being forced to the surface by a depth charge attack from HMS *Walker,* attempted to escape on the surface under cover of darkness. The U-100 was picked up by radar mounted on HMS *Vanco,* which then rammed and sank the U-boat.[45]

Unwittingly, the German naval command gave the Allies still another technological advantage. The system employed by the BdU in World War II called for each member of a U-boat patrol line to make an immediate radio report of any sighting of an Allied convoy and then shadow the convoy while using radio beacon signals to direct the other U-boats of the group to the Allied ships. At the same time the BdU used radio communications to order the other U-boats of the patrol line to concentrate on the convoy with the objective of making a mass night surface attack on the Allied ships. As each succeeding U-boat made contact with the convoy, German standard operating procedure called for a sighting report to be made to the BdU by radio. And, when the Axis first used these wolf pack tactics, they achieved a high rate of sinkings in convoy battles.

Within two years, however, the Allies were learning to exploit the technological advantage offered by the German pattern of frequent ship-to-shore radio communications. In 1941 the Allies began to mount HF/DF equipment on escorts, enabling them to take bearings on the ground waves of U-boat radio transmissions within a range of about 20 miles.[46] HF/DF, like radar, was a spin-off from research into the nature of the ionosphere by means of equipment using cathode ray tubes. This equipment incorporated a cathode ray tube which could give a very accurate visual bearing on a ground wave of a radio transmission. The Germans believed that if U-boat radio transmissions were very brief—thirty seconds—they would be impossible to pick up on conventional D/F equipment. The Germans did not know of HF/DF until after the war and blithely assumed that the Allied ships could not locate the sources of their radio transmissions. HF/DF aerials were generally a bird cage type mounted on the top of a mast, and even though German agents in Spain took hundreds of photographs of Allied warships entering Gibraltar, the Germans never figured out the true function of the aerials.[47]

This oversight was one of the great intelligence failures of the Battle of the Atlantic, for an Allied escort equipped with HF/DF was a deadly weapon against a U-boat. Wolf pack tactics required a large number of radio transmissions from a U-boat operating against a convoy. For instance, while attacking SC 118, the U-402 transmitted, over a period of four days, forty-one different radio messages which were intercepted by Allied ship-borne HF/DF. It took only three radio transmissions within an hour from the U-187, also attacking SC 118, for the convoy's escort to get a bearing with HF/DF on the German vessel and for two destroyers to run down the bearing, find the U-boat, and then sink the submarine.[48]

In 1941 Allied escorts began to be equipped with high frequency radio telephones, which permitted the commander of an escort group to communicate with the ships under his command and enabled members of an Allied escort group to work together as a team.[49] The Allies saw the advantages of escorts working cooperatively to fend off an attack on a convoy, and each escort was assigned to a group. The ships of an escort group were trained together and kept together as much as possible, functioning as a unit under the direction of an escort commander.[50] In September of 1942 the Allies organized support groups,[51] which sometimes included an escort carrier, whose

task it was to reinforce the escort of a convoy that was either threatened with or under attack by U-boats.[52] As the war progressed, the
sophistication and skill of the Allied escorts, owing to training and
experience, grew. Unlike the U-boats forming a patrol line, all the
ships which comprised an Allied convoy were under the direction of
a commander on the spot. The senior officer of the escort was in
command of all the ships which were escorting a convoy. This officer
was responsible for the safety and conduct of all the ships of the
convoy—both escorts and those ships being escorted. The ships under the escort's protection, usually merchant ships, were under the
command of the commodore of the convoy, in most North Atlantic
convoys this was a retired Royal Navy flag officer, who was em-
barked on a merchant ship with a small staff. This form of organization was established to insure proper command and control of every
ship in a convoy operation.[53]

The Allies' advantage in this efficient command system was com-
plemented by their evolution of effective air support for their convoys. At the beginning of the war, Doenitz stated "The U-boat has
no more to fear from aircraft than a mole from a cow." The German
admiral was to be proved wrong: during World War II, 312 Axis
U-boats (289 of them German) were sunk by aircraft.[54] As was discovered during World War I, even the presence of an aircraft had an
inhibiting effect on U-boats. Obviously, aircraft could sink a U-boat
on the surface with bombs, gunfire, rockets, torpedoes, and depth
charges; but equally important, aircraft could make U-boats submerge. Unlike modern nuclear submarines, World War II U-boats
were not true underwater craft. Instead, the German vessels operated
best on the surface and were capable of staying underwater only for
a limited amount of time. They could steam at 17 knots on the surface, but, underwater, could cruise at only 2 or 3 knots for limited
periods of time. German wolf pack tactics called for a convoy to be
located and then shadowed by one U-boat while others were summoned to attack the convoy. To get into favorable position for attack,
the shadower had to maintain contact with the convoy while the other
members of the pack made high-speed runs along the convoy's flanks
during the daylight hours to get into position to attack the convoy at
night. Aircraft carrying out searches around a convoy could not only
sink U-boats but also force them underwater, where a submerged

U-boat's speed would not match even the slowest of convoys, much less allow it to get ahead of a convoy into an attacking position. Moreover, if the shadower was forced to submerge, it usually lost contact with the convoy. Thus, if nothing else, Allied aircraft making searches and sweeps in front of a convoy, along its flanks, and behind it for several hours would force U-boats to dive and lose contact with their prey. It was the ability to force U-boats to lose contact with a convoy as well as their ability to sink U-boats that made aircraft so importance in the defense of convoys during World War II.[55]

Aircraft working with the surface escort of a convoy greatly strengthened the defense of the convoy from U-boat attack. In fact, very few ships sailing in convoys during World War II were sunk when the escort was comprised of both aircraft and surface ships.[56] Both the Allies and the Germans became aware of this early in the war, for it was aircraft working in conjunction with surface escorts that had driven the U-boats first from western approaches and then from American coastal waters. And this was a crucial factor in Doenitz's decision to redeploy his U-boats in the mid-Atlantic at the end of 1942. There, he reasoned, the wolf packs would be out of range of Allied aircraft, free to attack convoys running between North America and the British Isles. Doenitz decided on this deployment for U-boats because it permitted them to carry out wolf pack attacks without having to contend with Allied anti-U-boat aircraft.[57]

Even though the Allies knew that air escort of convoys would greatly reduce the losses of ships from U-boat attacks, they had great difficulty providing air escort to convoys in what they called the "air gap," or the "Greenland air gap" and what was known to the Germans as the "black hole."[58] Here, in the mid-Atlantic south of Greenland, there were still only a handful of VLR aircraft available for anti-U-boat operations as late as April and May 1943. Allied VLR aircraft were not operational in Newfoundland until June 1943.[59] Until then, the Allies had to rely on craft based in Iceland and Northern Ireland. On 1 March there were only eleven serviceable VLR B-24 Liberators from the RAF 120th Squadron in Iceland and twelve more of RAF 86th Squadron based in Northern Ireland. And by 10 May there were only seventeen serviceable VLR B-24 Liberators in Iceland and Northern Ireland.[60] This small force comprised the only land-based aircraft available to the Allies which were capable of operating against U-boats in the mid-Atlantic air gap south of Greenland.

This failure to provide sufficient air escort, which could have cost the Allies the war, was due simply to the Allies' inability to deploy the necessary aircraft of the right type to close the mid-Atlantic air gap. Before Pearl Harbor, the RAF Coastal Command obtained a number of B-24 Liberator aircraft from the United States, and it was found that by removing armor and self-sealing from the fuel tanks and adding "a minimum armament," these aircraft carrying 1,500 pounds of depth charges and acoustic homing torpedoes had an operational range of 2,600 nautical miles which enabled them to operate as air escorts for convoys in the mid-Atlantic air gap.[61] If enough modified B-24 Liberators, known as VLR aircraft after conversion, had been based in Northern Ireland, Iceland, and Newfoundland early enough, the air gap south of Greenland could have been closed and air cover provided for convoys throughout the North Atlantic crossing. But because of conflicts and misunderstandings between various Allied commands and commanders, it was found nearly impossible to obtain B-24 Liberators to be converted into VLR aircraft. As a result, only a handful of the versatile VLR B-24 Liberators were operating over convoys in the mid-Atlantic air gap in the spring of 1943.[62]

One contributing factor to the situation was the extreme reluctance of commanders of both the RAF and the United States Army Air Force (USAAF) to transfer aircraft suitable for strategic bombing to anti-U-boat operations. But these "Bomber Barons" were not the only problem, for the whole question of land-based aircraft for anti-U-boat operations was the subject of a huge disagreement between the US Navy and the USAAF.[63] Further, after the end of the U-boat offensive in American coastal waters at the beginning of 1942, the Americans would not deploy anti-U-boat aircraft away from the western Atlantic even though Allied intelligence knew that there were very few U-boats operating in the regions patrolled by American aircraft. In February 1943, for example, United States aircraft flew 20,067 hours on anti-U-boat operations in the Eastern and Gulf Sea frontiers without sighting a single U-boat.[64] And RAF Coastal Command, transfixed by the so-called Bay Offensive, would not release a number of B-24 Liberators from operations against the

U-boat transit routes in the Bay of Biscay for conversion into VLR aircraft suitable for operations in the mid-Atlantic air gap.[65] This represented a mistake in allocation of resources, as patrolling U-boat transit routes in the Bay of Biscay took an enormous amount of flying time to sink a single U-boat. During 1943, for instance,

> In the three months September to November, although the hours flown on escort in the area were steadily *reduced* and totalled less than one-seventh of the hours flown on patrol, the transit area air patrols accounted for four U-boats, air escorts for 15. In other words, while one kill on patrol absorbed 4,020 patrol hours one kill on escort and support absorbed only 160 hours.[66]

RAF Coastal Command instituted patrols over the Bay of Biscay in 1941 and, except for the period from May through August 1943, (when 25 U-boats were sunk by aircraft owing to the mistaken German tactic of remaining on the surface and fighting it out when attacked) kills by aircraft in the Bay of Biscay averaged about one a month.[67] Despite this short period of success, RAF Coastal Command's operations in the Bay of Biscay were not decisive for they never prevented all the U-boats from passing through the bay into the Atlantic where they could attack shipping. This confusion between various Allied commands over the allocation and proper deployment of B-24 aircraft almost cost the Allies victory in the Battle of the Atlantic.[68]

The Allies knew full well that the air gap south of Greenland could have been closed if a convoy were covered by an escort group built around an escort carrier. The Allies also knew how effective escort carriers could be in convoy battles from the success of HMS *Audacity,* the Royal Navy's first escort carrier.[69] But before deploying escort carriers, the Allies attempted to close the Greenland air gap by an odd assortment of schemes. For example, the British put into service a class of ships called merchant aircraft carriers—large bulk carriers such as grain ships with flight decks mounted on them to allow the operation of four Swordfish aircraft. The first merchant aircraft carrier went into operation in 1943.[70]

However, merchant aircraft carriers were only halfway measures, and the real solution lay in escort groups built around carriers. Not until March 1943 did the first such group go into action in the North Atlantic with the sailing of a convoy built around the escort carrier USS *Bogue*.[71] The usual explanation for not assigning escort carriers to North Atlantic convoys sooner was that these vessels were needed to support the invasion of North Africa.[72] However, of the fifteen escort carriers commissioned into the US Navy and the ten into the Royal Navy, only seven were involved in the North African campaign (HMS *Avenger*, HMS *Biter*, HMS *Dasher*, USS *Sangamon*, USS *Chenango*, USS *Suwannee*, USS *Santee*).[73] During the last months of 1942 and the first five months of 1943, American and British escort carriers were for the most part employed in activities that had nothing to do with the Battle of the Atlantic. Most American escort carriers were in the Pacific, while the British escort carriers were undergoing reconversion in British ports, and it was not until May 1943 that the British escort carriers HMS *Archer* and HMS *Biter* began operations against U-boats in the North Atlantic.[74] In the case of the American-built British escort carriers, the Royal Navy's director of construction had what was thought to be a good reason for reconverting the ships to Royal Navy standards: HMS *Avenger* went down with the loss of all but 17 of its crew after being hit by one torpedo, while HMS *Dasher* was destroyed in the River Clyde by a gasoline explosion that killed 378 men.[75] However, the failure to commit escort carriers to close the Greenland air gap shows, at best, the Allies lack of understanding of the importance of the Battle of the Atlantic.

At the beginning of March 1943 the Allies held the Atlantic Convoy Conference in Washington, D.C. This conference, attended mostly by American, British, and Canadian staff officers and experts on anti-U-boat warfare, corrected a large number of technical problems and misunderstandings among the Allies and brought a degree of rationalization to the war against the U-boats. The most important decision from the Conference came at the suggestion of Admiral Ernest J. King, the commander in chief of the US Fleet and chief of naval operations, who did not approve of mixing forces of different nationalities: the North Atlantic was divided into British Commonwealth and US regions of responsibility; Britain and Canada would be responsible for convoys north of the fortieth latitude, while the US Navy would be responsible for the protection of convoys south of that latitude. Task Force 24, the American naval command in New-foundland, would be abolished, and American forces would be with-drawn from the North Atlantic convoy routes.[76] This division of labor also set the stage for the Canadian armed forces being granted com-mand responsibility for the northwest Atlantic theater of opera-tions.[77] The new command arrangements agreed to at the Conference resulted in a much clearer demarcation of responsibilities among American, British, and Canadians for the future conduct of the Battle of the Atlantic.

The Allies subjected the German U-boats to a relentless intelli-gence attack. The main source of information available to the Allies was the numerous radio transmissions between the U-boats at sea and the BdU, required by the German methods of command and control. The Allies exploited German radio communications in three ways. Direction finding (or D/F) could locate a radio transmitter by obtaining simultaneous bearings on a transmission from several dif-ferent places by means of directional antennae and then calculate the point where the bearings intersect. The Allies could also identify a transmitter by means of the characteristics of the intercepted trans-mission, since an individual radio operator displayed unique sending characteristics much as a telegrapher uses a Morse key in an individ-ual fashion. Radio fingerprinting could also be used to identify an individual radio transmitter through analysis of the transmission it-self using high speed photography and the technology of cathode ray tubes. And lastly the content of a radio communication could be ob-tained by decrypting it.[78]

The Allies established a system of stations to intercept radio trans-missions in Britain, along the east coast of North America, in Africa, and on various islands such as Iceland, Bermuda, and Ascension Is-land.[79] D/F bearings and other materials required for radio traffic analysis plus texts for decryption were picked up by these stations and sent by secure means to Bletchley Park, London; Ottawa; and Washington, D.C., for study by Allied intelligence officers.

Just before the beginning of the war, the British established the Operational Intelligence Centre in the Admiralty.[80] In the campaign against the U-boats, the most important part of the Operational In-telligence Centre was the submarine tracking room, under Com-mander Rodger Winn, RNVR. From 1941 onwards, the submarine tracking room was at the center of the British intelligence effort against the U-boats. All operational intelligence relating to the U-boat war such as D/F bearings; results of the analysis of the characteristics of radio transmissions; decrypts of enemy radio communications; products of photographic reconnaissance and ship and aircraft sightings; and prisoner of war interrogations flowed into the tracking room. It was the task of the tracking room to take in this mass of information and produce a total intelligence picture of the state of the U-boat war. The product of the submarine tracking room was operational intelligence which was used by other sections of the Operational Intelligence Centre, such as the operations and trade sections, plus the naval staff in the Admiralty. The submarine tracking room also passed immediate operational intelligence to Headquarters RAF Coastal Command and Headquarters Western Approaches Command by direct secure telephone.[81]

At the suggestion of the British, the Canadians established an Operational Intelligence Centre with a submarine tracking room in Naval Service Headquarters, Ottawa, which was led by Lieutenant Commander John B. McDiarmid, RCNVR. The Canadians also developed a system of radio intercept stations which fed D/F fixes and other materials of radio traffic analysis into the submarine tracking room in Ottawa where it was combined with other intelligence materials to form a total picture of the U-boat war in the northwest Atlantic. After analysis, this intelligence was promulgated to various operational commands in the Canadian northwest Atlantic theater of operations. At first neither the Americans nor the British approved of the feasibility of an independently run Canadian intelligence operation and saw Canadian plots of German U-boat activity as a duplication of effort. But with the establishment of the Canadian northwest Atlantic theater of operations in 1943, there was an agreement to divide U-boat intelligence dissemination among the Americans, Canadians, and British. The Canadians were given the western Atlantic, the British the eastern Atlantic, and the Americans the Atlantic south of 40° north latitude.[82]

It was also at British urging that the US Navy set up a submarine tracking room, commanded by Commander Kenneth A. Knowles, USN, in COMINCH's Combat Intelligence Division shortly after Pearl Harbor. Like its British and Canadian counterparts, the American submarine tracking room's task was to build a total intelligence picture of the U-boat war in the Atlantic and then to promulgate intelligence to the staffs responsible for convoy routing and various operational commands.[83] Knowles, Winn, and McDiarmid exchanged information on U-boats by teleprinter on a daily basis.[84] These exchanges were "a completely free and unfettered exchange of ideas and information."[85]

In 1941 the British code breakers at Bletchley Park, north of London, broke the German naval codes. This achievement required a great deal of work, luck, and skill because although the German navy used the same basic code machine employed by the GAF and the German army—the enigma—naval radio communications were much more secure than those of other branches of the German armed forces. The information necessary to read the German naval codes came to the British code breakers in bits and pieces. In February 1940 three wheels of an enigma code machine were obtained from the U-33. Several months later cipher materials were recovered from the German patrol boat VP2623 enabling the British to read six days of German naval radio transmissions. On 4 March 1941, during a raid on the Lofoten Islands, additional cipher materials were found on the captured German trawler Krebs. But this was not enough information for the British code breakers, and in an effort to obtain more information on German naval codes, expeditions were mounted to capture two German weather ships. On 7 May 1941 the weather ship Munchen was captured, and on 28 June the weather ship Lauenburg was taken. Both of these ships yielded additional information about German codes. However, the biggest haul of materials was made two days after the capture of the Munchen, when the U-110 was forced to the surface by depth charges. Thinking their vessel was sinking fast, the U-110's crew abandoned the vessel without destroying the code and cipher materials. Unknown to the crew of the U-boat, however, a boarding party from HMS Bulldog managed to reach the submarine in time to remove all the code and cipher materials, including a naval enigma code machine. The U-110 later sank while being towed to Iceland.[86]

The information obtained from the two German weather ships and the U-110 enabled the code breakers at Bletchley Park to mount a successful attack on the German naval codes in 1941.[87] But on 1 February 1942 the Germans added a fourth wheel to the naval enigma code machine used for radio communications between U-boats at sea and the BdU. Fortunately for the Allies, though, the Germans did not change the codes used by U-boats in European coastal waters, which enabled the Allies to have knowledge of U-boat activities in the Baltic, the North Sea, and the Bay of Biscay. Still, it was not until December 1942 that the Allies broke the new German naval codes based on the four-wheel naval enigma code machine, and postwar experts considered the nine-month period when the Allies could not read that code "the most serious cryptanalytic failure" in the whole Allied attack on German naval codes. After breaking the code, however, the Allies could read radio transmissions to and from U-boats at sea with little difficulty.[88]

Intercepts of radio communications to and from U-boats were sent to the naval section of the Government Code and Cipher School at Bletchley Park for decryption. When a radio message had been reduced by code breakers to plain text, it was then dispatched by teleprinter to the submarine tracking room in the Operational Intelligence Centre in London. Upon receipt by the submarine tracking room, a decoded radio intercept was then combined with other intelligence materials to become part of the total intelligence picture. The submarine tracking room in London supplied the Canadian submarine tracking room with "digested and processed" decrypts of U-boat radio communications.[89]

Beginning in December 1942 the US Navy, not wanting to be dependent on the British for information, began to decrypt U-boat radio transmissions independently — but in continued cooperation with the British at Bletchley Park. The intercepts were sent to OP-20Y-G(A) (OP: office of the chief of naval operations; 20: communications division; Y: cryptanalysts; G: communications intelligence; A: Atlantic) which was located in a former young women's school, Mount Vernon Seminary in Washington, D.C. The intercepts were then deciphered, translated into English, and sent by teleprinter or by the hand of an officer to F-21 section of the Combat Intelligence Division of COMINCH at the Main Navy on the Mall near the Lincoln Memorial. Adjoining F-21's submarine tracking room was F-211 or the "secret room." Aside from several high ranking officers, such as the COMINCH himself — Admiral Ernest J. King, only five persons were permitted regularly into the secret room (Commander Kenneth Knowles, USN, commander F-21; Lieutenant John E. Parsons, USNR, commander secret room; Lieutenant (jg) John V. Boland, USNR; Ensign R. B. Chevalier, USNR; and Yeoman Samuel Livecchi, USN). It was in the secret room where the contents of the decrypts were married with other forms of intelligence such as D/F fixes, ship and aircraft sightings, and reports of U-boat attacks to produce a total intelligence picture. Intelligence, with its sources of information hidden, then moved out of the secret room to F-21's submarine tracking room. Further, OP-20Y-G(A) and the secret room in Washington, D.C., also exchanged by teleprinter cryptographic information with the naval section of the Government's Code and Cipher School at Bletchley Park and the Admiralty's submarine tracking room in London.[90]

Three submarine tracking rooms and two centers for decryption, all linked by teleprinters and telephones, resulted in some duplication of effort, but the system turned out mountains of intelligence on the U-boats. The best sources were decoded radio communications to and from the U-boats. The Germans sent thousands of radio communications which the Allies decrypted—the Americans alone deciphering 49,668 such messages during the war.[91] These intercepted and decrypted German radio messages gave the Allies operational intelligence such as foreknowledge of the deployments and locations of U-boat patrol lines in the North Atlantic. This information, when timely, was of great operational value to the Allies. However, on many occasions an intercepted German operational order of potentially great value to the Allies was not decrypted until hours or even days after the event occurred. For example, at 1116 on 14 December 1942 the Allies intercepted an order for fourteen U-boats to establish a patrol line, code named *Raufbold*, west of Ireland, and the order was not decrypted until 1754 on 16 December, more than twenty-four hours after Allied convoy ON 153 had been intercepted by the *Raufbold* patrol.[92] Nevertheless, even with lags caused by delays in decryption, the Allies time and time again gained priceless information about the deployment of U-boats in the North Atlantic from communications intelligence.

Intercepted and decrypted German radio communications not only gave the Allies operational intelligence, but also provided large amounts of valuable information regarding the German U-boat service. It was German standard operating procedure to include a U-boat's position, any defects, and fuel status in each report to the BdU. For example, on 3 May 1943 the U-614 radioed the BdU that "AM IN NAVAL GRID SQUARE AJ 6931. CRACK IN STARBOARD CYLINDER COVER. AM WITHDRAWING TO THE EASTWARD TO REPAIR. 49 CBM."[93] Such decoded radio messages thus revealed not only the location of the U-boats, but also the fuel status and general combat readiness of each vessel. These radio decrypts also provided Allied intelligence with insights into German tactics and strategy, command and control techniques, and standard operating procedures for such things as refueling at sea. Further, Allied access to German radio messages provided knowledge of the abilities and characters not only of the individual commanders of U-boats, but also of the commanders of the U-boat service itself. Communications intelligence offered the Allies a knowledge of the workings of the German U-boat service — unique in the history of naval warfare for its scope and completeness.

At the end of March 1943 German U-boats had successfully attacked Allied merchant shipping for forty-three months. During this period, the U-boats had sunk hundreds of Allied merchant ships totalling many thousands of tons at little cost to themselves.[94] This success, however, was usually achieved against ships which were sailing independently in areas such as the western approaches to Great Britain and in American coastal waters. When the Allies finally instituted defensive measures for shipping, in the form of convoys escorted by surface vessels and aircraft, the number of merchant ships sunk by U-boats decreased dramatically, while the number of U-boats lost to enemy action increased. Convoys supported by aircraft ended the so-called "happy times" for the U-boats first in the eastern Atlantic west of Great Britain and then off the east coast of North America.[95]

In early 1943 the mid-North Atlantic was the only area left where the U-boats could operate against Allied merchant shipping relatively free from Allied aircraft. And for the U-boats the mid-North Atlantic in 1943 was an area of great opportunity as well as one of great danger. Successful U-boat attacks on Allied shipping between North America and Great Britain would have a decisive effect on the Allied conduct of the war. The stakes were beyond calculation, for successful U-boat operations in the Atlantic during 1943 could at the least retard, and perhaps even prevent, the Allied buildup for the invasion of Europe in 1944. Operations in the mid-North Atlantic in 1943 were an opportunity for the U-boats to have a decisive impact on the war.

But there would be no easy victories for the U-boats against merchant vessels sailing independently in the mid-North Atlantic. Instead, shipping proceeding between North America and Great Britain would sail under convoy for the most part. To be successful in 1943, the German U-boat wolf packs would have to sink the ships in these Allied convoys, a far more difficult challenge than picking off independently routed ships. By the beginning of 1943, the U-boats were also being confronted and confounded by advances in Allied technology and intelligence. Further, in 1943, the Allies finally saw the importance of the North Atlantic convoys and began to deploy more and more resources in terms of personnel, surface escorts, and aircraft to defend transatlantic convoys. By April 1943 the issue of the Battle of the Atlantic hung in the balance and would be decided by a long series of battles between the U-boats and the convoy escorts which sprawled across the North Atlantic. In the end, the German wolf packs would be decisively defeated.

Chapter 2

The Battle of the Atlantic in the Balance

10–30 April 1943

March 1943 marked the point at which the German U-boats came closest to disrupting seaborne communications between North America and Great Britain.[1] During that month the U-boats sank 108 ships totaling 627,377 tons.[2] In one huge battle the U-boats destroyed twenty-one ships amounting to 140,842 tons belonging to convoys HX 229 and SC 122.[3] And in another battle at the beginning of April the U-boats sank six more ships from convoy HX 231.[4] During March the Germans lost only fourteen U-boats to enemy action.[5]

The Allies' strategic situation in the North Atlantic was bleak, with no end in sight to the sinkings and U-boat attacks on transatlantic convoys. On 5 April it was estimated by the US Navy that the Germans had 230 U-boats either in Norwegian and French ports or operating in the Atlantic.[6] And on 2 April another Allied intelligence appreciation report noted that the Germans were building "about 23 [U-boats] per month," which was almost double the rate at which the Allies were sinking them and that "unless our weapons or tactics are drastically improved, we can expect to lose three quarters as many ships during this year as in the whole war up to now."[7] To the Allies, the strategic situation in the North Atlantic at the end of March 1943 was filled with danger—if they lost in the North Atlantic, they could lose the war worldwide.

The Germans, on the other hand, had grounds for guarded optimism at the beginning of April. In March the Reich commissioned twenty-seven new U-boats, and on 1 April 411 U-boats were in service. During March the Germans had 194 operational U-boats in the

Atlantic theater—an average of 116 of these were at sea. Discounting those U-boats returning to or proceeding from their bases, the Germans maintained an average of forty-nine U-boats in operational areas in the North Atlantic during March.[8] The percentage of U-boats engaged in convoy operations steadily increased from 39 percent in the last six months of 1942 to 75 percent in the first quarter of 1943. Despite the fact that operations against convoys were much more difficult and dangerous for the U-boats than attacks on enemy ships sailing independently, German losses for this same period rose only slightly, from 8.9 percent to 9.2 percent.

Further, according to German analysis, the true operational effectiveness of each U-boat had been increasing, for in January 1943 U-boats sank 129 tons of shipping per U-boat per day while that figure had increased to 230 tons per day per U-boat in March.[9] Even though these figures were based on inflated claims of sinkings—the Germans claimed for March 780,000 tons when the actual figure was 625,377 tons—the BdU appeared to have grounds to be optimistic about the outcome of future operations against Allied convoys. However, at the beginning of April 1943 these facts and figures did not inform either Allies or Germans that the U-boats would suffer defeat by the end of May.

With the victory against convoys HX 229 and SC 122 in March and the battle over HX 231 in early April, the BdU decided to continue the campaign against Allied convoys running between North America and Great Britain, but with a reduced number of U-boats. After the big battles of March, many U-boats had to return to their bases to refuel, undergo repairs, and restock torpedoes. Therefore, the BdU undertook a number of battles in the first weeks of April with fewer U-boats until those at their bases could return to sea. However, by the end of the month, the BdU had some seventy U-boats operating against convoys in the North Atlantic.[10]

On 5 April the BdU ordered nine U-boats (U-188, U-257, U-86, U-615, U-627, U-404, U-662, U-571, U-618) to form a mid-Atlantic patrol line, code named *Adler*, at 0800 on 7 April to intercept a "CONVOY PROCEEDING NORTHWARDS" which is "EXPECTED FROM 7/4." Upon assuming their positions in the patrol line, the U-boats of the *Adler* group were to sweep on a course of 210° toward Flemish Cap at a rate of 100 miles per day. This order was decoded by the Allies at 2126 on 6 April.[11] The portion of this order which gave the position of the *Adler* patrol line was super-enciphered. However, the Allies could decode not only the Germans' routine radio transmissions, but also the super-encipherment of the positions given within them, and the Allies placed the *Adler* patrol line as running between 54°51'N, 44°35'W to 52°57'N, 39°55'W.[12] "Dead reckoning" indicated to the BdU that a slow eastbound North Atlantic convoy, SC 125, would be intercepted by the *Adler* patrol.[13]

Allied communications intelligence had identified the general location of the *Adler* patrol line, and SC 125 passed to the south of it.[14] The Germans learned from a radio intercept that SC 125 had bypassed the *Adler* patrol line. On 8 April the *Adler* group was reconstituted with fifteen U-boats (U-188, U-257, U-84, U-615, U-267, U-404, U-662, U-571, U-71, U-108, U-258, U-415, U-438, U-381, U-618) that formed a patrol line 300 miles long by 0800 on 11 April to sweep southeast in search of an HX (or fast eastbound) convoy. From "dead reckoning," the Germans concluded that an HX convoy was several days behind SC 125 and on approximately the same course.[15] There is no record that the Allies intercepted and decoded this order. German intelligence was also deficient, for the first convoy intercepted by the *Adler* group was not an HX convoy, but rather ON 176, a fast westbound convoy.

Convoy ON 176 consisted of forty-one merchant ships escorted by Escort Group B4—consisting of destroyers HMS *Highlander*, HMS *Vimy*, and HMS *Beverley*; and corvettes HMS *Anemone*, HMS *Asphodel*, HMS *Pennywort*, HMS *Abelia*, and HMS *Clover*—in which the destroyer HMS *Highlander*, the merchant ship *Ciarnwaluna*, and the rescue ship *Melrose Abbey* were all equipped with HF/DF.[16] The ocean escort met the convoy off northern Ireland on 1 April and the convoy proceeded in a general northwest direction. ON 176 was routed roughly along the northern great circle route to carry the convoy near air cover from Iceland as well as to allow it to pick up three ships from that island bound to North America on 4 April.

Serious problems were encountered at this point. Bad weather meant that the escorts could not be refueled at sea from tankers in the convoy, and HMS *Beverley* and HMS *Vimy* were detached to Iceland for fuel. On 7 April the convoy turned to a southwesterly course and, even though the sea was still rough, escort Commander E. C.

L. Day, RN, determined that they had to be refueled "before passing beyond air cover" from Iceland. In heavy seas and a freshening wind, HMS *Highlander*, HMS *Anemone*, and HMS *Asphodel* were fueled by the tankers *Hente Maersk* and *Luminetta*. On 8 April HMS *Beverley* and HMS *Vimy* rejoined the convoy at 59°25′N, 32°32′W. Dense fog was encountered, and HMS *Beverley* collided with the merchant ship *Ciarnvaluna* on 10 April. It was unclear to Day how this collision happened, and the British officer later reported that its cause "will now never be known." The Town class destroyer was holed forward on the starboard side. While it was still capable of making 15 knots, its sonar and depth charge gear were put out of action.[17]

At 1010Z on 10 April the HF/DF sets on the ships in the convoy picked up a radio transmission. This was the "first intimation" that Day had of U-boats being in the vicinity of the convoy. Several more radio transmissions were picked up which were coming from the southeast of ON 176 and were thought to be coming from the U-boats "concentrating on HX 231," the eastbound convoy. Then at 1315Z an HF/DF bearing of 120° was obtained at a range of between 12 and 15 miles from ON 176. This was the first of several sighting reports sent by the U-404.[18]

Upon receipt of the U-404's sighting report, the BdU ordered eight other U-boats (U-84, U-257, U-188, U-267, U-682, U-613, U-71, U-751) belonging to the *Adler* patrol line to operate against ON 176. The remaining U-boats of the *Adler* group (U-415, U-413, U-438, U-381, U-618, U-108, U-258) were ordered to set up another patrol line code named *Meise* by 0800 on 11 April to run between 52°09′N, 37°05′W and 49°51′N, 35°25′W. At the same time, a third patrol line was ordered set up consisting of ten U-boats (U-706, U-532, U-168, U-584, U-191, U-630, U-569, U-270, U-530, U-203) which were steaming west after breaking off the action against HX 231. This patrol was to be code named *Lerche* and was to run from 54°39′N, 34°35′N, to 51°45′N, 32°05′W. The U-boats of the *Lerche* group were further ordered to steam at "HIGH SPEED" to take up their assigned positions.[19] The objective of the *Meise* and *Lerche* patrol lines was an "expected HX convoy" which the BdU intended to intercept on 11 April.[20] The Allies decoded all three of these orders by 0841 on 11 April and were fully aware of the locations of the *Meise* and *Lerche* patrol lines.[21]

At 1315Z on 10 April, when the escort of ON 176 obtained an HF/DF bearing of 120° on the radio transmission made by the U-404, HMS *Vimy* and HMS *Pennywort* were ordered to "intercept" the U-boat. At 1340Z a bearing was obtained on a second U-boat, possibly the U-257, on a bearing of 98°. At 1406Z HMS *Vimy* sighted the U-404 and forced it to dive. Several minutes later another U-boat, probably the U-84, was sighted and also forced below. HMS *Vimy* and HMS *Pennywort*, reinforced by HMS *Clover*, attacked the U-boat several times with depth charges without result and remained searching for the U-boats until the convoy steamed past.[22]

In an attempt to throw off the U-boats, ON 176 changed course from 194° to 224° at 1400. But this maneuver did not work, for the ships of the convoy continued to obtain U-boat radio transmissions on their HF/DF sets throughout the afternoon. The bearings of these transmissions suggested to Day that the U-boats were southeast of the convoy and moving west to intercept. To give the impression that the convoy's route was southwest, ON 176's course was charged to 240° at 1600; to 220° at 2000Z; and to 174° at 2300Z. By this strategy, the convoy might pass astern of the U-boats or at least put the U-boats "up moon."[23]

During the afternoon of 10 April the BdU warned the U-boats that there was only a short time remaining to engage the convoy because of the "NEWFOUNDLAND FOG AND AIR PATROLS IN COASTAL AREAS." And later, at 0326 on 11 April, the U-boats were informed that the "CONVOY WILL PRESUMABLY PASS ALONG THE SOUTHERN EDGE OF NEWFOUNDLAND TO A NORTH AMERICAN PORT."[24] The BdU wanted the U-boats to attack ON 176 before the convoy came within range of Allied aircraft based in Newfoundland.

Even with the convoy's attempts to shake them off, the U-boats maintained contact with ON 176. Just after the convoy turned to a course of 174° at 2300Z on 10 April, HMS *Abelia* sighted a U-boat "in the moons path." This U-boat was chased, forced to dive, and attacked by HMS *Abelia* and HMS *Clover* before the warships returned to their stations on the starboard side of the convoy. At 0215Z it was clear from HF/DF bearings that two U-boats were attempting to close with the starboard bow of the convoy. A search was conducted and HMS *Highlander*, HMS *Abelia*, and HMS *Beverley* fired star shells, but nothing was seen. From its station on the starboard bow of the convoy, HMS *Clover* saw "a flash on the port bow" at 0352 and "immediately after a flare was seen in the water followed by a number of under water explosions in the same direction two miles off." This was thought to be HMS *Beverley* attacking, but in fact it was the destroyer blowing up after being torpedoed by the U-188. Seven minutes after HMS *Beverley* exploded, HMS *Clover* obtained a sonar contact bearing 215° "which was the approximate bearing of the flare." HMS *Clover* attacked, dropping ten depth charges. "Simultaneously with the dropping of the depth charges voices of survivors were heard. Immediately after the explosion of the last charge an overpowering smell of oil fuel was felt." HMS *Clover* ran out and turned but could not regain sonar contact with the target. The next contact with the enemy came at 0543 on 11 April, when HMS *Asphodel* obtained a radar target ahead of the port wing of the convoy. The British corvette attacked the U-boat, forced it to dive, and then followed the enemy vessel through the convoy and depth charged it astern of ON 176. The last action of the night of 10–11 April occurred when a U-boat was detected some 6 miles from the starboard bow of ON 176, but a search by HMS *Vimy* and HMS *Anemone* was without result.[25]

At 0800Z on 11 April the convoy altered course to 224° in an attempt to throw off the shadowing U-boats. At 1100 a B-17 Fortress aircraft from Newfoundland appeared over the convoy as an escort. A U-boat was next detected on the starboard beam of the convoy at a range of 10 miles. HMS *Abelia* and HMS *Clover* were sent to search for this U-boat, but nothing was found. HF/DF intercepts were "scant" throughout the daylight hours of 11 April, but Day thought that there was possibly a U-boat on the port quarter shadowing the convoy. At 2100Z the convoy went to a course of 230° "to look like a Navigational adjustment" and then at 0001 to a course of 200°.[26]

During the daylight hours and evening of 11 April, seven U-boats were in contact with ON 176, but the U-boats' operations were hampered by the appearance of Allied aircraft from Newfoundland over the convoy. At 1721, the U-404 reported "UNDERWATER BEFORE FLYING BOAT." Little more than three hours later, the U-257 radioed "AM BEING ATTACKED BY SHORE-BASED AIRCRAFT." Then the U-71, like the first two submarines, was forced to submerge because of aircraft.[27]

The BdU attempted to draw the Allies away from the *Adler* U-boats by misleading shore-based D/F stations. At 2158, the BdU ordered the U-84 to move off in a northwesterly direction to 53°15′N, 46°45′W, transmitting fake radio messages to make it appear that a group of U-boats were operating in the neighborhood. It was doubtful, however, that the Allies fell for this ruse, for they could identify an individual radio transmitter from the characteristics of the transmission.[28]

At 2320Z the escorts of ON 176 obtained an HF/DF bearing at a range of 6 miles on the starboard beam of the convoy. At this point Day made what he later called "a bad and costly mistake" by not immediately sending an escort down this bearing to hunt and attack this U-boat. This was the first HF/DF bearing picked up in several hours, and Day thought that the U-boat had just reestablished contact with ON 176. Day decided to postpone any action against the enemy vessel until 2345Z "so as to cover" a change of course by the convoy to 200° scheduled to take place at 0001. This inaction enabled the U-404 to torpedo and sink the merchant ship *Lancastrian Prince* at 2340Z. Screened by two escorts, the rescue ship *Melrose Abbey* stood by to pick up survivors, but none were found.[29]

At 0145Z on 12 April an HF/DF bearing placed a U-boat astern of the convoy. HMS *Vimy*, later joined by HMS *Abelia*, was sent down this bearing. After a fruitless two-hour hunt, both ships returned to their stations in the screen of ON 176. And at 0430 HMS *Clover* obtained a radar contact with a U-boat on the port quarter of the convoy. The U-boat was forced to dive by gunfire and was then depth charged several times before the British corvette lost contact and returned to the convoy. This was the last contact between the escorts of ON 176 and the U-boats. At 0800 the convoy encountered fog.[30]

One by one, the convoy's attackers fell back. The U-404 withdrew from the operation to conduct repairs. The U-71, overflown by an Allied aircraft, was not in contact with the convoy and reported that visibility had dropped to under 100 meters. And at 1629 the U-267 reported that it was not in contact with the convoy and that visibility was 500 meters to 2 miles.[31] The BdU ended the operation against ON 176 at 2022 because of the fog and the presence of Allied aircraft.[32]

Both sides pointed with pride to the ON 176 engagement. After the battle, Day claimed that "the value of two H/F D/F ships in the convoy is clearly born out." However, the number of U-boats in contact with the convoy and the small size of the escort prevented protracted hunts for U-boats. Still, with the exception of the torpedoing of the *Lancastrian Prince*, Day thought that the defense of the convoy had been "satisfactory."[33] The Germans, on the other hand, considered the battle with ON 176 a victory. Nine U-boats had chased the convoy over a distance of some 340 miles for several days. No U-boat was lost, only one was damaged, and the BdU wrongly thought that nine Allied ships had been sunk.[34]

At the same time that ON 176 was battling the U-boats of the *Adler* group, convoy HX 232, was under attack by ten U-boats of the *Lerche* group some miles to the east. HX 232 was an eastbound convoy, consisting of forty-six ships which sailed from New York on 2 April. Just before noon on 8 April, the convoy rendezvoused with Escort Group B3 consisting of the destroyers HMS *Escapade* (HF/DF) and ORP *Garland* (HF/DF) along with the corvettes HMS *Narcissus*, HMS *Azalea*, FFS *Roselys*, and FFS *Renoncule* (HMS *Keppel* was also a member of Escort Group B3, but was in port having its radar calibrated and did not join HX 232 until 14 April). That afternoon, HMS *Escapade* and ORP *Garland* were refueled from the tanker *Saintonge*, and just before dark the destroyer HMS *Witherington* joined the escort of the convoy.[35]

At 0142Z on the morning of 10 April, escort Commander M. J. Evans received a radio message from COMINCH stating that four radio transmissions had been intercepted from his vicinity. This was followed by an order from the commander in chief, western approaches, for the convoy to alter course. During 10 April there were no indications in the form of HF/DF bearings that the convoy had been sighted.[36]

As dawn broke on 11 April, HMS *Witherington* and ORP *Garland* were stationed as an extended screen 12 miles off the bow of the convoy. Evans claimed that visibility was so good that the convoy's smoke could be seen for 35 miles. At 0720 a radio message from the Admiralty was received stating that "D/F bearings at 101115Z 101213 and 102332Z indicate probable patrol line of U-boats approximately 055°59' North 034°01' West to approximately 050°58'

North 032°02' West."[37] This information was obviously based on the decoded text of the order from the BdU setting up the *Lerche* patrol line. Evans altered the course of HX 232 from 636° to 340° in a last minute attempt to avoid the U-boats. Shortly afterwards an HF/DF bearing of 334° was obtained coming from "within 50 miles" of the convoy. HX 232's course was again changed to the north "to clear this bearing." Evans then concluded that the convoy was already in the U-boat patrol line and by maintaining a course of north he would "only run up the line of submarines," so the convoy's course was again changed to 60 degree to pass through the patrol line as quickly as possible.

Aside from long-range HF/DF interceptions and the radio message from the Admiralty, Evans still had no evidence that HX 232 had been sighted by the enemy. In fact, "all bearings were consistent with reports and shadowing of ON 176 whose position had now been ascertained by direct communication on 2410 kc/s." But at 1547Z and 1603Z the HF/DF sets on the escorts picked up two U-boat radio transmissions bearing 179° and 337°, respectively. Evans thought that these were the first sighting reports of HX 232 made by the U-boats, with the sighting first reported by the U-584.[38] The Germans were able to intercept HX 232 because decoded Allied radio communications gave them foreknowledge of the route to be followed by the convoy.[39] The Allies, on the other hand, were not able to route HX 232 to avoid the *Lerche* line because they did not decode the order setting up that patrol group until 0733 on 11 April, when HX 232 was already upon the patrol line. At 0935 on 11 April the BdU ordered the U-boats of the *Lerche* group "TO GO FOR . . . CONVOY . . . AT MAXIMUM SPEED."[40]

After the transmission of the first sighting report, the HF/DF sets on HMS *Escapade* and ORP *Garland* picked up other radio transmissions coming from the port beam of the convoy, and at 1905Z HMS *Escapade* searched down a bearing of 19° in search of a U-boat. At 1945Z the British destroyer sighted a U-boat, probably the U-584. HMS *Escapade* did not open fire with its main armament, for the sea was rough and the "chances of a hit were infinitesimal," and the British wanted to keep the U-boat on the surface as long as possible to improve the chances of a shallow first depth charge attack. The U-boat dived 2 miles ahead of the British destroyer, which then attacked the enemy vessel with depth charges without result. Sonar contact was not gained and HMS *Escapade* hunted for the U-boat without success until 2230 and then returned to HX 232.[41]

In another attempt to throw off the U-boats, HX 232 changed course to 87° at 2130. But at 2225 a merchant ship of the convoy reported sighting a U-boat, although a search for the enemy vessel was fruitless. On the port side of the convoy, HMS *Witherington* obtained a "doubtful" sonar contact at a range of 400 yards at 2255. A depth charge attack was mounted, but before the attack could be carried out, a torpedo was heard approaching on a bearing of 140°. The torpedo missed the British destroyer, and a futile hunt was undertaken down the missile's track.[42]

Just before midnight, FFS *Renoncule*, on the convoy's port bow, obtained a sonar contact bearing 50° range with a range of 2,500 yards. The French corvette attacked with ten depth charges, at which point the ship's sonar momentarily broke down. But as the ship was running out after the attack, a radar contact was obtained at a range of 6,000 yards bearing 30°. As the corvette was running down this contact, two torpedoes were fired at the ship. FFS *Renoncule* then undertook a depth charge attack by eye. During the course of this attack, a radar contact was gained with another U-boat, which was illuminated with a star shell. FFS *Renoncule* closed with the second U-boat. FFS *Renoncule*'s sonar had been repaired, and when the submarine dived, sonar contact was established at a range of 1,000 yards. This contact was attacked with ten depth charges and then reattacked with another ten depth charges before it was lost. At 0114 FFS *Renoncule* was ordered to rejoin the screen of HX 232.[43]

At 0215 on 12 April, ORP *Garland* obtained a radar contact. As the contact was run down it disappeared and a sonar contact was gained, but this contact was classified as a "nonsubmarine" in the course of the hunt, and ORP *Garland* returned to its position in the screen on the starboard side of HX 232. As ORP *Garland* was steaming to resume its place, the U-563 torpedoed three merchant ships on the starboard side of the convoy between 0243Z and 0249Z. The *Ulysses* was hit in the starboard bow by a torpedo and sank within ten minutes. The *Pacific Grove* was hit amidships and burst into flames, sinking at 0710. And the *Fresco City* was torpedoed in the main hold on the starboard side. The ship went dead in the water and was abandoned by its crew. The *Fresco City*, later reboarded and again abandoned as being unsalvageable, was finished off later by the U-706. HMS *Azalea* picked up 158 crew members and passengers from the three ships. Evans later thought that the U-boat which had torpedoed these ships had slipped past the convoy's screen through a gap made when ORP *Garland* left its station to run down the radar contact at 0215.[44]

When the three merchant vessels were torpedoed, a nearby merchant ship sighted a U-boat which was taken under gunfire. The escorts on the starboard side of the convoy also began to hunt for the U-boat which had torpedoed the three ships, with the ORP *Garland* obtaining sonar contact in the region where the merchant ship had aimed its gunfire. This contact was attacked at 0253 with depth charges, but the contact was lost. At 0310 the hunt for the U-boat was given up and ORP *Garland* returned to its station. Forty minutes later, FFS *Roselys* received a radar contact which, when illuminated, revealed a submerging U-boat which was attacked with depth charges. Immediately thereafter, the French corvette obtained another radar contact. This contact was illuminated and began to escape from the corvette on the surface. However, ORP *Garland*, which had joined FFS *Roselys*, took up the chase, illuminated the enemy vessel, forced it to dive, and then attacked the U-boat with depth charges without result. ORP *Garland* rejoined HX 232 at 0625.[45]

At dawn on 12 April Evans concluded from HF/DF bearings that the convoy was being shadowed from four different directions, but the Allies turned the tables on the U-boats with the arrival of VLR B-24 Liberator aircraft from Iceland and Northern Ireland. Five of these planes operated over the convoy from 0900 to 2330.[46] At 1101 the U-203 radioed "AM CONTINUALLY BEING HARASSED BY AIR-CRAFT."[47] The U-584 reported that it had been forced to dive three times by aircraft.[48] And the U-191 had "A FAIRLY LONG AND SUC-CESSFUL MACHINE-GUN DEFENSE AGAINST THE CONSTANT AIR ES-CORT WITH THE CONVOY," during the course of which aircraft M/86 was forced to break off the action. The BdU retransmitted the report of this action to all the other U-boats at sea to encourage them to remain on the surface and fight back against aircraft.[49]

At 1100Z HX 232 altered course 20° to starboard in an effort to lose any U-boats which were shadowing the convoy, and at 1400 the

Allied force returned to a course of 87°. At 1850 the escort of HX 232 was reinforced by four destroyers of the 4th Escort Group (HMS *Inglefield*, HMS *Fury*, HMS *Eclipse*, HMS *Icarus*), but by the time they had arrived the battle was over, for no "hot D/F bearings" had been picked up by HX 232's escort since noon. Evans thought that "the attack on the convoy was finally abandoned because of the air cover."[50]

At 1548 on 12 April the BdU ordered the U-boats of the *Lerche* patrol line to attempt to get ahead of HX 232 by high speed surface runs, if necessary making a 30-mile detour around the convoy, to be in a position to attack that night. The U-boats were warned sternly that Allied aircraft would return over the convoy at daylight on 13 April. Although the *Lerche* U-boats were told later that HX 232 was steering for the "NORTH CHANNEL AND MAKE SURE YOU ARE AHEAD OF THE CONVOY AT FIRST LIGHT,"[51] the U-boats did not regain contact with HX 232, and the BdU called off the operation at 1044 on 13 April.[52] As Evans guessed, the arrival of aircraft over the convoy forced this decision. The operation had started well for the Germans, with seven out of ten U-boats gaining contact with the convoy on the first night and sinking three merchant ships, but on 12 April "Approach" to the convoy by the U-boats "was no longer possible as strong air cover came up."[53]

At the same time orders were issued to set up the *Lerche* patrol line, the BdU ordered seven U-boats (U-415, U-413, U-438, U-831, U-618, U-108, U-258) to form still another patrol line by 1800 on 11 April. Code named *Meise*, this line was to run between 52°09'N, 37°05'W to 49°15'N 35°25'W. The Allies decoded this order at 0841 on 11 April. The next day the BdU ordered the U-boats of the *Meise* group to steam southwest at a rate of 120 miles per day. Because of delays in decoding, the Allies did not read this order until 0502 on 16 April. On 12 April the BdU increased the *Meise* patrol line to twelve U-boats (U-84, U-613, U-404, U-571, U-415, U-413, U-662, U-381, U-618, U-108, U-258, U-831) and ordered them to form a patrol line by 0800 on 13 April running between 50°09'N, 40°15'W and 47°45'N, 38°35'W. The U-boats were to expect a northwest bound convoy on 13 April. This order was not decoded until 0848 on 16 April.[54] The Germans thought, based on "dead reckoning" and a "special Italian intercept message," that the U-boats would intercept convoy SC 126 on 13 April.[55]

By 11 April the Allies knew the general location of the major concentrations of U-boats including the *Meise* group,[56] and it was clear that the U-boats were moving westward toward Newfoundland and away from Ireland and Iceland. It was thought by the Allies that the U-boats were moving away from the VLR B-24 Liberator aircraft based on those islands because Allied aircraft at Newfoundland could operate only some 500 miles northeast of St. John's. In response to the German deployment, the Allies conducted what was termed a "somewhat bold expedient" by routing convoys northward and southward around the U-boats.

The main risk was thought to be run by those convoys routed to the south, for a great part of their voyage would be through "an area remote" from Allied air bases. The first convoy to risk the run past the *Meise* line was successful; westbound ON 177 sailed from Liverpool on 6 April on a northwest course to 60°10′N, 26°36′W before turning onto a southwest course. The convoy arrived safely at New York after a voyage of seventeen days without being contacted by any U-boats. At the same time, two eastbound convoys — HX 233 and SC 126 — were sent to Great Britain from North America along a southern route designed to pass southward of the known concentrations of U-boats.[57] This plan would have succeeded but for the fortuitous sighting of convoy HX 233 by the U-262.

The fifty-seven merchant ships of convoy HX 233 sailed on 6 April from New York escorted by Escort Group A3, commanded by Captain P. R. Heineman, USN, and consisted of the Coast Guard cutters USCGC *Spencer*, USCGC *Duane;* the destroyer HMCS *Skeena;* and the corvettes HMCS *Wetaskawin*, HMCS *Arvida*, HMS *Dianthus*, HMS *Bergamont*, and HMS *Bryony*. HMCS *Skeena* and the USCGC *Spencer* were equipped with HF/DF. HX 233 and its escort proceeded eastward without incident for ten days. Meanwhile, SC 126 sailed from Halifax on 8 April and proceeded behind HX 233 along approximately the same course.[58]

On 13 April the BdU ordered the *Meise* group to move westward and reinforced the formation to eighteen U-boats (U-267, U-257, U-188, U-71, U-84, *Koepke*, U-404, U-571, U-415, U-413, U-598, U-618, *Mueller*, U-831, U-618, U-258, U-610, U-108) which were told that "A NORTHEAST CONVOY IS EXPECTED." The next day, 14 April, convoys HX 233 and SC 126 still had not been located by the U-boats, and the BdU ordered them to steam northeast at 4 knots until 2300 and then to reverse course to the southwest and steam at 4 knots.[59] Not knowing that HX 233 and SC 126 were passing to the south of the *Meise* line, the BdU "intended that the group should proceed to meet the convoy next day."[60] At 0753 on 14 April the *Meise* group's position was given away when the U-188 radioed to report a damaged engine. The BdU rebuked the U-188 for breaking radio silence, but it was too late, for Allied shore-based D/F stations had obtained a fix on the transmission.[61] On 15 April the *Meise* group was reinforced by six U-boats (U-134, U-306, U-631, U-203, U-532, U-552) which extended the patrol line northward. The U-boats were ordered to maintain their positions and to watch out for a convoy.[62]

At 0434 on 15 April, U-262 by chance sighted HX 233 to the east and south of the *Meise* group. The U-262 was outward-bound to the Gulf of St. Lawrence to attempt to pick up a number of German prisoners of war who had informed the BdU of their plans to escape and requested that a U-boat pick them up.[63] After sighting HX 233, the U-262 was ordered to maintain contact with the convoy and was given freedom to attack. As the U-boats of the *Meise* group were too far to the west to intercept the convoy, five outward-bound U-boats (U-626, U-175, U-226, U-258, U-264) were ordered to attack HX 233. But these U-boats, being at some distance from the convoy, would need considerable time to intercept the Allied force.[64]

The first indication of U-boat activity came on 15 April, when four U-boat radio transmissions made at some distance from the convoy were intercepted. At 0340Z on 16 April the USCGC *Spencer*, 4,500 yards ahead of HX 233, obtained a radar contact. This was U-262 attempting to attack the convoy. The contact was at a range of 7,100 yards from the Coast Guard cutter bearing 150°. USCGC *Spencer* ran down the bearing and at a range of 3,200 yards the target disappeared. But at 0410Z sonar contact was obtained and a depth charge attack was undertaken without result. Sonar contact was quickly regained, and the American warship attacked the U-262 with a mouse-trap rocket launcher without effect.[65] HMCS *Wetaskawin* joined the hunt and at 0520Z the USCGC *Spencer* regained sonar contact and again attacked with a mousetrap without effect. Sonar contact was soon lost and after continuing the hunt for several more hours, the Allied warships resumed their positions on HX 233's screen once the convoy had steamed past the area.[66] After being driven off by the escort of HX 233, the U-262 continued westward on its mission to the Gulf of St. Lawrence.[67]

U-boat contacts with HX 233 multiplied overnight. At 2127Z on 16 April, the U-175 reported that it was in contact with a destroyer. Seven hours later the U-382, another outward-bound U-boat, reported "CONVOY IN SQ BE 4837, COURSE 090, SPEED 8." These radio transmissions were quickly followed by several more contact reports from other U-boats. The BdU at 1044Z ordered additional outward-bound U-boats to operate against HX 233 and "IN VIEW OF THE EXISTING AIRCRAFT SITUATION" to be ahead of the convoy that night or at daylight the next morning.[68]

The first contact on April 17 between the U-boats and HX 233 occurred at 0412Z when the USCGC *Spencer* obtained a radar contact ahead of the convoy. As the American warship ran down the bearing, the U-boat submerged. The USCGC *Spencer,* joined by HMS *Dianthus,* began a sonar hunt for the U-boat. Sonar contact was gained and at 0512Z the USCGC *Spencer* made a depth charge attack without result. The sonar hunt resumed, and another depth charge attack was made at 0754Z. At 0820Z sonar contact was again obtained and a fruitless attack was undertaken with a mousetrap. After this attack the hunt for the U-boat was abandoned, and the Allied warships steamed to rejoin the convoy, for HMS *Dianthus* and USCGC *Spencer* were now 10 miles astern of HX 233.[69]

While HMS *Dianthus* and USCGC *Spencer* still trailed HX 233, HMCS *Skeena* obtained an HF/DF bearing off the port bow of the convoy. This bearing was run down by the Canadian destroyer, but nothing was found. While the three Allied warships hunting U-boats were absent from the convoy's screen, the U-628 torpedoed the merchant ship *Fort Rampart* at 0605Z. After their vessel was hit aft on the starboard side, the crew of the *Fort Rampart* abandoned the ship and were picked up by HMCS *Arvida.* The merchant ship drifted clear of the convoy and was later sunk by Allied forces.[70]

At 1150Z the USCGC *Spencer,* now ahead of HX 233, obtained a sonar contact on the U-175 bearing 39° at a range of 1,500 yards. The American Coast Guard cutter immediately attacked with two depth charges six minutes apart. As the convoy overran the area, USCGC *Spencer* regained sonar contact and held it as the merchant ships steamed past, but could not attack because of the proximity of the convoy. At the same time the USCGC *Duane* steamed through the convoy to assist the USCGC *Spencer* in the hunt for the U-175. At 1217Z the USCGC *Spencer* attacked with a mousetrap, but sonar contact was then lost. The two Coast Guard cutters were preparing to resume the sonar hunt for the U-boat as the convoy cleared the area when, at 1238Z, the conning tower of the U-175 broke the surface just astern of HX 233.

Both Coast Guard cutters opened fire on the U-175 and were immediately followed by several merchant ships in the convoy. The USCGC *Spencer* turned toward the U-175 to ram, but Heineman, the escort commander, ordered ramming avoided if possible for the Germans could be seen abandoning the U-175. As the USCGC *Spencer* passed near the stern of the U-175, a number of Germans were visible in the water, and the U-boat appeared to be abandoned "but still afloat with way on and in fairly good trim." The Americans decided to attempt to capture the U-175 and sent a party aboard. However, as the Americans boarded the submarine began to sink stern first, and even though the Americans managed to get into the U-boat's control room, the enemy vessel could not be salvaged and soon sank. Some thirty Germans from the U-175 were later picked up by the Allies, and one Coast Guard member on the USCGC *Spencer* was killed by friendly fire.[71]

Even before the sinking of the U-175 in the early afternoon of 17 April, the Allies began to turn the tables on the U-boats. At 0847 four destroyers of the 3rd Escort Group (HMS *Panther*, HMS *Penn*, HMS *Impulsive*, HMS *Offa*) arrived to reinforce the convoy. The Allied destroyers swept along the port side of HX 233 and then went astern of the convoy. At 1130 a U-boat was sighted by HMS *Panther*, was forced to submerge, and was then hunted for several hours without result. At 1630 the first VLR B-24 Liberator from Northern Ireland arrived over the convoy to provide air escort through the next day.[72] There were several more contacts between the U-boats and the escorts of HX 233, but the threat to the convoy passed with the sinking of the U-175.[73] At 0024 on 18 April the BdU ended the operation against HX 233 because of "the anticipated intensified air activity that day."[74]

Astern of HX 233, convoy SC 126 passed to the south of the *Meise* group of U-boats and was not attacked. HF/DF intercepts indicated to the convoy's escorts that they had been sighted, but no attack developed.[75] On 16 April the Germans concluded, mostly from radio intelligence, that SC 126 was south of the *Meise* group, but found it "impossible to form a clear picture of the approximate convoy area or course." And by 17 April the BdU had concluded that "it can be no longer possible to intercept SC 126 with Group *Meise*."[76] SC 126 arrived in the United Kingdom on 23 April without incident.[77]

The passage of convoys ON 177 and SC 126 without loss and the HX 233's voyage with only one ship sunk were triumphs of Allied intelligence and routing. The Allies knew where the *Meise* group was operating and successfully routed ON 177 northward and SC 126 southward around these U-boats. HX 233 was successfully routed to the south of the *Meise* U-boats, but by chance ran into the U-262, thus enabling the BdU to divert several outward-bound U-boats to intercept the convoy. The resulting battle was not in favor of the U-boats because of the convoy's strong defense by the escorts and the Allies' ability to reinforce the convoy quickly with air and surface escorts—only one merchant ship was lost in exchange for the U-175.

On 16 April the BdU ordered the *Meise* patrol line to move to a position that ran from 53°57′N, 43°45′W through 50°30′N, 37°55′W to 48°15′N, 35°55′W by 1000 on 17 April. The Allies decoded this order at 2038 on 18 April.[78] By then, however, the BdU had moved the twenty-three U-boats (U-134, U-306, U-631, U-203, U-552, U-267, U-706, U-415, U-413, U-598, U-191, U-438, U-188, U-613, U-404, U-571, U-381, U-108, U-258, U-610, U-259, U-618, U-84) which now constituted the *Meise* group, ordering them northwest to take position in a patrol line running from 53°45′N, 46°15′S through 52°09′N, 43°25′W and through 51°03′N, 41°45′W to 49°45′N, 39°55′W by 0800 on 19 April. The U-boats were to maintain a distance of 15 miles between each vessel on the patrol line and were informed that they would be refueled at sea after contact had been made with a convoy. Further radio silence was to be maintained except for "REPORTS OF TACTICAL IMPORTANCE," and the U-boats were to permit themselves neither "TO BE SEEN NOR LOCATED BY

AIRCRAFT." This order was wholly decoded by the Allies by 0550 on 19 April.[79]

In addition, on 18 April the BdU established a new patrol line code named *Specht*, using seven U-boats (U-226, U-614, U-624, U-358, U-628, U-92, U-125) which had intercepted HX 233. This patrol line was formed north of the Azores and south and east of the *Meise* group and was to steam west at a rate of 220 miles per day. The BdU deployed the *Meise* group on the assumption that HX and SC convoys would proceed along the northern great circle route to Great Britain. The southern routing of HX 233 and SC 126 had taken the BdU by surprise, and the deployment of the *Specht* group, which was to be reinforced by six U-boats (U-270, U-260, U-168, U-584, U-630, U-662), was an attempt to cover the southern route as well. But on 18 April the Germans did not have any detailed intelligence as to Allied intentions.[80]

On 19 April Allied intelligence decoded the BdU's orders for the *Meise* and *Specht* groups. It appeared that the Germans had forty U-boats deployed in the northwest Atlantic. The Allies knew that the U-boat tanker, the U-487, was conducting refueling operations about halfway between Newfoundland and Iceland at 49°39'N, 31°45'S and that most of the U-boats were deployed in a patrol line about 500 miles northeast of Newfoundland.[81] Allied intelligence also noted that Allied anti-U-boat air power in Newfoundland was weak, and it was thought that the Germans' new deployment attempted to avoid the VLR B-24 Liberators based in Northern Ireland and Iceland. Further, Commander Rodger Winn, RNVR, head of the Admiralty's submarine tracking room in London, thought that the German deployment northeast of Newfoundland showed "the ever increasing apprehension of air attack and the enemy's recognition that pack tactics cannot be effectively employed when aircraft are with the convoy."[82]

On 19 April no fewer than five Allied convoys were threatened by the deployment of German U-boats northwest of Newfoundland. Three westbound convoys—ON 178, ONS 3 and ONS 4—were being routed to the extreme north, almost as far as Greenland, in an attempt to pass around the northwest end of the *Meise* group. The eastbound convoy HX 234 was routed north toward Greenland east of Newfoundland and Labrador in an attempt to pass the northwest end of the *Meise* patrol line, while SC 127, another eastbound convoy, would proceed in a general northeast direction to pass between the southern end of the *Meise* group and the northern tip of the *Specht* patrol.[83]

The success of this scheme would depend on the Germans' remaining ignorant of the northerly routes of HX 234, ON 178, ONS 3, and ONS 4. However, on 20 April decryption of an Allied radio message informed the Germans that HX 234 was proceeding east of Newfoundland and northward toward Greenland to circumvent the *Meise* patrol line. It also occurred to the Germans that the Allies knew, from aircraft sightings, of the location of the *Meise* U-boats. At the same time the Germans learned from another decrypt that convoy SC 127 was proceeding to Great Britain by a course that would carry the convoy far to the north. (Although the Germans also thought that it was possible to intercept a westbound convoy, they did not appear to have had hard or detailed intelligence on the routes of ON 178, ONS 3, and ONS 4.)

The BdU reacted to this information by sending nineteen U-boats (U-134, U-306, U-631, U-203, U-552, U-706, U-415, U-413, U-598, U-191, U-438, U-188, U-613, U-571, U-381, U-108, U-258, U-610, U-259) of the *Meise* group northwest to form a patrol line across HX 234's route between Newfoundland and Greenland. To deal with the slower-moving SC 127, the BdU detached four U-boats from the *Meise* group (U-84, U-267, U-404, U-618) which were low on fuel and ordered them to form a patrol line at 48°09′N, 38°05′W by 0800 on 22 April and to join with the *Specht* group which was steaming west.[84] The Allies apparently did not intercept and decode the order for the movement of the *Meise* patrol line, but on 22 April they did intercept and decode the orders for the augmentation of the *Specht* group as well as a message alerting the *Specht* U-boats to expect a convoy in the area of 46°05′N, 30°15′W on that day.[85]

The situation was complicated further when convoy ONS 3, consisting of twenty merchant ships, sailed from Liverpool on 6 April. ONS 3 was a small convoy whose average speed was 7 knots, and it was escorted by the 40th Escort Group comprised of the ex-USCG cutters HMS *Landguard* and HMS *Lulworth,* the sloops HMS *Hastings* and HMS *Bideford,* the corvettes HMS *Starwort* and HMS *Poppy,* the frigate HMS *Moyola,* and the trawler *Northern Gift.* ONS 3 sailed northwest from the North Channel in a great curving arc to a point south of Iceland and then west almost to the southern tip of Greenland before turning to run south for the ports of the east coast of Canada and the United States. The voyage was uneventful until 12 April, when heavy seas and force seven winds were encountered. For the next nine days ONS 3 battled heavy seas, encountering high winds and snow.[86]

The first indication of U-boats in the vicinity of ONS 3 came at 0230 on 21 April when the escort intercepted a number of radio transmissions, probably from the U-415. The commander of ONS 3's escort at this time "did not consider it wise to sweep away from the convoy except on firm information." In the next hour more U-boat radio transmissions were intercepted, and at 0324 HMS *Landguard* was ordered to run down a bearing of 340°. In the course of this sweep, HMS *Landguard* surprised the U-415 on the surface in a snow squall. At 0404 there were a series of explosions as the *Meise* group's U-415 torpedoed the *Ashantian* and *Wanstead*. One torpedo hit the *Ashantian* on the starboard side. The stokehold, No. 3 hold, and the engine room quickly filled with water, sinking the vessel in ten minutes. The *Wanstead* was hit by one torpedo in No. 1 hold and the ship began to buckle and settle. The crews abandoned both ships, and ninety-eight survivors were later picked up by HMS *Poppy* and the trawler *Northern Gift*.[87]

Immediately after the torpedoing of the *Ashantian* and *Wanstead*, the commander of the escort ordered the warships to sweep around the flanks and astern of the convoy, but the transmission of the order was delayed six minutes because of a snow squall. When the storm passed, the commander of the escort ordered that the escort fire star shells outward from the convoy. In the light of the star shells, several merchant ships sighted a U-boat within the convoy and opened fire on it as the enemy vessel submerged. ONS 3 was quickly clear of the danger area. Even though U-boat radio transmissions were picked up for the next several hours and several HF/DF bearings were obtained, the convoy was not again attacked nor did it sight any more U-boats.[88]

The convoy owed its reprieve to another change in strategy by the BdU. Shortly after the U-415 torpedoed the merchant ships *Ashantian* and *Wanstead*, the submarine reported the westbound convoy to be on a course of 240°. But by then the BdU had responded to a radio report from the U-306, which announced the sighting of another convoy in the same general area on an "EASTERLY COURSE." This convoy was HX 234. The BdU directed all the U-boats of the *Meise* group, except for the U-415 and U-706, to concentrate on HX 234, preferring to attack the eastbound convoy in a battle area that would move away from and not toward Allied air bases in Newfoundland.[89]

The newest U-boat target, convoy HX 234, had sailed from New York on 12 April bound for Liverpool. The group consisted of forty-two merchant ships including fifteen tankers, and its route was designed to pass north of the northwest end of the *Meise* patrol line. HX 234 steered northeast from New York to approximately 47°42′N, 48°02′W east of Newfoundland, where the local escort was detached and Escort Group B4 joined the convoy. The escort was commanded by Lieutenant Commander E. C. L. Day, RN, and consisted of the destroyers HMS *Highlander* and HMS *Vimy* (joining the convoy on 21 April), and the corvettes HMS *Asphodel*, HMS *Anemone*, HMS *Abelia*, HMS *Pennywort*, HMS *Clover*, and HMCS *Rosthern*. Once the convoy and its escort group had met, they took a course almost due north. Numerous icebergs were encountered, and the edge of the pack ice could be seen on the western horizon.[90]

At approximately 56°47′N, 47°46′W on 21 April HX 234 altered course to 76°. At 0400Z, just after the convoy changed course to the east, HMS *Pennywort* sighted the U-306, "timed down" up moon at a range of 1,500 yards. As the German submarine turned away, the British corvette fired a star shell and the U-boat dived. Sonar contact was obtained and a depth charge attack was undertaken without result. Sonar contact was not regained. A sonar hunt for the U-306 was then conducted until 0545Z when HMS *Pennywort* steamed to rejoin HX 234.[91]

Upon receipt of the U-306's sighting report on 21 April, the BdU issued a series of orders to the U-boats of the *Meise* group. The U-306 was ordered to shadow HX 234 but not to attack it, and seventeen other U-boats of the *Meise* group were also ordered to operate against HX 234. The U-306 remained in contact with HX 234 until 25 April, while the situation became even more complex for the strategists at the BdU: the *Meise* was soon faced with still another group of Allied ships.[92]

As the *Meise* U-boats did their best to follow their orders for dealing with the eastbound HX 234 and southbound ONS 3, two members of the German patrol line reported sighting a new party of Allied merchant ships steering south at 1543 on 21 April. The newest arrival on the scene was ON 178, about 80 miles astern of ONS 3. The BdU correctly realized that the *Meise* U-boats had now sighted three separate convoys, not stragglers from one of the earlier groups. The U-boats were commanded to "TAKE ADVANTAGE OF THE ELEMENTS OF SURPRISE TO ATTACK TONIGHT."[93]

The newcomer on the scene, ON 178, consisted of fifty-eight merchant ships which sailed from Liverpool for New York on 12 April. The convoy was escorted by Escort Group B1 which consisted of the destroyers HMS *Hurricane* and HMS *Rockingham*, the frigate HMS *Kale*, and the corvettes HMS *Dahlia*, HMS *Borage*, HMS *Monkshead*, HMS *Medowseat*, and HMS *Wallflower*. Like ONS 3, convoy ON 178 proceeded northwest from the North Channel and then west across the North Atlantic almost to Cape Farewell at the southern tip of Greenland before turning south toward the east coast of North America. The convoy steamed through gales and rough seas on the passage westward, and the ships encountered ice off Greenland before they turned on to a southerly course.[94]

Visibility was sufficient on 21 April for Commander E. C. Bayldon, RN, the commander of ON 178's escort, to see the whole convoy from the bridge of HMS *Hurricane* in the screen ahead of the convoy. In the forenoon the escort intercepted three radio transmissions from U-boats to the south of the convoy at an estimated range of between 30 and 50 miles.[95] ON 178 was first sighted by the U-483, and at 1752Z the U-191 torpedoed the merchant ship *Scebeli,* hitting the vessel on the port side and blowing the bow off the ship.[96] The crew took to the boats and were picked up by HMS *Kale*. The wreck of the *Scebeli* was salvageable, but Bayldon ordered it to be left. The escorts began to hunt for the U-boat and soon obtained a number of sonar contacts which were hunted and attacked without result.[97]

The HF/DF sets of ON 178's escorts obtained seventeen "ground-wave signals" during the evening of 21 April. It was estimated that there were three U-boats in contact with the convoy, one off the starboard quarter, and the other two off the port quarter of the convoy. Bayldon wanted to attempt to throw off the U-boats by conducting sweeps down the HF/DF bearings and altering the course of the convoy 40° to port. But just as these maneuvers were to be put into effect, ON 178 encountered a blizzard which lasted for three hours and prevented all signals between the ships of the convoy. After the blizzard stopped there were no more contacts between ON 178 and the U-boats, and the next day the convoy received an air escort from Newfoundland.[98]

The other members of the beleaguered trio of Allied convoys were being reinforced as well. At 0630Z on 21 April, HMS *Vimy* joined the escort of HX 234. Two hours later, in an attempt to lose the U-boats, the convoy changed course to 50° and then at 1215Z to 80°. Throughout the forenoon on 21 April, HMS *Highlander*'s HF/DF set picked up a number of U-boat radio transmissions. Day was just about to order HMS *Vimy* to sweep down an HF/DF bearing when a VLR B-24 Liberator aircraft from Iceland, M/120, appeared over the convoy. The U-306's sighting report had been intercepted and D/F'ed in England. Because there were three convoys in the area, an aircraft was dispatched from Iceland at extreme range to escort the convoys and then fly to Goose Bay, Labrador.[99]

Although the aircraft arrived over HX 234 unexpectedly, Day requested that it carry out a *python* on a bearing of 177° at a range of about 20 miles.[100] While conducting this search, aircraft M/120 sighted a U-boat which was probably the U-306. The plane's attempted attack miscarried when the depth charges failed to release from the bomb bay. Aircraft M/120 dropped a marker and asked Day to send an escort to hunt the U-boat. Circling the area, the plane homed in HMS *Vimy* by radio. After reaching the limit of its fuel, aircraft M/120 proceeded to Goose Bay. By 1919, when HMS *Vimy* arrived in the area, the U-boat had dived, and a sonar hunt was undertaken. Several "scaring attacks" were mounted with depth charges before HMS *Vimy* set course to rejoin the convoy at 2122.[101]

As night fell, the eastbound convoy was exposed to more risk as the time came for the evening attack ordered by the BdU. At dusk, HX 234 changed course to 47° as a snow storm descended on the convoy, dropping visibility to about 5 cables. In the first hours of 22

April, the U-boat assault began when the U-306 torpedoed and sank the merchant ship *Amerika*. Screened by HMS *Vimy*, HMS *Asphodel* rescued fifty-four survivors belonging to the merchant ship. Day thought the rescue to be a considerable "feat of seamanship" for it was dark and snowing, with a very heavy sea running. The heavy weather and the convoy's nighttime change of course had caused a number of merchant ships to wander from their places—Day estimated that the *Amerika* was 2 miles behind the convoy when it was torpedoed.[102] In the poor visibility and confusion of that night, still another straggler—the *Robert Gray*—was also sunk by the U-306.[103]

By daylight on 22 April the snow had ended. During the course of the day four VLR B-24 Liberator aircraft from Iceland operated over HX 234. One aircraft, T/120, returned to Iceland after escorting the convoy for several hours, while the other three planes conducted shuttle missions between Iceland and Goose Bay, Labrador. Nine sightings of U-boats in the vicinity of HX 234 were made by the aircraft and a number of air attacks were carried out. All of these failed because none of the depth charges would release from the bomb bays. Nevertheless, a number of U-boats were forced to submerge and no enemy vessels closed with the convoy. Still, during the afternoon, Day concluded from HF/DF bearings that there were a number of U-boats in the vicinity of HX 234.[104]

The situation in the northwest Atlantic on 22 April was somewhat confusing to the BdU. At 1024 the BdU ordered the U-boats of the *Meise* group which had not been in contact to report their positions by short signal. Aircraft over HX 234 had caused the U-boats to lose contact with the convoy, and the BdU ordered thirteen U-boats (U-610, U-552, U-631, U-598, U-89, U-267, U-378, U-732, U-648, U-209, U-306) to steam eastward and set up a new patrol line between 58°57'N, 32°36'W and 56°45'N, 32°36'W by 1400 on 23 April. Those U-boats attacking HX 234 not named in the order were to continue to operate against the convoy. However, if HX 234 was sighted, the new patrol line was to be canceled and all the U-boats were to operate on the basis of the sighting report. Several hours after this order was issued, the U-306 again sighted HX 234 and radioed that the convoy's course is "60 DEGREES, SPEED 8 KNOTS. AM SENDING BEACON SIGNALS IN ACCORDANCE WITH WAR ORDER."[105]

And the BdU informed the U-boats attacking HX 234 that they could be refueled at 51°25′N, 31°45′W after the operation.[106]

HX 234 was not attacked by U-boats during the night of 22 April, and at 2300Z the convoy altered course to 53°. While the convoy was changing course, HMS *Vimy* and HMS *Abelia* conducted offensive sweeps in an attempt to "throw off" the U-boat "pursuit for several hours." This maneuver was successful, for no HF/DF bearings were obtained until 23 April. At 0530 on 23 April it appeared to Day that the U-boats were again astern of the convoy and he sent HMS *Vimy* and HMS *Clover* to make a sweep while the course of the convoy was changed to 75°. But by 0930 Day was convinced that there were at least three U-boats—one ahead, one astern, and one on the port quarter—in contact with the convoy. Visibility was 30 miles and "with dismay" Day learned that bad weather had grounded all aircraft at Iceland.[107]

Day met this situation by conducting offensive sweeps. HMS *Highlander* ran down an HF/DF bearing off the bow of the convoy, while HMS *Vimy* was sent down a bearing off the convoy's starboard beam. HMS *Highlander* found nothing, but HMS *Vimy* sighted a U-boat at a range of 12 miles, and a second U-boat was sighted as HMS *Highlander* steamed to join HMS *Vimy*. Both U-boats dived as the British destroyers approached. The British warships attacked depth charges without result. Sonar hunts were undertaken, but before either U-boat could be located and successfully engaged, Day learned that the convoy had been attacked in another quarter.[108]

HX 234 was on a course of 75° and HMS *Abelia* was refueling from the tanker *Mosli* when a huge column of water shot up on the starboard side of the merchant ship *Silvermaple* at 1354. The U-954 had fired a torpedo at the merchant ship which exploded alongside the vessel slightly damaging it in the after peak, but it did not drop out of the formation and was able to proceed with the convoy. The escorts immediately began to search for the U-boat, and the convoy made an emergency change of course of 45° to port, quickly followed by another alteration of 45° to port. HMS *Anemone*, whose position in the screen was off the bow of HX 234, passed through the convoy searching for the U-boat. After clearing the stern of HX 234 and being joined by HMS *Abelia*, HMS *Anemone* obtained a sonar contact and at 1415 attacked with a ten depth charge pattern followed by an attack by HMS *Abelia*. After these attacks, "a large patch of oil" appeared on the surface and the two corvettes continued hunting for the U-boat with sonar. At 1455 HMS *Anemone* returned to the convoy, leaving HMS *Abelia* to continue the search for an additional thirty minutes before rejoining HX 234. At 1500 the convoy returned to a course of 75°.[109]

Aircraft from Iceland appeared over HX 234 during the forenoon of 23 April. The first aircraft, J/120, swept around the convoy, forcing one U-boat to submerge, and unsuccessfully attacked another U-boat with four depth charges as the vessel dived. Before returning to Iceland, aircraft J/120 reported to Day the sighting of a third U-boat's periscope. The second aircraft to reach HX 234 was V/120, which carried out a *cobra* (a search around the perimeter of the convoy) at Day's request, sighting a U-boat in the process and forcing the German vessel to submerge. Shortly after the first sighting of a U-boat, two others were spotted, and aircraft V/120 attacked one, the U-189, from a height of 50 feet. In the face of antiaircraft fire, the V/120 dropped four depth charges which straddled the vessel. After this attack the U-189 remained on the surface and appeared to the aircrew to be down by the stern. Aircraft V/120 circled and then attacked again with two depth charges. The crew of the aircraft saw the U-189 "sink vertically, stern first" leaving its crew in the water. Aircraft V/120 requested that Day send an escort to pick up the Germans, but the British officer refused, citing the large number of U-boats in the vicinity of the convoy. After sinking the U-189, aircraft V/120 remained with HX 234 for another thirty minutes before returning to Reykjavik.[110]

After the last aircraft had departed, there were several contacts between the convoy's escorts and the U-boats. Throughout 23 April the U-306 shadowed HX 234 sending a steady stream of reports to the BdU. At 1519 the BdU ordered the U-boats operating against HX 234 to get "AHEAD OF THE CONVOY IN ORDER TO CARRY OUT COMBINED SURFACE ATTACK AS SOON AS NIGHT BEGINS. SIMULTANEOUS ATTACK HAS THE BEST PROSPECTS OF SUCCESS." At 1830 HMCS *Rosthern* obtained a sonar contact off the port bow of the convoy, probably the U-378, and attacked several times with depth charges without result. At 2300 the convoy changed course to 70°. HMS *Pennywort*, off the starboard side of HX 234, picked up a radar contact bearing 160° at a range of 5,000 yards. This contact was run down and two star shells were fired, illuminating a U-boat, probably the U-108, which then dived. Sonar contact was obtained and at 0133Z on 24 April, a depth charge attack was conducted without result. After this attack, the sonar hunt was resumed and at 0207Z HMS *Pennywort* left the region to rejoin the convoy. At 0400Z HX 234 changed course to 100°.[111]

Even though the BdU determined that there were seven U-boats in the area of the convoy during the night of 23 April, the mass night attack did not "have the desired results." And the BdU was finding "it difficult to form a clear picture of the surface escort" of HX 234, for very few U-boats were reporting depth charge attacks by warships. In the late evening of 23 April the BdU revised its estimate to one of fifteen U-boats operating against HX 234.[112]

Just before dawn on 24 April, Day estimated from HF/DF bearings that there were U-boats off the port bow and ahead of the convoy and that four U-boats "had reached an attacking position." To the commander of the escort of HX 234, "This was the worst moment of the engagement and I feared that we were in for a concerted dawn attack." But no attack developed.[113]

The convoy could thank the Allied airfields in Iceland for its rescue. Air escort of HX 234 began at dawn on 24 April and lasted until 1730. All day, American PBY Catalinas based in Iceland flew over and around the convoy. U-boats were sighted, attacked, and forced to submerge by aircraft and Day later reported that the aircraft prevented the U-boats "from gaining bearing and getting into a favorable position for submerged daylight attack." The BdU quickly learned of the activities of the air escort on 24 April, for the U-boats made many reports of the effects of these aircraft. For example, the U-267 radioed "DRIVEN OFF CONTINUALLY BY AIR." The U-532 reported "PERMANENT AIR FROM ICELAND." The U-631 reported "AM EVADING PERMANENT AIR TO THE NORTHWARD." And the U-532 radioed "AM CONTINUALLY DRIVEN OFF BY PERMANENT AIR. AM MOVING OFF FOR REPAIRS." At 1531 the BdU radioed the U-boats operating against HX 234 that "WITH AIR GETTING STRONGER" they must get ahead of the convoy and make "SUBMERGED ATTACKS WITHOUT WAITING" and that "THE BEST SHADOWING IS USELESS WITHOUT SUCCESSFUL ATTACK."[114] However, even with twelve U-boats operating against the convoy, there would be no more attacks on HX 234.[115] The last U-boat to have contact with the convoy was the U-267 which reported at 2300 that it was astern of HX 234. And the next morning the BdU called off the operation and ordered the U-boats to withdraw to the southwest.[116]

The U-boat operations against HX 234 were a failure. The operations began with nineteen U-boats operating against the convoy. The U-306 doggedly shadowed the convoy from 21 to 25 April, homing in other U-boats over a distance of 700 nautical miles. At the end of the operation the BdU believed that only two Allied merchant ships had been sunk and another two damaged. It was thought by the BdU that this failure was owing to poor weather conditions—"hail, fog, rain, snow squalls," Allied air power, and the inexperience of the U-boat commanders.[117]

One westbound Allied convoy remained a U-boat target. On 23 April, the U-732, attempting to close with HX 234 from the southwest, sighted a westbound convoy at 57°45′N, 33°48′W. Immediately after sighting the convoy, the U-732 was forced to dive by "BIPLANE."[118] The BdU wrongly thought that the aircraft was probably a scouting plane catapulted from a warship and tentatively, but correctly, identified the convoy as ONS 4.[119] In response to this sighting, the BdU ordered the *Specht* group of U-boats, which were 600 miles to the south, to intercept. Four members (U-84, U-257, U-415, U-618) of the *Specht* group which were running low on fuel were directed to proceed to the U-487 at 51°25′N, 31°45′W to refuel before returning to base. And a little later the BdU ordered seventeen U-boats (U-203, U-438, U-706, U-630, U-662, U-584, U-168, U-720, U-620, U-92, U-628, U-707, U-358, U-264, U-614, U-226, U-125) of the *Specht* group to steam north and establish a patrol line running between 54°15′N, 43°15′W and 51°15′N, 38°55′W across the estimated course of ONS 4 by 1400 on 25 April. This order was decoded by the Allies at 0408 on 24 April.[120]

Convoy ONS 4, consisting of thirty-four merchant ships, sailed from Liverpool on 13 April for New York. The convoy was escorted by Escort Group B2 led by Commander Donald Macintyre, RN, consisting of the destroyers HMS *Hesperus* and HMS *Whitehall*; the sloop HMS *Gentian*; and the corvettes HMS *Heather*, HMS *Sweetbriar*, HMS *Campanula*, HMS *Clematis*, and HM Trawler *Cape Ar-*

gona. ONS 4 steamed northwest from the North Channel to 60°15'N, 19°42'W, south of Iceland, on 19 April when it turned to a west southwest course. The convoy proceeded at a speed of 4 or 5 knots owing to a number of very slow ships which Macintyre thought could "only be described as coasters, which were certainly not built for the Atlantic trade." On 17 April a full westerly gale was encountered, and by 21 April Macintyre was "getting most anxious as to the fuel situation in all the escorts." However, by the evening of 21 April the weather moderated, and HMS *Whitehall* was refueled from the tanker *Athol Prince*. The next day HMS *Hesperus*, HMS *Gentian*, HMS *Sweetbriar*, and HMS *Clematis* were refueled from the tanker *Scottish Heather*.[121]

On 22 April Macintyre expected that ONS 4 would be joined by the 5th Escort Group led by Captain E. M. C. Abel Smith, RN, consisting of the escort carrier HMS *Biter*, and the destroyers HMS *Pathfinder*, HMS *Opportune*, and HMS *Obdurate*. The formation of the convoy had been adjusted to accommodate the aircraft carrier, but the 5th Escort Group did not join ONS 4, and when Macintyre attempted to contact HMS *Biter* on the radio telephone there was no answer. The radio silence stemmed from Abel Smith's reluctance to give away his escort group's position before it was in flying range of ONS 4. Abel Smith believed that it would be dangerous for an aircraft carrier to be stationed within a slow convoy for "under these circumstances . . . it is considered that the obvious prize, the carrier, would fall an easy prey to the more aggressive submarine captain, no avoiding and little evasive action being possible." The captain also believed that the need for a carrier to charge course, when flying aircraft on and off, would greatly hinder flying operations if HMS *Biter* were to be stationed within the confines of a slow convoy.[122] It was Abel Smith's intention that the 5th Escort Group should operate at a distance from and in support of ONS 4 and not become a part of that formation.

On 23 April Macintyre concluded that ONS 4 was passing through a U-boat patrol line, for at 0800 the escorts intercepted a sighting report transmitted by the U-732 at a range of 20 miles bearing 69°. HMS *Whitehall* and HMS *Campanula* were sent down this bearing and did not sight a U-boat, but the two escorts did sight the

5th Escort Group. The U-732 had been forced to dive by an aircraft from HMS *Biter*.[123]

HMS *Hesperus* at 1649 obtained an HF/DF bearing at 321° on a U-boat transmitting a sighting report at a range of 20 miles: the U-191.[124] The British destroyer ran down the bearing and at 1714 the U-191 was sighted and several minutes later the U-boat dived. HMS *Hesperus* mounted a sonar hunt and almost immediately contact was gained. Sonar "conditions were perfect and the contact was easily held" while the British destroyer mounted a hedgehog attack at 1740. HMS *Hesperus* ran in for the attack, the order to fire was given, and nothing happened owing to a mix-up among the crew of the hedgehog. At 1749 a second hedgehog attack was mounted by HMS *Hesperus*. This time the weapon was fired, but there was no result. Sonar contact was lost for a short time and then regained at 1803. However, this contact appeared to be a decoy fired by the U-191. At 1813 sonar contact was regained. Four minutes later a depth charge attack was undertaken against the U-boat which was now thought to have "gone deep," and the target was then lost. But HMS *Clematis*, which had joined the hunt, immediately obtained sonar contact as did HMS *Hesperus*, which directed HMS *Clematis* to the U-boat for a hedgehog attack, but again the weapon malfunctioned. Believing that the U-boat was deep, Macintyre next attacked at 1834 with conventional depth charges set to go off at 500 feet and a Mark X depth charge[125.]

The effects of this attack were "most impressive," for the explosions of the depth charges were "followed by reverberating rumbles." Sonar contact following the attack was lost for a short time, and just as HMS *Clematis* regained sonar contact, HMS *Hesperus* crossed the corvette's bow causing the contact to be lost once again. Not to be discouraged, HMS *Hesperus* remained in "firm contact" and attacked with a hedgehog at 1858. Twenty-four seconds after firing the weapon, there was "a violent explosion . . . followed by several concussions at intervals which, on earphones sounded like muffled explosions and to people standing on the bridge can best be described as bumps." HMS *Hesperus* and HMS *Clematis* swept through the area conducting sonar searches, but contact was not again obtained. This was the end of the U-191.[126]

At the beginning of the U-191 operation, Macintyre had requested air support from HMS *Biter*. However, at that time, the 5th Escort

Group was 50 miles away from ONS 4, and poor communications delayed the dispatch of a Swordfish aircraft. Although the plane did not arrive in the area of the hunt for the U-191 until the submarine had been sunk, the pilot did drop a smoke marker on what was thought to be "a possible wake" of a U-boat some 10 miles from HMS *Hesperus* and HMS *Clematis*. HMS *Hesperus* steamed to the smoke marker, found nothing, and then departed from the area. For Macintyre, this incident proved "the weakness of the stationing of the carrier away from the convoy, a move that forced the aircraft to arrive late without any knowledge of the tactical situation."[127]

There were no contacts with U-boats on 24 April. Nine sorties were flown by aircraft from HMS *Biter* before air operations were curtailed to conserve aircraft as there were no HF/DF bearings on U-boats in the vicinity of the convoy. At 0953 on 25 April, at 54°12′N, 34°35′W, the convoy altered course from approximately south to a few degrees north of west to reach 55°40′N, 43°38′W — the first step in a maneuver designed to skirt the northern end of the *Specht* patrol line. The 5th Escort Group encountered several U-boats that day. At 0246Z HMS *Biter* obtained a radar contact at a range of 4,600 yards. The escort carrier altered course away from the target, and HMS *Opportune* was sent down the bearing which faded from the destroyer's screen at a range of 3,000 yards. This might have been the U-404.[128]

One of the more bizarre episodes of the North Atlantic campaign came during the morning of 25 April, when the U-404 reported sighting, torpedoing, and sinking the aircraft carrier USS *Ranger*, escorted by four destroyers, at 54°21′N, 38°55′W.[129] The report of the *Ranger*'s sinking was passed quickly up the chain of command in Berlin and announced to the public. Indeed, the commander of the U-404 was awarded the Knights Cross of the Iron Cross by Adolf Hitler.[130] In fact, however, the aircraft carrier seen by the U-404 was HMS *Biter*, and there was no mention of any attack in Allied records.[131] The BdU "did not uphold the claim [of sinking the USS *Ranger*] and was irritated at the premature announcement."[132]

The real action of that morning began when the HMS *Hesperus* obtained an HF/DF bearing which indicated that there was a U-boat near the 5th Escort Group. This information was transmitted to HMS *Biter*. Aircraft were dispatched to search for the U-boat, but nothing was found. At 1812Z HMS *Opportune* picked up what was thought to be a sonar contact on a U-boat. The 5th Escort Group altered course away from the target, but "the contact was not confirmed." Twelve minutes later, one of HMS *Biter*'s Swordfish aircraft reported a U-boat on the surface 6 miles from the escort carrier. The Swordfish attacked with two depth charges twenty seconds after the conning tower of the U-203 disappeared under the water. After the attack, the aircraft dropped a marker on the position where the U-boat had submerged. HMS *Pathfinder* was then sent to the region to hunt for the U-boat.[133]

Twenty-five minutes after the U-203 had submerged, HMS *Pathfinder* arrived in the area of the marker and began a sonar search. At about 1718 sonar contact was gained at a range of 1,700 yards. An attack was undertaken on a north-south course without result. Sonar contact was quickly regained and a second attack with depth charges was mounted on a south-north course, again without result. The next two depth charge attacks were on easterly and westerly courses. The third attack was undertaken with settings on the depth charges set at "very deep." After this attack the U-203 could be heard blowing its tanks. Sonar contact was obtained, but the U-boat attempted to escape inside the turning circle of the destroyer. Nevertheless, HMS *Pathfinder* mounted a fourth attack with the depth charge settings on shallow. Shortly after this attack, as a fifth attack was being mounted, engines could be heard ahead of the destroyer as the U-203 used its diesels to drive herself to the surface. As HMS *Pathfinder* moved in for the attack, the U-203 rose out of the water on the starboard bow of the destroyer, bow first at a 45 degree angle. One or two sailors appeared in the conning tower of the U-boat as HMS *Pathfinder* engaged it with gunfire. While HMS *Pathfinder* passed astern of the U-203, the destroyer's starboard throwers fired two depth charges at the enemy vessel, killing several Germans who were in the water. It was all over in three minutes. The U-boat broke the surface at 1834, and the U-203 sank at 1837. HMS *Pathfinder* later picked up forty-two crew members of the U-203.[134]

That night ONS 4 encountered fog, and the convoy's escort was reinforced by the five ships of the 1st Escort Group (Sloop HMS *Pelican*, frigates HMS *Jed*, HMS *Wear*, HMS *Sprey*, and the ex-US Coast Guard cutter HMS *Sennen*) the next day. On 26 April, ONS

northwest from the North Channel until it reached 58°09′N, 22°30′W on 22 April. The convoy then turned to a southwest course which, over the next two days, carried it to 55°33′N, 32°43′W, the northern end of the soon-to-be-deployed *Amsel* patrol line. For the next three days, ON 179 steered west, skirting around the northern end of the *Specht* group. On reaching 56°49′N, 46°28′W on 27 April, the convoy turned south and then southwest for New York, where the convoy arrived safely on 6 May.[147]

Knowing that the bulk of the U-boats in the North Atlantic were now north of 50°N and west of 30°W, the Allies routed three convoys from North America to Great Britain by southerly courses.[148] Convoy HX 235, consisting of forty merchant ships, sailed from New York on 18 April, shepherded by Escort Group C4 consisting of the destroyers HMS *Churchill* and HMCS *Restigouche* and the corvettes HMCS *Collingwood*, HMCS *Baddeck*, HMCS *Trent*, and HMCS *Brandon*. The escort of HX 235 was further strengthened when Task Group 92.3, consisting of the escort carrier USS *Bogue* and the destroyers USS *Belknop*, USS *Greene*, USS *Lea*, and USS *Osmond Ingram*, joined the convoy on 25 April. The American destroyers were placed in the screen of HX 235, and the USS *Bogue* was stationed between columns six and seven within the main body of the convoy. HX 235 steered east southeast to 43°20′N, 34°48′W northwest of the Azores before turning on to a northeast course for the North Channel where the convoy arrived on 3 May.[149] During the voyage, the USS *Bogue* conducted extensive air operations from its position within the convoy, and the only contact between the Allied force and the U-boats occurred on 28 April when a TBF Avenger aircraft from the USS *Bogue* sighted a U-boat on the surface some 50 miles from the convoy. The aircraft attacked the U-boat with machine-gun fire and four depth charges which ricocheted on the water before exploding. The U-boat escaped damage. The next day, Task Group 92.3 operated ahead of HX 235 as a separate unit from the convoy, ready to sweep the U-boats out of the path of the Allied force with offensive air patrols, but no U-boats were encountered. HX 235 and Task Group 92.3 arrived in the British Isles without any further incident.[150] Later in April, the Allied convoy HX 236 sailed from North America to Great Britain along the southern route without any contact with U-boats.[151]

Cryptographic intelligence made the Germans aware that the Allies knew the location of their patrol lines in the North Atlantic and were routing convoys around them. What aroused German suspicions was an American "U-boat situation report" which showed that the Allies knew of the demarcation line between the *Specht* and *Amsel* patrol lines. However, the Germans did not suspect that the Allies were reading their command radio communications, but thought instead "this confirms, more than ever, the suspicion that the enemy has at his disposal a radar device especially effective for aircraft, which our boats are powerless to intercept."[152] From the beginning to the end of the war, the German navy communications security officers simply refused to believe that their codes could be broken.[153] This mistaken, but rocklike, belief on the part of German communications security specialists led the BdU to embrace mistaken theories such as an all-seeing Allied airborne radar as the source of Allied knowledge of the deployments of the U-boats.

At the end of April 1943 the U-boats had problems other than insecure radio communications that should have been recognized. On 15 April the Allies estimated that there were forty U-boats in the North Atlantic operating against convoys, and by 1 May this number had grown to sixty U-boats.[154] Yet Germany saw little return on this great increase in vessels. In the period between 10 and 30 April, the U-boats intercepted seven convoys (ON 176, ON 178, HX 232, HX 233, HX 234, ONS 3, ONS 4) and engaged in battles that sprawled across the North Atlantic, but they had sunk only eleven ships (HMS *Beverley* and the merchant ships *Lancastrian Prince, Pacific Grove, Ulysses, Fresco City, Fort Rampart, Ashantian, Wanstead, Scebeli, Amerika, and Robert Gray*) in these combats while losing four U-boats (U-175, U-189, U-191, U-203) to the escorts of Allied merchant ships. This was not a very favorable exchange for the submarine patrols.

The problem for the U-boats was simple in concept, but it proved extremely difficult for the Germans to solve. The Allies knew that German doctrine was to undertake "NIGHT ATTACKS FROM FAVORABLE POSITIONS UTILIZING DAYLIGHT SURFACE RUNS TO GAIN POSITION AHEAD OF THE CONVOY." Allied intelligence had concluded that "weather and air cover, together with evasive routing, saved the [April] convoys [HX 234, ON 176, ON 178, and ONS 4] from any such disastrous attacks as those of March."[155] This pinpointed the major problem confronting the Germans in April 1943: the U-boat was an obsolete weapons system whose effectiveness was severely compromised in heavy weather and which was nearly helpless when confronted with Allied aircraft.

The Allies could not control the weather, but they could and did provide aircraft to harass the U-boats, and these planes were decisive in the Allied defense of convoys. The U-boats could not defend themselves against aircraft, and not only could Allied aircraft sink U-boats, but they could also, by their mere presence, force a U-boat to submerge. The Allied tactic of employing aircraft to conduct searches in front of and around the flanks of a convoy forced any nearby U-boat to dive and thus to lose contact with the convoy. It was the presence of aircraft that prevented the U-boats of the *Meise* group from overpowering HX 234. The Germans saw the power of aircraft and, by deploying the bulk of their U-boats in the northwest Atlantic, they attempted to escape the VLR B-24 Liberator aircraft based in Northern Ireland and Iceland. The Allies, on the other hand, were deploying more and more VLR aircraft against the U-boats and had begun to introduce escort carriers into the North Atlantic to cover areas which could not be reached by land-based aircraft.

But aircraft were only part of the problem confronting the U-boats, for even with no aircraft present, Allied radar made it very difficult if not impossible for the German submarines to approach a well-escorted convoy on the surface. Further, unknown to the Germans, the Allies were capitalizing tactically on the U-boats' habit of making numerous radio transmissions. It was one of the Allies principal tactics to use HF/DF to detect a U-boat at a distance from a convoy, then send a surface escort down the bearing to attack the U-boat or at least to force the enemy vessel to submerge. Even when this move did not result in a U-boat sinking, it forced the enemy submarines to lose contact with a convoy by going underwater. Ignorant of the existence of shipborne HF/DF, the Germans never understood the connection between a recent radio transmission and the unexpected appearance of an Allied escort. Communications intelligence, electronic warfare, and the increasing strength of the Allied escorts were preventing the U-boats from successfully intercepting and attacking convoys. By April 1943, the Allies were fighting the Battle of the Atlantic with the tools of the age of aircraft and electronic warfare. Unless the Germans could develop and deploy new tactics and technology, the U-boats would be defeated.

Chapter 3

The Battle for Convoy ONS 5

22 April–6 May 1943

The westbound voyage of convoy ONS 5 was the prize the Germans sought in the biggest convoy battle of World War II. At the beginning of May the battle between the Allies and the Germans along the transatlantic convoy routes hung in the balance. If the U-boats could overcome the convoy defenses and sink a significant number of merchant ships, they would be the victors in this campaign. If, on the other hand, the convoy escorts could prevent merchant ships from being sunk and at the same time greatly increase the rate of U-boat losses, then the Germans would be defeated.

During the last days of April, the Allies lacked any detailed knowledge of German U-boat deployments when a failure in the decoding process cut off cryptographic intelligence from the North Atlantic. However, at the beginning of May, Allied intelligence estimated that the Germans had some sixty U-boats stationed in the northwest Atlantic, with most of them operating in an arc some 600 miles east of the Allied air base at Gander, Newfoundland. It was assumed that this deployment was adopted by the BdU to avoid Allied VLR aircraft based in Iceland and Northern Ireland and that the northwest Atlantic "will receive the enemy's main attention" and will be the most dangerous area for Allied convoys.[1] In fact, on 27 April, the Germans ordered fifteen U-boats (U-710, U-650, U-533, U-386, U-528, U-231, U-532, U-378, U-381, U-191, U-258, U-552, U-954, U-648, U-209, U-413) to establish a patrol line, code named *Star*, south of Greenland to reinforce the *Specht* and *Amsel* lines in blocking the northern convoy route between North America and Great Britain.[2]

Despite the absence of cryptographic intelligence, the Allies used a combination of skill and luck to route two convoys clear of the U-boats at the end of April. Convoy SC 128 sailed from Halifax on 25 April and headed northeast along the southern coast of New-foundland, and then turned almost due north toward southern Greenland to 54° north, then turning northeast to 60° north before turning east for the run to Britain.[3] This route was chosen so that SC 128 would pass west and then north of the U-boats of the *Specht-Amsel* groups which Allied intelligence showed were deployed in a line running roughly from 56°N, 47°W to 54°N, 37°W.[4] On 1 May one of the escorts of SC 128 sighted two U-boats while running down one of the numerous HF/DF bearings that had been picked up. And on 4 May SC 128's escorts intercepted a number of radio transmissions from U-boats operating against ONS 5, which was about 100 miles away from SC 128. There was, however, no further contact with the U-boats, and the convoy arrived without further incident on 13 May at Liverpool.[5]

Convoy ON 180 sailed from Liverpool on 24 April and took ap-proximately the reverse of the route followed by SC 128 — northwest to 61°N almost to the tip of Greenland, then in a southwest arc toward Newfoundland, passing safely to the north and west of the *Specht-Amsel* groups, before proceeding to New York where the con-voy arrived on 14 May. In the heavy seas, gales, and fog, four mer-chant ships were damaged by running into icebergs. Still, even though a number of radio transmissions were intercepted from U-boats operating on ONS 5, there were no contacts with the U-boats.[6] The Allies were to some extent very lucky with ONS 180 and SC 128, for there were at least thirty-one U-boats operating against ONS 5 just east of the routes followed by both convoys.[7] The battle for ONS 5 probably preoccupied the BdU ashore and U-boats at sea, thus distracting attention from SC 128 and ON 180.

Convoy ONS 5, formed on 22 April off the island of Islay west of Scotland at the entrance of the North Channel, consisted of forty-three merchant ships. The convoy was escorted by Escort Group B7 consisting of the destroyer HMS *Duncan* (senior officer); the frigate *Tay;* the corvettes HMS *Sunflower,* HMS *Snowflake,* HMS *Loosestrife,* and HMS *Pink;* and the trawlers *Northern Gem* and *Northern Spray.* HMS *Duncan* and HMS *Tay* were equipped with HF/DF. The tank-ers *Argon* and *British Lady* were to serve as oilers for the escorts.[8] The convoy was lucky enough to have Commander Peter Gretton, RN, who was one of the most skillful and hard driving commanders of any escort group.[9]

During the afternoon of 22 April ONS 5 headed northwest out into the Atlantic. The convoy would take a course similar to that followed by SC 128 and ON 180—northwest to 61°45′N, and then west almost to Cape Farewell before returning south southwest to run across the Grand Banks of Newfoundland just west of Flemish Cap, then turning southwest for the east coast of North America. This route was chosen to avoid known concentrations of U-boats and to take the greatest possible advantage of air cover provided by aircraft based in Iceland. After the fact, though, Allied intelligence concluded that this north-about route was a mistake in the case of ONS 5 because bad weather forced the convoy "to hove to for almost two days off Greenland and thereby give the U-boats more time to get into a favorable position."[10]

After departing from Islay, Gretton practiced oiling HMS *Duncan* from the tanker *British Lady,* and then stationed HMS *Duncan* within the body of the convoy as the destroyer "had a bad reputation for oil consumption." It was discovered at this time that the American tanker *Argon*'s canvas hoses could only refuel another ship alongside (rather than astern as was the practice with British warships) which would make it impossible to oil escorts except in a "flat calm." This meant that the escorts of ONS 5 could be refueled only from the tanker *British Lady,* and this in turn would effect the operational capabilities of the escorts.[11]

The convoy's troubles multiplied. Having engine trouble, the freighter *Modlin* left the convoy at 2200 on 22 April and returned to the Clyde. On 25 April ONS 5 encountered moderate gales and the merchant ships of the convoy, being for the most part in ballast and light in the water, had difficulty keeping station which would be a problem throughout the voyage. On 26 April HMS *Vidette,* escorting the tanker USS *Sapelo* and the freighters *Gudvor* and *Bosworth,* joined the convoy from Iceland. That evening, the merchant ships *Bornholm* and *Berkel* collided with each other in heavy seas, and the *Bornholm* had a hole smashed in its engine room above the water line which required it to be detached to Iceland. The *Berkel,* though damaged, remained with the convoy. As ONS 5 proceeded northwest in heavy seas, the weather gave Gretton grave concerns about refueling some of the escorts, but on 27 April the weather moderated enough to allow him to refuel HMS *Duncan* and HMS *Vidette* from the tanker *British Lady*. Later that day the merchant ship *Penhale* dropped astern of ONS 5, and, unable to regain its station, had to be sent to Iceland.[12]

At 0530 on 28 April HMS *Duncan* obtained an HF/DF bearing of 159°. This radio transmission was from a U-boat of the *Meise* group hunting for convoy SC 127 to the south of ONS 5.[13] Gretton thought it possible that the U-boats would concentrate against SC 127 and that, perhaps, ONS 5 would escape attack.[14] But at 1110 HMS *Duncan* obtained an HF/DF bearing "close ahead" of the convoy and Gretton concluded that ONS 5 was being shadowed.[15] ONS 5 was coming into contact with the northern most U-boats of the new *Star* group, which were deploying into a patrol line as ordered by the BdU on 27 April.[16] The Germans knew that convoys ONS 3 and ONS 4 had followed a very northern route to North America, and the deployment of the *Star* group in a patrol line along 30°W and as far north as 60°N was an attempt to intercept convoys following this route. However, bad weather and errors in navigation on the part of some U-boats would make it very difficult for the U-boats of the *Star* group to operate against ONS 5.[17] Further, magnetic interference with U-boat radio transmissions hampered the BdU in exercising command and control over the *Star* U-boats operating against ONS 5.[18]

When HMS *Duncan* obtained an HF/DF bearing "close ahead" of the convoy just before noon on 28 April, Gretton ordered HMS *Snowflake* to search down the bearing, and the convoy altered course 35° to starboard. The search, however, was without result. At 1230 both HMS *Duncan* and HMS *Tay* obtained bearings on a strong radio transmission at 275° from the convoy. HMS *Duncan*, which had left the main body of the convoy for a position in the forward screen, made a sweep ahead of the convoy to the depth of 10 miles. Nothing was found and the destroyer returned to its position in the convoy's screen. At 1600, ONS 5 returned to its original course. Ten minutes later HMS *Duncan* picked up on its HF/DF set another radio transmission which indicated to Gretton that "the U-boats were now astern of us." HMS *Tay* was sent to hunt for this U-boat. At 1641 another HF/DF bearing was picked up on a bearing of 13° and HMS *Vidette* was sent down this bearing. Both searches were "fruitless."[19]

At 1838 more radio transmissions were obtained by the escort's HF/DF sets and HMS *Duncan* and HMS *Tay* searched down the bearings on parallel sweeps. During this sweep HMS *Duncan* picked up another bearing and sighted a U-boat on the surface which could be seen in the rough seas only by the spray around its conning tower. HMS *Duncan* turned toward the U-boat, which dived at a range of 2,000 yards. No sonar contact was obtained and a ten depth charge pattern was dropped on the estimated position of the U-boat. HMS *Tay* was then ordered to "sit" on the U-boat until one hour after sunset to keep the enemy vessel away from the convoy.[20]

As night fell, HF/DF bearings indicated to Gretton that there were U-boats on the port bow, port beam, and astern of ONS 5. For night stations, HMS *Vidette* was ahead of the convoy; HMS *Sunflower,* off the port bow; HMS *Snowflake,* on the port beam; HMS *Duncan,* off the port stern quarter; HMS *Tay,* astern; HMS *Loosestrife,* off the starboard stern quarter; and the two trawlers, astern of the wing columns. This formation left the starboard bow of ONS 5 somewhat unprotected.[21]

At 2140 HMS *Sunflower* obtained a radar contact. The corvette tuned toward the contact, the U-boat submerged, and a box search was carried out. At 2204 a "doubtful" contact was picked up and HMS *Sunflower* dropped two depth charges on what was "classified as a non-sub, principally to scare any submarine in the vicinity." By mistake a calcium flare was also dropped along with the depth charges, which "seemed rather an unnecessary advertisement," and the corvette then had to extinguish this flare by running over it to draw the flare into the ship's propeller. When the flare had been put out, HMS *Sunflower* returned to its position on the port bow of the convoy.[22]

HMS *Duncan* obtained a radar contact at a range of 3,500 yards at 2245. The British destroyer turned to attack the U-boat, which then dived. A sonar contact was gained at 1,500 yards range and then lost. A depth charge was dropped on the estimated position of the U-boat by HMS *Duncan*. But at 2314, as the destroyer was returning to its station, another radar contact appeared at a range of 2,500 yards. The U-boat was chased before it dived. A ten depth charge pattern was then dropped in the U-boat's wake. As HMS *Duncan* ran out to mount a second depth charge attack, another radar contact was obtained at a range of 4,340 yards. As the destroyer turned into the sea toward the new contact, the ship's bow threw spray over the masthead. The U-boat sighted the British warship and dived at a range of 3,000 yards. No sonar contact was gained, but one depth charge was dropped where the U-boat was thought to be. At 2335, as HMS *Duncan* was turning to set a course to return to its station, another radar contact was picked up at a range of 4,000 yards. HMS *Duncan* began to chase the U-boat, which was steering toward the convoy at a speed of about 12 knots, but the U-boat dived at a range of 1,500 yards. HMS *Duncan* obtained a sonar contact which was attacked with a ten depth charge pattern. At the time the depth charges were dropped, the U-boat's wake could be seen under the destroyer's port bow. The contact was quickly regained, but then lost several times. Before regaining its station with the convoy at 0110, HMS *Duncan* dropped two more depth charges where Gretton estimated the U-boat to be located.[23]

HMS *Snowflake* gained a sonar contact off the port bow of the convoy at 0132 on 29 April. Then radar contact was made at a range of 1,300 yards, and the U-boat began to dive. But as the corvette was attacking with depth charges at a range of 200 yards from the target, the ship's wheel was put "hard-a-starboard" by a misunderstanding of commands by the quartermaster. The U-boat passed at a range of 200 yards down the side of HMS *Snowflake,* and no depth charges were dropped owing to another "mistake" in the confusion of the action. Contact was lost and HMS *Snowflake* maneuvered to get between the U-boat and the convoy. At 0135 three depth charges were dropped between the U-boat and the convoy. A minute later sonar contact was gained at a range of 2,000 yards. As HMS *Snowflake* turned to attack, the U-boat fired a torpedo at the corvette, which missed by 20 yards, as it passed down the side of the ship. HMS *Snowflake* dropped a ten depth charge pattern on the sonar contact which was "not considered particularly accurate." The contact was then regained at a range of 1,400 yards and attacked with ten depth charges. The contact was next regained astern but was thought to be "doubtful." HMS *Snowflake* then broke off the action because it was thought that the U-boat was now not "in a position to menace the

Convoy." The attempted night attacks on ONS 5 ended with HMS *Tay* gaining a sonar contact astern of the convoy which was attacked without result. Gretton thought that the U-boats must have been discouraged by the escorts' aggressive tactics, but that they might attempt a dawn or daylight attack on the convoy.[24]

When the sun rose on the morning of 29 April, HMS *Tay* was sent astern of the convoy to hunt for any U-boats attempting to shadow ONS 5. This would also provide a better baseline for triangulations of HF/DF bearings obtained by HMS *Duncan* and HMS *Tay*. At 0338 HMS *Duncan*'s HF/DF set picked up a bearing of a radio transmission ahead of ONS 5. HMS *Vidette* was sent down this bearing for a distance of 15 miles, but nothing was found. The destroyer returned to its station at 0525.[25]

At 0529 the U-258 torpedoed the merchant ship *McKeesport* in the starboard side.[26] Gretton in HMS *Duncan*, whose station was ahead of the convoy on the port bow, turned into the convoy, passing between columns of merchant ships. He did not know from what direction the torpedo had been fired until he saw a second torpedo explode at the end of its run on the port quarter of the convoy, indicating that the attack came from the starboard side of ONS 5. When the *McKeesport* was torpedoed, HMS *Snowflake,* stationed to port of HMS *Duncan*, turned and steamed down the port side of ONS 5. HMS *Snowflake* was ordered to screen a straggler, the *West Maximus*, which was some 5 miles behind the convoy. When HMS *Snowflake* reached the *West Maximus* the corvette obtained a sonar contact at a range of 2,600 yards. This contact was thought to be doubtful, but because an enemy vessel at this spot could have threatened the *West Maximus*, one depth charge was dropped. The contact was regained ten minutes later and HMS *Snowflake* attacked with two depth charges. Several minutes after this attack, HMS *Snowflake* regained the sonar contact, now astern of the *West Maximus*. Because of the need to conserve depth charges and because the contact was now astern of both the convoy and the *West Maximus*, HMS *Snowflake* did not attack and returned to its station in the screen of the convoy.[27]

After passing though the convoy, HMS *Duncan* came upon the trawler *Northern Gem* which was attacking a sonar contact. HMS *Duncan* searched the area with its sonar without result for five minutes and then circled the location where Gretton thought the

U-boat that had torpedoed the *McKeesport* was hiding. Gretton, however, quickly ended the search when he concluded that he was in error. And at 0620 HMS *Duncan*'s HF/DF set picked up a bearing on a radio transmission. HMS *Vidette* was ordered to search down the bearing but found nothing, and HMS *Duncan* began to return to its station off the port bow of the convoy. As HMS *Duncan* steamed back through the ships of the convoy, it passed the trawler *Northern Gem* picking up survivors from the *McKeesport* which was sinking but still afloat. As Gretton passed the trawler *Northern Gem* and *McKeesport*, he reminded the master of the merchant ship by loud hailer to destroy his confidential books before abandoning the ship. After picking up the crew of the *McKeesport*, the trawler *Northern Gem* tried unsuccessfully to sink the freighter with gunfire. At this point the master of the *McKeesport* remembered that he had left on board not only the ships logs but also charts which showed the western ocean meeting point for ONS 5. *Northern Gem* tried to radio this information to HMS *Duncan*, but the radio transmission was indecipherable and Gretton did not learn about the *McKeesport*'s charts and logs until the *Northern Gem* rejoined ONS 5. The upshot was that HMS *Tay*, still astern of the convoy, was ordered to sink the merchant ship. After sinking the *McKeesport* with depth charges, HMS *Tay* began steaming to overtake the convoy. The frigate did not rejoin ONS 5 until 0600 on 30 April.[28]

After the torpedoing of the *McKeesport*, Gretton interpreted HF/DF bearings to indicate that there were possibly three or four U-boats attempting to work around the bow of the convoy into attack positions. But there were no contacts or attacks. At 1630, HF/DF activity showed two U-boats moving along the port side of ONS 5 to get into position ahead of the convoy. HMS *Sunflower* was sent down one of these bearings looking for U-boats, but did not make contact. The corvette dropped five depth charges "for propaganda purposes" before returning to its station in the convoy's screen. After being detached from SC 127, the destroyer HMS *Oribi* of the 3rd Escort Group joined ONS 5 at 2300. And, some 49 miles astern, HMS *Tay* was steaming to rejoin the convoy. During the night of 29 April some HF/DF bearings were obtained on U-boat radio transmissions, and HMS *Duncan* and HMS *Sunflower* made several attacks on sonar contacts with depth charges. Gretton expected a dawn U-boat attack on

ONS 5, but it did not materialize "and no more ground ray signals were received for twenty hours so that the SCARE tactics appeared to be successful."[29]

Iceland-based air cover for ONS 5 resumed at 0445 on 30 April when a VLR B-24 Liberator aircraft, M/120, appeared over the convoy. When the planes sighted no U-boats for three days, it was thought that the convoy was not being shadowed, and at midnight on 27 April the air cover was discontinued. But late on 28 April a USN PBY Catalina from Iceland sighted ONS 5 and then discovered that the convoy was being followed by a U-boat. This was the U-560, and its radio transmissions, along with those of other U-boats of the *Star* group in ONS 5's neighborhood, were D/F'ed in England. Escort of ONS 5 by VLR B-24 Liberator aircraft of 120th Squadron was ordered for 29 April, but the missions were canceled because of bad weather at the air base at Reykjavik. On 30 April two VLR B-24 Liberators were dispatched from Iceland to escort ONS 5. One aircraft did not sight the convoy and returned to base, while the other, M/120, made contact with ONS 5 and conducted an *Adder* search in front of the convoy at Gretton's request without sighting any U-boats. Then, because of poor visibility, aircraft M/120 had to return to Iceland.[30]

During the morning of 30 April HMS *Oribi* was refueled from the tanker *British Lady*. Around noon the weather began to turn bad and the other escorts could not be refueled. By 1900 the convoy was encountering a full gale blowing out of the west. At about 2200, HMS *Duncan* picked up some HF/DF bearings which were considered distant. An hour later HMS *Snowflake* obtained a radar contact at a range of 3,300 yards. The corvette altered course toward the target, and a U-boat was seen and attacked with gunfire before submerging. A sonar contact was not obtained, but one depth charge was dropped by HMS *Snowflake* on the estimated position of the U-boat. Gretton thought that the HF/DF bearings picked up at 2200 were in fact ground wave transmissions from a U-boat near the convoy and "it will be the first case of a night attack I have met without previous H/F warning." At 2314 HMS *Duncan* obtained another HF/DF bearing from a U-boat just ahead of the convoy. HMS *Vidette*, on the starboard bow of ONS 5, was ordered to drop several depth charges, and at the same time HMS *Duncan* on the port bow of ONS 5 also dropped several depth charges. It was Gretton's intention to scare the U-boat. This tactic apparently was successful for no attack took place and no further HF/DF bearings were obtained for several days.[31]

On 1 May ONS 5 encountered a force ten gale and the ships of the convoy were scattered. As the ships were battling through 30 foot waves, Allied aircraft appeared over the convoy. In the forenoon two US Army aircraft, thought by Gretton to be from Greenland, were sighted and one of these aircraft attacked a U-boat 60 miles south of the convoy. One VLR B-24 Liberator of 120th Squadron was dispatched to ONS 5 on a shuttle mission from Goose Bay, Labrador, to Iceland, but did not find the convoy. After conducting a search for the Allied ships, the Liberator continued on its way to Iceland. Two other VLR B-24 Liberators reached the convoy during the dog watch from Reykjavik. At the direction of Gretton, several searches were conducted "in appalling weather" during the course of which one freighter was sighted 30 miles astern of ONS 5. No U-boats were spotted.[32]

The bad weather also affected the operations of the U-boats. The U-954 radioed the BdU that the "OPERATION IS USELESS BECAUSE OF THE WEATHER SITUATION" and the vessel had been constantly overflown by aircraft.[33] The BdU ended the operations of the *Star* group against ONS 5 because of the bad weather in the battle area and the failure of the U-boats to maintain contact with the convoy. The BdU calculated that only five U-boats had gained contact with ONS 5 during this phase of the battle and that successful attacks on the convoy had been prevented by the weather and not the escorts.[34]

The BdU was having problems of command and control because radio messages from the U-boats were being greatly delayed by atmospheric conditions in the northwest Atlantic that interfered with radio transmissions. However, at 2029 on 1 May, the U-628, a member of the *Specht* group northeast of Newfoundland, reported seeing several clouds of smoke. The BdU thought that the U-268 had sighted SC 128 and ordered seventeen U-boats (U-260, U-438, U-662, U-630, U-584, U-168, U-514, U-270, U-268, U-732, U-92, U-628, U-707, U-358, U-264, U-614, U-226, U-125) of the *Specht* group to chase it.[35] The U-628 reported at 0256Z on 2 May that a hydrophone bearing showed the convoy was steering a course between 000° and 020°. About two hours later the U-628 radioed that it had lost the convoy and thought that it had changed course to the east. And at 0912Z the BdU received a report that star shells had been sighted. As a result of these reports the BdU at 0928Z ordered thirteen U-boats (U-648, U-533, U-531, U-954, U-192, U-231, U-419, U-592, U-378, U-269, U-258, U-560) of the *Star* group to move south southwest toward the *Specht* group to intercept convoy ONS 5. The U-707 reported that it had been "FORCED OFF BY DE-STROYER" and at 2019Z another U-boat radioed that it had seen star shells.[36] From these reports the BdU concluded that the convoy was steering between 10° and 50° at a speed of 6.8 knots.[37]

The U-boats did not sight SC 128 again on 3 May, but the Germans did not give up the hope of intercepting the convoy. At 1029 on 3 May, still wishing to intercept SC 128, the BdU ordered the U-boats of the *Specht* and *Star* groups to form a patrol line by 1800 running from 56°21'N, 44°35'W to 54°57'N, 39°35'W. Several hours later the U-boats were ordered to steam from the assigned patrol line on a course of 280° at a speed of 4 knots until 0001 and then maintain the positions reached. At the same time the U-boats were informed that it was possible that the convoy would not reach the patrol line until darkness on 3 May. However, SC 128 was not intercepted by the U-boats, for the convoy passed to the west of their patrol line.[38] Neither the Allies nor the Germans realized that the *Specht-Star* patrol line was positioned across the intended route of ONS 5.

At the same time that the U-boats of the *Specht* and *Star* groups were moving into their positions in the patrol line, the BdU was forming another seventeen-U-boat patrol line to the south of the *Specht-Star* line, across the intended route of ONS 5. At 1646 the BdU ordered the *Amsel* group of U-boats divided into subgroups of five U-boats each, code named *Amsel 1* through *Amsel 4*. *Amsel 1* (U-638, U-621, U-404, U-575, U-504) was to form a patrol line running from 51°51'N, 49°05'W to 51°39'N, 46°25'W; *Amsel 2* (U-634, U-223, U-266, U-377, U-393) was to take station from 51°33'N, 43°25'W to 50°27'N, 41°25'W; *Amsel 3* (U-709, U-569, U-525, U-468, U-448) was to form a patrol line from 48°45'N, 41°54'W to 47°45'N, 41°25'W; and *Amsel 4* (U-466, U-454, U-359, U-186, U-403) was to be stationed from 45°56'N, 39°35'W to 44°15'N, 39°35'W.[39] By dividing the *Amsel* group into four subdivisions, the

BdU hoped to persuade Allied intelligence that there was a patrol line "stretching right around the Newfoundland Banks." According to BdU theory, when Allied intelligence discovered the "gaps" between the *Amsel* subdivisions, the enemy would attempt to run convoys between the *Amsel* subgroups of U-boats, and the BdU could then combine the *Amsel* components into one patrol line to attack the convoy.[40]

On May 4 the U-boats of the *Specht-Star* patrol line sighted some ships of the escort for ONS 5. At 1419Z the U-264 radioed that it had seen two destroyers on a course of 180°. This was quickly followed by reports of destroyers from two other U-boats. And at 1818Z the U-628 reported sighting the convoy. Then at 1915Z the U-707 also reported a convoy. Both U-boats placed ONS 5 at about 55°N, 42°W steering a southerly course.[41] Thereupon, at 1637, the BdU ordered seventeen U-boats of the *Specht-Star* group to form a patrol line running from 56°45'N, 47°12'W to 54°09'N, 36°55'S by 1,000 on 5 May. This patrol line was coded named *Fink,* and the U-boats were informed that a "S.W. BOUND CONVOY EXPECTED TO-MORROW ONWARDS." Several hours later at 2051 the BdU informed the U-boats of *Amsel 1* and *Amsel 2* of ONS 5's course and position at 2020 and ordered these ten U-boats to operate against the convoy. Even though the Allies did not decode these two orders until 1158 and 1241 on 5 May, they already knew the location of the *Fink* group in general terms, for every one of the sighting reports made by the U-boats had been D/F'ed by shore-based intercept stations.[42]

At dawn on 2 May the weather moderated and ONS 5's escorts began to round up the stragglers. By 0900Z there were twenty merchant ships of the convoy in company with HMS *Duncan*. Gretton was becoming worried about the state of the fuel in some of the escorts. While the weather and sea would permit refueling, the convoy had encountered ice. The tanker *British Lady* had to alter course constantly to avoid growlers and pack ice, thus making refueling operations impossible. By the time the ships were clear of the ice the weather would not permit the escorts to fuel. At 2000 the 3rd Escort Group, consisting of the destroyers HMS *Penn*, HMS *Panther*, HMS *Impulsive*, and HMS *Offa*, joined the escort of ONS 5. Gretton stationed these destroyers in an extended screen across the bow of the convoy. At first glance, these four destroyers appeared to be a considerable reinforcement to the escort of ONS 5, but these ships had not been designed or modified for long-range escort work. Having steamed to the convoy from St. John's, Newfoundland, they were already low on fuel by the time they joined the convoy.[43]

At dawn on 3 May the convoy encountered another gale and ONS 5 was again scattered. As a result of the gale, Gretton only knew the location of thirty-two ships. The four destroyers of the 3rd Escort Group were ahead of the convoy forming an extended screen. HMS *Offa* was astern of ONS 5 hunting for stragglers. And HMS *Pink* with six merchant ships was an estimated 50 miles behind the convoy. The major problem confronting Gretton was not the scattering of the convoy, but rather the fuel status of some of the escorts. The weather and the American tanker *Argon*'s equipment made it impossible to refuel the escorts from that ship. And, even if the weather would permit refueling from the tanker *British Lady*, little assistance could be obtained, for it had only an estimated 100 tons of oil remaining on board. Because of the state of fuel in some of the escorts, Gretton had no choice but to detach some of the warships to obtain fuel. At 1400 Gretton handed command of the escort of ONS 5 over to Lieutenant Commander R. E. Sherwood, RNR, in HMS *Tay* and proceeded to St. John's in HMS *Duncan*. That night, on orders from the commander in chief, western approaches, the fuel-short HMS *Impulsive* was sent to Iceland. The next morning HMS *Panther* and HMS *Penn* left the convoy and went to Newfoundland for fuel. The trawler *Northern Gem*, with the survivors of the *McKeesport* on board, was also dispatched to St. John's.[44] Because of the shortage of fuel and the inability to refuel at sea, the escort of ONS 5 was reduced in strength by four destroyers and one armed trawler just at the time when the Germans were amassing some thirty-seven U-boats across the convoy's intended route.

Throughout 4 May the escorts of ONS 5 obtained a number of HF/DF bearings from off the convoy's port bow and beam. No attacks on the convoy developed during the daylight hours of 4 May. The only contact between the surface escorts of ONS 5 and the U-boats before nightfall occurred at 1915, when HMS *Oribi*, some 14 miles off the port bow of the convoy, obtained an HF/DF bearing of 195°. The destroyer ran down the bearing and sighted a U-boat at 1951 at a range of 7 miles. The U-boat dived, and HMS *Oribi* hunted the submarine until 2230 when the destroyer returned to its station in the screen of the convoy.[45]

One reason for this lack of contact by the U-boats with the convoy was Allied air activity in the vicinity of ONS 5. US Army B-17 aircraft from Newfoundland were sweeping the area in front of ONS 5, but the honors on 4 May go to the Canadians.[46] Flying from Torbay in Newfoundland at the extreme limit of their range, Cansos (the Canadian variant of an American PBY Catalina aircraft) of RCAF 5th (BR) Squadron flew air cover for ONS 5. About 30 miles astern of ONS 5, a Canso obtained a radar contact. As the aircraft dived, a U-boat (the U-630) was sighted and attacked with four depth charges. Two exploded on the port side of the enemy vessel; the third, "off the conning tower"; while the fourth missed. The explosions forced the U-630 to the surface from its crash dive and sank the submarine within ten seconds. After the sinking of the U-630, the Canso's air crew could see debris and an oil slick on the surface of the sea which "grew to 200 by 800 feet." Another Canso sighted a U-boat, most likely the U-438, and attacked by diving out of the sun and dropping depth charges at a height of 20 feet. According to the Germans, these missed by only 15 meters.[47] In the face of antiaircraft fire, the Canadian aircraft again attacked the U-boat with machine-gun fire. As the aircraft climbed and turned, the U-boat submerged. In addition, two more U-boats were sighted, with one of them attacked by Canso's before the end of the sweep.[49]

At dusk on 4 May ONS 5 consisted of thirty merchant ships in ten columns steering a course of 202° steaming at 7 knots. HMS *Offa* and HMS *Oribi* were stationed off the port and starboard bows of the convoy at a distance of 5 miles. The inner screen consisted of HMS *Sunflower* on the port bow of the convoy and HMS *Vidette* on the starboard bow. While HMS *Snowflake*'s and HMS *Loosestrife*'s stations were on the port and starboard beams of the convoy, HMS *Tay*'s station was off the port stern quarter of the convoy and the trawler *Northern Spray* was positioned off the starboard stern quarter. However, the trawler *Northern Spray* was not in its station, but astern of the convoy. Much farther astern was HMS *Pink* escorting four stragglers. Sherwood had requested by radio that HMS *Pink* and the four stragglers be routed as a separate convoy.[49]

At 2228 the *Northern Spray* reported that a merchant ship had been torpedoed while straggling 6 miles behind the convoy.[50] This freighter, the *North Britain,* had a defective boiler which had just been repaired, and was attempting to rejoin ONS 5 when it was torpedoed and sunk in two minutes by the U-707.[51] There were only eleven survivors who were picked up by the *Northern Spray.* Before rescuing the crew from the *North Britain,* the trawler circled the area searching for a U-boat, but nothing was found.[52]

At 2109 HMS *Vidette* obtained a radar contact bearing 200° at a range of 5,100 yards. The destroyer steamed down this bearing. At 2117 a second target was obtained on the ship's radar bearing 190° at a range of 7,200 yards. At 2123 a U-boat was sighted on the surface steaming at high speed. At a range of 700 yards the U-boat began to dive. HMS *Vidette* attacked, dropping ten depth charges on the swirl of the submerging U-boat. Immediately after the depth charges went off, there was another large explosion, and the depth charge party on the stern of the destroyer saw a column of dark water rise out of the sea at a range of between 300 and 600 yards. HMS *Vidette* did not reattack this U-boat but headed for the second radar contact. At a range of 900 yards another U-boat was sighted. The submarine appeared to alter course 30° to starboard and then dive. HMS *Vidette* then attacked the estimated position of the U-boat with five depth charges at 2133. The destroyer ran out, turned, and began searching the area with sonar, but did not obtain a target. HMS *Vidette* then resumed its position in the screen of ONS 5.[53]

After returning to its station on the starboard bow of ONS 5, HMS *Vidette* obtained another radar contact bearing 205° at a range of 3,600 yards at 2220. HMS *Vidette* ran down the bearing at a speed of 22 knots. At 2225 a U-boat was sighted on the surface. Three minutes later the U-boat dived at a range of 700 yards. An attack was undertaken immediately with fourteen depth charges "fired by eye" dropped close ahead of the diving position of the U-boat. HMS *Vidette* then hunted the U-boat with sonar, but at 2250 another radar contact was gained at a range of 3,600 yards bearing 285°. As HMS *Vidette* ran down this bearing the ship's speed was increased to 20 knots. At 2258 a U-boat was sighted drawing slowly to the right— 1,000 yards ahead of the destroyer. HMS *Vidette* opened fire with 20mm Oerlikons. The U-boat appeared to be "reluctant" to dive and the conning tower did not disappear into the sea until the range had closed to 80 yards. HMS *Vidette* passed through the swirl of the sub-merging U-boat and dropped fourteen depth charges. The destroyer then ran out, turned, and began to hunt the U-boat with sonar. At 2325 a sonar contact was obtained. As the British destroyer moved in to attack "the target had no movement and produced no Doppler, but it was classified . . . as a U-boat." Fourteen depth charges were dropped. HMS *Vidette* ran out and turned to attack a third time. As the range closed "one good echo" was obtained at a range of 750 yards from the position of the last attack. However, no further sonar contact was gained as the destroyer moved through the area of the last attack. At 2350 HMS *Vidette* returned to its station.[54]

At 2254 Sherwood saw the freighters *Harperly* and *Harbury* torpedoed. He later discovered that the merchant ship *West Maximus* had been torpedoed as well. The *Harbury* was hit by one torpedo fired by the U-628 on the starboard side in the No. 5 hold. The ship did not sink, but as the *Harbury* settled into the water the crew abandoned the vessel. Minutes later the *West Maximus* was torpedoed and sunk by the U-264. Fifty-one members of the crew disembarked before the *West Maximus* sank. Next the freighter *Harperly* was hit on the port side by two torpedoes fired by the U-264. One torpedo hit the ship in the engine room and the other near the foremast. Thirty-nine members of the crew took to the life boats. Twenty minutes later the *Harperly* sank. The *Northern Spray* coming up from astern of the convoy later picked up 132 survivors from the three merchant ships. The *Harbury*, which did not sink immediately, was later finished off by gunfire from the U-264.[55]

Just as HMS *Vidette* was attacking two U-boats, HMS *Snowflake*, on the port beam of the convoy, obtained a radar contact at a range of 3,000 yards bearing 255°. The corvette ran down this bearing and at 2301 heard the U-boat fire two torpedoes on its sonar. Three minutes later HMS *Snowflake* opened fire with star shells down the bearing. The corvette's sonar could hear the U-boat and it was still in radar contact. Not knowing if the target was a decoy or a U-boat, HMS *Snowflake* attacked with ten depth charges. After the attack the captain of the British warship thought that he had been "bluffed" into attacking. After this depth charge attack, HMS *Snowflake* was still in radar contact with the U-boat, and the corvette began to fire star and high explosive shells at the enemy vessel. The U-boat dived at 2323 and HMS *Snowflake* dropped five depth charges in the area where the enemy vessel had disappeared. At 2329 a torpedo passed from port to starboard at a range of 125 yards from HMS *Snowflake*. Unable to gain sonar contact with the U-boat which had fired the torpedo, HMS *Snowflake* began to return to its station off the port beam of ONS 5 at 2334.[56]

Off the port bow of the convoy, HMS *Sunflower* picked up a radar contact at a range of 4,000 yards bearing 150°. When HMS *Sunflower* investigated the target it quickly obtained a sonar contact which was thought to be doubtful. Four depth charges were dropped of which one failed to explode. The contact after the attack was classified as a non-U-boat, and HMS *Sunflower* returned to its station on the screen of the convoy.

Back off the port beam of ONS 5, HMS *Snowflake* obtained a radar contact at a range of 3,400 yards bearing 175° at 0122 on 5 May. The corvette began to run down the bearing and a star shell was fired at 0124. HMS *Oribi* was ordered to assist HMS *Snowflake,* and at 0154 HMS *Oribi* fired a star shell. Five minutes later, a U-boat submerged 900 yards ahead of HMS *Snowflake* and the corvette attacked with five depth charges set on shallow. At 0200 HMS *Snowflake* ran in for a second attack but the run was "inaccurate" and no depth charges were dropped. HMS *Snowflake* then attacked again with four depth charges. But at 0215 HMS *Oribi* was in visual contact with the corvette. Because it was running short of depth charges, HMS *Snowflake* requested that the destroyer take over the hunt for the U-boat. HMS *Oribi*'s gyro compass repeaters were not working, so for the next hour HMS *Snowflake* directed the destroyer to the target as HMS *Oribi* attacked the U-boat with depth charges. At 0320 HMS *Snowflake* departed from the area to return to ONS 5, while HMS *Oribi* continued to hunt the U-boat vainly for another hour before returning to its station on the distant screen.[57]

At 0306 HMS *Tay* obtained an HF/DF bearing on a U-boat just off the port bow of the convoy. Nine minutes later the U-358 torpedoed two merchant ships.[58] The *Bristol City,* the lead ship in the port most column of the convoy, was hit on the port side in the No. 4 hold by the first torpedo. A second torpedo hit the ship in the No. 1 hold. The crew of the *Bristol City* went over the side as the ship sank. The merchant ship *Wentworth,* also on the port side of the convoy in column three, was hit by a torpedo on the port side amidships in the stokehold. The crew of the *Wentworth* abandoned the ship, which did not sink.[59]

When the *Bristol City* and the *Wentworth* were torpedoed, the escorts began to hunt for the U-358. But, on the starboard beam of ONS 5, HMS *Loosestrife* obtained a radar contact at 0312 and fired a star shell down the bearing three minutes later. A U-boat was then sighted and when it dived, the corvette attacked with ten depth charges which exploded as the U-boat passed down the starboard side of HMS *Loosestrife* at a range of 100 yards. Before HMS *Loosestrife* could mount a second attack, a second radar contact was obtained at a range of 2,400 yards at 0324. The corvette turned toward the target and fired a star shell. A U-boat was sighted and the British warship opened fire with 20mm Oerlikons. The U-boat dived and HMS *Loosestrife* attacked with nine depth charges about 100 yards ahead of the swirl left by the submerging U-boat. Even though HMS *Loosestrife*'s sonar recorder was not working, the corvette swept back through the area of the attack, hunting vainly for the U-boat. HMS *Loosestrife* then began to return to its station on the starboard beam of ONS 5, but, at 0340, the corvette sighted the still floating freighter *Wentworth* with its survivors and those from the *Bristol City*. The corvette picked up sixty-one survivors from the two freighters and attempted to sink the *Wentworth* with a depth charge and gunfire. The commander of HMS *Loosestrife* thought that it had left the *Wentworth* in a sinking condition, but the merchant ship was later sunk by gunfire from the U-628 astern of ONS 5.[60] At 0850 HMS *Loosestrife* was back in its station off the starboard beam of the convoy. Just as HMS *Loosestrife* was conducting depth charge attacks astern of ONS 5, HMS *Tay* carried out a number of depth charge attacks on the starboard quarter of the convoy.[61]

At 0500 ONS 5's escorts took up their day stations for 5 May. HMS *Offa* and HMS *Oribi* were ahead of the convoy as an extended screen. The inner screen consisted of HMS *Tay* off the bow of the convoy, with HMS *Vidette* and HMS *Sunflower* stationed off the starboard and port bows of ONS 5 and HMS *Loosestrife* and HMS *Snowflake* off the starboard and port beams of the convoy. At 0700 the *Northern Spray*, with 143 survivors from sunk merchant ships on board, was detached to St. John's. During the morning of 5 May heavy enemy radio traffic was intercepted by the convoy's escorts. At 1010 a "first class" HF/DF bearing at 155° was obtained. HMS *Oribi*, 5 miles in front of the port wing of the convoy, was ordered to search down this bearing to a depth of 12 miles. At 0857 a U-boat was sighted at a range of 7 miles, and HMS *Oribi* increased speed to 30 knots. And at 0907 and 0910 two more U-boats were sighted. The three U-boats appeared to be steering away at high speed from the destroyer "roughly in line abreast" formation, but when the three U-boats saw they were being "overhauled" by HMS *Oribi*, they submerged. At 1120 HMS *Oribi* began to hunt the first U-boat with sonar. Contact was quickly gained, but a malfunctioning gyro repeater hampered the destroyer's hunt for the U-boat. The only available substitute was a magnetic compass, whose use made it very difficult to ascertain whether a target was moving left or right. At 0948 HMS *Oribi* attacked with depth charges. It was thought that the U-boat was moving left. But only four depth charges were dropped when it was learned that the U-boat was moving down the left side of the ship. After this attack, sonar contact was lost but then regained at 1243. Four minutes later HMS *Oribi* attacked with ten depth charges. About two minutes after the first depth charges exploded "two unexplained explosions were heard, one heavy and one less intensity, resulting in a large visible eruption of air." HMS *Oribi* ran out, turned, and attacked again with five depth charges. There were "no visible results." The contact was held through the disturbances of the exploding depth charges, but it then faded before another attack could be mounted. At 1140 HMS *Oribi* left the area to resume its station.[62]

At about 0900 HMS *Tay* and HMS *Offa* moved into the main body of the convoy to refuel from the tankers *Argon* and *British Lady*. It had been discovered that if the *British Lady* remained with the convoy, instead of proceeding to St. John's, it could supply the escorts with 250 tons of oil as opposed to the 100 tons it was originally thought. And the fuel situation among the escorts was so critical that an attempt had to be made to obtain fuel from the *Argon* even if it was not equipped to refuel ships over the stern. HMS *Tay* was refueled by the *British Lady*, but when HMS *Offa* approached the *Argon*, the crew learned that the tanker would not be ready to refuel for another hour.

At 1,100 HMS *Offa* again closed with the *Argon*, but after "receiving one gallon of oil the hose parted."[63]

As HMS *Offa* was getting clear of the *Argon*, the merchant ship *Dolius* was torpedoed in the engine room on the starboard side, probably by the U-638.[64] The crew of the *Dolius* abandoned the ship, which was "floating well down, with the after well deck awash." Sherwood thought that the U-boat had fired the torpedo from within the convoy, and the escorts began hunting for the U-boat, with HMS *Sunflower* sweeping down through the convoy between columns two and three at full speed. Slightly astern of the *Dolius*, a sonar contact was obtained and attacked with ten depth charges. Joined by HMS *Tay*, the corvette mounted a sonar search for the U-boat, but no contact was obtained. HMS *Sunflower*, while being screened by HMS *Snowflake*, then picked up sixty-six survivors from the *Dolius*.[65]

Eighty miles astern of the main body of ONS 5, HMS *Pink* was escorting four merchant ships which had separated from the convoy in bad weather, which now formed a separate convoy proceeding independently toward Newfoundland. HMS *Pink* was about 3,000 yards ahead of the merchant ships which were in line-abreast formation when, at 0954Z, the corvette obtained a sonar contact off the starboard bow at a range of 2,200 yards. Sonar conditions were "splendid," and HMS *Pink* carried out four depth charge attacks in rapid succession. The U-boat, the U-192, was then heard to blow its tanks, and large air bubbles were soon seen on the surface of the ocean. Two more depth charge attacks were carried out on the U-boat, which appeared to be motionless, but the contact was lost after the seventh attack. HMS *Pink* then gave up the hunt for the U-192 and set course to rejoin the four merchant ships—now about 10 miles ahead of the warship. Some fourteen minutes after breaking off the action, "a dull and most powerful underwater explosion shook the ship." Officers and crew of HMS *Pink* realized that this was the death throes of the U-boat exploding deep underwater. HMS *Pink* had destroyed the U-192.[66]

At 1452Z, when HMS *Pink* was 3 miles astern of the four merchant ships, "a huge column of smoke" burst from the merchant ship *West Market*. This ship was torpedoed by the U-584.[67] The *West Market*'s crew abandoned the ship, its back broken. HMS *Pink* circled the wrecked *West Market* and its life boats, dropping several depth charges "to keep the U-boat down." Believing that the U-boat might still be in the vicinity, HMS *Pink* steamed around "at various courses and speeds" before picking up the survivors. By 1600Z the corvette had picked up sixty-one members of *West Market*'s crew, and the merchant ship was then sunk by two depth charges.[68]

An hour and a half later HMS *Pink* rejoined the little convoy and took station astern of the remaining three merchant ships. At 1850Z a sonar contact 1000 yards ahead of the convoy was obtained and attacked with four depth charges. Further attacks were not undertaken because HMS *Pink* was down to twenty-one depth charges and was running short of fuel as well. But at 1945Z another sonar contact was picked up which was later considered to be "probably nonsubmarine." This contact was attacked with two depth charges. As darkness was approaching, the commander of HMS *Pink*, Lieutenant Roger Atkinson, RNVR, thought it likely that he would have to fight off a night attack. Atkinson thought that his best weapon "for the night to be evasive tactics," and in the darkness the small convoy steered "various alterations" in courses and was not attacked. The rest of the voyage was quiet, and HMS *Pink*'s convoy arrived off St. John's without further incident on 9 May.[69]

Allied intelligence after the battle for ONS 5 estimated that during the period 1200 on 4 May to 1200 on 5 May, twenty-eight U-boats were in contact with the convoy at various times. Several U-boats had been damaged by the escorts and the U-358, U-378, and U-514 were forced to withdraw from the action because of damage received at the hands of the escorts. On 5 May the BdU thought that there was the possibility that the U-boats could destroy ONS 5, and at 1126Z the BdU directed the U-boats to make submerged attacks during the daylight hours while simultaneously getting ahead of ONS 5 in order to be in a position for night attacks. The U-boats were ordered to "HURRY. OTHERWISE THERE WILL BE NOTHING LEFT OF THE CONVOY FOR THE 40 SUBS. THE BATTLE WILL NOT LAST LONG BECAUSE OF THE SHORT SEA AREA WHICH IS LEFT." At 1830Z two U-boats in contact with ONS 5 were ordered to send beacon signals so additional U-boats could home in on the convoy. And the U-boats were directed to remain on the surface and fight Allied planes with antiaircraft guns to ensure gaining attacking positions before the onset of darkness. The U-boats, the BdU decreed, "MUST UTILIZE THIS GREAT OPPORTUNITY."[70]

Even though HF/DF bearings indicated that there were U-boats ahead and astern of ONS 5, HMS *Oribi* began to take oil from the *British Lady* at 1220. However, the destroyer stopped refueling at 1500 because of HF/DF activity. A half hour later, Sherwood concluded that he "did not think an attack was imminent," and HMS *Offa* proceeded to take oil again from the *British Lady*. After receiving about thirty tons of oil, the destroyer ended the operation and began to move away from the tanker. Eleven minutes after HMS *Offa* ended refueling the U-266 torpedoed the merchant ship *Selvistan*, followed almost immediately by the merchant ships *Gharinda* and *Bonde*.[71] The *Selvistan* was hit by two torpedoes on the port side in the No. 4 hold and sunk within two minutes, while the crew was abandoning the ship. The *Gharinda* was hit on the port side in the No. 1 hold. The ship began to settle by the bow and the crew abandoned the vessel. A periscope was seen by the *Bonde* just a few seconds before it was torpedoed, and the *Bonde* opened fire on the periscope with 20mm Oerlikons. But it was too late, for the vessel was hit by a torpedo in the starboard side.[72]

At 1745 the convoy made an emergency turn of 90° to port, returning to its base course at 1838. Aircraft J/120, a VLR B-24 Liberator from Iceland operating at the extreme limit of its range, appeared over ONS 5 at 1754. At Sherwood's request, the aircraft carried out two searches, sighting merchant ships and the debris of battle. After some two hours over the battle area, aircraft J/120 began its return to Reykjavik.[73]

The torpedoes which hit the *Selvistan*, *Ghanida*, and *Bonde* appeared to have come from within the body of the convoy. HMS *Tay*, whose sonar was now out of action, rescued the survivors from the three torpedoed merchant ships, while HMS *Oribi* and HMS *Offa* circled the frigate, the survivors, and the wreck of the *Ghanida* hunting for the U-boat. At 1839, HMS *Offa* obtained a firm sonar contact at a range of 1,500 yards. An attack was carried out with depth charges and two minutes after they exploded, "large air bubbles were seen rising from the position." HMS *Offa* then carried out four more depth charge attacks. After the fifth attack, however, HMS *Offa* and HMS *Oribi* broke off the action and returned to their stations because the commander of HMS *Offa* thought that the heavy enemy radio traffic coming from the vicinity of ONS 5 "indicated that the convoy was threatened with annihilation."[74]

Enemy radio activity in the vicinity of the convoy convinced Sherwood that the U-boats would make a night attack on ONS 5. HMS *Oribi* and *Offa* were stationed in an extended screen 5 miles off each bow of the convoy. The close escort consisted of HMS *Tay* ahead of ONS 5, with HMS *Sunflower* and HMS *Vidette* off the port and starboard bows, and HMS *Snowflake* and HMS *Loosestrife* off the port and starboard stern quarters of the convoy. The convoy was steaming at 7 knots on a course of 180° until 2359 when it was altered to 156°. Shortly before the escorts took up their night stations, the convoy found itself in thick fog and the visibility dropped almost to nil.[75]

The first action of the night of 5 May began in heavy fog at 2040 when HMS *Sunflower* picked up a radar contact off its port bow. As HMS *Sunflower* closed with the target to investigate, the radar contact faded, but the ship's sonar picked up the contact. At 2053 HMS *Sunflower* attacked the U-boat, which appeared to be moving from left to right, with a ten depth charge pattern. Just before the depth charges were dropped, HMS *Sunflower*'s radar obtained a contact on a second U-boat at a range of 3,400 yards. This U-boat was beyond the U-boat under attack and, after dropping the depth charges, HMS *Sunflower* headed for the second U-boat. At 2055 HMS *Sunflower*'s sonar revealed a torpedo being fired at the ship on a bearing of 20° to starboard. HMS *Sunflower* turned toward the torpedo which passed down the port side of the ship. As HMS *Sunflower* turned to avoid the torpedo, the ship's radar showed a third U-boat bearing 30° from the other U-boat. HMS *Sunflower* continued to steam toward the U-boat which had fired on her. At 2058 the U-boat was sighted and HMS *Sunflower* opened fire with its main armament, but after two rounds the gun jammed. With its main armament out of action, HMS *Sunflower* turned to starboard toward the third U-boat to attempt to force it to submerge. Then at 2107 HMS *Sunflower* heard on its sonar a "full salvo" of torpedoes being fired. The helm was put hard to port and then back to starboard, while the torpedoes passed down the port side of the warship. HMS *Sunflower* then veered away from the U-boats and radioed HMS *Tay* that it was returning to its station. Only minutes later, the jam in HMS *Sunflower*'s gun was cleared, and one minute later a radar contact was obtained at a range of 3,800 yards. HMS *Sunflower* ran down the bearing, but the contact disappeared. The British warship continued to run down the bearing. At 2129 a flash came on starboard, and HMS *Sunflower* altered course toward it. HMS *Sunflower* then saw HMS *Snowflake* firing star shells through the fog and darkness. *Sunflower* then returned to its position on the port bow of ONS 5.[76]

HMS *Snowflake* was on the way to assist HMS *Sunflower*, but when it learned that the other corvette was returning to its station, HMS *Snowflake* returned to its station as well. At 2123 a radar contact was obtained on a bearing of 190° at a range of 2,400 yards. HMS *Snowflake* ran down the bearing, and the U-boat altered course to the eastward as the range closed. HMS *Snowflake* began to fire high explosive and star shells. When the U-boat dived, the corvette ran in to attack with depth charges. As HMS *Snowflake* was running in to attack, a radar contact was obtained at a range of 2,100 yards bearing 160°. Two depth charges were dropped on the first U-boat while HMS *Snowflake*'s radar held the second contact. At 2134 the second U-boat dived at a range of 1,800 yards on a bearing of 160°. A sonar contact was immediately obtained and HMS *Snowflake* ran into attack. The target was moving to port, and it was anticipated that the enemy vessel would turn hard to port, but the U-boat turned to starboard and passed down the starboard side of the British warship. Sonar contact was held until 2139 when it was lost. HMS *Snowflake* then turned on to the bearing of the first U-boat and four minutes later dropped one depth charge "to persuade U-boats to stay down for a while." HMS *Snowflake* then set course to rejoin ONS 5, but at 2147 a doubtful sonar contact was obtained on a U-boat which was attacked with two depth charges. Sonar contact was then regained, but the echoes were "doubtful." At 2156 HMS *Snowflake* broke off the action and at 2230 had returned to its station on the port stern quarter of the convoy.[77]

At 2134 HMS *Sunflower*, off the starboard bow of ONS 5, obtained a sonar contact off its starboard bow at a range of 700 yards. The corvette ran down the bearing which was classified as a non-U-boat. As HMS *Sunflower* was returning to its station in the screen of the convoy, another sonar contact was picked up at 2215 and a hedgehog attack was mounted without result. A second sonar contact was obtained, but it was immediately lost. A radar contact was then obtained at 2230, and a star shell was fired down the bearing, but nothing was seen and the contact faded at a range of 1,000 yards. HMS *Sunflower* next obtained what was thought to be a sonar contact ahead of the ship, but there was some confusion over the nature of the target and position. At the same time a U-boat was sighted, but HMS *Sunflower* was steaming away at full speed and the enemy vessel disappeared before an attack could be mounted. At 2344 the corvette returned to its station.[78]

HMS *Loosestrife*, on the starboard beam of the convoy, obtained a radar contact at a range of 4,700 yards at 2126. The corvette turned toward the target and ran down the bearing. At 2134 a U-boat was sighted moving from left to right. Fire was opened with the ship's 20mm Oerlikons and main armament. One round appeared to hit the superstructure of the U-boat before it dived at a range of 800 yards. A sonar contact was immediately obtained at a range of 800 yards, and HMS *Loosestrife* attacked with ten depth charges. But the U-boat escaped, sonar contact was not regained, and HMS *Loosestrife* at 2209 took station, as ordered, off the starboard stern quarter of ONS 5. Twenty-five minutes later HMS *Loosestrife* obtained a radar contact to starboard at a range of 5,200 yards. It was the U-638, which was soon sighted at a range of 500 yards. Simultaneously, the enemy vessel saw the British warship, turned away from HMS *Loosestrife* and fired a torpedo from its aft torpedo tube as it to zigzagged in flight. HMS *Loosestrife* followed the U-638 in the vessel's wake. The U-boat crash dived right in front of the corvette and, as the U-638 submerged, HMS *Loosestrife* ran up the U-boat's wake passing over the enemy vessel and dropping ten depth charges. As the depth charges exploded, the U-638 broke the surface and burst apart in "a vivid green-blue flash" with such force that the sailors in the corvette's engine room thought, for a moment, that the ship's stern had been blown off. HMS *Loosestrife* turned and passed through an "immense patch of oil" and debris before returning to its station on the screen of ONS 5 at 2305.[79]

Less than ninety minutes later, at 0026 on 6 May, HMS *Vidette* obtained a radar contact bearing 230° at a range of 1,500 yards on the starboard bow of ONS 5. HMS *Vidette* increased speed to 20 knots and ran toward the contact. The target disappeared at a range of 700 yards. A star shell was fired, "but had little effect in view of the prevailing fog." The destroyer dropped one depth charge and began to return toward its station. As HMS *Vidette* was steaming to its station, a sonar contact was obtained at 0207. The destroyer turned toward the target, classified as a U-boat, as its prey moved slowly to starboard. It was then decided to attack with a hedgehog. HMS *Vidette*'s speed was decreased to 9 knots as it approached the submerged U-boat. At 0208 the hedgehog was fired: approximately three seconds later, after the last of the bombs hit the water, there were "two distinct underwater explosions, and flashes observed." Then what appeared to be a "U-boat blowing tanks" was heard on the sonar followed by "metallic banging noises." On the starboard side of the destroyer, the crew saw "a large disturbance and upheaval which might have been caused by the escape of air from the U-boat." HMS *Vidette* then swept through the area with sonar but could not regain contact.[80]

On ONS 5's port flank in the early hours of 6 May, the escorts were still heavily engaged with the U-boats that doggedly tried to close with the convoy for an attack. At 0001 ONS 5 altered course to 186° in an attempt to throw off the U-boats. To reinforce the port side of the screen, Sherwood ordered HMS *Offa* to take station off the port bow of ONS 5, replacing HMS *Oribi*, which had gone to assist HMS *Sunflower*. This maneuver required HMS *Offa* to make a dash across the front of the convoy.[81]

Off the port beam of the convoy, HMS *Snowflake* obtained a radar contact at a range of 4,000 yards bearing 90° at 0022. The corvette began to chase the U-boat, firing alternatively high explosive and star shells. At 0030 the U-boat dived at a range of 600 yards and HMS *Snowflake* attacked with depth charges. The corvette ran out, turned, and then ran over the target at 0035 holding sonar contact with "instantaneous echoes." At 0038 a second attack was mounted with one depth charge. HMS *Snowflake* regained sonar contact astern at 0039 but did not attack again, for it "had insufficient time or charges," and returned to its station in the screen of the convoy. At 0130 HMS *Snowflake* obtained another radar contact at a range of 4,100 yards bearing 30°. This contact was reported by radio to HMS *Tay*. HMS *Snowflake* began to chase the U-boat. Using the ship's search radar to aim the gun, it fired high explosive shells, for "by this time fog had closed in and star shell were useless." At 0140 the U-boat dived at a range of 400 yards. One minute later the corvette attacked, dropping one depth charge. As this attack was being made, a radar contact was obtained at a range of 2,400 yards bearing 170°. HMS *Snowflake* began to chase this U-boat which was moving "rapidly left." This second U-boat was reported to HMS *Tay* which fired on the submarine with high explosive shells. At 0145 the U-boat dived, and at the same time a radar contact was obtained on a third U-boat at a range of 1,000 yards bearing 180°. HMS *Snowflake* turned toward the U-boat to chase it and reported the vessel to HMS *Tay*. At 0146 the third U-boat dived. Sonar contact was obtained at a range of 700 yards and HMS *Snowflake* ran in to attack with the ship's last depth charge. Contact was lost and the depth charge was not dropped.[82]

At 0149 HMS *Sunflower* was ordered to assist HMS *Snowflake*. At 0151 HMS *Snowflake* began a radar sweep through the area where the three U-boats had submerged, hoping to learn whether any of the trio had surfaced. At 0154 HMS *Snowflake* obtained a radar contact bearing 150°, range 3,200 yards, on what would prove to be the U-125. On the corvette's radar, the enemy vessel appeared to be stopped, low in the water. The range was closed to 500 yards and contact was gained by the corvette's sonar. At 0200 HMS *Snowflake* closed with the U-125 and illuminated the U-boat with a searchlight. The U-boat was then seen to turn rapidly to starboard. The corvette's "wheel was put hard-a-starboard" in an attempt to ram, and HMS *Snowflake* opened fire with its guns. As the U-125 turned to starboard, HMS *Snowflake* "turned inside the U-boat's turning circle and came up alongside her starboard side with only a few feet separating the two." The U-125 was badly damaged with its "conning tower buckled, periscope standards twisted, A. A. gun wrecked." The two ships were so close that HMS *Snowflake*'s guns could not be depressed enough to hit the U-boat. When the two ships drew apart, it was seen that the U-125's stern had settled and air bubbles were coming out of the aft hatch. The crew of the U-125 attempted to use the vessel's deck gun, but were beaten off by fire from HMS *Snowflake*'s port 20mm Oerlikon and two pounder pom-pom guns. Some of the Germans "waved their arms, presumably as a signal to cease fire, this was ignored." But in the confusion, darkness, and fog, the U-125 managed to break away. The commander of the corvette reported that it had rammed and sank a U-boat, assuming incorrectly that the port bilge keel of HMS *Snowflake* "had torn a hole in the U-boat's starboard side."[83]

After escaping from HMS *Snowflake*, the U-125 radioed BdU "HAVE BEEN RAMMED—UNABLE TO DIVE . . . REQUEST AID."[84] When the U-125 disappeared, HMS *Snowflake* obtained a radar contact at a range of 1,400 yards bearing 160°. The corvette "set course to ram being the only means left to deal with U-boats." At 2213, HMS *Snowflake*'s spotlight revealed that its target was HMS *Sunflower*. HMS *Snowflake*'s wheel was "put hard-a-port and a collision was successfully averted." Almost immediately, HMS *Snowflake* heard several explosions which were thought to be the U-125's scuttling charges. The corvette swept through the area, its light illuminating a number of Germans in the water. HMS *Snowflake* requested permission to pick up the Germans "for interrogation," but this request was turned down and the crew of the U-125 was left to die in the water. At 0218 HMS *Snowflake* obtained a sonar contact which was lost three minutes later, and the corvette returned to its station on the screen of ONS 5.[85]

HMS *Sunflower*, which so narrowly escaped ramming by the *Snowflake*, had left its station on the port bow of ONS 5 upon receiving the order to assist the other corvette. At 0243 HMS *Sunflower* obtained a sonar contact at 1,200 yards range. The ship's radar picked up the U-boat as the enemy vessel, the U-533, surfaced. HMS *Sunflower* drew alongside the U-533, illuminating the submarine with a searchlight. The corvette then turned toward the U-boat and rammed it in the stern. It was a glancing blow and the U-533 escaped with only minor damage. At 0258 HMS *Sunflower* began to return to its station.[86]

Meanwhile, HMS *Oribi* was ordered to assist HMS *Sunflower*. As the destroyer steamed from its station on the port bow of ONS 5 toward the reported position of the corvette, an unknown escort was sighted about a mile away firing star shells. At 0252 HMS *Oribi* obtained a sonar contact which was thought by the destroyer's commander to be either a U-boat or HMS *Sunflower*. As HMS *Oribi* turned toward the target, a U-boat was sighted coming out of the fog. This was the U-531 which was off HMS *Oribi*'s starboard bow at a range of one cable. HMS *Oribi* rammed the U-531 just aft of the

U-boat's conning tower. The U-531 "slewed" around the port side of the destroyer, "heeled over with her bows and conning tower out of the water," and then disappeared. After ramming and sinking the U-531, HMS *Oribi* searched for wreckage of the U-boat, but nothing was found in the darkness and fog except "a very strong smell of oil over a very large area." HMS *Oribi*, damaged forward from the ramming and capable of only 12 knots, remained off the port side of ONS 5 until daylight on 6 May.[87]

Off the starboard stern quarter of ONS 5, HMS *Loosestrife* obtained a radar contact at a range of 4,000 yards. The corvette turned toward the target. At a range of 2,500 yards, the echo disappeared, and at 2,000 yards sonar contact was gained. HMS *Loosestrife* attacked dropping ten depth charges at 0130. Sonar contact was quickly regained and, as the corvette ran in for a second attack, HMS *Loosestrife*'s radar obtained a contact at a range of 4,600 yards. It was then decided not to attack the radar contact which was quickly classified as a side echo. At 0139 HMS *Loosestrife* was back at its station. At 0327 another radar contact was obtained at a range of 4,000 yards and HMS *Loosestrife* turned toward it to investigate and run down the bearing. The contact faded from the ship's radar "almost immediately," but it was decided to run down the range of the echo and drop two depth charges "with a view to keeping submarine down." At 0342, while running in to drop the depth charges, the corvette obtained another radar contact. It was a U-boat moving across the stern of ONS 5 from starboard to port. At 0402, HMS *Loosestrife* radioed HMS *Snowflake*, off the port quarter of ONS 5, that a U-boat was heading its way. HMS *Snowflake* then steamed to intercept the U-boat. Four minutes later HMS *Loosestrife* was sighted "in the half light of dawn," steering 45°. While HMS *Snowflake*'s radar swept ahead of HMS *Loosestrife*, it obtained a radar contact at 0412 bearing 47° at a range of 3,000 yards. HMS *Snowflake* fired a star shell followed by high explosive shells, using search radar to aim the rounds. At 0416 HMS *Snowflake* gained sonar contact with the target. One minute later the sonar brought in a "very loud whistle effect," and at 0418 two torpedoes passed down the port side of the corvette. Two more torpedoes followed three minutes later. At 0421 the U-boat submerged and nine minutes later HMS *Loosestrife* attacked with depth charges. The contact after this attack was not regained and both corvettes resumed their stations on the screen of ONS 5.[88]

At 1200 on 4 May, the 1st Escort Group—consisting of the sloop HMS *Pelican;* the frigates HMS *Wear*, HMS *Spey*, HMS *Jed;* and the ex-US Coast Guard cutter HMS *Sennen*—sailed from St. John's to reinforce the escort of ONS 5, moving on the orders of the commander in chief, western approaches. The vessels proceeded east and then north at a speed of 14 knots. Learning that ONS 5 was under heavy attack, the group increased speed to 16 knots on 5 May. Because of slow speed, HMS *Sennen* was detached and sent to join HMS *Pink*'s convoy astern of the main body of ONS 5. After attacking two U-boats en route, HMS *Sennen* joined HMS *Pink* at 2300 on 6 May.[89]

During the early hours of 6 May, the four remaining ships of the 1st Escort Group steamed toward ONS 5 in a line-abreast formation with 4 miles between each ship. The plan was for the 1st Escort Group to join ONS 5 at 0400, sweep around the stern of the convoy at first light, and then form an extended screen ahead of ONS 5. The commander of the 1st Escort Group, Commander G. N. Brewen, RN, knew from radio telephone intercepts that ONS 5 was under heavy attack, and his tactic of sweeping toward ONS 5 in line-abreast formation was designed to intercept any U-boats that might be in front of the convoy.[90]

In thick fog at 0350 on 6 May HMS *Wear* obtained an HF/DF bearing, and two minutes later HMS *Pelican* picked up a radar contact at a range of 5,300 yards bearing 40°. HMS *Pelican* quickly obtained a sonar contact with the target at a range of 3,000 yards and sighted the U-431 off the starboard bow at a range of 300 yards at 0407. Apparently unaware of the British warship, the U-boat was steering 180°, fully surfaced and steaming at only 9 knots. HMS *Pelican* opened fire with A and B guns and its port 20mm Oerlikon. At a range of 100 yards the U-431 crash dived. HMS *Pelican* attacked, dropping ten depth charges into the swirl of the submerging U-boat, and thirty seconds to one minute after the depth charges exploded, there were "two thin founts of water, resembling shell splashes, astern, close to where the pattern had exploded." The sloop ran out 800 yards, sonar contact was regained, and a second attack was made with nine depth charges. Sonar contact could not be regained and about a minute after the depth charges exploded, three "small sharp explosions were heard." Eight minutes later there were two more explosions, "the second one being violent enough to shake the ship." The U-431 was destroyed. HMS *Pelican* swept through the area but could not gain sonar contact and no wreckage was found. Brewen thought that the U-boat had either been destroyed or damaged so badly that it was no longer a threat to ONS 5 and discontinued the hunt for the U-boat, bowing to the greater need to reinforce the convoy's escort.[91]

HMS *Pelican* and HMS *Jed* joined the close screen of ONS 5 while HMS *Spey* and HMS *Wear* conducted a sweep 20 miles astern of the convoy. In the course of this sweep, HMS *Spey* obtained a radar contact at a range of 5,200 yards some 15 miles astern of ONS 5. Course was altered toward the contact and a U-boat was sighted at a range of 800 or 900 yards. The U-boat was thought to be "almost certainly an Italian one and resembled the 'Dessie' class." HMS *Spey* opened fire on the U-boat, and "two definite hits" were made on the conning tower before the enemy vessel dived at a range of 400 yards. HMS *Spey* attacked, dropping ten depth charges by eye in the swirl of the submerging U-boat. Sonar contact was obtained, but the U-boat had apparently gone deep. A hedgehog attack was undertaken, followed by a depth charge attack, but both were without result. After the depth charge attack sonar contact was not regained. HMS *Spey*, joined by HMS *Wear*, continued the hunt and at 0915 sonar contact was regained. Although the contact was not very reliable, it was decided to attack. The contact was held to a range of 400 yards and "the attack was delivered without conviction and the contact was not regained." The whole area was then swept through by the two frigates. Nothing was found. And at 1015 it was decided to conduct a sweep toward ONS 5, which was now some 40 miles distant.[92]

Through 6 May, the BdU received radio reports from damaged U-boats attacked on the surface in the fog. Four U-boats (U-264, U-358, U-552, and U-954) had to break off the action and withdraw from the battle. The U-266 radioed "AM MOVING OFF TO REPAIR D/C DAMAGE." The U-634 reported that at 1142B "A FULL HIT BY DESTROYER ARTILLERY AFTER SURFACING." The U-264 radioed "SURPRIZED BY DESTROYER COMING OUT OF FOG. SHELL-FIRE AND

D/C." The U-377 reported "GUN-FIRE, SEARCH LIGHTS AND D/C FROM DD [destroyer]." From these reports and others, the BdU learned that the U-boats were being roughly handled in fog by the escorts. And at 1214Z the BdU ordered the U-boats operating against ONS 5 to break off the action. The U-boats of the *Fink* group were directed to move off in an easterly direction and those of *Amsel 1* and *Amsel 2* were ordered to the area of 50°33′N, 39°15′W.[93]

The battle for ONS 5 was the largest convoy action of the entire North Atlantic campaign. At the time, the battle was seen as "possibly the most decisive of all the convoy engagements." The Admiralty's Operational Intelligence Centre concluded, mostly from cryptographic sources, that forty U-boats had been ordered to operate against ONS 5 and that they made over forty separate attacks on the convoy, while the escorts carried out "approximately the same number of counterattacks." During these counterattacks, Allied intelligence thought that six U-boats (U-125, U-192, U-438, U-531, U-630, U-631) were sunk, five U-boats were severely damaged, and twelve U-boats "reported varying degrees of lesser damage, and on 20 separate occasions U/B's reported being driven off or forced to dive." The U-boats sank thirteen merchant ships (*McKeesport, North Britain, Harbury, West Maximus, Bristol City, Wentworth, Dolius, West Market, Selvistan, Gharinda, Bonde,* and the straggler *Lorient*) during the battle, a tradeoff of a little over one U-boat for every two Allied merchant ship sunk, which Allied intelligence considered "heavy punishment for results which in the circumstances must have seemed meager to the B.D.U."[94]

The key to the Allied defense of ONS 5, especially on the night of 5 May, was radar. Allied radar not only detected the U-boats in the fog and darkness but also enabled the escorts to attack and fend off the U-boats before they were in a position to attack the convoy. Or, as Sherwood put it: "The group tactics of hitting all submarines quickly and hard and then rejoining at full speed achieved most satisfactory results."[95] The BdU also concluded that it was Allied radar which prevented the U-boats from achieving success against ONS 5, remarking that the operations against "Convoy . . . [ONS 5] . . . had to be broken off because of radar" and that if "fog had held off for 6 more hours more ships would certainly have been sunk. As it was, the fog ruined everything" because the U-boats "had no countermeasures against [radar] location, the boats were definitely at a disadvantage and had little prospect of success." The BdU further thought that the U-boats "had a bad time" and agreed that the "loss of 6 boats is very high and grave considering the short duration of the attack."[96]

Grand Admiral Karl Doenitz, commander in chief of the German Navy, thought that the battle for ONS 5 was a defeat for the U-boats and blamed Allied radar and aircraft for the outcome.[97] In the wake of the operations against ONS 5, the BdU reassessed the role of Allied radar and aircraft in the conduct of the U-boat campaign against Allied convoys in the North Atlantic. The BdU concluded that radar gave the Allies the ability to attack U-boats approaching a convoy on the surface, and also to locate U-boat patrol lines and to reroute convoys to avoid them. In short, "Radar location is thus robbing the submarine of her most important characteristic — ability to remain undetected." And the BdU realized, as well, that in the near future Allied aircraft would be capable of operating over all areas of the North Atlantic and that aircraft have "always forced our submarines to lag hopelessly behind the convoy and prevented them from achieving any successes." It is clear that at the beginning of May the BdU understood some of the problems confronting the U-boats in the North Atlantic in their battles against Allied convoys. But in this reassessment, the BdU ignored the possibility of insecure radio communications, and the only schemes put forward to counter Allied convoy defenses were those for the accelerated development and deployment of new types of torpedoes, heavier antiaircraft armament of U-boats, and the deployment of antiaircraft U-boats.[98]

None of these measures even addressed the problems posed by insecure radio communications or radar. And the BdU's efforts to meet the threat of aircraft ignored the fact that, no matter how powerful the guns employed, a U-boat would never be a suitable platform for antiaircraft guns. This was especially true against the smaller, faster carrier-borne aircraft the Allies were sending against the wolf packs that preyed on convoys in the Atlantic. After the battle for ONS 5, the BdU saw the problems posed to the U-boats by Allied radar and aircraft but failed to adopt a single measure — strategic, tactical, or technological — which would overcome these threats.

Chapter 4

The First Defeat of the Wolf Packs

3–24 May 1943

The battle for convoy ONS 5 marked the beginning of the defeat of the U-boats in the North Atlantic. From this point forward, the U-boats found it increasingly difficult and eventually almost impossible to launch successful attacks upon Allied merchant ships in North Atlantic convoys. This stemmed in part from the Germans' failure to realize that the Allies were reading their command radio communications. But, more importantly, the U-boats were confronted and confounded by growing numbers of skillful surface escorts supported by aircraft which hounded, hunted, and sank the German vessels in the vicinity of the convoys. Increasingly, the U-boats found that they did not have the ability, and in fact lacked the technological means, to better or to just break even in combat with the Allies.

ONS 5 was followed shortly by two more convoys—ONS 6 and ON 181—which were westbound along the same northern route to North America. Convoy ONS 6, consisting of thirty merchant ships, was assembled on 30 April near the island of Altacarry off the west coast of Scotland. The convoy was escorted by Escort Group B6, consisting of the destroyer HMS *Viscount;* the corvettes HNorMS *Acanthus,* HNorMS *Potentilla,* HNorMS *Eglantine,* HNorMS *Rose,* HMS *Vervain,* HMS *Kingcup;* and the trawlers *Northern Pride* and *Northern Reward.*[1]

ONS 6 steamed northwest to 59°N and then west, with air support provided by aircraft from Iceland from 3 May. During the morning of 6 May the U-418 and U-956, two U-boats en route to take up station south of Greenland, sighted and reported ONS 6. These transmissions were picked up by HF/DF on the convoy and were D/F'ed by shore stations. Air cover from Iceland was then increased, with two USN PBY Catalina aircraft providing close support, while RAF Hudson aircraft of 296th Squadron made numerous sweeps over the area. By 1800 some ten sightings of U-boats had been made and several were attacked. The convoy changed course at 2300 to 225°. At 0023 on 7 May an HF/DF bearing was obtained, and HNorMS *Potentilla* searched for the U-boat without success. The convoy's course was again altered to 283° at 0615. More HF/DF bearings were picked up and HNorMS *Potentilla* again searched down the bearings without result. The convoy's course was again changed at noon to 270°. At 2012 on 8 May, HMS *Viscount* obtained an HF/DF bearing and ran it down, sighting a U-boat (probably the U-952) at a range of 7,000 yards. The U-boat submerged, and a depth charge attack was carried out without result. This was the last contact between the U-boats and ONS 6.[2]

During the evening of 8 May the escort carrier HMS *Archer* and three destroyers (HMS *Onslaught*, HMS *Impulsive*, HMS *Faueknor*) reinforced the escort of ONS 6, and the convoy's escort was further reinforced the next morning by the arrival of the four frigates of the 1st Escort Group. However, ONS 6 was out of danger and the ships of the 1st Escort Group were detached on 10 May, while HMS *Archer* and its escorts left the convoy on 11 May. ONS 6 was routed westward along 58°N until it reached 58°50'N, 39°25'W on 9 May when the convoy turned to a southwest course. On 11 May the Allied force turned to a southerly course to carry the convoy through the area where the battle for ONS 5 had been fought and across the Grand Banks of Newfoundland before turning to run to the ports of the east coast of North America.[3]

From cryptographic intelligence, the Allies knew that the U-boats which had operated against ONS 5 had been ordered eastward and this route carried ONS 6 well to the west of the known concentrations of U-boats. Convoy ON 181 sailed from Britain one day after ONS 6, following roughly the same route and enjoying what the convoy's commodore described as "a quiet voyage" without any contacts with U-boats.[4]

The next two eastbound convoys—HX 237 and SC 129—were

sent to Great Britain by the southern route. SC 129 began its voyage first, sailing from Halifax, Nova Scotia, on 2 May, but this slow-moving convoy would take far longer to reach U-boat patrolled waters, and it was HX 237 and its escorts that first encountered the German wolf packs. In the evening of 5 May, two escort groups set sail from St. John's, Newfoundland, to rendezvous with convoy HX 237 for its voyage from New York to Britain. The first was Escort Group C2 consisting of the destroyer HMS *Broadway;* the frigate *Lagan;* the corvettes HMS *Primrose,* HMCS *Chambly,* HMCS *Modern,* HMCS *Drumheller,* HM Tug *Dexterous;* and HMS Trawler *Vizalma.* The second, two hours later, was the 5th Escort Group consisting of the escort carrier HMS *Biter* and the destroyers HMS *Pathfinder,* HMS *Obdurate,* and HMS *Opportune.*[5] The plan called for the two escort groups to meet the eastbound convoy on 6 May southwest of Newfoundland at the Western Ocean Meeting Point (WESTOMP), there to relieve the local escort which shepherded the convoy north-eastward along the coast of North America. But immediately after departing from Newfoundland, both escort groups encountered heavy fog which delayed the meeting with the convoy. After the fog had finally lifted and countless radio transmissions exchanged among various ships, Escort Group C2 met the convoy at 1400 on 7 May and relieved the local escort.

Convoy HX 237 consisted of thirty-eight ships and nine stragglers. Two of these stragglers returned to North America, four quickly joined the convoy, and three — *Fort Concord, Brand,* and *Sandanger* — proceeded independently across the Atlantic along the same general route as the convoy. In addition, the escort itself had two stragglers: HM Tug *Dexterous* and HM Trawler *Vizalma,* which had sailed from St. John's shortly before the rest of Escort Group C2 and traveled so slowly that they were never able to join HX 237, instead proceeded independently and followed the same general route as the convoy.[6]

As the two Allied escort groups struggled through the fog to meet the escort, the German naval command was moving quickly. On 7 May the BdU concluded, by means of "dead reckoning," that "2 Eastbound convoys may be expected about 8.5 [8 May] roughly in position 42° west."[7] It is not known whether the BdU reached this conclusion by means of cryptographic intelligence or through a knowledge of Allied convoy cycles. During the morning of 7 May the BdU redeployed the U-boats east of Newfoundland which had been operating against ONS 5. At 1015 on 7 May the BdU ordered ten U-boats to form a patrol line, code named *Rhein*, by 0800 on 8 May to run from 47°33′N, 40°55′W to 43°57′N, 40°05′W. And at 1048 seventeen U-boats (U-634, U-575, U-584, U-650, U-614, U-266, U-533, U-231, U-514, U-267, U-621, U-223, U-504, U-377, U-107, U-383, U-402) were ordered to form a patrol line code named *Elbe* by 0800 on 8 May, running between 52°45′N, 43°55′W to 47°51′N, 41°05′W Shortly after sending these orders the BdU informed the U-boats which were to form the *Rhein* and *Elbe* patrol lines that "FROM 8/5 ONWARDS ONE FAST AND ONE SLOW CONVOY EXPECTED. BOTH ON EASTERLY TO NORTHERLY COURSES." The U-boats were also directed to space themselves at 20-mile intervals in the patrol lines, and no radio reports were to be made by those U-boats arriving late on station. The U-boats were to "EXPECT EASTBOUND CONVOY FROM NOON TOMORROW ONWARDS."[8]

Later in the day on 7 May the BdU received "high priority" radio intercept intelligence that the expected convoy, HX 237, was in "BC 7684" at 2330 on 6 May. The BdU considered this information to be "fairly definite" and concluded that the convoy was to proceed to Great Britain on "the southerly route."[9] At 2133Z the BdU informed the *Rhein-Elbe* groups that "AN EXPECTED CONVOY WAS IN—[BC 7684 43°57N 48°25W] ON 6 MAY ON 2330B. PRECISE COURSE NOT KNOWN, BUT APPROXIMATELY EASTWARD; SPEED 9.3." Within an hour of sending this message the BdU decided to send the *Rhein-Elbe* patrol lines 90 miles to the south. Orders were radioed to the *Rhein* group to move its patrol line to run from 45°45′N, 40°25′W to 42°03′N, 40°14′W, while group *Elbe* was simultaneously ordered to move its patrol line to 56°39′N, 42°55′W running to 45°57′N, 40°35′W. The U-boats were again directed to maintain 20 miles separation and radio silence for those U-boats late in taking up their positions. All were alerted to "BE READY FOR EAST-BOUND CONVOY FROM TOMORROW NOON ON."[10] The BdU also concluded from "former experience" that the convoy expected on 8 May would be followed two days later by an SC convoy.[11]

The BdU expected the U-boats of the *Rhein-Elbe* groups to intercept HX 237 during the morning of 8 May, but by evening of that

day the convoy had not appeared.[12] Not knowing the course and location of HX 237 and thinking that the convoy might have taken a
northeast route, the BdU issued new orders at 1950 that evening.
The U-boats of the *Rhein-Elbe* groups were to proceed on a course of
60° at a speed of 8 knots until 0900 on 9 May, when the U-boat were
to "STAY PUT ON PATROL LINE IN THE POSITION LINE REACHED."[13]

But shortly after this order was issued, the BdU received intelligence based on decryption of two Allied coded radio messages that
HX 237 was further southeast than expected and steering a course
of 180° at a speed of 9 knots. SC 129, the same intelligence reported,
was ordered to follow a route which would carry the convoy around
the southern end of the *Rhein-Elbe* patrol line.[14] As a result of this
intelligence, the BdU canceled the first orders and instead directed
the *Rhein* group of U-boats to turn around and steer "AT ONCE
COURSE 120 DEGREES, BEST SPEED."[15] At 2304 on 8 May, the *Rhein*
group was directed to establish a new patrol line running from
43°33′N, 34°55′W to 39°45′N, 35°02′W by 2000 on 9 May. The
Rhein group was also told that "ACCORDING TO A RELIABLE REPORT
THE EXPECTED CONVOY IS FURTHER SOUTH AND FURTHER AHEAD
THAN ASSUMED," and several hours later the *Rhein* group was informed "ENEMY SPEED IN NO CASE LESS THAN 9. DO NOT FALL BE-
HIND."[16] At 2228 the *Elbe* group was directed to steam at 10 knots on
a course of 120° beginning at 0100 on 9 May. And at the same time
the BdU ordered west a group of six U-boats, code named *Drossel,*
which were operating against convoys running between Gibraltar,
West Africa, and Great Britain.[17] It was the BdU's intention that the
Rhein U-boats be in position to intercept HX 237; that the *Elbe* group
form a patrol line later to intercept SC 129; and that the U-boats of
the *Drossel* group, by moving west, be in position to operate against
both convoys.[18]

On 8 May, when the BdU learned that HX 237 had taken a southern route, the Germans believed that this proved there was a "definite
avoidance" of the *Rhein-Elbe* patrol lines on the part of the Allies. And
the BdU considered that it was "most important to demand how the
enemy was able to intercept our patrol strip." The BdU believed that
the Allies could have discovered the location of the *Rhein-Elbe* patrol
line by some sophisticated method of location by aircraft of which
the Germans had no knowledge. They also hypothesized that the

Allies had possibly deduced the position of the patrol line from the radio traffic to and from U-boats attacking ONS 5 or from a weather report made by an *Amsel 4* U-boat on 5 May. But "it was also considered unlikely," by the BdU, "that the enemy has cracked our ciphers unless he has captured one of our boats." To guard against the possibility that the Allies had obtained the settings of a code machine on a captured U-boat, the BdU ordered an immediate change of settings, thinking that "the possibility of . . . [the Allies] . . . having cracked our ciphers has been canceled out by an immediate change of cipher settings."[19] The BdU refused to recognize the possibility that the Allies were in fact reading their coded command radio communications and assumed that without such cipher settings, the Allies could not read the German codes even if they had possession of the code machine itself.

In fact, there is no evidence that the Allies knew the location of the *Rhein-Elbe* groups of U-boats before they gained contact with HX 237 or that the Allies knew that the *Drossel* group was moving west. Of all the BdU's radio messages creating and positioning the *Rhein-Elbe* groups and redeploying the *Drossel* ships, only one, the message creating the *Rhein* group on 7 May, was decoded before the fourth week of May, several days after the U-boats' operations had been concluded. On 6 May the Allies knew that there were thirty-nine U-boats operating against ONS 5 northeast of Newfoundland.[20] Even as late as 10 May, when the U-boats had already obtained contact with HX 237, the Allies believed their convoy had passed south of a German patrol line of twelve U-boats running along 40°30′W between 44°00′N, and 47°00′N. The remaining thirty-odd U-boats were thought to be north of this patrol line between "latitudes 50°00′N, and 55°00′N, and longitudes 30°00′W and 40°00′W being refueled and resupplied at sea."[21] Thus it is most likely HX 237 was sent on a southerly route simply to avoid the known concentrations of U-boats east of Newfoundland and to gain good flying weather for escort carrier operations, not because of a foreknowledge of the location of the *Rhein-Elbe* patrol line.

The presence of a carrier among the convoy's escorts required careful planning for HX 237 during the voyage east. As HX 237 departed from WESTOMP, steering in a general southeasterly direction, the 5th Escort Group took up a position southwest of the convoy to form a distant covering force. In the course of a radio telephone conversation, Captain E. M. C. Abel Smith, RN, the commander of the 5th Escort Group, and Lieutenant Commander E. H. Chavasse, RN, the commander of Escort Group C2, decided to limit aircraft operations to a "few close patrols" in order to conserve aircraft and the strength of the aircrews as well as to prevent U-boats from learning of the presence of the convoy by sighting carrier-borne aircraft. Abel Smith thought "that submarines more often sight an aircraft first and in many cases can dive without themselves being detected." This was probably a wise decision, for two Martlet (British name for a F4F Wildcat fighter aircraft) fighter aircraft were lost when they ran out of fuel astern of the convoy, owing to a navigational error, and were forced to crash land in the water.[22]

On 8 May, because of poor visibility, only three sorties were flown by HMS *Biter*'s aircraft, and the 5th Escort Group remained out of sight to the southwest of HX 237. At 1900 HM Trawler *Vizalma* joined the convoy and reported to Chavasse that it had parted company with HM Tug *Dexterous* some distance from the convoy. Chavasse thought that the tug probably did not have the latest straggler's route information, and he "considered it urgent" that HM Tug *Dexterous* join the convoy. The commander vainly attempted to reach HMS *Biter* by radio telephone to request an air search for the missing tug. Because of the low visibility, Chavasse had not seen an aircraft since the morning of 7 May and did not know HMS *Biter*'s position. The commander of Escort Group C2 observed that "had U-boat transmissions on H/F been received at this period, crossing-bearings would have been of no use for fixing the U-boat, since the relative positions of Biter and Broadway were not known to either of us, as must always be the case in a prolonged period of low visibility with a carrier operating at some distance from the convoy." Chavasse was only expressing an escort commander's natural desire to have all the ships of a convoy in one group to increase the protection of the formation. Chavasse thought that if an escort carrier operated at a distance from a convoy, the amount of radio traffic would increase, HF/DF bearings would be of decreased value, the escort carrier would itself be at greater risk of being torpedoed, time would be required for aircraft to reach the convoy, and, perhaps most important, additional escorts would be required to screen an independently sailing escort carrier. Abel Smith, on the other hand, thought that an escort carrier should operate independently of a convoy to use its operational flexibility to hunt down and destroy U-boats before they could get near to the convoy. The commander of the carrier *Biter* did not like a policy which gave a higher priority to the "safe and timely arrival of the convoy" than to the "early detection and destruction of U-boats." In the case of HX 237, this question was settled by a 9 May order from the commander in chief, western approaches, directing that HMS *Biter* take station within the convoy and remain there for the rest of the voyage.[23]

On 9 May HX 237 and its escorts first encountered part of the German U-boat fleet. At 0800 HMS *Broadway* began refueling from the tanker *British Valour*. In order to facilitate oiling, the convoy's speed was decreased to 8 knots. At 1108, while still taking on oil, HMS *Broadway* obtained an HF/DF bearing astern of the convoy. HMS *Broadway* stopped refueling, the convoy increased speed to 10 knots, and Chavasse ordered the convoy to make a 40 degree evasive turn to starboard "in the fog to get 20 miles off our route. I thought the U-boat might expect us to turn to port, i.e. homeward." The submarine was the U-359, a member of the *Rhein* group which sighted HX 237 northwest of the Azores at 41°09′N, 26°54′W at 1306 as it moved into position in the U-boat patrol line.[24]

Chavasse sent HMS *Primrose*, whose station was astern of the starboard wing of the convoy, down the HF/DF bearing to hunt the U-boat. The visibility was about 3 miles and the corvette, making 15.5 knots into the sea, sighted the U-boat at a range of about 3 miles. The U-359 was barely visible with its decks awash in the heavy seas. With heavy seas breaking across the bridge and foredeck as it approached the U-359, HMS *Primrose* could not fire its main armament unless it reduced speed. At a range of 5,000 yards the U-359 submerged. HMS *Primrose* reduced speed, obtained sonar contact, and twenty minutes after first sighting the U-359, attacked with a ten depth charge pattern. The contact was quickly regained and the corvette began to make another attack with a hedgehog. But just before the attack was to be carried out, HMS *Primrose*'s sonar broke down. It took thirty-six minutes to repair the sonar before the hunt could resume. The corvette then continued the search for the U-359 without result for another fifty minutes, and HMS *Primrose* was then ordered to return to the convoy.[25]

At 1350 the British destroyer HMS *Broadway* picked up another HF/DF bearing astern of the convoy. Chavasse thought it was the same U-boat which HMS *Primrose* had been hunting. The corvette, still astern of the convoy, was ordered to conduct a 5-mile-deep sweep to search for the U-boat before rejoining HX 237. While HMS *Biter* and the other ships of its escort group closed with the convoy in poor visibility to join the formation, it picked up the same HF/DF bearing astern of the convoy. Not knowing that HMS *Primrose* was astern of the convoy, Abel Smith sent HMS *Opportune* to search for the U-boat, making this transmission before informing Chavasse. At 1518 both HMS *Biter* and HMS *Broadway* obtained another HF/DF bearing. Chavasse thought this transmission was "undoubtedly made by a different operator and the bearing was widely different from the first one." (This U-boat may have been the U-186.) HMCS *Drumheller* was sent down the bearing for 5 miles but found nothing. Chavasse, nevertheless, believed that "it was clear, however, that there were two U-boats in the vicinity." But poor weather and severely limited visibility meant that HMS *Biter*'s aircraft could not be used to hunt down these U-boats.[26]

Both sides bolstered their forces in the area after this first contact between HX 237 and the U-boats. The U-359 was ordered not to attack until another U-boat gained contact in order not to lose the convoy, and it was forced to submerge when the convoy's escort appeared on the scene. From hydrophone bearings, the U-359 deduced that HX 237 had made a turn to the north. At 1726 the U-186 picked up a wide hydrophone ban from 320–350 meters, but contact was not regained with the convoy. The BdU ordered the *Drossel* group to increase speed and close with HX 237 from the east. The *Rhein* group U-boats were then commanded to steam at their "best speed" and set up a patrol line north and east of the point where the U-359 had sighted the convoy by 0900 on 10 May. The BdU thought that because the convoy's destination was Great Britain and its speed was 9 or 10 knots, HX 237 would have to take an easterly or northern route. Unaware that HX 237 was escorted by an aircraft carrier, the BdU discounted the effects of Allied air power, for the *Rhein* group was assured that "IN THE PRESENT AREA WHERE BUT LITTLE AIR CAN

JOIN THE CONVOY, WE MUST CONTACT AND ENGAGE IT AS FAST AS POSSIBLE." But the BdU also confided to its war diary that "the chance of picking up the convoy is slim as a long leg to the North or South can be made by the convoy under cover of the constant fog."[27]

And, in all this, the BdU did not forget its other target among eastbound Allied convoys. At 1524 on 9 May the *Elbe* group was ordered to form a patrol line to the southwest of the position where HX 237 had been sighted. The BdU concluded from a decoded Allied radio transmission that SC 129 would be sighted by the new *Elbe* patrol line during the evening of 10 May. At this time the BdU also signified that the members of the *Elbe* group were to be refueled from the U-119 some several hundred miles north of the new patrol line.[28]

On the Allied side, HMS *Biter* and its escorts, as ordered by the commander in chief, western approaches, joined the convoy during the afternoon of 9 May, and the escorts were refueled by tankers in the convoy. HMS *Biter* took station astern of the Commodore's merchant ship. The command of the three destroyers in the escort, except during flying operations, was turned over to Chavasse. During the night of 9 May there were several contacts with U-boats obtained by radar, HF/DF, and sonar. But searches undertaken by the convoy's escorts proved all these contacts to be false.[29]

On the morning of 10 May the U-403 sighted HM Tug *Dexterous* as it was approaching HX 237. The U-boat followed the tug in the hope of discovering a convoy. At 1645 HMS *Pathfinder* sighted HM Tug *Dexterous* as it neared the starboard side of the convoy. Two minutes later HMCS *Chambly* sighted the U-403 on the surface to starboard and gave chase. At this time Chavasse also ordered HMS *Obdurate* to join the chase, but one of HMS *Biter*'s Swordfish aircraft attacked the U-403 before the two British warships could reach the U-boat. The U-boat opened fire with antiaircraft guns before diving, hitting the aircraft, which attacked with depth charges. When HMCS *Chambly* and HMS *Obdurate* arrived on the scene, the two warships could not obtain a contact with their sonar.[30]

The U-403 radioed the BdU: "WHILE FOLLOWING TUG DISCOVERED CONVOY. AFTER M/G FIGHT WITH WHEELED A/C . . . PUT DOWN BY A/C BOMBS, NAVAL GRID SQUARE 2191 [position on German grid map—approximately 42°04'N, 30°59'W]. LAST HYDROPHONE BEARING 025 DEGREES TRUE."[31] When the BdU received the U-403's radio transmission, it was thought that the *Rhein* group was about 90 miles astern of HX 237. The BdU decided to call off the operation against HX 237 and to deploy the U-boats of the *Rhein* group against SC 129 which had not yet been sighted and was now "considered to offer better chances of success." The U-403 was to remain in contact with HX 237, and the *Drossel* group, which was steaming west at high speed, was to attempt to intercept and attack the convoy.[32] The only U-boats which now had any chance of attacking HX 237 were the U-403, six U-boats belonging to the *Drossel* group, and those U-boats that could be vectored on to the convoy from the east after leaving the Bay of Biscay from their bases in France.

HMS *Biter*'s aircraft patrolled around the convoy during the afternoon of 10 May, but no U-boats were sighted. In the late afternoon a Swordfish aircraft was lost through a navigational error when it apparently overshot the convoy and was forced to crash-land in the sea from lack of fuel. HMS *Broadway* made an extensive search for the aircrew without result, but the crew was later picked up by a warship of the Western Approaches Command.[33]

When U-boat activity around HX 237 dropped off on the morning of 11 May, Chavasse took the opportunity to refuel HMS *Broadway* and HMCS *Chambly* from a tanker in the convoy. On the orders of commander in chief, western approaches, the base course of the convoy was altered to intercept the merchant ship *Roslin Castle*, which was independently routed, so that it could join the convoy.[34] The BdU mistakenly thought that this change of course was an "avoiding action."[35]

During the afternoon of 11 May the U-boat activity around HX 237 resumed when the *Drossel* group closed with HX 237 from the east.[36] At 1240 HMS *Lagan* was sent down an HF/DF bearing to hunt a U-boat. Shortly thereafter HMS *Pathfinder* also conducted a search for a U-boat in front of the convoy, but these searches were unsuccessful, and Chavasse decided "to discontinue surface sorties as wasteful to fuel and unduly weakening to the close screen." Instead he decided to send the destroyers HMS *Pathfinder* and HMS *Obdurate* to make a prolonged search for U-boats ahead of the convoy. The two warships did not find any U-boats and returned to HX 237 after dark. As there was a fairly heavy sea running with poor flying weather, Abel Smith did not want to run the risk of aircraft crashing on takeoff and landing. But at Chavasse's insistence, two aircraft were flown off HMS *Biter* because of the increased HF/DF activity.[37] The U-89 sighted one aircraft and the U-436 was attacked by another. It was from the U-89 that the BdU first learned that an aircraft carrier was operating with HX 237, even though the U-403 had been attacked by a carrier-borne aircraft the day before. While the BdU thought that seven U-boats (U-89, U-403, U-436, U-230, U-456, U-607, U-603) were "stalking" the convoy on the afternoon of 11 May, in fact, only the U-436 was in firm contact with it for two hours before being driven off. During the night of 11 May the U-402 torpedoed the merchant ship, *Sandanger*, one of the stragglers independently following the same route as HX 237.[38]

On 12 May flying conditions were difficult because of a heavy swell which made HMS *Biter*'s deck pitch wildly. Nevertheless, nine sorties were flown. While conducting a search, the first Swordfish aircraft airborne in the morning sighted and attacked a U-boat, the U-230, but antiaircraft fire from the U-boat brought down the plane. This resulted in a change of British tactics, for after this loss, Swordfish aircraft were considered too old and weakly constructed to attack U-boats alone in the face of antiaircraft fire. HMS *Biter*'s planes were now instructed not to attack a U-boat on the surface unless the vessel was seen to be diving. Otherwise the aircraft had to await reinforcements before attacking. On 12 May the carrier-borne aircraft were reinforced by the arrival over the convoy of shore-based VLR B-24 Liberator aircraft from Ireland. However, owing to a failure of radio communications between these shore-based aircraft and HMS *Broadway*, Chavasse could not coordinate his forces with them. Nevertheless, even with the loss of the Swordfish and this failure in coordination, the presence of aircraft over HX 237 was quickly reflected in the radio reports of various U-boats. For example, the U-230 radioed: "CARRIER-BORNE AIRCRAFT WITH CONVOY." The U-221 reported: "HAVE DRIVEN OFF A LARGE 4 ENGINE FLYING BOAT. IT IS CRUISING AROUND THE SQUARE," and a third U-boat radioed: "DRIVEN UNDERWATER BY CARRIER-BORNE AIRCRAFT. AIRCRAFT BOMBS, HYDROPHONE HUNT."[39]

At 1115 Chavasse received a report that a VLR B-24 Liberator, aircraft B/86, had attacked a submerging U-boat with an acoustic homing torpedo and three depth charges astern of the convoy.[40] Then

HMS *Broadway* picked up an HF/DF bearing which confirmed the report, and HMS *Pathfinder* was sent to investigate. Aircraft B/86 next reported that the U-boat (the U-456) had submerged and then resurfaced and was apparently damaged and could not dive. At 1151 the U-456 radioed "AM UNABLE TO DIVE. NAVAL GRID SQUARE BD 6646." Several minutes later the U-456 again radioed "AM STEERING COURSE 300 DEGREES AT HIGH SPEED. HEAVY IN RUSH OF WATER IN AFTER COMPARTMENT. REQUIRE URGENT ASSISTANCE." At 1248 the U-456 again requested assistance. Not knowing that this U-boat was about to be attacked and sunk by the Allies, the BdU ordered the U-89 to assist the U-456 at 1252. And at 1428 the U-456 radioed "AIRCRAFT MAINTAINING CONTACT HAS NO BOMBS LEFT . . . AM STEERING COURSE OF 200 DEGREES. IN RUSH OF WATER CAN STILL BE KEPT UNDER CONTROL FOR PRESENT." This was the U-456's last radio transmission before it sank. The U-182 radioed that it was going to the assistance of the U-456, and the BdU ordered two additional U-boats to aid the stricken submarine, but it was too late. HMS *Pathfinder* was recalled to HX 237 before it reached the U-456, but HMS *Opportune,* which had been vectored to the area at the request of aircraft B/86, sighted the U-456, which dived before the British destroyer could attack. HMS *Opportune* did not obtain a sonar contact,[41] and the U-456 was never seen again nor did it report to the BdU. In fact, it sank while attempting to dive.[42]

At 1232 a Swordfish aircraft from HMS *Biter* reported to HMS *Broadway* that there was a U-boat, the U-89, on the surface about 6 miles ahead of HX 237. Chavasse ordered the convoy to make a 90 degree turn to starboard to avoid the U-boat and proceeded himself in HMS *Broadway* with HMS *Lagan* to attack the enemy vessel. Before the two British warships reached the U-89, the Swordfish attacked with depth charges, forcing the U-boat to dive and marking the location with a marker. Chavasse was convinced that the Swordfish had damaged the U-boat, for by the time HMS *Broadway* arrived on the scene the submarine had not moved away from the aircraft's marker HMS *Broadway* quickly obtained a sonar contact near the marker and mounted a hedgehog attack without result. Then at 1318 HMS *Lagan* attacked with a hedgehog which also missed. Thirty-eight minutes later HMS *Lagan* conducted a second hedgehog attack which again failed. Then at 1400 HMS *Broadway* undertook still another hedgehog attack. Sixteen seconds after the hedgehog bombs hit the water, there was "a sharp explosion" followed by a "fainter" second explosion. But at 1410 HMS *Lagan* gained sonar contact and carried out a third hedgehog attack without result. At 1434 the two British warships began a box search, and at 1445 HMS *Lagan* obtained a sonar contact which it attacked. Chavasse in his report says that this was "probably non-sub," but at 1447 HMS *Lagan* saw "lots of pieces of wood floating about." Without a sonar contact, HMS *Broadway* then dropped a pattern of depth charges with settings of 150 and 300 feet on the floating wood. Immediately after this attack HMS *Broadway* gained sonar and again attacked with depth charges, but only five were dropped because the rails on the port side of the ship had jammed. Then much more wood, pieces too large to fit through a torpedo tube, plus bits of clothing and paper appeared on the surface. HMS *Lagan* reported "seeing some substance resembling flesh." HMS *Broadway* and HMS *Lagan* had sunk the U-89 at 46°49'N, 25°33'E.[43]

While HMS *Broadway* and HMS *Lagan* were hunting and then sinking the U-89, a Swordfish aircraft from HMS *Biter* sighted a lifeboat. HMCS *Drumheller* was sent to investigate and picked up fifteen members of the crew of the merchant ship *Fort Concord*, one of the stragglers that had become separated from HX 237 off Newfoundland. Proceeding independently along the same track as HX 237, it was torpedoed by the U-403. After picking up the survivors from the *Fort Concord*, the Canadian corvette returned to the convoy.[44]

At 1651, just after returning to the convoy, HMS *Broadway* picked up an HF/DF bearing. HMS *Biter* and HMS *Pathfinder* simultaneously obtained HF/DF fixes on the same bearing. Chavasse sent HMS *Pathfinder* down these bearings, but the destroyer found nothing. During the remainder of 12 May, the escorts of HX 237 picked up more HF/DF bearings which were investigated, but no U-boats were found. U-boat activity during the evening of 12 May stopped even though a night attack was expected. Chavasse thought, "it was possible that the multifarious gyrations of escorts had disorganized them and put them off their stroke."[45]

While conducting one of the last sweeps of the day around HX 237, a Swordfish aircraft saw four landing craft and three lifeboats. HMCS *Morden* was detached from the convoy to investigate. The

Canadian corvette discovered four empty landing craft, which had been carried as a deck load on the Norwegian merchant ship *Brand*, as well as three lifeboats with forty members of the ship's crew on board. Like the *Fort Concord* and *Sandanger*, the *Brand* had become separated from HX 237 in the fog off Newfoundland on 5 May and proceeded independently until it was sunk by the U-603 on 12 May. HMCS *Morden* picked up the survivors from the *Brand* and rejoined the convoy at 2158.[46]

The U-boats attacking HX 237 were roughly handled by air and surface escorts on 12 May. Two U-boats were sunk, and at least five were damaged. The U-569 reported "PORT OUTER EXHAUST CUT OUT ROD UPPER DECK UNCOUPLED." The U-603 had a defective gyro. Another U-boat radioed that it was "REPAIRING STARBOARD DIESEL COUPLING." The U-190 was "MOVING OFF FOR AIRCRAFT DAMAGE ON UPPER DECK." And the starboard shaft in the U-230 was "KNOCKING." Radio reports made it clear to the BdU that the escorts had the upper hand around HX 237 and that the U-boats were being hunted and hounded by Allied aircraft, not only the HMS *Biter*'s planes but also the three VLR B-24 Liberators from Ireland. In the early morning of 13 May, the BdU ordered the *Drossel* U-boats to withdraw and redeploy to attack SC 129, if there were still Allied aircraft in the area and no contact with the convoy. Several hours later the BdU directed four other U-boats to suspend their operations and "MOVE OFF TO THE SOUTHWEST" toward SC 129 if they were not in a position ahead of HX 237.[47]

During the morning of 13 May, HF/DF was "moderate" around HX 237. A RCAF Sunderland, aircraft G/423, was homed in on the convoy by HMS *Broadway*, while two Swordfish aircraft were flown off HMS *Biter*. About 10 miles ahead of the convoy, aircraft G/423 sighted a U-boat which was attacked with depth charges at 48°35'N, 22°50'W.[48] HMCS *Drumheller* sighted the U-boat and, along with HMS *Lagan*, was sent ahead to attack the enemy vessel. One of the Swordfish also sighted this U-boat. The enemy vessel then submerged. When HMCS *Drumheller* arrived on the scene, it obtained a sonar contact and attacked with depth charges. This attack was followed by a hedgehog attack by HMS *Lagan* which claimed two hits. Bits of wood, a large patch of oil, and two large bubbles appeared on the surface, and Chavasse concluded rightly a U-boat, the U-753, had been sunk.[49] Later in the morning, aircraft from HMS *Biter* found and attacked several more U-boats and then, in Chavasse's words, "enemy activity in our vicinity abruptly ceased, and I was able to get on with the paper war and produce this report." The BdU ordered the remaining U-boats to break off the action and to attack SC 129. In the late morning of 13 May, the 5th Escort Group left HX 237 and sailed southwest to support convoy SC 129.[50]

This slow eastbound convoy trailed just behind HX 237 along approximately the same route. SC 129 sailed from Halifax, Nova Scotia, on 2 May and proceeded roughly due east to WESTOMP at 45°38'N, 48°55'W, where it was joined on 6 May by Escort Group B2. This escort group was led by Commander Donald Macintyre, RN, and consisted of the destroyers HMS *Hesperus* and HMS *Whitehall;* the corvettes HMS *Clematis,* HMS *Campanula,* HMS *Heather,* HMS *Sweetbriar,* HMS *Gentian;* and the trawlers *Lady Madeleine* and HMS *Sapper.* The weather southeast of Newfoundland was foggy, and a change of course of 50° to starboard ordered by commander in chief, western approaches, for 1500 on 5 May was postponed until 1300 on 6 May in the hope that the weather would improve. But the weather did not clear and the turn was made by the convoy in heavy fog. Only the Greek merchant ship *Kyklades* became separated from the main body of the convoy when the change of course was made. The *Kyklades,* after falling out from the convoy, made its own way eastward across the Atlantic to Horta in the Azores.[51]

German intelligence learned of SC 129's change of course to the southeast on 8 May, and the Germans expected to intercept SC 129 on 10 May. The BdU ordered the *Elbe* group to form a patrol line northwest of the Azores running from 45°33'N, 33°55'W to 40°33'N, 33°58'W. A number of other U-boats were directed to take part in this operation, even though they might be low on fuel, with the expectation that they could be refueled from a U-boat tanker in "THE SAME AREA AFTER CONTACTING THE CONVOY." The Allies did not decode the order for setting up this patrol line until 21 May, long after the end of the battle. Realizing that SC 129 could not be intercepted until the afternoon of 11 May, the BdU on 10 May dissolved the *Elbe* group and formed two new groups called *Elbe 1* and *Elbe 2.* These two groups consisted of those U-boats from the *Rhein-Elbe* groups (with the exception of the U-584 and U-614) that had enough fuel remaining to intercept SC 129 on 11 May. The BdU radioed the twenty-seven U-boats deployed to attack SC 129: "SLOW EAST-BOUND CONVOY EXPECTED WITH CERTAINTY TOMORROW. BE SURE NOT TO MISS IT."[52]

The first HF/DF bearing was picked up by SC 129's escort at 41°03′N, 33°36′W during the afternoon of 11 May. The U-boat appeared to be some 20 miles away from the port side of the convoy. At 1800 the merchant ships *Antigone* and *Grado* were torpedoed by the U-402, and a sonar hunt off the port quarter of the convoy by the escorts produced a contact by HMS *Gentian*. Along with HMS *Hesperus*, HMS *Gentian* attacked this contact with hedgehogs without result. HMS *Hesperus* returned to SC 129 and HMS *Gentian* continued the hunt without success until dusk.[53]

At 2315 HMS *Hesperus* obtained a radar contact astern of the convoy. As the destroyer turned toward the contact, a U-boat was sighted at a range of 3,300 yards. The U-boat dived and as HMS *Hesperus* passed over the spot where the U-boat was last seen, a pattern of depth charges was dropped. The contact was regained on the sonar as the destroyer turned for another attack which was made with a hedgehog without result at 2336. A third attack was made just after midnight at 0016 with fourteen standard depth charges and a one-ton Mark X depth charge.[54] The contact was regained and HMS *Hesperus* attacked with fourteen standard depth charges and a Mark X depth charge. After this attack at 0040, the U-boat (the U-223) was sighted surfacing and was taken under fire by 20mm Oerlikon guns. HMS *Hesperus'* main armament could not depress low enough to engage the U-223 as it passed down the starboard side of the destroyer, but a number of depth charges set at 50 feet were dropped, landing close aboard the U-223. HMS *Hesperus* ran past the U-223 and turned to attack again. As the destroyer was bearing down on her, the U-223 fired several torpedoes at HMS *Hesperus*. The torpedoes missed, and when the U-223 crossed the bows of the British destroyer at 0102, Macintyre decided to "deal her a rather half-hearted ram." Just as the British destroyer was about to ram the U-223, it stopped both engines, and the U-223 was hit at an estimated speed of about 10 knots just aft of the conning tower. Macintyre decided not to ram the U-boat at full speed because he still had a long voyage to Britain and did not want to damage HMS *Hesperus'* sonar. He also remembered the fate of HMS *Harvester,* which had rammed and sunk the U-423 in March, but was then torpedoed and sunk by another U-boat when it lost all power. When HMS *Hesperus* rammed the U-223, the British could see a number of the U-boat's crew in the conning tower and it was thought to be in a sinking condition. At this point Macintyre decided to break off the action because of the large number of U-boats thought to be in the area and the need to return to the convoy, feeling he "was not justified in remaining to hasten the end of the damaged U-boat." Macintyre mistakenly believed that he had critically damaged if not sunk the U-223, which, in fact, managed to return to base.[55]

During the night of 11 to 12 May some twenty-two U-boats still stalked SC 129, but after the action between the U-223 and HMS *Hesperus* there were no meaningful contacts with the submarines. The convoy's escorts did, however, pick up a number of HF/DF bearings, and HMS *Hesperus* and HMS *Whitehall* both made unsuccessful searches astern of SC 129 on the basis of HF/DF fixes. Macintyre concluded from HF/DF bearings that the U-boats were mostly astern or on the flanks of the convoy. Knowing that he could outstrip those enemy vessels, he decided only to search for those U-boats which were in front of SC 129.[56]

A number of U-boats were apparently running short of fuel and falling behind SC 129 and the BdU made arrangements for them to be refueled at sea. At the same time the U-boats were directed: "DO NOT SLIP ASTERN. PROCEED AHEAD AT BEST SPEED." During 12 May U-boats broadcast a stream of contact reports, but the BdU, still unsatisfied, ordered the U-boats to "REPORT CONTACT FORTH-WITH."[57] The problem confronting the BdU was one of turning contacts into sunken Allied merchant ships, which meant that the U-boats had to get ahead of SC 129 into effective attacking positions.

At 1133 HMS *Hesperus* obtained an HF/DF bearing ahead of the convoy. The British destroyer ran down the bearing at 20 knots and gained a sonar contact at the estimated position of the U-boat. A hedgehog attack was undertaken without result, but two and a half minutes later a periscope was sighted crossing the bow of HMS *Hesperus* from starboard to port. A ten depth charge pattern was then dropped by eye which "must have straddled the U-boat." HMS *Hesperus* than ran out, turned, and delivered a hedgehog attack which was followed by another ten depth charge attack. Minutes later the British heard a series of "distant underwater explosions of unknown origin." HMS *Hesperus* then attacked again, dropping a ten depth charge pattern and the contact "faded." But twelve minutes later the British heard "a single sharp explosion . . . though evidently quite close, [that] produced no disturbance on the surface of the sea." HMS *Hesperus* then "swept" through the area of the last attack and found "a considerable area covered with floating wreckage and slight traces of oil." The U-186 had been sunk and HMS *Hesperus* rejoined SC 129.[58]

From the "constant stream" of HF/DF bearings being picked up, Macintyre concluded that the U-boats were "gradually working around the front" of the convoy. At 1508 HMS *Whitehall* and HMS *Heather* were sent down an HF/DF bearing ahead of SC 129. A U-boat was sighted which submerged and was then attacked without result. HMS *Heather* then sighted a second U-boat which was also forced to dive and was unsuccessfully attacked. From their positions on SC 129's screen, HMS *Clematis* and HMS *Sweetbriar* next sighted three U-boats between them. This trio was chased away from the convoy but not overtaken and attacked. At 1830 HMS *Whitehall* was again sent ahead of the convoy to run down an HF/DF bearing. At 1903 a U-boat was sighted and shortly thereafter two more U-boats were seen from the British warship. One U-boat dived, another withdrew in a northerly direction, and HMS *Whitehall* chased and attacked the third U-boat with gunfire. HMS *Hesperus* had joined HMS *Whitehall* by this time. The U-boat dived, and the British destroyers then attacked with depth charges and hedgehogs, but HMS *Hesperus* had to break off the operation and return to the convoy because it was running short of depth charges. HMS *Whitehall* continued to hunt and to attack the U-boat without result until it returned to the screen of SC 129 at 2233.[59]

At dusk SC 129's course had been changed 40° to port "not so much in any hope of evading the U-boats but rather to throw them out of position or so cut down the time available for them to attack in the short night prevailing." This stratagem must have worked, for during the night only one U-boat was contacted. At 2353 a radar contact was obtained on a U-boat which was run down by HMS *Hesperus*. The U-boat was forced to dive and then hunted and at-

tacked until 0715 the morning of 13 May by HMS *Clematis*. Macintyre expected a "strong mass attack" during the night, and this
probably failed to materialize because of the aggressive HF/DF-
guided sweeps ahead of the convoy which forced the U-boats to lose
contact. At least one U-boat was sunk and several others damaged as
a result of these sweeps, while others were driven off. For example,
the U-454 reported "AM BEING DRIVEN OFF." The U-621 radioed
"DIVED FROM CORVETTE." And the U-525 was forced "UNDER WA-
TER BY DESTROYER." The BdU noted in its war diary that contact
was not made during the night of 12 May with SC 129 and that all
the U-boats had been "forced away by escort vessels," but even
though contact with the convoy had been lost, the operation would
continue.[60]

On the morning of 13 May the BdU ordered the U-boats operating
against SC 129 "TO CONTINUE TO SEARCH TENACIOUSLY FOR EN-
EMY, COURSE ABOUT 40 DEGREES." But before the U-boats could
regain contact with SC 129, VLR B-24 Liberator aircraft appeared
in the region. Even though the convoy was not sighted by these aircraft they did attack several U-boats operating against SC 129, and
the presence of Allied aircraft was quickly felt by the submarines.
For example, the U-569 radioed the BdU "DIVED TO AVOID LOCA-
TION BY AIR," while the U-454 reported: "DIVED TO AVOID A/C."
Nevertheless, the BdU continued to urge the U-boats to seek and
make contact with SC 129, for the "CONVOY ABSOLUTELY MUST BE
FOUND AGAIN WHILE VISIBILITY IS GOOD. DO YOUR BEST. SUCCESS
MUST COME THIS COMING NIGHT." Still, the BdU also realized that
any chances of operating successfully against SC 129 were greatly
reduced, if not destroyed, when the U-642 reported sighting an aircraft carrier approaching from the northeast.[61] Because of the impending threat of strong air support from the carrier's aircraft, the
BdU decided to call off operations against SC 129 on 14 May.[62]

Even though there were no contacts between the escorts of SC 129
and the U-boats on 14 May, a number of HF/DF transmissions were
picked up by the escorts of SC 129. At 1330 HMS *Biter* and other
members of the 5th Escort Group joined the convoy. The U-403
managed to sight SC 129, but was driven off by aircraft. During the
night the U-607 sank the neutral Irish merchant ship *Irish Oak*, mis-
taking the vessel for a straggler as it passed astern of the convoy. On

the whole the U-boats were rendered ineffectual by carrier-borne and shore-based aircraft. In the afternoon of 14 May the BdU radioed the U-boats operating against SC 129 "BREAK OFF OPERATION AGAINST CONVOY."[63]

At the beginning of the operation against HX 237 and SC 129, the Germans had very good intelligence on the locations, speeds, and courses of the convoys. In fact American naval intelligence remarked of the deployments against the convoys: "No U/B operation of which we have any record was so evidently guided by continuing intelligence of convoy movements." The Germans deployed some thirty-six U-boats, including those of the *Drossel* group, against HX 237 and SC 129 and, according to American naval intelligence, the two convoys "should have been enveloped in mid-ocean south of 45°N. The conditions had never been more ideal for U/B command."[64]

But every time that the U-boats of the *Rhein, Elbe,* and *Drossel* groups appeared to be closing in on HX 237 and SC 129, the Germans saw the two convoys slipping through their fingers. Whenever the U-boats gained contact or even approached HX 237 and SC 129, the Germans found it nearly impossible to engage and attack the two convoys, for they were placed at a great disadvantage by Allied technology, weapon systems, and tactics. For example, the Germans never discovered the connection between their radio transmissions and the appearance of an Allied escort. HF/DF enabled the escorts to hunt down, attack, or at least force the U-boats to submerge while approaching the convoys, before they had gained contact and could attack. And aircraft, either carrier-borne or shore-based, was an Allied weapon system which the U-boat found almost impossible to counter. Tactically, the U-boats stalking HX 237 and SC 129 were confronted with very aggressive air and surface escorts employing radar and HF/DF to locate and then attack U-boats and neutralize them as they approached the convoys. In the operations against HX 237 and SC 129, the BdU failed to comprehend that the U-boats themselves could not overcome the tactical defense of the convoys, and as a result the Germans were incapable of attacking HX 237 and SC 129 effectively.

In the days after the battle for HX 237 and SC 129, American naval intelligence officers studying decrypts of the orders sent to the U-boats from the BdU concluded that there was a possibility that the

Germans had foreknowledge of the convoys' movements. It had been clear for some time that the BdU had a good knowledge of Allied ship and convoy movements, and the phrase "convoy expected" had been a regular feature of the BdU's radio transmissions. The movement of U-boats and patrol lines always appeared to Allied intelligence to be guided by advance information, such as a knowledge of Allied convoy routes and cycles. In a theater as huge as the Atlantic Ocean, they argued, it would be nearly impossible for U-boats to intercept a convoy without the assistance of intelligence. The basic questions that had to be answered were how accurate and timely was such intelligence and, even more important, what were the sources of the BdU's knowledge of the movements of Allied convoys.

From a cursory study of German decrypts and U-boat operations, it would appear that the BdU's intelligence was not, in fact, very good. Certainly the intelligence was maddeningly inconsistent for the purposes of the U-boats and their commanders. The "convoy expected" messages were routine, and at times the BdU appeared to be well informed about Allied convoy movements and successfully deployed U-boats to intercept the convoys. At other times, however, Allied diversions and routings appeared to be successful, for the U-boats failed to intercept various convoys.

These inconsistencies baffled the Allies as well. Convoy departures, cycles, and other routine matters could not be kept from the Germans, and Allied convoys did not maintain anything like radio silence. Still, as Allied skills in decrypting enemy command radio traffic improved, it seemed to some that Allied diversions of convoys were more and more successful. But then the sudden movements and deployments of the *Rhein, Elbe,* and *Drossel* groups in response to the movements of HX 237 and SC 129 caused American naval intelligence to become suspicious.

American naval intelligence knew very little about the organization of German naval intelligence. The possible sources of German intelligence were many and varied: agents, prisoners, U-boat and aircraft sightings, and the analysis of Allied radio traffic. It was also logical to assume that the Germans were attempting to read Allied codes. American naval intelligence officers decided that the most likely source of German intelligence on the movement of convoys was the coded Allied radio transmissions themselves. Still, they needed proof that the Germans were in fact reading a particular code before they could overcome a natural reluctance of various command authorities to authorize the expense, work, and trouble involved in a major change of compromised codes. Proving that a particular code had been broken was a difficult problem, for the Germans had a wide and varied choice of sources of coded information. Even a preliminary identification of the particular system that the enemy was reading demanded a complete knowledge of Allied communications, codes, actual movements, plans, and standard operating procedures. And the American naval intelligence realized that merely reading the enemy's command radio communications themselves would not necessarily provide the required information, "*unless* the enemy fails to observe elementary precautions." Such a failure would provide the conclusive proof required for an effective demand for a major change of Allied codes.

American naval intelligence undertook a massive paper chase in the files of COMINCH and the 10th Fleet's Convoy and Routing Division for evidence that Allied command radio communications were being read by the Germans. After studying all the papers and messages concerning HX 237 and SC 129, American naval intelligence concluded that, among others, the BdU's orders of 8 and 9 May to the *Rhein* group directing those U-boats to change course and to establish a new patrol line were based on information that could have only come from a knowledge of the contents of a radio message sent to the Western Local Escort Group or a transmission made by the convoy's escort. It was further concluded that the BdU's 11 May order to the *Drossel* group giving the expected position of HX 237 at 1600B on 11 May was apparently based on the contents of a radio message sent to HM Tug *Dexterous*. These examples and other evidence pointed to the conclusion that the Germans were able to read "Combined Naval Cipher No. 3 (tables S and M)," but the evidence was inconclusive, and American naval intelligence would continue to do research into the security of Allied command radio transmissions for several more weeks.[65]

On 11 and 12 May, when the U-boats were closing in to attack HX 237 and SC 129 northwest of the Azores, the BdU issued orders for twenty-five U-boats to be deployed south southeast of Greenland. The bulk of these U-boats were to be drawn from those vessels which were being refueled at sea and also from a number of U-boats which were just entering the North Atlantic from their European bases.[66] The *Lech* group, consisting of five U-boats (U-109, U-202, U-91, U-340, U-731), was to set up a patrol line running from 55°75'N, 37°25'W to 55°09'N, 36°25'W. Group *Isar*, with five U-boats (U-304, U-227, U-645, U-952, U-418), was to establish a patrol line running from 58°09'N, 40°27'W to 57°03'N, 38°48'W. Group *Inn*, made up of four U-boats (U-258, U-381, U-954, U-92), was to form a patrol line running from 56°09'N, 40°55'W to 55°15'N, 40°05'W. Group *Iller*, consisting of six U-boats (U-760, U-636, U-340, U-731, U-657, U-640), was to set up a patrol line running from 55°51'N, 34°25'W to 54°33'N, 37°35'W. And the six U-boats of Group *Nab* (U-707, U-413, U-552, U-264, U-378, U-218) were to make a patrol line running from roughly 51°N, 35°W to 53°N, 36°W. This deployment would result in five patrol lines southeast of Greenland by 15 May, with this simple objective: interdiction of the northern convoy route between Great Britain and North America.

The Allies did not decode the first order for setting up the patrol lines until 0958 on 14 May, and the bulk of these orders were read by the Allies late in the day on 15 May and in the early hours of 16 May. The first Allied convoy to run the gauntlet of these new U-boat patrol lines, westbound ON 182, sailed from Liverpool on 6 May and reached New York on 22 May. After passing through the North Channel into the Atlantic ON 182 headed northwest along a northern arc that carried its fifty-seven merchant ships as far north and west as 59°55'N, 39°06'W before turning southwest for the east coast ports of North America. Although ON 182 passed through the area where the northern wing of the *Isar* group was to be deployed, the U-boats were not in place until the convoy had passed to the westward. The convoy's voyage was uneventful but for encounters with icebergs and fog.[67]

The first convoy to actually encounter the U-boats bound for these patrol lines was the westbound ONS 7 which assembled off Oban west of Scotland on 8 May. The convoy comprised some fifty merchant ships escorted by Escort Group B5 consisting of the frigates HMS *Swale* and HMS *Nene;* the sloop *Wren;* the corvettes HMS *Buttercup,* HMS *Pimpernel,* HMS *Lavender,* HMS *Godetia;* and the trawlers HMS *Stafnes* and *Northern Wave.* ONS 7 proceeded northwest from Great Britain along the northern convoy route to North America, and on 10 May nine more merchant ships joined the convoy from Iceland. At 2355Z on 12 May, HMS *Wren* sighted a U-boat on the surface—the U-640. The U-boat dived ahead of ONS 7, and HMS *Wren*, accompanied by HMS *Swale*, hunted and attacked the U-640 with depth charges while the convoy made a 90 degree emergency turn to port in an attempt to lose the U-boat. At 0305Z on 13 May, ONS 7 returned to a base course of 275°, and HMS *Wren* continued to hunt the U-640 until daylight.[68]

The U-640 was steaming west to take up its assigned position in the *Iller* patrol line when it sighted ONS 7. The convoy was quickly identified by the BdU, but at this point the bulk of the U-boats belonging to the *Lech, Inn, Iller, Isar,* and *Nab* groups were south of Greenland and west of the convoy.[69] At 0353 on 13 May, the BdU ordered the U-boats of these five patrol groups to steam at 5 knots on a course of 30° to attempt to intercept ONS 7. Throughout 13 May the U-640 maintained contact with the convoy. At 1417Z the BdU informed the U-boats that it thought that ONS 7 would pass through 61°21'N, 29°63'W before turning to a west and then southwest course. Half an hour later the U-boats of the *Isar* and *Inn* groups were ordered to form themselves into a new group called *Donau 1* and to establish a patrol line running from 60°09'N, 38°48'W to 58°27'N, 36°48'W. Groups *Lech* and *Nab* were now to be called *Donau 2,* forming a patrol line running from 58°15'N, 36°W to 56°21'N, 34°25'W. These patrol lines were to be established by 0800B on 15 May. (This order was decoded by the Allies at 0115 on 15 May.) Several hours later the U-boats of the *Iller* group, which was the closest to ONS 7, were ordered to "OPERATE INDEPENDENTLY" against the convoy.[70]

There was no contact between the U-boats and ONS 7 on 13 May. However, at 1812 the U-640 reported firing two torpedoes at the ships of the convoy and hearing those torpedoes explode. No ship was hit, and the U-640 probably heard, instead, the torpedoes exploding at the end of their runs, for no mention of this attack was made in the after action reports of the convoy's escorts. Most of the U-boats were to the west and south of ONS 7 on 13 May. Air support for ONS 7 was provided by USN PBY Catalina aircraft from Iceland, and the U-640 reported being bombed by a PBY Catalina late on 13 May.[71]

Because of the sightings of the U-640, air cover for ONS 7 was increased on 14 May. Six USN PBY Catalinas and a VLR B-24 Liberator of RAF 120th Squadron were dispatched. The aircraft sighted six U-boats and made four attacks. During one of these attacks, a USN PBY Catalina attacked and sank the U-657 with an acoustic homing torpedo. This air activity kept the U-boats submerged and away from the convoy and helped mask a strategic rerouting. Both the commander of Escort Group B5 and the commander in chief, western approaches, thought that the main danger from the U-boats to ONS 7 came from the south, and the convoy's course was changed to the northward from 275° to 288°, which would carry ONS 7 as far north as 61°15'N, on 15 May.[72]

At 1854Z on 14 May, the BdU ordered the U-640 and the U-657 to "FURTHER SEARCH INDEPENDENTLY" for ONS 7, while four other U-boats (U-340, U-731, U-760, U-636) of the *Iller* group were directed to form a patrol line running from 60°51'N, 40°24'W to 60°15'N, 39°12'W by 1000B on 15 May. And the U-boats were further directed: "IN CASE OF DIFFICULTY WITH ICE, REMAIN AT ICE-LINE ((BOUNDARY))." It is clear that the BdU hoped to intercept ONS 7 just east of the southern tip of Greenland, immediately after the convoy had turned to a southwest course. However, there was no contact between ONS 7 and the U-boats for the next two days. On 15 May ONS 7 reached 61°15'N, 37°18'W and turned on to a course of approximately 228°. On 16 May the convoy passed just to the north of the northern wing of the *Donau 1* patrol line and through the *Iller* patrol line without being intercepted.[73]

Even though ONS 7 had passed beyond the *Donau 1* and *Iller* patrol lines, the U-640 was still in contact with the convoy. At 0037Z on 17 May the U-640 torpedoed the merchant ship *Aymeric*.[74] One torpedo hit the *Aymeric* in the No. 1 hold on the port side. Two minutes later a second torpedo struck the ship, again on the port side, forward of the bridge. The crew of the *Aymeric* abandoned the ship which sank rapidly. When the *Aymeric* was torpedoed, the convoy's escorts swept back through the formation hunting for the U-640. HMS *Swale* obtained a sonar contact which was immediately attacked with depth charges and hedgehogs. Thirty-three seconds after the second hedgehog attack, there was an explosion followed two minutes and forty seconds later by "two muffled explosions." The

U-640 had been destroyed. The rescue ship *Copeland* and the trawler *Northern Wave* picked up twenty-five survivors from the *Aymeric*. After the sinking of the *Aymeric* there were no further contacts between ONS 7 and the U-boats, and the convoy arrived at Halifax on 25 May.[75]

The new German patrol lines were quickly tested by more Allied convoys. The day before ONS 7 departed from the Island of Oban for North America, convoy HX 238, consisting of forty-six merchant ships, left New York for Great Britain. The convoy proceeded roughly northeast along the coast of North America and across the Grand Banks of Newfoundland to 52°17'N, 47°15'W, where it changed to an easterly course, passing to the south of the *Donau 2* patrol line. It arrived at Liverpool on 22 May without encountering any U-boats. When another westbound convoy, ON 183, sailed from Great Britain on 10 May, this group, like HX 238, was successfully routed around the southern end of the *Donau 1* patrol line.[76]

However, SC 130, an eastbound convoy that sailed from Halifax, Nova Scotia, for Great Britain on 11 May was not so lucky. For four days SC 130 and a local escort group proceeded northeast to approximately 46°56'N, 47°56'W some 150 miles southeast of Cape Race, Newfoundland, where Escort Group B7 relieved the local escort. Escort Group B7, led by Commander Peter Gretton, RN, consisted of the destroyers HMS *Duncan* and HMS *Vidette*; the corvettes HMS *Snowflake*, HMS *Pink*, and HMS *Loosestrife*; the frigate HMS *Tay*; and the trawler *Northern Spray*. HMCS *Kitchener* was also assigned to the group as an "extra corvette." (The corvette HMS *Sunflower*, a regular member of Escort Group B7, remained in St. John's, Newfoundland, for repairs to its damaged bow.) The captains and the ships of this group had worked and trained together before and, according to Gretton, "each ship knew what the other would do in all circumstances and I had to make very few signals—ships acted at once and reported what they were doing. They never waited for orders."[77] Escort Group B7 would provide SC 130 with a powerful escort. The convoy itself consisted of thirty-nine merchant ships, including the rescue ship *Zamalek* which, like HMS *Duncan* and HMS *Tay* in the escort, was equipped with HF/DF.[78]

At 0655Z on 15 May the local escort departed, and SC 130 headed for Great Britain, making 7.5 knots on a base course of 81°. During that afternoon, the convoy encountered fog and icebergs, and night-time fog and icebergs prevented any rapid emergency turns. Thus, when HMS *Vidette*'s radar picked up a large iceberg in the path of the convoy which could not be avoided, the destroyer had to become a beacon station for the convoy and its escort. Standing by the iceberg with navigation lights on, the *Vidette* sounded its siren and trained its searchlight on the iceberg as columns of merchant ships steamed by. The merchant ship *Tamaha* that night, for reasons which are not known, "deliberately broke convoy."[79]

The fog cleared by 1100 on 16 May, and the convoy encountered "perfect weather" for the following several days. HMS *Sunflower* rejoined the convoy from Newfoundland, and Gretton took advantage of the good weather and lack of enemy contacts to top off the fuel of the escorts. On 16 May HMS *Duncan*, HMS *Vidette*, and HMS *Sunflower* were refueled from a tanker in the convoy and on 18 May HMS *Snowflake*, HMS *Pink*, and HMS *Loosestrife* were refueled. During the morning of 18 May, the merchant ship *Essex Lance* broke down and dropped astern of the convoy. Gretton assigned the trawler *Northern Spray* to escort the disabled ship independently to port and the ships did not rejoin SC 130. As SC 130 proceeded away from North America at a speed of about 8 knots, it received air cover from the RCAF. Even though the Canadians provided SC 130 with airborne protection up to a point of some 600 miles east of Newfoundland, Gretton did not consider the air support "as satisfactory as it might have been" because of the aircrews' lack of training and a failure of coordination between the air force and navy authorities in Newfoundland.[80]

On 17 May, the BdU received a decrypt of a 14 May "Admiralty U-boat Situation Report" to convoy commodores which gave SC 130's speed as 7.5 knots and course as 76° with a position of 150 miles southeast of Cape Race, Newfoundland. On the basis of this information, the BdU concluded that SC 130 was proceeding to Great Britain by a southerly route. Thus, at 1023 on 17 May, the BdU began to issue the orders required to intercept SC 130. A new patrol line code named *Oder*, consisting of eight U-boats (U-221, U-666, U-558, U-752, U-336, U-642, U-603, U-228), was to be established between 50°21′N, 33°25′W and 48°39′N, 32°35′W by 18 May. And twenty-five U-boats of the *Donau 1* (U-640, U-657, U-760,

U-636, U-340, U-731, U-304, U-227, U-645, U-952, U-418, U-258, U-318, the BdU was unaware that the U-640 and U-657 had been sunk) and *Donau 2* (U-954, U-92, U-109, U-202, U-664, U-91, U-707, U-413, U-553, U-264, U-378, U-532) groups were moved to the south to form two new patrol lines running from 56°03'N, 37°55'W to 53°21'N, 35°25'W and from 53°09'N, 35°15'W to 50°33'N, 33°35'W. The U-boats were ordered to maintain radio silence. They were also told that they could expect to intercept another convoy.[81]

Good cryptographic intelligence enabled the BdU to deploy U-boat lines right across the route of SC 130, but Allied cryptographers moved too slowly to warn the convoy: decoding of the BdU's orders of 17 May did not begin until the evening of 19 May and was not completed until the morning of 22 May. Thus, the commander of SC 130's escort received his first warning of the U-boats from HF/DF on the convoy's rescue ship. At 2019 on 18 May, the *Zamalek* picked up a "ground ray signal" bearing north on the HF/DF set, and Gretton sent HMS *Vidette* to run down this bearing for 20 miles in an unsuccessful attempt to locate the U-boat making this radio transmission. This was probably the U-304.[82]

There is some confusion as to exactly when the Allies discovered that the Germans were going to attack SC 130. After the battle, Gretton stated that he was "puzzled" by running into a concentration of U-boats without first being warned by the Admiralty, which he thought should have been alerted by shore-based D/F fixes. Gretton also thought it possible that the convoy "had run by misadventure, into a concentration" of U-boats and that the Germans might be using radio frequencies, not detected by his force or by "British Shore Organizations."[83] In fact, the Allies did know of the new redeployment of U-boats to intercept SC 130, for on 17 May Allied intelligence noted:

> The next development will be the establishment of new patrols on an arch between 020° and 140° from Virgin Rocks at a radius of 600 miles from Gander Newfoundland. Twenty or more U/boats are now moving to take these up and the apparent gap through which SC 130 has

been routed is rapidly closing: it will be touch and go whether this convoy scrapes through.[84]

As a result of this assessment the 1st Escort Group, consisting of the frigates HMS *Jed*, HMS *Wear*, HMS *Spey*, and the ex-US Coast Guard cutter HMS *Sennen*, was dispatched from St. John's, Newfoundland, to reinforce SC 130's escort.[85]

Meanwhile, Gretton's escort group fought alone through the evening of 18 May. At 2316 the escorts of SC 130 picked up more and more H/F signals, and Gretton "quickly appreciated" that there were two U-boats close ahead of the convoy and one on each quarter of it. But there was a full moon, a light sea running, and a slight breeze out of the northwest—all of which the BdU considered to be "especially unfavorable" conditions for U-boat operations. Thus the convoy was not attacked at this time. At 0134 on 19 May the rescue ship *Zamalek* and HMS *Duncan* both obtained a good HF/DF fix at 54°45′N, 35°36′W, which placed a U-boat 4 miles ahead on the port bow of the convoy. HMS *Duncan* increased speed and steered to intercept the U-boat (probably the U-91), obtaining a radar contact at a range of 5,000 yards. But the U-boat dived at a range of 4,000 yards, and the contact was lost. HMS *Duncan* dropped five depth charges on the U-boat's estimated position without regaining contact but continued to hunt the enemy vessel until the convoy was past and out of danger. Gretton then informed the Admiralty that "convoy shadowed by at least 4 submarines . . . Duncan has attacked one." Even before HMS *Duncan* had conducted the first attack of the battle, U-boats began reporting to the BdU the course, position, and speed of SC 130. For example, at 0400 the U-304 radioed "CONVOY IN SQUARE 4675. EASTERLY COURSE. SPEED 7 KNOTS."[86]

At 0300 on 19 May Gretton ordered the convoy to make two emergency turns to starboard with the hope of "foxing the intended dawn submerged attacker." The convoy then returned to the base course of 81° at 0400. In the early daylight, the first VLR B-24 Liberator aircraft of RAF 120th Squadron from Reykjavik, Iceland, appeared over the convoy at 0340. The plane sighted a U-boat in what Gretton thought "would have been the ideal firing position" if the convoy had not made a change of course, and aircraft T/120 attacked the U-boat with three 250-pound depth charges which straddled the vessel. Just after the U-boat submerged, the plane attacked again with two acoustic homing torpedoes which were dropped into the U-boat's wake. There were two small explosions 70 yards from where the torpedoes entered the water, sinking the U-954 without a trace. Just before the U-954 was sunk, it sent the following radio message: "CONVOY IN NAVAL GRID SQUARE AK 5482, HAVE SIGHTED AN AIRCRAFT."[87]

At 0415 aircraft T/120 sighted two U-boats off the port quarter of the convoy. Having expended all its depth charges and acoustic homing torpedoes during the attack on the U-954, the aircraft dived in a mock attack that made both U-boats submerge. A marker was dropped, and the plane informed Gretton of the position of the two U-boats. HMS *Tay* was sent to investigate, sighting a U-boat and forcing it to submerge. HMS *Tay* carried out an attack on the U-boat without result and then remained in the area for several hours to keep the U-boat down until the convoy passed safely.[88]

At 0524 aircraft T/120 sighted another U-boat and carried out a mock attack. This U-boat did not dive but instead opened fire with antiaircraft guns. The plane then banked to port, and its rear gunner raked the conning tower of the U-boat with machine-gun fire, forcing the U-boat to "crash dive." A marker was dropped on the spot, and when Gretton was informed of the action, he dispatched HMS *Vidette* to the area, but no contact was gained. Aircraft T/120 next sighted a U-boat submerging 14 miles ahead of SC 130. The aircraft dropped a marker on the position, and HMS *Pink* was ordered to investigate. The corvette dropped some depth charges and then rejoined the convoy. At 0642 the convoy made an emergency turn to starboard to avoid the U-boat forced down by aircraft T/120. The convoy returned to the base course of 81° at 0726.[89]

At 0648 HMS *Sunflower* sighted a surfaced U-boat bearing 70° about 10 miles distant. At the same time, aircraft T/120 sighted the same U-boat, forced it to dive, and dropped a marker on the position. HMS *Sunflower* did not continue the chase but returned to its station in the convoy's screen because the commander thought that it was "rather thin." After forcing this U-boat to dive, aircraft T/120 returned to Iceland, the pilot noting in his log that "during all this time destroyers seem to be continuously depth charging on receipt of reports from A/C and on their own initiative." In the short time that aircraft T/120 provided air support to SC 130, it sank one U-boat, forced five others to dive, and directed escorts to attack four submarines. While Gretton thought that aircraft T/120 "did great work," he also believed that the pilot of the aircraft "marred the result" by closing down his radio telephone to report the attacks immediately to his base in Iceland, thus preventing Gretton from contacting the aircraft on the radio telephone on several "vital" occasions.[90]

Other vessels in the convoy had been at work without air assistance. At 0550 HMS *Snowflake* obtained a sonar contact ahead of the ninth column of merchant ships in the convoy. Then the U-boat's periscope was sighted about 50 yards off the corvette's starboard beam, just as the ship was undertaking a depth charge attack with no apparent result. By then, HMS *Duncan* had joined in the hunt and Gretton ordered HMS *Snowflake* to return to its station while HMS *Duncan* delivered a deliberate ten depth charge attack between two columns of merchant ships. As HMS *Duncan* fell astern of the convoy, another depth charge attack was undertaken, followed by three hedgehog attacks, one of which hit its target, with "a good deal of oil" appearing on the surface of the ocean. Gretton correctly credited HMS *Duncan* and HMS *Snowflake* with sinking a U-boat, which proved to be the U-381.[91]

At 0818 the escorts' crews saw two columns of water shoot up near HMS *Sunflower* and HMCS *Kitchener,* which they assumed to be two torpedoes exploding at the end of their runs. Gretton thought that the U-boat that fired these torpedoes was "very timorous for the explosions were some five thousand yards from the convoy."[92] These torpedoes were probably fired by the U-92, which claimed to have sunk a ship in this action, and this incident shows that the tactics employed by Allied air and surface escorts were keeping the U-boats at a distance from SC 130.[93] For example, the U-952 reported that it was "CONTINUALLY FORCED UNDER WATER BY CATALINA [aircraft] FROM 0750 TO 1130." And another U-boat radioed that "CONVOY DESTROYERS IN NAVAL GRID SQUARE AK 5468. FLOWN AT CONTINUOUSLY FROM LOW CLOUDS." At the same time, the BdU urged the U-boats attacking SC 130 not to "REMAIN SUBMERGED TOO LONG. REMEMBER DELUSIVE DEPTH CHARGES. AS SOON AS POSSIBLE COME TO PERISCOPE DEPTH AND LOOK FOR THE ENEMY."[94]

At 0839 a U-boat's conning tower was sighted from the bridge of HMS *Duncan* at a range of 5 miles. The British destroyer came to full speed and steamed toward the U-boat which submerged. A depth charge was dropped, and an unsuccessful hunt was conducted without sonar contact until 0949. But, as HMS *Duncan* was leaving the area to rejoin the convoy, a sonar contact was obtained and hunted without result. At 1100 HMS *Duncan* returned to its station on the screen.[95]

At 0915 the second VLR B-24 Liberator aircraft, P/120, arrived from Iceland. At Gretton's request, the plane carried out a *mamba* (a search for 30 miles down a particular bearing from the convoy) on the port beam of SC 130. In the course of this search, aircraft P/120 sighted a U-boat which submerged within twenty seconds of being seen. The aircraft dived and dropped four depth charges from a height of 50 feet, about 250 feet ahead of the swirl made by the submerging U-boat. Shortly thereafter another U-boat was sighted, diving before it could be attacked. Nineteen minutes later the aircraft sighted another U-boat which also dived before it could be attacked. The aircraft then continued the patrol for thirty-five minutes when another U-boat was sighted and forced to dive before being attacked. And before aircraft P/120 left SC 130, three more U-boats were sighted and forced to dive.[96] During the course of operations around the convoy, aircraft P/120 attacked one U-boat and forced six others to dive, almost certainly losing contact with SC 130.

While aircraft P/120 was forcing U-boats underwater around SC 130, Gretton could hear on the radio telephone that the ships of the 1st Escort Group were closing with the stern of SC 130. They sailed in a line-abreast formation with 4 miles between each ship, their objective to sweep across the stern of the convoy and force any shadowing U-boats to lose contact. At 0930 HMS *Wear* sighted a U-boat at a range of 12 miles. The four escort vessels closed formation to 3,000 yards. The U-boat dived and HMS *Jed* and HMS *Wear* began a hunt with sonar. Four minutes later, HMS *Jed* sighted another U-boat and along with HMS *Wear* steamed toward the enemy vessel, but the U-boat dived. Then at 1027 HMS *Jed* sighted yet another U-boat on the surface at a range of 8 miles. HMS *Jed* and HMS *Wear* proceeded toward it at full speed. HMS *Jed* was ahead of HMS *Wear*, and at 1033 two or three torpedoes passed between the two frigates.

The two British warships turned into the torpedo tracks. HMS *Wear* quickly picked up a sonar contact at the end of the torpedo tracks, but at 1039 HMS *Jed* sighted another U-boat 5 miles away and steamed toward the enemy vessel. HMS *Wear* continued to track the contact until 1045 when it attacked with a hedgehog. Thirty seconds later HMS *Wear*'s helm jammed hard to port.[97]

To the north of where HMS *Wear* lay with damaged steering gear, HMS *Jed* continued to hunt and attack the U-boat it had sighted at 1039. HMS *Sennen* quickly joined the hunt, and the two British warships continued to track the U-boat with sonar and depth charges until 1325, when a "very large oil patch, increasing in size, also oil and air bubbles and wreckage [were] observed in the vicinity of the attack."[98] HMS *Jed* and HMS *Sennen* had finally sunk the U-209.

Immediately after HMS *Wear*'s steering gear had been repaired, it steamed to meet HMS *Spey*. A periscope was sighted, but no sonar contact was obtained. At 1305 HMS *Wear* joined HMS *Spey* in attacking the U-boat. Their efforts were fruitless, and sonar contact was lost. Both frigates broke off the action and steamed toward SC 130. By 1725 the ships of the 1st Escort Group had joined the screen of SC 130.[99]

In the afternoon of 19 May there was a lull in U-boat activity near SC 130, and radio transmissions around the convoy had dropped off somewhat. Gretton took this opportunity "to top up" the fuel of HMS *Duncan* and HMS *Vidette*. Later HMS *Spey* was also refueled. At this time a third VLR B-24 Liberator, aircraft Y/120, appeared over the convoy, sighted a U-boat while conducting a *mamba* search, and attacked the vessel with an acoustic homing torpedo. After patrolling around the convoy to the limit of its fuel, aircraft P/120 returned to Iceland.[100]

By 1615 HF/DF bearings persuaded Gretton that there were two U-boats off the starboard bow of SC 130. The commander of the escort ordered the convoy to make an emergency turn to port to avoid these submarines and an hour later SC 130 returned to its base course of 81°. By changing the convoy's course, Gretton was forcing U-boats to lose contact with it; for example, the U-413 reported to the BdU "SUBMERGED ATTACK FAILED ON ACCOUNT OF TURN TO NORTHEAST."[101]

A fourth VLR B-24 Liberator, aircraft O/120, arrived over the convoy just before it returned to its base course. At Gretton's request, aircraft 0/120 conducted a *frog* search (a sweep across the stern of the convoy). During the course of this search a U-boat was sighted, forced to dive, and attacked with an acoustic homing torpedo. Gretton then obtained several other aerial searches during the course of which another U-boat was sighted, forced to dive, and attacked with an acoustic homing torpedo. Aircraft 0/120 circled over the position where the U-boat submerged until HMS *Tay* arrived to continue the hunt, which was without result. When aircraft 0/120 left the convoy for its base in Iceland it was replaced by another VLR B-24 Liberator H/120, which conducted an additional number of patrols around SC 130, including an *adder* (a search within visual distance around all four sides of the convoy). Aircraft H/120 did not sight any U-boats before returning to base.[102] The VLR B-24 Liberator aircraft patrolling around SC 130 during the daylight hours of 19 May greatly assisted the surface escorts of the convoy in defeating and breaking up U-boat attacks.

The effects of air attacks and the successful tactics employed by the surface escorts are reflected in the radio transmissions made by U-boats attacking SC 130. The U-645 radioed "UP TO NOW HAVE BEEN DRIVEN UNDER WATER CONTINUALLY BY AIRCRAFT OUT OF LOW CLOUDS AND BY DESTROYERS." The same U-boat later radioed "LOCATED BY AIRCRAFT." While the U-707 was "CONTINUOUSLY DRIVEN UNDERWATER," the U-304 was attacked by "DEPTH CHARGES. NEGATIVE BUOYANCY TANKS DEFECTIVE . . . HAVE LOST CONTACT." Another U-boat radioed: "CORVETTES DEPTH CHARGES . . . PORT FORWARD ELECTRICAL MACHINERY BEARING DEFECTIVE AM REPAIRING." By the evening of 19 May, the BdU had concluded "THAT IT WAS NOT POSSIBLE TO STAY ON CONVOY ON ACCOUNT OF AIR," and the U-boats attacking SC 130 were ordered "TO MOVE OFF AND PROCEED AHEAD AROUND THE CONVOY AT BEST SPEED OUTSIDE CLOSE AIR ((ESCORTS)), I.E. PRESUMABLY AT A DISTANCE OF ABOUT 30 OR 40 MILES, IN ORDER TO DIVE AHEAD OF THE CONVOY FOR DAY ATTACK."[103]

Later that evening the U-boats were ordered to steam to a position to intercept SC 130 at night in order to avoid air attacks but at the same time "PROCEED WITH M/G READY FOR FIRING AND MANNED IN CASE OF SURPRISE ATTACKS." However, SC 130 was not attacked during the night of 19 May, and, indeed, there was not even a radar contact on a U-boat. Early in the voyage HMS *Sunflower*'s sonar recorder broke down; the radar failed as well during the evening of 19 May and could not be repaired. That same evening, HMCS *Kitchener* was detached to reinforce the escort of convoy ON 184. At 0054 and 0107 HMS *Jed* and HMS *Spey* were ordered to search down HF/DF bearings. Two U-boats were found on the surface, forced to dive, and attacked. At dawn SC 130 conducted two emergency turns to port and seventy-one minutes later the convoy returned to its base course: "The ruse was again successful . . . no attacks were attempted."[104]

Shortly after dawn on 20 May, the first VLR B-24 Liberator of the day, aircraft N/120, appeared over SC 130 and conducted an *adder* search at Gretton's request. A U-boat was sighted and attacked before it dived. Aircraft N/120 dropped three depth charges in the swirl of the submerging U-boat, and five minutes later the aircraft saw the bow of the U-boat protruding from the sea at a 30 degree angle. An acoustic homing torpedo was dropped near the damaged U-boat with no observed result. One hour and forty minutes later another U-boat was sighted. As aircraft N/120 dived, the U-boat opened fire with antiaircraft guns. Aircraft N/120 took evasive action and its rear gunner fired on the enemy vessel. Even while attacking this U-boat, aircraft N/120 spotted a third U-boat. The plane circled out of range of the vessel's antiaircraft guns and then informed Gretton that the third U-boat was circling on the surface, but this submarine then crash dived. While carrying out a *mamba*, aircraft N/120 sighted a fourth U-boat whose conning tower was raked with machine-gun fire before it "dived rather slowly." Before aircraft N/120 left SC 130, a fifth U-boat was sighted and forced to dive.[105] In the four hours and twenty-six minutes spent over SC 130, aircraft N/120 attacked one U-boat and forced four others to submerge.

At 1315 Gretton ordered another emergency turn to port to avoid a U-boat which HF/DF had picked up close ahead of the convoy. After a half hour SC 130 returned to its base course. While the convoy made the emergency turn, HMS *Sennen* obtained a sonar contact astern of SC 130 and attacked it without result.[106]

During the afternoon of 20 May another VLR B-24 Liberator, aircraft P/120, appeared over SC 130, and Gretton requested a second *mamba* search. The plane sighted a U-boat which submerged in twenty-three seconds before it could be attacked. Two hours later a second U-boat (the U-256) was sighted, and the aircraft attacked with four depth charges, obtaining a straddle around the partly submerged U-boat. The aircraft continued the patrol, sighting a third U-boat which it attacked in a dive, machine guns firing. This U-boat returned the fire with antiaircraft guns, and the British plane attacked a second time, firing 180 rounds of cannon fire into the base of the U-boat's conning tower and foredeck. A third attack was made with an acoustic homing torpedo, and after this attack the U-boat "seemed in difficulties" being down at the stern. The pilot of the aircraft contacted Gretton, and the commander of the escort began to steam toward the damaged U-boat, taking bearings on homing signals transmitted by aircraft P/120. The operation was canceled, however, when the U-boat dived and it was realized that it was over 20 miles from SC 130. Aircraft P/120 had, in fact, destroyed the U-256. While returning to Iceland, aircraft P/120 sighted a fourth U-boat which dived and was "lost in sun and haze." All in all, the plane had sighted four U-boats, attacked one with depth charges and sunk another one with gunfire and an acoustic homing torpedo.[107]

The U-boats, on the other hand, did not achieve anything during 20 May and, in fact, were heavily handled by air and surface escorts. The U-952 radioed "HEAVY DEPTH CHARGING BY 2 DESTROYERS. DIESEL HEAD VALVE DAMAGED. TUBS 2, 3, 5, AUXILIARY BILGE PUMP DEFECTIVE. SEVERAL LEAKS IN CONTROL ROOM." Another U-boat reported "HEAVY DEPTH CHARGES FROM BOEING [AIRCRAFT]. DEFECTS RECTIFIED EXCEPT FOR ATTACK PERISCOPE." The U-413 was "HEAVILY DEPTH CHARGED FOR 90 MINUTES." And a fourth U-boat radioed that it had "BEEN CONSTANTLY DIVING FROM AIRCRAFT."[108] Sunset of 20 May marked the end of the battle for SC 130.

SC 130 was not attacked during that evening although several escorts made nighttime attacks on sonar contacts with no results. HF/DF did not pick up any enemy radio transmissions after 0100 on 21 May. At dawn, the convoy made the "usual 90 degree turn . . . in case there were some U-boats still ahead who did not talk on H/F; but no further attempts were made to molest the convoy." Unknown to the escort of SC 130, the Germans had called off the battle, and the BdU had radioed the U-boats attacking the convoy "BREAK OFF OPERATIONS AGAINST CONVOY. MOVE AWAY WESTWARD."[109] SC 130 arrived with thirty-seven merchant ships in Great Britain on 25 May without further incident.

The Germans were utterly defeated in the battle for SC 130. The U-boats did not sink one Allied merchant ship but lost four submarines (U-954, U-381, U-209, U-258). Even if the Allies had sunk no enemy vessels, they would have still won the battle for SC 130, for their main objective was the safe and timely arrival of merchant ships at their destination, while the overriding German objective in the Battle of the Atlantic was to prevent the Allies from sailing merchant ships across that ocean. By these and any other criteria, the Allies were the clear victors in the battle for SC 130.

The Allies won because they simply outfought the Germans. At every turn in their attacks on SC 130, the U-boats were confronted with weapon systems and tactics which they could not counter. The Germans, for example, did not know of the Allies' use of airborne acoustic homing torpedoes. Nor did they know of the existence and importance of HF/DF. It was HF/DF which enabled Gretton to locate a U-boat before the convoy came within torpedo range and avoid the enemy vessel by making an emergency turn. And HF/DF gave Gretton the ability to send a warship or an aircraft down the bearing of U-boat radio transmission, where it could either attack or force the U-boat to submerge, causing it to lose contact with the convoy.

The VLR B-24 Liberator aircraft of RAF 120th Squadron were the weapon system which tipped the battle in favor of the Allies. What made aircraft such an effective weapon against U-boats was their high speed relative to a surface vessel, a speed which permitted them to search a much greater area than a ship. And with HF/DF, Gretton "was able to get fixes on U-boats transmitting near us with great accuracy and to send aircraft quickly after them."[110] At the end of the battle the BdU noted the effectiveness of air support for SC 130 when it stated in its war diary:

> that the boats could not approach near owing to continuous air cover being too strong, and it was also not possible to maintain contact and proceed in the vicinity of the convoy owing to the continual surprise attacks from low-lying clouds. . . . The amazing thing is that apparently at the time only 1 to 2 machines in all were escorting the convoy,

according to intercepted messages of aircraft operating. Each machine detected, however, during the whole day one boat more frequently than every quarter-hour, from which it must be concluded that the enemy's radar hardly missed a boat. With about 20 boats in the vicinity of the convoy this was quite possible, since the boats were scattered around the convoy at quite short distances apart for an aircraft.[111]

Convoy HX 239, consisting of forty-four merchant ships sailed from New York on 13 May. At 1450Z on 19 May at 45°50'N, 44°42'W Escort Group B3 relieved the convoy's local escort. Commander M. J. Evans, RN, led the escort group: the destroyers HMS *Keppel*, HMS *Escapade*, ORP *Garland*; the corvettes HMS *Orchis*, FFS *Roselys*, FFS *Lobelia*, FFS *Renoncule*, FFS *Aconit*; the trawler *Northern Gem*; and HM Tug *Growler*. As HX 239 and the escort group headed eastward into the Atlantic, they encountered a "heavy North Westerly gale."[112]

On the day that the convoy rendezvoused with the escort group, the BdU learned the position, course, and speed of HX 239 from an intercepted and decrypted Allied radio transmission.[113] As a result of this intelligence, the BdU ordered twenty-one U-boats (U-552, U-264, U-378, U-607, U-218, U-221, U-666, U-752, U-558, U-650, U-336, U-642, U-603, U-228, U-575, U-621, U-229, U-641, U-305, U-567, U-458, U-231) to establish a patrol line, code named *Mosel*, running from 55°15'N, 44°25'W to 52°09'N, 37°15'W. The U-boats were to be in place at 2000B on 21 May, and their orders informed them tersely: "NORTHEAST BOUND CONVOY IS EXPECTED FROM 2000B ON."

At first it seemed that HX 239 might be spared an encounter with this new U-boat line. Even though the BdU's order establishing the *Mosel* line was not decoded by the Allies until 1443 on 20 May, the convoy's route would have taken the merchant ships and their escort around the new line of U-boats. By 0800 BST on 20 May, HX 239 had reached 47°50'N, 48°59'W, a point well south of the southern end of the planned *Mosel* patrol line.[114] But eleven hours later, the BdU received cryptographic intelligence giving the course and positions of HX 239 through 22 May. From this information, the BdU concluded that the convoy was "proceeding much further to the S. than the first course instructions indicated."[115] Accordingly, at 2216Z on 20 May, the BdU ordered the *Mosel* patrol moved east and extended to the south—it would now run from 55°15'N, 44°25'W to 52°15'N, 37°35'W with the move to be completed by 2000B on 21 May. The next day, 21 May, the BdU received additional intelligence which resulted in the *Mosel* patrol line being moved again, this time to the northeast, while its length contracted. At 1220Z, the U-boats were ordered to establish a patrol line running from 54°45'N, 43°15'W to 51°45'N, 36°25'W by 2000B. Several hours later the U-boats of the *Donau* group were ordered to steam toward 51°25'N, 30°15'W to attempt to intercept HX 239. Then at 2214 the BdU informed the U-boats of the *Mosel* group that "THE EXPECTED CONVOY" was at 49°27'N, 43°45'W at 1700B on 20 May; and that HX 239 will "BE IN" 50°27'N, 35°15'W at 1700B on 21 May. Further, the convoy "IS TO HEAD FROM THERE FOR" 52°09'N, 33°25'W. And the speed of HX 239 is "9-9.5." Next, at 2132Z on 22 May, the BdU radioed the *Mosel* group that it "ASSUMES THAT NORTHEAST CONVOY WAS IN ((AK 8557 = 52.15N—33.25W)) ON 22 MAY 1700B."[116]

Here the Germans had a real intelligence advantage. The Allies did not begin reading decoded versions of any of the BdU's orders redeploying the *Mosel* line until 22 May, and the last of the radio messages was not decoded until 3 June.[117] The Germans, on the other hand, were acting on very reliable and accurate intelligence reports that enabled the BdU to deploy a number of U-boats across the route of HX 239. Convoy HX 239 and its escort group thus spent two days sailing directly toward a newly stationed U-boat line of which the Allied merchant ships and the British escort were completely ignorant.

But the situation was filled with irony for the Germans: their communications intelligence was getting better and better, giving the BdU very accurate information on Allied North Atlantic convoys at the very time that the U-boat campaign against Allied convoys was faltering, and on the verge of collapse because of heavy losses and rare successes. Further, the Germans' poor communications security was about to deny them further communications intelligence as a steady source of information on Allied convoy movements. American naval intelligence was close to proving that the Germans were reading the Combined Naval Cipher No. 3. When American intelligence officers studied the decrypts of the BdU's orders and messages to the *Mosel* group on HX 239 and then compared them to the texts of various Allied radio transmissions, they deduced correctly that the Germans had decoded and read "a dispatch containing R/V positions for May 20, 21, 22 sent by CINCCNWA [Commander in Chief Canadian Northwest Atlantic]." At this time, however, American naval intelligence could not say whether this dispatch and several others were the Germans' *sole* cryptographic sources of information.[118] Further study would be required to prove that Allied codes were in fact broken and that the Germans were gaining knowledge of Allied command radio transmissions.

However, this intelligence breakthrough lay in the future and was of no consequence to the Allied convoys in the North Atlantic in the third week of May 1943. HX 239 was joined in the area by convoy ON 184, a westbound convoy of thirty-nine merchant ships that sailed from Great Britain on 15 May. The escort of the convoy was Escort Group C1, consisting of the frigate HMS *Itchen;* the destroyers HMS *Burwell,* HMCS *St. Croix,* and HMCS *St. Laurent;* and the corvettes HMCS *Agassiz,* HMCS *Sackville,* and HMCS *Woodstock.* ON 184 steered northwest from the North Channel until it reached 58°43'N, 26°47'W where the convoy turned to a southwest course.[119] On 19 May the escort carrier USS *Bogue;* the destroyers USS *Belknap,* USS *Badger,* USS *Greene,* USS *Lea,* USS *Osmond Ingram;* and the merchant ship *Toltec* joined ON 184 from Iceland. The *Toltec* became a member of the convoy while the USS *Bogue* took station within the body of the convoy and the five American destroyers joined ON 184's screen.[120] HMCS *Kitchener,* detached from SC 130, joined ON 184 on 20 May.

Like the HX 239, ON 184 continued to steer a southwesterly course toward the *Mosel* patrol line, denied any warnings by laggardly Allied decoding of German radio transmissions. In fact, ON 184 had contact with the U-boats before the HX 239. During the afternoon of 21 May, one of the USS *Bogue*'s TBF Avenger aircraft sighted a U-boat on the surface some 60 miles in front of the convoy. As the U-boat began to submerge, this aircraft dived and dropped four depth charges just ahead of the vessel's swirl at a height of 50 feet.

After attacking this U-boat, the aircraft circled the area and then returned to the USS *Bogue* when the limit of its fuel was reached.[121]

Meanwhile, the escort of HX 239 was being reinforced before the unsuspecting convoy had its first contact with the *Mosel* line. On the first leg of the voyage to Great Britain, air cover had been provided to HX 239 by RCAF aircraft based in Newfoundland. However, just before the convoy passed out of range of the Canadian aircraft, it was joined on 21 May at 49°17′N, 40°30′W by the 4th Escort Group consisting of the escort carrier HMS *Archer;* the destroyers HMS *Onslaught,* HMS *Faulknor,* HMS *Impulsive;* and the sloop HMS *Pelican.* HMS *Archer* took station within the convoy where it remained except when operating aircraft, while the ships of its escort joined the screen of the convoy.[122]

The next day, 22 May, the escorts of HX 239 began to pick up numerous HF/DF bearings in the vicinity of the convoy. These HF/DF intercepts revealed the presence not only of a number of U-boats near HX 239 but also of the eastbound convoy ON 184 to the north. Because of the HF/DF activity, HMS *Archer* sent out a Swordfish. Aircraft A/819 conducted a *cobra* (a search around the perimeter of the convoy) during the course of which the plane sighted some of ON 184's ships about 30 miles to the north of HX 239. Aircraft A/819 was relieved by aircraft F/819, which sighted two corvettes belonging to ON 184's escort about 20 miles on the port beam of HX 239. About 10 miles astern of the two corvettes, aircraft F/819, "using cloud cover," approached within 2 miles of a U-boat which "did not show signs of submerging, but commenced to zig-zag." At this moment, the plane received a radio message from HMS *Archer* that additional aircraft were being sent, and the pilot decided to await reinforcements before attacking. But then the U-boat began to dive, and aircraft F/819 dropped two depth charges in front of the swirl of the submerging U-boat. Aircraft F/819 then circled the area until an escort arrived to sit on the U-boat.[123]

The U-boat attacked by aircraft F/819 was the U-305,[124] part of the southern wing of the *Mosel* patrol line. Before being attacked by aircraft F/819, the submarine reported sighting a destroyer, probably part of ON 184's escort. The U-218 also reported that it had to submerge when a destroyer came out of a rain squall. And at 1726 the U-569 radioed that "SINCE 1000 CONTINUALLY UNDERWATER BY AIR.

DESTROYER(S), AIRCRAFT BOMBS. HYDROPHONE, EXPLOSIVE LO-
CATION, DEPTH CHARGES. SOUTHWESTBOUND CONVOY ACCORDING
TO HYDROPHONE BEARING AT 1730." This was the first sighting report that notified the BdU that the U-boats of the *Mosel* group had
intercepted a convoy other than HX 239—ON 184. These radio messages prompted the BdU to issue this stern order to the U-boats that
formed the southern portion of the *Mosel* patrol line: "HALT! STOP IN
AREA REACHED."[125]

The *Mosel* U-boats hardly needed a warning that they were involved in an unusual action. On 22 May, the patrol line had not only
unexpectedly intercepted two different Allied convoys but also found
itself facing planes from two different aircraft carriers, one escorting
each of the convoys. That day aircraft from the USS *Bogue*, attached
to westbound convoy On 184, attacked four U-boats. In the face of
antiaircraft fire, a TBF Avenger attacked a U-boat on the surface
with machine-gun fire and four depth charges at 0540. This U-boat
was most likely damaged, and the Americans described the early-
morning attack as "probably a kill." Another U-boat was sighted by
a TBF Avenger at 0950 some 16 miles ahead of ON 184. The
U-boat was attacked with depth charges, again in the face of antiaircraft fire. Just after the four depth charges exploded alongside the
U-boat, it dived. A third U-boat was sighted and attacked with gunfire and depth charges at 1230 by an American plane astern of the
convoy.

At 1727A the USS *Bogue* obtained an HF/DF bearing at 160° from
the convoy. A plane was sent down this bearing, and the U-569 was
sighted at a range of 20 miles from the convoy. The aircraft circled
into the clouds and then attacked this U-boat from the stern. The
U-569 was taken by surprise and four depth charges—two on each
side—exploded, straddling the U-boat. The U-569 dived and the
American aircraft then dropped a smoke marker before departing for
the USS *Bogue*. A second TBF Avenger arrived in the area and was
circling the smoke marker when the U-569 surfaced about thirty
minutes after the attack. The American aircraft immediately attacked, dropping four depth charges which exploded alongside the
enemy vessel. The bow of the U-569 was seen to rise at an angle out
of the water before settling back into the sea. When the American
aircrew saw the crew of the U-boat coming out of the conning tower

of the U-569, the U-boat was taken under machine-gun fire which kept the Germans inside the vessel to prevent them from scuttling. Between bursts of gunfire, a number of Germans appeared on the deck of the U-569 waving white flags. The surrender was reported to the USS *Bogue* and the aircraft continued to circle. HMCS *St. Laurent* arrived just as the U-569 disappeared into the sea, followed by two underwater explosions. Twenty-five Germans, including the commander of the U-569, were then picked up by the Canadian warship.[126]

After dark ON 184's course was changed from southwest to west to hinder any U-boats which might be shadowing the convoy. Even though aircraft conducted searches to the depth of 60 miles around ON 184 on 23 May, there were no more contacts with U-boats.[127] There was no submarine pursuit of ON 184 in part because the U-boats had been overpowered by American carrier aircraft. But the Germans were also hampered because their communications intelligence system remained ignorant of the presence of ON 184 until 21 May. By that time, in the opinion of the BdU, "operations on this convoy were hopeless in view of the boats being too far behind."[128]

However, to the south of ON 184, HX 239 was still in contact with the U-boats on 23 May. Just before midnight on 22 May Commander M. J. Evans, RN, of the eastbound convoy's escort, thought that HX 239 had not been sighted by the U-boats. Nevertheless, at dawn on 23 May , Evans requested HMS *Archer* to fly off two Swordfish aircraft to conduct patrols astern and off the beam of HX 239. Shortly afterwards, a VLR B-24 Liberator, aircraft P/86, appeared over the convoy. At 0650, the Liberator was sent down an HF/DF bearing of 355° which had been obtained by HMS *Keppel*. Aircraft P/86 sighted a surfaced U-boat which it attacked and forced to dive. HMS *Onslaught* was then sent to hunt for this U-boat, which was not found. Just as he was about to return to Iceland, the Liberator's pilot then reported to Evans that he had sighted a second U-boat which was being attacked by a Swordfish that forced the enemy vessel to dive.[129]

The attacking Swordfish, aircraft F/819, had been searching down an HF/DF bearing before sighting the U-boat on the surface. On seeing the Swordfish, the U-boat dived to periscope depth. Aircraft F/819 dropped four depth charges, and the aircrew "saw the periscope feather pass between the two center explosions of the stick."

Meanwhile, another Swordfish and a Martlet fighter were flown off HMS *Archer* to support aircraft F/819. As they proceeded toward the area where aircraft F/819 had forced a U-boat to dive, the two planes sighted another U-boat. Both attacked immediately. The Martlet, being much faster than the Swordfish, came in first with machine-gun fire, forcing the U-boat to dive. Twenty-five seconds after the U-boat had submerged, the Swordfish attacked with depth charges. After this attack the Swordfish remained in the area for forty-five minutes, but nothing was sighted.[130]

At 1002 a third Swordfish, aircraft B/819, was flown off HMS *Archer* to search down a bearing of 206°. While conducting this search, the plane sighted a U-boat at a range of 10 miles. Using cloud cover, aircraft B/819 got within a mile of the U-boat (the U-752) before diving to attack. The Swordfish employed a new weapon which had not been used before in the Battle of the Atlantic — an air-to-surface rocket. Four salvos of two rockets each were fired. The first two rockets hit the water 150 yards short of the U-752, and the second two hit the surface of the sea about 30 feet short of the U-boat's conning tower. The third salvo landed in the water 10 feet short and aft of the conning tower, but the fourth salvo, fired at a range of 200 yards, hit the U-752 on the water line about 20 feet forward of the rudder as it dived bow first at an angle of 30°. The U-752 continued to dive and then slowly returned to the surface, beginning "to circle to port exuding large quantities of oil." The crew of the U-752 then manned the vessel's antiaircraft guns, and aircraft B/819 retreated out of range, requesting assistance. One minute later a Martlet fighter aircraft appeared on the scene and attacked the U-752 with machine-gun fire, killing the captain and gun crew. HMS *Escapade* arrived just as the U-752 sank and picked up thirteen Germans who had escaped from the submarine. An estimated twenty to thirty Germans were left in the water by the British, but later some of these sailors were rescued by the U-91. No further U-boats were sighted by the ships and aircraft of HX 239's escort and during the afternoon, HF/DF bearings "indicated that the submarines were dropping further and further astern and [because of the] heavy air cover failed to make any sightings."[131]

The BdU ended the battle for HX 239 at 0934Z on 23 May when it ordered the U-boats to "DISCONTINUE OPERATION ON NORTHEAST

CONVOY, SET OFF TO THE WEST."[132] The BdU really had no choice but to end the operation against HX 239, for a steady stream of radio reports during the early hours of 23 May made it clear that the U-boats were achieving little or nothing while being hammered by Allied aircraft.[133] Like those U-boats which had operated against ON 184, the U-boats attempting to attack HX 239 were overwhelmed by Allied air power. The commander of the escort of HX 239 contended after the battle that the main body of the convoy had not even been sighted by the U-boats.[134] Certainly the U-boats in the operations against ON 184 and HX 239 had been totally defeated. No Allied ships had been sunk, while the U-569 and U-752 were destroyed.

The almost total lack of success for U-boats during April and May of 1943—culminating in the defeats in the battles against convoys SC 130, ON 184, and HX 239—forced the Germans to rethink and then to recast the whole U-boat campaign in the Atlantic. In the fighting between the U-boats and the convoys along the North Atlantic convoy route between Great Britain and North America, the U-boats had not had a major success in a convoy battle since the beginning of April. In the period 10 April to 23 May the Germans had fought some twelve convoy battles in the North Atlantic along the Great Britain–North American convoy route and had sunk only twenty-nine ships (HMS *Beverley, Ingerfire, Lancastrian Prince, Pacific Grove, Fresno City, Ulysses, Fort Rampart, Ashantian, Wenstead, Scebeli, Amerika, Robert Grey, McKeesport, Harbury, West Maximus, Harperley, Bristol City, Wentworth, Dolius, West Market, Selvistan, Charinda, Bonde, Antigone, Grado, Standanger, Brand, Aymeric, Fort Concord*) while losing twenty-two U-boats (U-175, U-189, U-191, U-203, U-630, U-638, U-125, U-531, U-438, U-186, U-84, U-456, U-266, U-657, U-753, U-640, U-954, U-209, U-381, U-258, U-569, U-752) to the escorts. Roughly one U-boat had been sunk for every one-and-a-quarter Allied ships lost in these battles. At the time, the Germans calculated that they had lost fourteen U-boats in the Atlantic in February, thirteen in March, twelve in April, and thirty-one in the first twenty-two days of May. Thus, even according to German calculations, the exchange rate in May was one U-boat for every 10,000 tons of Allied shipping sunk. The BdU concluded that these "losses in May have, therefore, reached an impossible height."[135]

During that month, the BdU estimated that twenty U-boats had been "almost certainly" lost to Allied aircraft; six more "possibly" destroyed by aircraft; and eight U-boats sunk by surface escorts. Therefore, the BdU concluded that aircraft "played an important part in causing such high losses." Further, even before the disastrous engagements with the escorts of On 184 and HX 239, the BdU was convinced that the key to the Allies' success was their ability to locate U-boats at sea by means of some kind of location device unknown to the Germans. On 21 May, the BdU drew up a memorandum entitled "Effects of Radar used by Enemy Forces in U-boat Warfare and Necessary Countermeasures"[136] which stated that the Allies had some kind of radar and/or infrared location device which gave a single Allied aircraft the ability to discover the location of an entire U-boat patrol line, thus giving Allied convoys the ability to avoid the U-boats. This mythical device also enabled Allied escorts and aircraft to detect a U-boat on the surface as the vessel approached a convoy. The result was that "the U-boat is deprived of its most effective characteristic by radar location, i.e. that it cannot be sighted."[137]

This memorandum then directed various technical commands of the German navy, such as the Communications Research Department and Communications Experimental Command, to eliminate "all pulses emanating from the U-boat" which the enemy could use to locate the vessel and either to destroy, divert, or disturb "the pulses sent out by the enemy for the purposes of location" of a U-boat. To achieve these objectives, it was further ordered that research be undertaken to determine the nature of the radar and infrared devices used by the Allies to detect U-boats so that the required jammers, detectors, and decoys required to counter these devices could be produced. While "the re-establishment of the 'invisibility' of the U-boat" remained their first priority, agencies such as the Naval Weapons Department were also ordered to develop the weapons required to "fight" off Allied aircraft and surface vessels.[138]

The radar memorandum of 21 May shows that the Germans did not even consider the possibility that the Allies were reading their command radio transmissions. Apparently the BdU, like all other German command authorities, simply accepted as axiomatic the assertion of the specialists in communications security that German codes were so good that they would be impossible to break. And, unlike American naval intelligence, German naval intelligence never conducted a proper investigation into U-boat radio communication security.[139] If the Germans had seriously considered the possibility that the Allies were reading their coded command radio communications, World War II might have turned out a little differently.

But the radar memorandum of 21 May betrayed another intellectual limitation of the BdU and its technical advisers. Allied radar was better than German radar, but an all-seeing device capable of locating all the U-boats on patrol line in the mid-Atlantic was far beyond the limits of 1943 technology. The Allies were just not that far ahead of the Germans in technology of radar that year.

The problem confronting the Germans in May 1943 was far more complex than some "secret" radar weapon. Because of the limitations of existing U-boat technology, the German vessels just could not overcome Allied weapon systems, intelligence advantages, and tactics. After the war, Doenitz, referring to the May 1943 crisis, said that because of Allied air power, wolf pack tactics were "no longer possible" unless the Germans "succeeded in radically increasing the fighting power of the U-boats." In May 1943 the Germans needed a revolution in U-boat technology, not just an increase in the fighting capability of existing U-boats. The Germans, however, had missed their chances for a revolution in U-boat technology when they failed to develop the Walter U-boat, which could remain submerged almost indefinitely while sprinting at high speeds.[140]

Considering all the circumstances, the BdU felt compelled to break off U-boat operations in the North Atlantic against convoys running between Great Britain and North America until new weapons were developed to counter Allied radar, aircraft, and surface escorts. Those U-boats with enough fuel were ordered to proceed to an area southwest of the Azores to operate against Allied convoys running between the United States and Gibraltar. The BdU believed this to be the one region in the North Atlantic where Allied anti-U-boat aircraft could not operate. At the same time, those U-boats lacking fuel for operations southwest of the Azores were directed to remain at sea in the North Atlantic, there to deceive the Allies with fake radio transmissions as to the true deployment of the submarines.

This was an admission of defeat for as the BdU noted in its war diary:

> This decision denotes a temporary abandonment of the fundamental principles which have so far governed the U-boat campaign. The change of policy is dictated by the need to avoid unnecessary losses in a period when our weapons are shown to be at a disadvantage. It must be realized, however, that as soon as our boats have been equipped with new weapons, the battle in the North Atlantic—the decisive area—will be resumed.[141]

Chapter 5

Escort Carriers and U-Boats

June–September 1943

The German decision to suspend U-boat operations against the North Atlantic convoys, running between North America and Great Britain, was an admission of defeat. By this order of 24 May 1943, the Germans conceded their submarines were incapable of overcoming or eluding the escorts and successfully attacking Allied convoys in the North Atlantic.

What could the Germans do next, if U-boat operations in the North Atlantic were to be suspended? It appeared that it would take several months to develop and deploy new weapons required for the U-boats to combat the Allied escorts successfully. It was thought that the Walter U-boat, with its high underwater speed, could not enter the U-boat service until late 1944. One alternative would have been to suspend U-boat operations in the Atlantic until the vessels could be reequipped with the weapons required to overcome the Allied escorts or replaced by boats of the Walter design. This course was rejected by Doenitz and his advisers who reasoned that if the U-boats conceded the battle in the Atlantic, the Allies could then redeploy all the men, ships, and aircraft used to combat the U-boats directly against Germany. There were other considerations as well. There were not enough bombproof shelters to accommodate the whole fleet, and if the U-boats were simply recalled and remained idle in port, the vessels themselves would be vulnerable to Allied air attack. Further, the morale of the U-boat crews would also suffer from a long period of idleness, and the U-boat service as a whole would lose its familiarity with the latest Allied anti-U-boat techniques. In view of these considerations, Doenitz decided that he had no choice but to continue the battle until the U-boats could be equipped with new weapons even if "there was no longer any chance of major success" and there was a good possibility that the U-boats would suffer heavy losses. Years later Doenitz stated that this was "the most difficult decision of the war."[1]

Instead of permanently suspending the submarine offensive in the Atlantic, the BdU decided that the U-boats would simply be deployed to attack convoys sailing between North America and Gibraltar. The Allies had been running such convoys at regular intervals for about six months and the BdU knew the times of departures on each side of the Atlantic, although the Germans had little knowledge of the mid-Atlantic courses followed by the Allied ships. Although several previous operations against North American-Gibraltar convoys had been failures, now the Germans had no choice.

The area west of the Azores was the only region in the Atlantic where the U-boats could hope for even minor success, for it was the only major shipping route beyond the range of Allied shore-based anti-U-boat aircraft.[2] Thus, on 24 May the BdU ordered sixteen U-boats (U-569, U-641, U-228, U-603, U-642, U-336, U-558, U-666, U-211, U-608, U-221, U-953, U-951, U-232, U-435, U-217) to proceed to an area southwest of the Azores.[3] However, the German belief that shifting operations southward to the United States-Gibraltar convoy routes would protect the U-boats from Allied aircraft was a major miscalculation, for these convoys were to be the beneficiaries of expanded Allied use of carrier-based, not land-based, aircraft. The US Navy was responsible for the protection of North American-Gibraltar convoys, and the Americans intended to guard these convoys by a new strategy based on hunter-killer groups built around escort carriers. This was a departure from the British doctrine of protecting a convoy by close escort, which occasionally included an escort carrier supported by shore-based VLR aircraft. By contrast, the US Navy intended to protect the convoys themselves not only with a close surface escort but also with escort groups built around carriers that would provide distant support. These carrier groups could not only provide close escort when convoys moved through waters infested with U-boats but could also provide defensive, distant escort. They could send out planes to search for German submarine wolf packs in advance of the convoy's arrival, attacking and sinking U-boats before the convoy's merchant ships approached a region where the BdU had stationed patrol lines.[4] The success of this strategy, of course, depended in a large part on accurate and effective communications intelligence to locate U-boats.

By June 1943 the Americans boasted both the escort carriers and the communications intelligence needed to institute a strategy of this type. Indeed, British intelligence authorities argued that if information from the decryption of enemy radio communications was used to target U-boats for sinking by these escort carrier groups, the Germans might finally realize that the Allies owed part of their success against the U-boats to breaking the supposedly impenetrable German codes and not to some mysterious secret weapon.[5] However, the Americans disagreed with this assessment and disregarded British objections to the hunter-killer strategy.

At the beginning of June American naval intelligence officers inflicted a new and decisive blow when they proved conclusively that the Germans were reading Naval Cipher No. 3. On 28 May Commander Kenneth A. Knowles, USN, the head of American anti-U-boat intelligence, issued an intelligence summary pointing out that the Germans apparently had foreknowledge of the route of the freighter *Sydney Star* which was proceeding independently from Montevideo to the Clyde. It was thought that the Germans had obtained this information from either agents in South America or "a break of the route signal to Cominch." This conclusion was based on a decrypted German message stating: "SIDNEY STAR LEFT MONTEVIDEO 12 MAY FOR THE CLYDE VIA NAV. SQ. FK 4391 AND DS 4212: WILL ARRIVE (CLYDE) 1 JUNE. SPEED 14.5."[6] The transmission of this message in this form was a serious lapse of communications security on the part of the Germans. This phraseology pinpointed the source of the information as a message employing Naval Cipher No. 3. This nonmachine cipher was employed by American, Canadian, and British forces involved in protection of the North Atlantic convoys, but its primary use was in transmissions between New York and Great Britain.

In the next few days there were several other breaches in German communications security showing that the Germans were reading Cipher No. 3. American intelligence deduced that the Germans had knowledge of the route for stragglers from convoy HX 240. Next, American naval intelligence read a decrypt from the BdU, dated 27

May, stating that "AMERICAN SUB WAS IN AK 5445 ON 24 MAY AT 2100B PROCEEDING TO ITS PATROL AREA NEAR AK 7657. ANOTHER AMERICAN SUB WAS ON PATROL ON 24TH AT 2100B NEAR AD 7182." From this radio message the Americans concluded that the submarine warning "CONF 241705 COMINCH NCR" was compromised. This too had been sent in Naval Cipher No. 3. The Americans concluded further from studying additional decrypts that the Germans had read another Allied radio dispatch giving the positions of the American submarines *Herring, Hado,* and *Hake* as well as the order directing the SS *Lombardy* to deviate from its course. All of these messages had been sent in Naval Cipher No. 3.[7]

The Allies had long suspected that cipher was not secure as the official account of the matter explained, because "USN-British Naval Communications were so complex, and often repetitious," no one authority knew "how many times a thing might be sent and by whom—and in what system." Thus it was extremely difficult to prove beyond a doubt from what source the Germans had gained a particular piece of information. Perhaps the German reading of Naval Cipher No. 3 would have been discovered sooner, US Naval intelligence concluded, if the Allied "Combined Communications system had been less obscure and had there been closer cooperation between the British and the U.S. in such matters."[8] Despite these factors, the Allies began a gradual elimination of Naval Cipher No. 3 on 10 June.[9] When the Allies began to change their codes, the Germans did not suffer a blackout, but rather a fade out, for the large number of users of the cipher made conversion to new systems more time-consuming than would otherwise have been the case. This was a major defeat for the Germans. After the war the US Navy estimated that 70 percent of the convoys intercepted by the Germans between 1 December 1942 and 31 May 1943 were located by intelligence obtained from decryption of Naval Cipher No. 3.[10]

The planners of the BdU were still confident of their intelligence advantage when they set up their newest patrol line. The sixteen U-boats ordered on 24 May to assemble southwest of the Azores had been joined by the U-92. On 26 May this group was directed to form a patrol line, code named *Trutz,* running from 38°45'N, 43°26'W to 32°03'N, 43°26'W by 0008B on 1 June. The U-boats were to maintain a distance of 25 miles between each vessel. (This order was not decrypted by the Allies until 0145 on 7 June.) Three days later the BdU informed the *Trutz* group that an eastbound convoy with a speed of 8 to 8.5 knots was expected between 1 and 6 June. The U-boats were ordered: "DO NOT LET YOURSELVES BE SEEN. TRANSMIT ONLY IF YOU HAVE BEEN OBSERVED" and at the same time directed not to attack another Allied convoy consisting mainly of landing craft that would be in the area. On 1 June the U-boats were ordered to attack an expected westbound convoy, and at 1230 the patrol line was ordered to move 90 miles to the south. The Allies did not decode the first of the orders detailing the movements of their convoys until 1325 on 4 June, and their decryption was a significant confirmation that the Germans were obtaining their intelligence on North American-Gibraltar convoys from reading Naval Cipher No. 3.[11]

On 31 May the task group, TG 21.12, sailed from Argentia, Newfoundland, "to operate offensively in appropriate areas in support of African convoys." This force was commanded by Captain Giles E. Short, USN, and consisted of the escort carrier USS *Bogue* and the "flush deck" American destroyers *Clemson, Osmond Ingram, George E. Badger,* and *Greene.* Short's orders called for TG 21.12 to protect America-Gibraltar convoys in the mid-Atlantic while hunting and attacking U-boats "as long as logistic requirements permitted." This meant that the ships of TG 21.12 would have to be positioned so that the aircraft of the USS *Bogue* could, if necessary, support the convoys while at the same time conducting offensive searches for U-boats. The general area in which a U-boat or U-boats were operating would be determined by means of intelligence from decrypted German radio messages. Within this region the U-boats would then be hunted down using D/F, HF/DF, radar, and aircraft. A limiting factor to the task force's operations was the fuel capacity of the destroyers. Short decided that the destroyers must always have on board enough fuel either to reach a friendly port or an Allied convoy in case the USS *Bogue* was sunk.[12]

During the evening of 1 June TG 21.12 arrived in the vicinity of 40°N, 50°W, north and west of the position of the *Trutz* patrol line. There were now three convoys in the vicinity: GUS-7A proceeding west at 29°59'N, 43°45'W, UGS-9 heading east at 30°10'N, 60°08'W, and the eastbound landing craft in convoy Flight 10 (a group of nineteen British landing craft infantry) at 32°53'N, 58°55'W. Intelligence based on the decryption of the BdU's order of 24 May placed the main body of the U-boats within a 300-mile circle centered at 35°N, 50°W.[13] To Short there appeared to be two alternative courses of action: either to steam into the center of the circle, begin hunting for the U-boats, and then move south to be in a position to support UGS-9; or to pass through the western part of the circle reaching a position to support directly either UGS-9 or GUS-7A. On the afternoon of 2 June the American officer decided to pass through the western part of the circle using aircraft to search a path 120 miles wide for U-boats while refueling the task group's destroyers.[14]

On 2 June the ships and aircraft of TG 21.12 swept south, searching for U-boats, while GUS-7A was routed southward to avoid the suspected concentration of U-boats.[15] No U-boats were sighted. On 3 June the task group searched to the eastward in front of convoys UGS-9 and Flight 10, moving toward the center of the suspected concentration of U-boats—"hoping to locate and develop" those enemy vessels which might be ahead of the convoys. Again there was no contact with the U-boats and TG 21.12 withdrew to the northeast at night.[16]

On 4 June the hunt for the U-boats was continued. During the morning and early afternoon aircraft searched in front of the American warships. At 1815 five TBF Avengers were launched to conduct searches on an arc of 350° and 150° from the ship to a distance of 80 miles.[17] At 1842 two TBF Avengers searching down an HF/DF bearing sighted the U-228 50 miles away from the USS *Bogue*. Both aircraft dived on the U-boat, taking it by surprise and attacking from a height of 50 feet with a total of eight depth charges which were seen to explode around the U-boat, throwing water into the air. Still, the U-228 escaped by diving.[18]

While returning to the USS *Bogue*, twenty-seven minutes after the attack, another TBF Avenger sighted the U-603. The U-boat was about 50 miles north of the escort carrier and 10 miles south of convoy Flight 10. The American aircraft immediately attacked the U-603, passing over the U-boat from stern to bow at a height of 50 feet and dropping four depth charges which exploded across the bow of the enemy vessel. As the TBF Avenger turned to attack with machine guns, the U-603 opened fire with antiaircraft guns. The American aircraft then attacked the U-boat twice more with machine gunfire, but as the TBF Avenger was turning to mount a third strafing attack, the U-603 submerged.[19]

Only one minute after the U-603 had been sighted, another aircraft from the USS *Bogue* sighted the U-641. The U-boat was on a bearing of 112° from the escort carrier at a range of about 25 miles. The TBF Avenger took the U-641 by surprise, diving out of the sun at a speed of 200 knots toward the port quarter of the U-boat. However, when the release point for the depth charges was reached, the pilot thought the aircraft was going too fast for an attack and passed over the U-boat without striking, then circled and climbed to try again. The Germans manned the vessel's guns and the second attack was made in the face of antiaircraft fire. Two depth charges never left the aircraft's bomb bay and the other two exploded along the starboard side of the U-boat between its bow and conning tower. After this attack the U-641 began circling to starboard and appeared down at the stern. The U-boat did not submerge, and the American aircraft radioed the USS *Bogue* for assistance and continued to circle the enemy vessel. Twenty-two minutes later another TBF Avenger appeared over the U-641. Both aircraft then dived on the U-boat in the face of antiaircraft fire. While one Avenger attempted to distract the attention of the enemy gunners, the other aircraft dropped four depth charges which exploded along the port side of the U-boat. Just after this attack the U-641 submerged. The crews of the American aircraft thought that the U-boat had been destroyed, but it had escaped.[20]

At dusk on 4 June TG 21.12 withdrew to the westward for the night. From the positions of the three U-boats which had been attacked that evening by aircraft, Short concluded that he had found a U-boat patrol line "extending from about 350T to 170T."[21] On the basis of this conclusion, he decided to search for U-boats the next day southward along the suspected patrol line in the path of convoy UGS-9. Upon receiving reports of the attacks by the USS *Bogue*'s aircraft, the BdU concluded that the "expected America-Gibraltar convoy is approaching," but that the convoy's position could be either "immediately off the patrol line or 200 miles W. of it." In Doenitz's absence, the BdU decided to reduce the distance between each

U-boat to 20 miles, but not to move the *Trutz* submarines north or south. Such a redeployment could make it easier for the expected convoy to "evade" the *Trutz* U-boats by passing either north or south of their patrol line. When Doenitz learned of this decision he strongly disagreed, saying that after news of the aircraft attacks he would have ordered the U-boats eastward under cover of darkness "so as to prevent at all costs the convoy from passing the patrol line."[22]

At 0736 on 5 June aircraft from the USS *Bogue* began to search southward along the axis of the suspected patrol line.[23] At 0850 a returning TBF Avenger and F4F Wildcat sighted the U-217 on the surface at a range of 63 miles from the USS *Bogue*. The U-217 opened fire and the American aircraft attacked, with the F4F Wildcat strafing the U-217 three times from a height of 25 feet. During the first run, a fire broke out in the U-boat's conning tower and the vessel began to turn to starboard. After the third strafing attack, the pilot of the TBF Avenger saw that the U-boat's antiaircraft fire had ceased. He then attacked coming out of the sun and dropped four depth charges which straddled the U-boat forward of the conning tower. Just after the depth charges exploded, the Americans saw the U-boat disappear, bow first, under the surface of the sea.[24] After the sinking of the U-217, further searches by the USS *Bogue*'s aircraft on 5 and 6 June produced no contacts with the enemy, even though an HF/DF bearing "indicated" that there was a U-boat to the south of TG 21.12. The USS *Bogue* and its escorts then moved south to cover convoy UGS-9 "directly."[25]

By attacking the U-228, U-603, and U-641 on 4 June and sinking the U-217 on 5 June, TG 21.12 neutralized the southern end of the *Trutz* patrol line. Even though the Germans' communications intelligence gave them advance knowledge of the route of convoy Flight 10's route and possibly also of GUS-7A, neither of these convoys nor convoy UGS-9 was attacked.[26] Convoys GUS-7A and UGS-9 were routed around the southern end of the *Trutz* patrol line, while Flight 10 passed through a hole punched in the line by the American carrier aircraft attack on the U-603.[27]

The BdU ignored the significance of this episode, preferring to believe that the convoys had evaded the *Trutz* patrol line through sheer luck, either passing through it unnoticed or sailing to the north or south of the U-boats. After dark on 5 June the Germans dissolved the patrol line, sending the U-92 and the U-569 back to base and ordering the other U-boats of the *Trutz* group to leave the area and refuel from the U-488.[28] This refueling operation was to begin at 37°57'N, 44°30'W, and the U-boats were notified that the U-488 would "ALWAYS STAND BY AT PROVISIONING POINT AT EXACTLY 1200B," ready to supply each U-boat with ninety cubic meters of fuel plus spare parts for its metox radar detectors. The U-boats were to maintain radio silence and were warned not to use beacon signals to effect a meeting with the U-488 until two days had passed. When the fueling had been completed the next day, the U-boats were ordered to take up stations west of the Azores.

The information contained in these orders would have been a gold mine to American naval intelligence, but at this time the Allies were encountering delays in decrypting German radio messages. The orders for disbanding the *Trutz* patrol line, refueling from the U-488, and taking station west of the Azores were not decrypted until 22 and 23 June.[29] Thus, ignorant of the redeployment of the U-boats belonging to the *Trutz* group, TG 21.12 provided cover to UGS-9 during the night of 5 June and the daylight hours of 6 June. Short then "estimated that the most likely area of [U-boat activity] was latitude 29-00 to 35-00N and 42-00 to 44-00W." Therefore, on the evening of 6 June the USS *Bogue* and its escorts left UGS-9 and steamed westward, conducting a fruitless aircraft search to the west at dawn on 7 June. Believing that the convoy had been sighted and that it was threatened by a U-boat concentration to the northeast, Short then ordered TG 21.12 to sweep eastward along the 30th parallel. No U-boats were sighted on 7 June and TG 21.12 made contact with UGS-9 on 8 June. HF/DF activity that day convinced Short that these signals were radio sighting reports from U-boats still in contact with UGS-9 and that TG 21.12 must "endeavor to keep the submarines down and to prevent trailing or the forming of concentrations which might develop into a pack attack on the convoy." To this end the aircraft of the USS *Bogue* conducted searches around and in front of the convoy.[30]

There was no contact with the U-boats on 8 June until the mid-afternoon, when the *Bogue*'s HF/DF picked up a bearing of 242° on a radio transmission. A TBF Avenger was sent down this bearing and sighted the U-758 at a range of 10 miles from UGS-9.[31] When the U-758 was sighted, Short thought that it was shadowing UGS-9 for a wolf pack. However, unknown to the commander of TG 21.12, the only U-boats operating in the area were those of the *Trutz* group, at that time some miles to the west of UGS-9. The U-758's encounter with UGS-9 was entirely accidental, for the submarine was outward-bound to the Caribbean.[32]

After sighting the U-758, the TBF Avenger circled and then attacked by diving on the U-boat from the direction of the sun. As the aircraft dived it was taken under "extremely heavy tracer fire" by the U-boat. It was no accident that the American plane found the U-758 a more formidable foe than anticipated: in the U-758, the Avenger had unwittingly taken on the first U-boat fitted with a quadruple mount of 20mm guns for the specific purpose of fighting off aircraft. Still, at a height of 60 feet, the plane dropped four depth charges which appeared to straddle the U-758 aft of the conning tower. The U-boat's stern was lifted out of the water by the explosions, and the American aircrew saw "3 to 5" sailors in the water, thought to have been blown overboard by the explosions. The aircraft circled and then attacked the enemy vessel again with machine-gun fire. The antiaircraft fire was heavy, but it appeared to be silenced by the machine-gun bursts. After this attack the aircraft circled the U-758 which was steaming in circles at a speed of 4 or 5 knots and appeared to be unable to submerge. After some difficulty, the USS *Bogue* was radioed and reinforcements requested.[33]

Three more aircraft came from the USS *Bogue* to assist in the attack on the U-758. The first to arrive on the scene was another TBF Avenger which immediately dived from a height of 2,500 feet to attack the U-boat. The U-758 withheld its antiaircraft fire until the aircraft had closed to within a range of 250 yards, then opened fire and hit the attacking aircraft in the engine, starboard wing, and wheel, and wounded a crew member. Nevertheless, the attack was pressed home, and depth charges exploded around the stern of the U-boat. Because of the battle damage, the aircraft returned to the USS *Bogue*.[34]

After the second depth charge attack the U-758, though damaged, could still make headway and the vessel's antiaircraft guns still worked. A third TBF Avenger continued to circle around the U-758 awaiting reinforcements. After some minutes it was joined by a F4F Wildcat fighter which began to strafe the U-758. The first attack was carried out with heavy antiaircraft fire which was quickly silenced by the plane's machine-gun bursts. Just after the F4F Wildcat made its third strafing attack, the U-758 began to submerge. As the U-758 began to dive, the TBF Avenger attacked, dropping four depth charges as the U-boat's conning tower disappeared under the water. The two American aircraft circled approximately eight minutes after the U-boat had submerged, and they saw a large air bubble rise out of the water as the U-758 surfaced. The U-boat opened antiaircraft fire on the two American aircraft and began to move forward very slowly, trailing oil. The U-758 was then strafed two more times by the F4F Wildcat before slowly submerging, leaving a trail of oil in its wake. Owing to a confusion of radio messages among the American forces, the destroyer USS *Clemson* did not arrive in the area and begin to hunt the U-758 until forty minutes after the U-boat had submerged for a second time. Several hours after the end of the action, the U-758 radioed the BdU: "BOAT HEAVILY DAMAGED, IS SINKING,"[35] but the U-758 did not sink and finally escaped from TG 21.12.

The American attacks on the U-758 were neither very effective nor skillful. The aircraft attacked the enemy vessel alone and without coordination or cooperation between air and surface forces. Fearing an attack on UGS-9, Short would not commit more aircraft to attack the U-758 and held his last four TBF Avengers on the deck of the USS *Bogue* in order to conduct an anti-U-boat search just before sunset.[36] The U-758, on the other hand, employed skillful handling of antiaircraft guns and cagey tactics to escape destruction. Ironically, the U-758's good luck proved unfortunate for the Germans in the long run. The successful defense of the U-758 convinced the BdU that U-boats equipped with quadruple 20mm antiaircraft guns could beat the attacks from carrier aircraft.[37] This encouraged the disastrous German policy of requiring U-boats to remain on the surface and fight back against Allied aircraft.[38]

The most important immediate consequence of the action with the U-758 was the delay and confusion that ultimately prevented the American task group from making effective contact with the main body of the *Trutz* patrol line. Short's initial misapprehension that the

U-758's radio transmissions were a call for attack on the convoy by a U-boat wolf pack was reinforced in the early evening of 8 June when the USS *Bogue*'s HF/DF equipment intercepted more U-boat transmissions. These convinced Short that "there remained the danger—and at the time it seemed a probability—of concentrations forming ahead in preparation for an attack on the night of June 9th or 10th." As a result, TG 21.12 proceeded eastward, guarding UGS-9 from possible attack until the evening of 10 June, when a land-based B-24 Liberator appeared over the convoy. Only then, at 2025Z, did the USS *Bogue* and its escorts leave convoy UGS-9 and head west along the 30th parallel toward "the center of reported concentrations of submarines," the real location of Short's phantom wolf pack.[39]

Short was not solely to blame for this delay. On 8 June the Allies were not decrypting German radio messages promptly and had no clear understanding either of the deployment of the U-boats or of the problems created for the BdU by the crippling of the U-758. In the late evening of 8 June the BdU ordered the U-118, the U-460, and the U-92 to assist the U-758, whose position was given to rescuers as 29°09'N, 33°32'W. The U-118 was a minelaying U-boat being used as a tanker with orders to refuel the U-333 and the U-592—two outward-bound vessels sailing under orders to conduct operations in distant seas. The U-460 was a U-boat tanker returning from the South Atlantic and carrying on board some extra fuel which it had been ordered to turn over to the U-118 before returning to base. These four vessels—the two tankers and the outward-bound U-boats—were scheduled to meet at 30°45'N, 33°40'W. The Allies, however, did not even begin decoding these orders until the early afternoon of 11 June.[40]

These lags in decoding German radio transmissions meant that the Allies missed several golden opportunities to gain a clear picture of the BdU's plans and the hasty revisions of those plans after the U-758 accidentally encountered the aircraft from the *Bogue*. At 0707 on 9 June, for instance, the tanker U-118 sent a message acknowledging its position. The BdU then radioed another U-boat, the U-214, to refuel the U-333, leaving the U-118 to refuel the U-92. These orders were not read by the Allies until 13 June. Next the U-118 radioed that it could not find the U-758 and then later that

day it radioed that it had found the damaged U-boat. On 10 June
the U-640 reported that it had met the U-118 and the U-758 and
turned over the extra fuel to the U-118 before beginning to escort
the U-758 back to Europe. The U-118 then received orders to proceed to 30°45'N, 33°40'W to refuel the U-530, U-172, U-572, and
U-795 between 12 and 18 June. None of these messages were read
by the Allies until 13 June. Fortunately, Allied shore-based D/F
equipment picked up the transmissions, giving the Allies the locations of the broadcasting submarines, even if they had no knowledge
of the messages' contents.[41]

Thus, when TG 21.12 left UGS-9 on the morning of 12 June,
Short and his crew believed they were steaming west toward a
U-boat patrol line an assumption based on the D/F fixes on the flurry
of radio signals arising from the damage to U-758 resulting in the
rescheduling of U-boat tanker operations. In fact, the Allied task
group was heading toward the U-118's refueling rendezvous, not the
Trutz wolf pack it sought.[42] This mission began at 0657 on 12 June
when the *Bogue* flew off eight aircraft to conduct searches for
U-boats. Nothing was found and the aircraft returned to the escort
carrier. At 1207 seven more aircraft were flown off to continue the
search. One aircraft had to return to the escort carrier almost at once
because of generator problems, but the other six continued searching
for U-boats.[43] At 1347 the U-118 was sighted by a TBF Avenger and
a F4F Wildcat at a range of 20 miles from the USS *Bogue*. Flying
only 15 feet above the water, the F4F Wildcat launched a strafing
attack on the enemy vessel from bow to stern, and the U-118 began
to submerge. After the strafing attack, the TBF Avenger dived on the
U-boat dropping four depth charges which straddled the U-118 just
before the vessel's conning tower disappeared under the water. The
U-118 continued to submerge but then "resurfaced almost at once"
moving forward very slowly and trailing oil. The F4F Wildcat then
attacked the enemy vessel a second time with machine-gun fire as the
U-boat sank back into the water, trailing oil and air bubbles. The
water was clear enough so that the American aircraft could see the
U-boat under the surface.

About five minutes after the first attack, as the U-118 again surfaced, a second pair of aircraft—a TBF Avenger and a F4F Wildcat—appeared on the scene. The TBF Avenger promptly attacked

the U-118 with four depth charges just as the U-boat was breaking the surface. The F4F Wildcat then strafed the enemy vessel twice. The U-118 remained on the surface as the American aircraft circled the U-boat, intermittently strafing the vessel and subjecting it to machine-gun fire from the ball turrets of the TBF Avengers. The crew of the U-118, prevented from using the ship's guns by machine-gun fire, could be seen putting on life jackets. About twenty minutes after the U-118 had been sighted, a third TBF Avenger arrived and attacked with two depth charges which straddled the U-boat amidship. After this attack the U-118 began to list to starboard and sink by the stern. The crew began to abandon the vessel, and the U-118 was then strafed twice and attacked by a fourth TBF Avenger which dropped two depth charges that exploded under the ship's conning tower. After this attack, the TBF Avenger "made a sharp left turn" and attacked again with two more depth charges which exploded under the vessel. The U-118 then exploded "sending large pieces of metal and debris high into the air. Huge amounts of oil rose high into the air." The Americans used six aircraft, sixteen depth charges, and 5,210 rounds of machine-gun ammunition to destroy the U-118. Later the destroyer USS *Osmond Ingram* picked up seventeen survivors from the U-boat tanker.[44]

After the sinking of the U-118, TG 21.12 continued to search for U-boats, still acting on the misapprehension that the U-118 was a member of a patrol line or a "concentration of U-boats" located approximately in a 200-mile square area with 29°N, 40°W at its center. Although there was no wolf pack at hand, sinking the single tanker U-118 seriously disrupted the BdU's plans for refueling U-boats at sea. The U-118 had on board about 300 cubic meters of fuel intended for use by four other U-boats: the U-172, U-530, U-572, and U-795. The first hint of trouble came to the BdU on 12 June when the U-172 radioed that there were carrier aircraft over the point for its rendezvous with the U-118. Ignorant of the loss of the U-118, the BdU accordingly moved the refueling point 100 miles south.[45] Then, when the BdU learned of the loss of the U-118, the plans for fueling the U-boat quartet had to be altered once again. The U-172 was refueled from the U-530 between the Azores and the Bulge of Brazil, while the U-530 was then ordered to break off its cruise altogether. The U-795 and the U-752 continued on their voyages to Cuba and the northeast coast of Brazil without being refueled. Thus the sinking of the U-118 not only cost the Germans a valuable U-boat tanker but also forced another U-boat to return to Europe and required two more to carry on with dangerously low fuel reserves. "The net result," according to US Naval Intelligence, "over and above the permanent loss by actually sinking, was to reduce the fighting power of the U/B fleet at sea by a considerable margin."[46]

However, as the Allies were not currently decrypting German radio messages, the officers and crew of TG 21.12 remained ignorant of the happy effects of the sinking of the U-118 until long after the event. For two days after the engagement with the U-118, the task group steamed west and south searching fruitlessly for U-boats. Delays in decrypting German radio messages meant that the Americans were unaware that the *Trutz* group of U-boats had again been ordered to maintain radio silence as they moved to new positions to the north and west of the area being searched by TG 21.12.[47] During the evening of 14 June, TG 21.12's logistic constraints and problems with the USS *Bogue*'s catapult persuaded the task group to break off the operation and steam home for Hampton Roads, Virginia.[48]

Meanwhile, another escort group was on its way to match wits with the U-boats along the America-Gibraltar sea lanes. On 13 June, TG 21.11, consisting of the escort carrier USS *Santee* and the American destroyers *Bainbridge*, *Overton*, and *MacLeish*, sailed from New York to escort convoy UGS-10 from North America to the Mediterranean. TG 21.11 provided close escort to UGS-10, and for a good part of the voyage the USS *Santee* remained within the main body of the convoy except when conducting flight operations. The convoy reaped significant rewards from Allied intelligence. Once the U-boats of the *Trutz* group had been refueled, the BdU radioed on 11 June to order the submarines to a new position along 48°06′W running north to south between 33°27′N, to 28°57′N. The Allies decrypted this order on 15 June, and UGS-10 was routed as far south as 22°N to avoid the redeployed *Trutz* line.[49] The voyage of UGS-10 was uneventful until 22 June, when the U-752 penetrated the convoy's screen, where it torpedoed and sank the French tanker *Lot*.[50] The U-572 was proceeding independently to the West Indies and had intercepted UGS-10 by sheer accident. After the sinking of the *Lot*, the escorts of the convoy hunted for the U-572 for several hours without result, and UGS-10 continued on its way to the Mediterranean without further incident, while the USS *Santee* arrived in the North African port of Casablanca on 3 July.[51]

Even though it maintained station for ten days, the *Trutz* group failed to intercept a convoy, for UGS-10's rerouting successfully took the Allied ships far to the south of the waiting U-boats. On 21 June the BdU radioed the *Trutz* group to steam on a course of 80° at a rate of 160 miles per day, a message decrypted by the Allies at 1430 on 27 June.[52] The BdU's plans called for the *Trutz* group to intercept a Gibraltar-bound convoy running from the United States south of the Azores on 29 June.[53] This maneuver, however, was largely a matter of guesswork, for the Germans lacked adequate intelligence on the movement of convoys running back and forth between the United States and Gibraltar. For convoys running between North America and Great Britain in the North Atlantic and for isolated cases such as that of the British convoy Flight 10 proceeding to the Mediterranean, the Germans had gained intelligence by decrypting Naval Cipher No. 3, used primarily for intercommunication among the United States, Royal Canadian, and British Royal Navies.[54] However, the UGS and GUS convoys shuttling between Gibraltar and North America were wholly controlled and escorted by the US Navy, which enciphered its radio transmissions with the US electrical cipher machine. These transmissions could not be read by German naval intelligence, and the BdU was left with almost no information about the routes taken by these convoys.[55] Instead, the BdU had to fall back to guesswork based on dead reckoning, a process that would make it nearly impossible for U-boats of the *Trutz* group to intercept a convoy.

The fortuitous encounter with the French tanker *Lot* prompted the BdU to make another of these uninformed guesses. On 26 June the BdU again moved the *Trutz* group, this time forming two patrol lines which ran from 36°03'N, 31°58'W to 30°03'N, 31°58'W and from 35°39'N, 31°18'W to 30°33'N, 31°15'W. The Allies decoded this order on 3 July.[56] By this move, the Germans expected to intercept a convoy on 28 June, for they had persuaded themselves that the *Lot* had been torpedoed within convoy UGS-10 while that convoy was on a "southerly evasive movement." The BdU also deduced that it was possible that the Allies had D/F'ed several radio transmissions by U-boats to the south of the *Trutz* patrol lines and concluded that these transmission signals would prompt the next Allied convoy to follow a more northerly course. However, the BdU admitted that these calculations were "pure speculation" and that without "aerial reconnaissance and also without deciphered intelligence," the interception of a convoy "is extremely tricky and more or less a matter of luck."[57]

When there was no contact between the *Trutz* group of U-boats and a convoy by 28 June, the BdU concluded that the Allied force had evaded the patrol line.[58] Even before this point, on 27 June, the U-boats had been ordered to move, steaming on a course of 270° at 8 knots until 0900B. At 2218 on 29 June the BdU gave up any hope of intercepting a North American-Gibraltar convoy with the *Trutz* patrol line and disbanded the group and ordered the U-boats eastward to operate off the coast of Portugal. The first of these radio messages were not read by the Allies until 4 July.[59]

In the next two weeks the Germans made a major reassessment of their strategy against the Gibraltar convoys. The lack of communications intelligence from decrypted Allied radio messages had made it impossible to intercept these convoys with the traditional tactics of wolf packs and patrol lines employing a large number of U-boats. However, after the event, the BdU cited several other reasons for their failure in the mid-Atlantic in June 1943. Prominent among these was the theory that the Americans had first pinpointed the location of the *Trutz* patrol lines by sightings of high flying carrier aircraft and then routed the convoys to skirt the U-boats. There was so much sea room between North America and Gibraltar that the convoys could make "extensive evading movements" without greatly prolonging their voyages. According to this theory, there was no purpose in continuing to use wolf pack tactics while the U-boats were unable to detect "enemy radar transmissions from aircraft." More practically, from the very beginning of the campaign the BdU had "no illusions as to the difficulties of finding convoys in the area *without reconnaissance by our aircraft*."[60]

Weighing all of these considerations, the BdU halted further wolf pack missions against transatlantic Allied convoys until September. Then, it was hoped, U-boats would be equipped not only with the newly developed *zaunkonig* torpedoes but also with effective radar detectors. In disbanding the *Trutz* group and breaking off patrol line operations, the BdU acknowledged defeat in the face of its inability to obtain the intelligence for this type of attack. Because of the failure of the *Trutz* group, the BdU next instituted a strategy of dispersal as compared to one of concentrated attacks against transatlantic convoys.

U-boats would now be ordered in increasing numbers to the West Indies, the coasts of West Africa and Brazil, and the Indian Ocean as a means of harassing the Allies and holding down Allied resources in remote regions until wolf pack operations against convoys proceeding between Great Britain and North America could be resumed in September. This decision was taken even though the BdU knew that the Type VIIC U-boats which formed a majority of the German fleet lacked the fuel capacity to operate in regions remote from Europe without being refueled at sea.[61]

The BdU apparently did not realize that the complexities of organizing such refueling would make the U-boats and their tankers easy and tempting targets for the Allies. The first such opportunity came in mid-July. The fifty-nine-ship convoy UGS-11, sailed from Hampton Roads for Gibraltar on 27 June.[62] In addition to a close escort, this eastbound convoy was also protected by TG 21.15 consisting of the escort carrier USS *Core* and the American destroyers *Barker*, *Bulmer*, and *Badger*. Ten days after convoy UGS-11 left Virginia, TG 21.11 sailed from Casablanca and joined the escort of the westbound convoy GUS-9. TG 21.11 remained with GUS-9, providing air cover from the carrier *Santee* until 12 July. TG 21.11 then separated from the convoy at a point south of Sao Miguel in the Azores and headed north to hunt U-boats.[63] At the same time, TG 21.15, having left UGS-11, joined GUS-9 to escort that convoy on the next leg of its voyage to the United States.

At 1421 on 13 July two aircraft in this task group flying from the USS *Core* sighted the U-487, a U-boat tanker which was part of a complex BdU plan to refuel U-boats at sea.[64] Before being sighted by the American aircraft from the USS *Core*, the U-487 had already refueled six U-boats (U-604, U-591, U-598, U-662, U-406, U-195) at sea and had orders to refuel eleven of the U-boats (U-168, U-516, U-514, U-183, U-188, U-506, U-533, U-532, U-509, U-523, U-847) of the *Monsun* group bound to the Indian Ocean. It was originally intended to refuel the U-boats of the *Monsun* group from another U-boat tanker, but that vessel was damaged in an air attack in the Bay of Biscay and forced to return to France.[65] When the BdU ordered the U-487 to refuel the *Monsun* U-boats, the tanker's reserves were already depleted by other refueling missions, and there was insufficient fuel on board to supply all the needs of the *Monsun* group. Therefore, an outward-bound U-boat was ordered to turn over all fuel to the U-487, retaining only enough to return to base. Although the Allies did not decrypt the orders setting up the rendezvous for the transfer of the fuel until 1 August, the number of radio transmissions required to arrange the U-boats' meeting enabled American naval intelligence to discern the approximate position of the U-487, and TG 21.15 was directed toward the U-boat.[66]

The U-487 was taken completely by surprise when a F4F Wildcat dived and strafed it with machine-gun fire. The fighter was immediately followed by a TBF Avenger which dropped four depth charges, of which two exploded off the port side of the U-boat while the other two straddled the vessel's bow. As the American aircraft pulled out of the attack and circled, the U-487 opened fire with antiaircraft guns and was seen to leak oil and turn slowly to starboard. The attack on the U-boat was reported to the USS *Core*, and several more aircraft and the destroyer USS *Barker* were sent to the scene. A second strafing attack was then undertaken, but as the F4F Wildcat dived on the U-487, the aircraft swerved to the left and crashed into the sea off the U-boat's bow, killing the pilot. Just after the American fighter crashed, more American aircraft arrived over the U-487. The U-boat was strafed again by another F4F Wildcat and a TBF Avenger, and then attacked with four depth charges from a height of 100 feet. Two depth charges exploded under the U-boat, one off the starboard bow, and one off the port quarter. The U-487 was covered with plumes of water by the explosions and then was seen to sink bow first. The USS *Barker* later picked up thirty-three survivors from the U-487.[67]

The sinking of the U-487 on 13 July disrupted the BdU's plans for refueling the U-boats of the *Monsun* group. When the BdU finally learned of the loss of the U-boat tanker on 18 July, a desperate reshuffling of submarines and tankers began.[68] The U-648 was ordered to turn fuel over to the U-257, while the U-155 was to refuel the

U-188, U-183, and U-186 of the *Monsun* group on 21 July and then return to base. The U-160 was to supply fuel to the *Monsun* vessels U-509, U-523, U-516, and U-533 and then return to France. This order was not decoded by the Allies until 30 July, too late for them to allow exploitation of the information that it contained, but the sinking of the U-487 itself not only forced the U-160 and U-155 to return to base but also created a situation in which each of the *Monsun* U-boats received only thirty-five cubic meters of fuel, a scant ration that forced them to be refueled again in the western Indian Ocean.[69]

Nor was this the end of the mounting number of Allied successes that month. On 13 July, the same day the U-487 was sunk, the U-67 radioed the BdU that it could not find the U-527 at the planned rendezvous point prior to sailing across the Bay of Biscay to base. The U-67 also radioed that it would return to the meeting point on 23 July. Although the Allies did not decrypt this message until 28 August, their D/F equipment did pick up the transmission, thus revealing the location of the U-67. The USS *Core*'s aircraft were immediately tasked to search for the U-67. A TBF Avenger found the U-67 at 0525 on 16 July, some 27 miles from the westbound GUS-9. Using cloud cover to close the range with the U-boat, the TBF Avenger attacked with four depth charges, taking the U-67 by surprise. One depth charge exploded under the U-boat aft of the conning tower and the other three exploded along the port side. As the U-67 sank, its bow rose out of the water at a 35 degree angle and then disappeared in four or five seconds leaving an oil slick, wreckage, and several survivors on the surface. Later the destroyer USS *McCormick* rescued three members of the U-67's crew.[70] On 17 July TG 21.15 departed from GUS-9 and proceeded to Norfolk, Virginia where it arrived on 30 July.[71]

Meanwhile, after leaving GUS-9, TG 21.11 headed north toward suspected "enemy submarine concentrations south of the Azores." On 13 July aircraft from the USS *Santee* searched to the northward on a 200-mile front beginning at 29°N, 29°W but made no contact with the U-boats. However, about midnight on 13 July, the commander of TG 21.11, Captain Harold F. Fick, USN, received "a special report of a D/F of a submarine located about 200 miles to the northeast from Washington, D.C." This D/F fix was probably obtained from an exchange of radio messages between the BdU and the U-160 concerning that vessel's transfer of fuel to the U-487, which was then to use it to refuel the *Monsun* U-boats. At first daylight on 14 July, the USS *Santee*'s aircraft began to search for U-boats, and at 0803 a F4F Wildcat and a TBF Avenger sighted the U-160 at a range of 144 miles from the carrier. The Wildcat strafed the U-160, twice forcing the vessel to dive, and the Avenger then dropped an acoustic homing torpedo 200 yards ahead of the swirl of the submerging U-boat. Seventy-five seconds after the torpedo entered the water there was an explosion 300 yards ahead of the swirl, the blast destroying the U-160. The sinking of the U-160 disrupted once again the BdU's schemes for refueling the *Monsun* U-boats. When the BdU learned of the loss of the U-160 on 21 July, the U-516, one of the *Monsun* U-boats, was ordered to refuel three other submarines in the group from reserves and then return to base.[72] Thus, the U-160's sinking cost the Germans the services of another vessel when the U-516 sailed back to France.

The *Santee*'s aircraft continued to search the seas after the U-160 was destroyed. During the afternoon of 14 July, two SBD Dauntless aircraft sighted a periscope wake and attacked with depth charges without result. Before the two planes returned to the USS *Santee*, a TBF Avenger appeared on the scene and continued circling and hunting for the U-boat. About two hours after the first attack, a U-boat was seen to surface about 6 miles from the aircraft, and the Avenger strafed it three times before it began to submerge. As the U-boat was disappearing under the water the TBF Avenger attacked again with an acoustic torpedo, but there was no explosion.[73] The U-boat, probably the U-168, escaped.[74]

On 15 July the USS *Santee*'s aircraft conducted operations on the basis of more intelligence received from Washington. At 0818, 14 miles from the carrier, a F4F Wildcat and a TBF Avenger sighted the U-509, a member of the *Monsun* group. In the face of antiaircraft fire, the F4F Wildcat strafed the U-boat four times until the U-509 began to submerge. Then the TBF Avenger attacked, dropping an acoustic torpedo 250 feet ahead and 250 feet to starboard of the swirl of the U-boat about seven seconds after the conning tower had disappeared. Forty-five seconds later and 500 feet ahead of the swirl, there was an explosion followed by oil appearing on the surface of the ocean. The U-509 had been destroyed.[75]

Later that afternoon at 1546 a pair of aircraft from the USS *Santee* sighted another U-boat, probably the U-532, surfacing at 31°51'N, 27°25'W.[76] After three strafing attacks by the F4F Wildcat in the team, the U-boat dived and a TBF Avenger attacked with an acoustic homing torpedo. But the torpedo was not released on the first two passes over the U-boat because "the selector switch was in the wrong station." Finally, on the third attack, the torpedo was dropped and hit the water 900 yards ahead of the swirl, exploding thirty-five seconds later. The U-boat, however, escaped.[77]

For days TG 21.11 doggedly searched the area south of the Azores for U-boats without obtaining any contacts. At 0819 on 24 July USS *Santee* aircraft on a leg of the search that reached almost as far east as Madeira spotted the U-373, which was on a mission to mine Port Lautey in West Africa.[78] A TBF Avenger and F4F Wildcat spotted the U-boat 90 miles from the *Santee*. The F4F Wildcat made three strafing attacks, forcing the U-boat to dive. Sixty seconds after the U-373 disappeared, the TBF Avenger attacked with an acoustic torpedo which entered the water 600 feet ahead and 100 feet to the right of the swirl. There was no explosion. Shortly afterwards the USS *Bainbridge* arrived in the area where the elusive U-boat had submerged and conducted a hunt for the enemy vessel. The American destroyer obtained several sonar contacts which were attacked with "numerous depth charges," but the U-373 escaped.[79] Just after midnight the U-373 radioed the BdU that it had been attacked by two carrier-borne aircraft, leaving the U-boat with two sailors killed and seven wounded and with its diving ability so impaired that the U-373 had to return to base.

This radio transmission from the U-373 was not decoded by the Allies until 0845 on 4 August.[80] Such long delays in decrypting German radio messages were characteristic of the period of TG 21.11's operations south of the Azores. Despite this handicap, the Allied task group persevered. On 25 July at 32°45'N, 16°25'W, TG 21.11 joined convoy GUS-10 and provided air cover to that convoy as it proceeded west toward the United States. Sixty miles from the USS *Santee*, at 1711 on 30 July, a F4F Wildcat and a TBF Avenger sighted two U-boats "steaming in column approximately 500 yards apart, course 200, speed about 12 knots." The position was 34°54′N, 35°07′W, and the U-boats were the U-43 and the U-403. The larger of the two U-boats, the U-43, was a Type IXA minelayer en route to West Africa that had been detailed to refuel the smaller Type VIIC U-403.[81] The F4F Wildcat strafed both U-boats and the TBF Avenger then attacked, dropping two depth charges that exploded near the U-43, which then dived, trailing oil. Next the TBF Avenger dropped an acoustic torpedo 100 feet ahead of the swirl of the U-43 as it disappeared under the surface, and two minutes later "an explosion was observed followed by a small amount of debris and some oil." The U-43 had been sunk, while the smaller U-403 escaped. On the morning of 2 August, TG 21.11 left GUS-10 and proceeded to Hampton Roads where the warships arrived on 6 August.[82]

The next task group to face the U-boats on the United States-Gibraltar convoy run was TG 21.13. Organized around the carrier USS *Bogue*, TG 21.13 also included the American destroyers *George E. Badger, Osmond Ingram,* and *Clemson* when the group sailed from Chesapeake Bay on 13 July to escort the eastbound convoy UGS-12 to Gibraltar. At 0500 that day, TG 21.13 joined the eastbound convoy with the USS *Bogue* taking position within the main body of the convoy and the task group's destroyers joining its escort. However, at about 1500 on 14 July, TG 21.13 left UGS-12 to scout ahead of the convoy toward "the vicinity of Latitude 30N and Longitude 45W where possible concentration of submarines was reported."[83]

For the next six days, TG 21.13 proceeded eastward with the aircraft of the USS *Bogue* conducting sweeps ahead of and to the southward of UGS-12. Only one HF/DF bearing was obtained before 19 July, but after that date, as TG 21.13 "approached the reported submarine concentration," HF/DF "activity increased." On 20 July TG 21.13 rejoined convoy UGS-12 to refuel the task group's destroyers, leaving the convoy again the next day to hunt U-boats. That day the task group received information that there was a "concentration" of U-boats "600 miles south of the Azores between Longitude 29W and 25W which was moving southwest."[84] As the Allies were not reading German radio messages immediately at this time, the report of this U-boat concentration was likely drawn from D/F fixes.[85]

There was no actual contact between TG 21.13 and the Germans until 0800Z on 23 July, when a U-boat was sighted by a F4F Wildcat and a TBF Avenger about 11 miles from the escort carrier. The F4F Wildcat strafed the U-boat, and, as the enemy vessel was submerging, the Avenger attacked, dropping four depth charges whose explosion produced an oil slick which was still visible from the air half an hour after the attack.[86] Still, the U-boat escaped. Two hours later, the USS *George E. Badger* obtained a sonar contact bearing 148°. The USS *Bogue* immediately took evasive action, and at 1020Z the USS *George E. Badger* attacked the U-boat with depth charges. The U-boat was thought by the Americans to be at a depth of 600 feet, and the USS *George E. Badger* conducted three more depth charge attacks dropping a total of forty depth charges. After the last attack, debris—wood, "articles of personal gear," some oil, and "fragments of dismembered bodies"—began to appear on the surface. This debris was still rising to the surface when the USS *George E. Badger* departed from the area.[87] This was the end of the U-613.

At 1302Z on 23 July aircraft from the USS *Bogue* sighted the U-527 and the U-648. The precise source of the intelligence that allowed the planes to locate this pair of German submarines is unclear. Both had expected to be refueled by the U-487, which had been sunk on 15 July by aircraft from the USS *Core*. The U-183's 17 June radio messages informing the BdU that it and three other U-boats were looking for the U-487 provided the Allies with D/F fixes locating the transmitter at 26°30'N, 33°30'W. When the BdU learned of the loss of the U-487 the next day, the U-527 and U-648 were directed to return jointly to base after the U-648 had supplied the U-527 with the fuel required for the voyage. The rendezvous between the U-527 and the U-648 was to be "SUFFICIENTLY REMOVED FROM THE PRESENT AREA." On 21 July the U-527 reported to the BdU that its position was 28°39'N, 30°38'W, but this radio transmission was apparently not D/F'ed by an Allied shore intercept station, and none of these radio messages was decrypted by the Allies until 30 July. While there is no direct evidence just how the U-527 and U-648 (as well as the U-613) were located, it was probably by a combination of shipborne HF/DF and shore-based D/F: the U-527 and U-648 are listed in OP-20Y-G(A)'s history of communications intelligence in the Battle of the Atlantic as among "U/B'S SUNK BY U.S. FORCES WITH THE AID OF RADIO INTELLIGENCE."[88]

The two ill-fated submarines were sighted by a TBF Avenger from the USS *Bogue* steaming on parallel courses a few yards apart about 45 miles from the escort carrier. Both U-boats were surprised by the aircraft, and the U-648 began to submerge while the U-527 attempted to escape into a fog bank. However, the TBF Avenger was too quick for the U-527 and dropped four depth charges which bracketed the U-boat with explosions. The U-527 lost forward movement, turned slowly to starboard, and sank stern first with the vessel's bow rising out of the water at a 30 to 40 degree angle. Later the USS *Clemson* picked up thirteen survivors from the U-527.[89] After this action, the TG 21.13 continued to support UGS-12 while searching the area south of the Azores for U-boats. However, no further contact was made with the U-boats, and on 29 July the American task group steamed to Casablanca, arriving in the North African port on 1 August.[90]

TG 21.13's successes in the last week of July were largely due to the carelessness of German U-boat commanders. The BdU had warned the U-boats that there was an aircraft carrier operating south of the Azores on 21 July. And, in a second warning radioed the same day, the U-boats were told to stay far to the west of the Azores because of enemy aircraft. Those U-boats that had operated to the south of those islands were "TO CRUISE WITH SPECIAL CAUTION." Obviously the U-527 and the U-648 had disregarded these warning, for they too were caught by surprise on the surface by an American carrier-based aircraft. Once sighted by carrier aircraft, a U-boat had two choices: submerge or remain on the surface and fight it out. Neither of these alternatives were tactically viable. A submerging U-boat could be successfully attacked with airborne depth charges and was wide open to an attack with an acoustic torpedo. On the other hand, a U-boat commander ran an equally grave risk when he followed the official BdU doctrine: "IN CASE OF DOUBT, STAY UPSTAIRS AND SHOOT."[91] If a U-boat remained on the surface and beat off an initial aircraft attack, then more aircraft would probably appear and continue to attack until the U-boat was destroyed, as U-boat antiaircraft guns were proving tragically ineffective in the face of machine-gun fire from F4F Wildcat fighters.

The vulnerable U-boats were soon engaged by still another group of unwelcome American visitors: the ships of TG 21.14. This task group sailed from Hampton Roads on 27 July, consisting of the escort carrier USS *Card* and the destroyers USS *Barry,* USS *Borie,* and USS *Goff.* After refueling at Bermuda, TG 21.14 joined convoy UGS-13 on 1 August, remaining only long enough to refuel the task group's destroyers from a tanker in the convoy. TG 21.14 then sailed off, "en route to submarine concentration to conduct offensive action." The plan called for TG 21.14 to proceed during daylight right through the center of a suspected concentration of U-boats, with aircraft from the USS *Card* searching to the depth of 100 miles in front and along the flanks of the American force. This procedure produced results quickly, for on 3 August communications intelligence enabled an aircraft from the USS *Card* to locate and sight the U-66.[92]

Pinpointing the U-66 reflected long overdue improvements in Allied methods. On 24 July, the U-117, a U-boat minelayer refitted as a tanker, was directed to proceed to 40°04'N, 30°05'W: this order was not decrypted by the Allies until 7 September. However, when the BdU sent a 27 July radio message to the U-66 directing the submarine to be refueled by the U-117 in the region of 38°51'N, 40°54'W, Allied cryptographers decoded the message on 2 August. Later transmissions were also processed in more timely fashion. On 30 July the BdU directed the U-117 to "STAND BY" at 38°50'N, 37°20'W. The next day the U-66 was ordered to "CONTINUE TO CRUISE" to 38°51'N, 36°06'W, and the U-84 was told on the same day to proceed to 38°51'N, 44°30'W because "REFUELLING FROM NEWMANN ((117)) PLANNED APPROXIMATELY THERE." All of these directions were read by the Allies on 1 August. Next, the U-117 was directed to proceed to 37°57'N, 38°30'W on 1 August, and several hours later the BdU radioed that the U-66 was to be refueled by the U-117 at 37°57'N, 38°30'W at 2000B on 3 August. These radio messages were decrypted at 1305 and 1320 on 1 August. In transmissions of 2 August, the U-66 informed the BdU that it could not carry out the plan, and the BdU pushed this objection aside and ordered the U-66 to carry out the scheme as directed. Fortunately, these last radio transmissions were of no significance, for the new-found efficiency of Allied intelligence collapsed temporarily, and these messages were not decrypted until 21 and 28 August.[93]

At 1618 on 3 August four F4F Wildcats and four TBF Avengers were flown from the USS *Card* at 37°27'N, 40°18'W. While conducting a search at a distance of 75 miles from the carrier, a F4F Wildcat and a TBF Avenger sighted the U-66. Because there was no cloud cover, both aircraft attacked at once, with the Wildcat first strafing the U-boat, and the Avenger following to attack with two depth charges which failed to leave the aircraft's bomb bay. As this attack was being mounted, the Germans opened up with antiaircraft fire. Both aircraft next attacked a second time in the face of the submarine's antiaircraft fire, and this time the TBF Avenger successfully dropped two depth charges and an acoustic torpedo. Although there was a heavy explosion off the starboard side forward of the U-boat's conning tower and a column of water shot into the air, the U-66 escaped by diving.[94]

Later the U-66 reported to the BdU that it had been attacked by two aircraft, was damaged, and had suffered "heavy casualties."[95] The U-66 was thereupon ordered to again attempt to meet the U-117, which had a physician on board, at 1200B on 4 August at 38°51′N, 40°30′W. This rendezvous was not kept, and at 0023 on 6 August the U-66 radioed the BdU that it would meet the U-117 at 1200B at 38°51′N, 38°14′W. This transmission was D/F'ed by the Allies as coming from 42°30′N, 33°00′W. Several hours later, at 0535, the BdU radioed confirming the rendezvous between the two submarines. The U-117 was to "REPORT TIME OF ARRIVAL AT ONCE," and the U-760 was to join the two U-boats at the meeting point. Then at 0727 and 0827, the U-117 radioed the BdU that "R/V AT 1200B." These telltale radio exchanges had no real significance for either side. Although the second of these transmissions was D/F'ed by the Allies as coming from 41°25′N, 34°30′W, none of these radio messages was decrypted by the Allies before 14 September.[96] This proved to be inconsequential, for the planned meeting between the U-66 and the U-117 on 6 August never took place. For reasons which are unclear from the existing record (probably the result of what Clausewitz termed friction), the two U-boats did not join forces until the morning of 7 August.

That juncture proved to be a rendezvous with an Allied task group as well. After attacking the U-66, TG 21.14 continued to hunt for U-boats using intelligence from Washington. On 5 August the USS *Card* obtained a good HF/DF bearing on a radio transmission thought to have come from a U-boat, but nothing came of it. The following day, TG 21.14 briefly rejoined UGS-13 to refuel the force's destroyers before leaving the convoy at 1306 to "head toward [the] area of submarine concentration."[97]

On the morning of 7 August, a TBF Avenger from the USS *Card* sighted the U-66 and the U-117 at a range of 82 miles from the escort carrier. The U-boats were about 200 feet apart, barely moving forward, and the U-117 apparently had just begun to refuel the U-66. As the American aircraft attacked, the Germans did not see the TBF Avenger until it was 400 yards away. The two U-boats quickly opened antiaircraft fire. From a height of 125 feet, the TBF Avenger attacked the U-117 with two depth charges that straddled the U-boat. The U-117 was badly damaged by the assault and began to make "erratic turns," trailing oil and smoking. As the American aircraft turned and climbed to gain position for a second attack, the U-66 appeared to be attempting to assist the damaged U-117. After several minutes, however, the U-66 began to submerge and the TBF Avenger attacked a second time in the face of the U-117's antiaircraft fire. The aircraft dropped an acoustic torpedo which entered the water 50 yards to starboard and 150 yards ahead of the swirl left by the diving U-66. There was no explosion, and the U-66 escaped. After this attack the TBF Avenger climbed to 6,400 feet to await the arrival of additional aircraft from the USS *Card*.[98]

After the initial air attack, the U-117 attempted to submerge but almost immediately reappeared on the surface and radioed the BdU "AM BEING ATTACKED BY AIR PLANE IN NAV SQ CD 6155 ((39.45N—38.30W))." This radio transmission was D/F'ed by Allied shore-based intercept stations as coming from 42°00′N, 42°00′W.[99] At 0927, in response to the report of the sighting of the two submarines the USS *Card* flew off two F4F Wildcats and two TBF Avengers to support the attacking aircraft.[100] About twenty minutes after the first attack on the U-117, these aircraft arrived over the damaged U-boat. The two F4F Wildcats strafed the U-117 unmercifully, and the TBF Avengers then attacked with depth charges. Two depth charges exploded along the port side of the U-117 and then two more off the starboard quarter of the vessel. The U-117 began to turn to the right and then attempted to submerge again. As the U-117 tried to dive, the two TBF Avengers attacked, but just as the drop point for the depth charges was reached, the U-117 began to surface and the two

American aircraft broke off the attack. After several minutes the U-117 disappeared under the water again stern first, trailing large quantities of oil. The two American aircraft renewed the attack, dropping two acoustic torpedoes along side the oil slick left by the U-boat. Shortly after the acoustic homing torpedo entered the water, the American aircrews saw "a very light blue bubbly area 100 feet in diameter suddenly appear about 300 feet ahead to starboard of where the U-boat had gone under."[101]

The sinking of the U-117 was still another serious disruption of the BdU's plans for refueling U-boats at sea. It was several days before the Germans realized that the U-117 had been lost. At 0017 on 8 August the U-66 radioed the BdU that it had been attacked by carrier aircraft at the rendezvous with the U-117 and suggested another meeting with the U-117 at a position to the north. This transmission was D/F'ed by the Allies and placed as coming from 39°45'N, 30°30'W.[102] The U-66 later requested that it be allowed to put into the Spanish port of El Ferrol, but the BdU turned down this idea and directed the U-66 to attempt to refuel a second time from the U-117.[103] Indeed, the BdU was still counting on the U-117 to refuel a number of U-boats returning to base from distant seas. The U-117's role in the BdU's refueling plans became more critical when the BdU learned on 11 August of the loss of another U-boat tanker, the U-489. This news forced the BdU to decide that the U-117 would be used to refuel thirteen more U-boats in addition to the U-66 (U-84, U-415, U-653, U-510, U-333, U-571, U-600, U-257, U-508, U-358, U-618, U-525, U-230), which needed fuel for its return voyage to France. But by 13 August the BdU had concluded that the U-117 was lost. This forced a major change in the BdU's plans for refueling U-boats in the central Atlantic. The new scheme called for four different vessels to assume the U-117's refueling duties: the U-847 to refuel the U-66; the U-760 to refuel the U-84; the U-525 to refuel four U-boats; and the U-219 to refuel the remaining quartet of submarines earlier assigned to the U-117.[104] The orders for putting these plans into effect went out from the BdU on 14 August, but they were not decrypted by the Allies until 19 and 25 September.[105]

Meanwhile, the aircraft of USS *Card* pursued submarines in their neighborhood without mercy. At 0615 on 8 August two F4F Wildcats and two TBF Avengers flew from the carrier to search for

U-boats. About an hour later, a F4F Wildcat and a TBF Avenger sighted the U-262 and U-664, a U-boat tanker fueling another vessel.[106] The location of this pair of U-boats may have been betrayed by radio transmissions of 4 and 6 August that ordered the German submarines to their rendezvous at 41°33′N, 38°20′W on 7 August. The first order was not decoded by the Allies until 16 August, but D/F fixes were obtained on the second message from 44°00′N, 39°00′W.[107] It is unclear whether this provided enough information to draw TG 21.14 toward the two U-boats.

When the two American pilots sighted the U-664 and U-264, they attacked immediately with such speed that the aircraft did not inform the USS *Card* of the sighting. The F4F Wildcat strafed the two U-boats first, followed by the Avenger, which was hit at least twice by antiaircraft fire that knocked out the aircraft's electrical systems. Because of this damage, it was impossible to release the two depth charges from the bomb bay on the first pass. The Avenger next circled and attacked again in the face of enemy fire, dropping two depth charges which straddled the U-664. The TBF Avenger was further damaged by enemy gunfire, and the aircraft ditched its acoustic torpedo and made a forced landing in the sea. The USS *Barry* later picked up the pilot and gunner. The radioman of the TBF Avenger was killed in the action. The F4F Wildcat continued strafing the U-boats, but the U-262 then shot down the fighter, killing the pilot. Both U-boats escaped and there was no reaction from TG 21.14 for several hours because the American force had no knowledge of the attacks.[108] This was one of the few times that the "fight back" tactics of the U-boats were successful.

After the loss of the two aircraft to gunfire and the evident increase in the antiaircraft armament of the U-boats, the commander of TG 21.14 temporarily changed the makeup of aircraft anti-U-boat patrols. Hitherto, the standard patrol consisted of one F4F Wildcat and one TBF Avenger. In the future, patrols would consist of one F4F Wildcat, one TBF Avenger armed with two "instantaneous 500 lb. bombs," and another TBF Avenger armed with two depth charges and an acoustic torpedo. The bombs were to break the enemy's morale. But increasing the number of aircraft in a patrol would decrease the number of patrols that could be undertaken by the limited aircraft available on the escort carrier.[109]

At 1330 on 9 August a three-aircraft patrol from the USS *Card* sighted the U-664 65 miles from the escort carrier. The sighting was reported to the USS *Card,* and the aircraft attacked. The U-boat was first strafed by the F4F Wildcat and then immediately after attacked by the two TBF Avengers. The first TBF Avenger dropped a 500-pound bomb which exploded off the port bow of the U-664. Seconds later, as the U-boat was beginning to submerge, the second TBF Avenger dropped two depth charges from an altitude of about 100 feet. These exploded under the stern of the U-664, effectively stopping the dive and forcing the U-boat back to the surface. A number of Germans began to leave the U-boat's conning tower and they were "mowed down" as the F4F Wildcat made a second strafing attack. The U-boat then began to submerge again, leaving about ten survivors in the water, and at this time the first TBF Avenger attacked again, dropping a second bomb off the submarine's port quarter. About fifteen minutes later, the U-664 surfaced again and remained dead in the water with its stern down, gushing oil. At this point six more aircraft arrived with orders to "continue the attack until the sub was definitely sunk." These aircraft "went wild." The U-boat was then strafed, and three bombs and two depth charges were dropped, all missing the sinking U-664. Forty-four survivors from the U-664 were later picked up by the destroyer USS *Borie.*[110]

On 10 August TG 21.14 confidently "headed north toward best submarine areas."[111] The reasons for this northward movement are not really clear. One authority says that it was because of HF/DF activity, but there is no real evidence for this other than a single D/F of a transmission from the U-760 which was fixed at 41°45′N, 46°20′W; the conclusion in the official OP-20-G history of communication intelligence is probably the correct one: "Because of lags in decryption, RI played no part in this sinking [U-525], except in the wide sense that U/B's could be presumed to be concentrated in this general area."[112] Whatever the reasons for the maneuver, it was well justified, for on 11 August aircraft from the USS *Card* sighted another German tanker, the U-525, about 15 miles from the Allied carrier. The first attack was made by a F4F Wildcat, which strafed the U-boat, starting a fire in the vessel's conning tower. Right behind the fighter was a TBF Avenger, attacking with two depth charges that exploded on the port beam of the submerging U-boat. The U-525, now trailing oil, continued the dive and disappeared within thirty-five seconds. The TBF Avenger then attacked a second time, dropping an acoustic torpedo just ahead of the spot where the pilot of the aircraft estimated the U-boat had disappeared. Ten seconds after the torpedo hit the water there "was a big underwater explosion throwing a geyser of water approximately 150 feet ahead of the spot where the U-boat was last seen." This was followed by oil which formed a slick "500 to 600 feet long and 200 feet wide."[113]

After sinking the U-525, TG 21.14 continued to search for U-boats without result and on 14 August proceeded to Casablanca where the American task group arrived on 16 August.[114] However, by eliminating that single U-boat tanker, the Allied carrier group had inflicted another costly blow to the BdU's plans for refueling U-boats at sea. Ignorant of the U-525's destruction on 11 August, the BdU assigned the tanker new duties as one of the replacements for the U-117. But when the sinking of the U-525 became known to the BdU on 18 August, the four U-boats assigned for refueling were reassigned to the U-487.[115] This U-boat was a member of the *Monsun* group and its detention to refuel U-boats in the Atlantic kept it from its mission to the Indian Ocean.[116]

Next in the train of US Navy task groups came TG 21.15, consisting of the escort carrier USS *Croatan* and the "flush deck" destroyers USS *Belknap*, USS *Paul Jones*, and USS *Parrott*. Sailing from Bermuda on 9 August, TG 21.15 was assigned to hunt U-boats and to provide cover to convoy UGS-14. First, the task group conducted a series of searches for the U-760. On 9 and 10 August this submarine was D/F'ed by Allied shore-based intercept stations as being located at 41°45′N, 46°20′W and at 39°30′N, 46°15′W, and on 11 August the U-boat was sighted by the USCGC *Menemsha*. However, this hunt came to nothing, in part because of squally weather, and TG 21.15 joined UGS-14 on 15 August.[117]

For a few days, TG 21.15 provided close air escort to the convoy. For example, on 18 August, the aircraft of the USS *Croatan* flew U-boat searches which reached 80 miles ahead and astern of UGS-14 and 48 miles on each flank of the convoy. However, on 19 August TG 21.15 departed from UGS-14 "to operate against U-boats estimated to be in area 30–35N, 20–25W."[118] The U-161 was ordered to the north of the region to be searched by TG 21.15 as the Japanese submarine I-151 was passing through the region, but it is not known just how much the Allies knew of U-boat activities in the area to be searched or what intelligence was the basis of the USS *Croatan*'s orders.[119] The operation did, however, produce a U-boat sighting.

Over the next two days, TG 21.15 searched the area north and east of the Azores, and on 21 August at 42°05′N, 24°00′W, a F4F Wildcat and a TBF Avenger from the USS *Croatan* sighted the U-134 83 miles from the escort carrier. The aircraft attacked immediately in the face of antiaircraft fire, with the F4F first strafing the U-boat and the TBF Avenger then nearly missing the enemy vessel with four depth charges. After these attacks, the American aircraft circled the U-134 awaiting the arrival of additional aircraft to continue the attacks, and after fifty-five minutes the U-boat submerged and disappeared. When the U-boat sighting report arrived on the USS *Croatan*, additional planes were ordered to attack the U-134, and as these aircraft were flying off the escort carrier, an HF/DF bearing was obtained on a radio transmission from the U-134. This bearing, however, was misinterpreted, and the aircraft were sent in the wrong direction and did not arrive at the scene of the attack until after the U-134 had dived. After the failed attack on the U-134 the USS *Croatan* suffered a series of mishaps: a deck crash in which several aircraft were lost, a main fuel pump failure that reduced the ship's speed to 10 knots, and loss of the ship's radar. Finally, the escort carrier's catapult broke down. On 26 August, the hapless TG 21.15 put into Casablanca, soon to be placed by TG 21.12.[120]

The BdU's crisis in refueling U-boats produced still more targets for TG 21.12 and the planes of the USS *Core*, the group's carrier. For most of the third week of August, the *Core* and its companion destroyers—USS *Barker*, USS *Badger*, and USS *Bulmer*—occupied themselves providing cover for the fifty-eight-ship eastbound convoy UGS-15 which had sailed from Norfolk, Virginia, for Gibraltar on 16 August. When the convoy neared the comparative safety of the Azores, the task group was free to leave and begin a freewheeling hunt for U-boats assisted by Allied communications intelligence.[121]

Decryptions of Axis radio transmissions allowed Allied experts to track arrangements for German refueling rendezvous involving a pair of U-boat tankers—the U-847 and U-760. The telltale radio messages began on 11 August, when the BdU ordered the U-847 to refuel the U-66 at 41°38'N, 28°54'W on 16 August and then radioed the U-760 to 35°33'N, 43°18'W to supply the U-84 with enough fuel to reach Bergen. On 17 August the rendezvous for the U-760 and U-84 was changed to 39°09'N, 44°46'W in another radio transmission. When the U-66 reported that it had already been refueled from the U-857, the BdU gave that tanker new radio orders. On 18 August, the U-857 was ordered to change course, and the following day, it was given still another destination, 28°21'N, 38°06'W, where it was to be ready to begin refueling the U-185 and several other U-boats on 23 August. The Allies had decrypted all of these radio orders by 21 August.[122]

On 23 August aircraft from the USS *Core* spotted the U-84, the submarine that was to meet the tanker U-760. The U-boat managed to elude the Americans that day, but at 0705 the next morning, the U-185 was sighted by a F4F Wildcat and a TBF Avenger from the USS *Core* at a distance of 100 miles from TG 21.12. Using cloud cover to take the U-boat by surprise, the two aircraft attacked the U-185 from the stern. The F4F Wildcat first strafed the U-boat, and the TBF Avenger attacked next, dropping four depth charges which straddled the U-boat and exploded under the vessel. The U-185 turned to port, smoke coming out of its conning tower, and began to settle by the stern. The F4F Wildcat strafed the U-185 a second time. Two more aircraft, a F4F Wildcat and a TBF Avenger, then appeared over the U-185, and the U-boat was strafed twice. An attack by the TBF Avenger failed when the depth charges would not leave the aircraft because of an electrical fault. There were no more attacks on the U-185 because the American aircrews could see clearly that the vessel was sinking. Several hours after the U-185 sank stern first, six Germans were picked up by the USS *Barker*.[123] About 10 miles from where the U-185 had sunk, the U-84 was sighted again by a TBF Avenger from the USS *Core* around noon on 24 August. The U-boat attempted to escape by diving, but the aircraft attacked with an acoustic torpedo which destroyed the U-84. However, after these successes, TG 21.12 had to cut short operations and return to the United States because the USS *Core* developed a vibration in its turbines.[124]

In the search for U-boats southwest of the Azores, TG 21.12 was replaced by TG 21.14, led by the carrier USS *Card* which had sailed from Casablanca on 22 August.[125] The objective of this search was the U-847. At 0945 on 27 August, the USS *Card* flew off four aircraft to search for U-boats at 28°18′N, 37°10′W. At 1129 a TBF Avenger sighted the U-508 about 70 miles from the escort carrier. As the aircraft closed with the U-boat, the sighting was reported to the USS *Card*, and another three aircraft were flown off and ordered to the scene of the sighting. The TBF Avenger launched a 500-pound bomb which fell 200 feet away from the U-508, which responded with antiaircraft fire. The U-508 then dived, and the TBF circled and attacked with an acoustic torpedo which entered the water near the swirl of the U-boat. There was no explosion: the U-508 had escaped. As the other three aircraft—two F4F Wildcats and a TBF Avenger— approached the area where the U-508 had submerged, they sighted a second U-boat, the tanker U-847. The two F4F Wildcats strafed the U-boat twice, forcing it to submerge. Then the TBF Avenger attacked with an acoustic torpedo which entered the water 100 feet to starboard and ahead of the swirl. Several seconds later there was an underwater explosion destroying the U-847.[126]

This engagement effectively ended this phase of the campaign against U-boats in the central Atlantic. For the next several days TG 21.14 continued to search for U-boats before departing for Norfolk. TG 21.14 was followed by TG 21.15 which sailed from Casablanca on 30 August, cruised back and forth south and west of the Azores, and attacked only one U-boat before putting into Hampton Roads on 22 September.[127]

In three months of operations in the central Atlantic, the Germans sunk one ship (the *Lot*) from an Allied convoy and shot down three carrier-based aircraft. In exchange for this small bag, the U-boat service had lost to American hunter-killer groups fifteen U-boats, of which eight were refuelers or U-boat tankers (U-117, U-118, U-487, U-67, U-167, U-509, U-43, U-527, U-525, U-185, U-847, U-613, U-664, U-84). This was a major defeat for the Germans not only in terms of the number of U-boats lost, but also in the grave disruption of U-boat deployments to distant seas. Because of the heavy losses of U-boat refueling craft and the limited fuel capacity of the majority of their U-boats, German schemes for posting U-boats to the Indian Ocean, West Indies, and the South Atlantic were seriously hampered. A number of U-boats were forced to return to port, and, of much greater importance, the U-boat service's ability to sustain operations in distant seas was greatly curtailed.[128]

The U-boats found that not only was it almost impossible to locate Allied convoys proceeding between the United States and Gibraltar but it was, in fact, very dangerous for a U-boat even to linger in the region transited by these convoys. The American codes could not be read, thus denying the BdU cryptographic intelligence on the movement of these convoys. Without this type of intelligence, it was nearly impossible for the U-boats to find the convoys to attack. On the other hand, while the U-boats could not find convoys, the Allies could and did find and sink the U-boats. In the majority of instances, cryptographic intelligence did not play a big role in these successes, for there were still lags and delays in the reading of German radio messages at this time. What cryptographic intelligence could provide Allied commanders for this period was a picture—even if somewhat delayed—of the general pattern of U-boat deployments, with D/F providing numerous hints or pointers as to the location of particular U-boats. Using this information, the US Navy deployed escort or hunter-killer groups built around escort carriers into regions of known U-boat concentrations. When a hunter-killer group entered a region known to be frequented by U-boats, American carrier-borne aircraft sought out the U-boats over a wide area and attacked them. Communications intelligence, combined with the ability of carrier aircraft to search vast stretches of ocean, was the basis of American success against the U-boats along the North American-Gibraltar convoy route in the summer of 1943.

In September the U-boats would again be deployed against North America-Great Britain convoys in the North Atlantic. Summer had brought the German submarines nothing but heavy losses and failures against Allied convoys along the Gibraltar route. Now the German naval command would see whether their new weapons and technology would give the U-boats another chance for success in the North Atlantic, the most decisive area of this war at sea.

Chapter 6

More Battles along the North American-United Kingdom Convoy Route

15 September–7 November 1943

In mid-September 1943 German U-boats returned to the North Atlantic, the theater of operations from which they had been withdrawn on 24 May 1943 after forty-five months of battle. Their unacceptably heavy losses at the hands of Allied convoy escorts had forced the BdU to abandon the campaign in those waters temporarily, resolved to renew their attacks on Allied convoys proceeding between Great Britain and North America as soon as they had developed new weapons and tactics to overcome Allied convoy defenses.[1] Their interim strategy was an attempt to step up assault on the Allies' supposed weak spots in mid-Atlantic waters during the summer, simultaneously conducting operations in distant seas such as the Caribbean, South Atlantic, and Indian Ocean. But the Germans learned that there were no Allied weak spots and, in fact, it was the Allies who found a German "weak spot" and attacked it with great effect. Not only were U-boat attacks on United States-Mediterranean convoys a failure that summer, but the operations of American hunter-killer groups built around escort aircraft carriers totally disrupted German U-boat refueling operations in the central Atlantic, forcing the Germans to abandon large-scale U-boat operations in distant seas.[2]

Against this bleak strategic background, the Germans doggedly pursued their plan to renew operations against Allied convoys in the North Atlantic, hoping against hope that their scientists and technicians had used the hiatus to good purpose by developing new technological weapons for the U-boats. The gamble was a desperate one, but the chance of disrupting trade routes between Britain and the United States made it one worth taking.

U-boat success against Allied convoys in the North Atlantic in September of 1943 would be problematic at best. Allied defenses of North Atlantic convoys were far stronger now than in May. By September the Allies had acquired a marked superiority over the Germans in intelligence. The Allies could now read coded German command radio communications with increasing speed and skill, thus gaining hints—or even foreknowledge—of the deployment and movement of German U-boats. On the other hand, German intelligence on Allied movements and deployments was considerably weaker in September than it had been when attacks on Allied North Atlantic convoys were suspended at the end of May. Until June 1943 the Germans had been reading Allied codes, and these sources had given the BdU most of the intelligence required to deploy U-boats to intercept Allied convoys.[3] But in June 1943 the Allies discovered the weakness in their codes and changed them. By September, the Germans had managed to break only enough new Allied codes to gain a foreknowledge of some routes taken by stragglers that had parted company from the convoys. This intelligence, when combined with other low grade communications intelligence, gave the BdU merely a general and, in some cases, a misleading knowledge of the routes to be employed by Allied convoys. It was certainly not good enough to ensure the interception of convoys.[4]

By September of 1943 the Allies were not only superior to the Germans in the realm of communications intelligence but also had greatly increased the number of Allied VLR anti-U-boat aircraft. RAF Coastal Command had deployed three squadrons, consisting of some forty-five VLR B-24 Liberators, in Iceland and Northern Ireland.[5] The RCAF had based a number of VLR B-24 Liberators in Newfoundland as well.[6] The Greenland Air Gap was now closed, and there was no area on the convoy route between North America and Great Britain where Allied aircraft could not support the convoys in strength.

Apparently the Germans either underestimated or discounted their own weakness and the growing strength of the Allies in the North Atlantic. What the Germans needed now to overcome Allied convoy defenses was a revolution in the tactics and technology of U-boat warfare, but they had only marginally increased the effectiveness of the existing types of U-boats over the summer. Still, the Germans clung to the hope that new or improved weapons and tactics offered a possibility of success against the Allies. To combat enemy aircraft, one additional quadruple and two additional twin 20mm antiaircraft guns were mounted on each U-boat. To mislead Allied radar, the U-boats were equipped with the *aphrodite* radar decoy and the *wanze* radar detector. However, the Germans placed their greatest reliance on the *zaunkonig* acoustic homing torpedo. The *zaunkonig* was originally not scheduled to begin operational service until the beginning of 1944, but at the request of the German Navy, production was speeded up and some eighty of these torpedoes arrived at the U-boat bases in France by 1 August 1943. During July and early August the commanding officers and crews of the U-boats which were to renew operations against the North American-Great Britain convoys were given special training to familiarize them with new weapons and tactics to be employed in the coming offensive.[7]

The Germans thought that North Atlantic convoys would be weakly escorted in the fall of 1943 because of "Allied Mediterranean operations." Their plan called for a number of U-boats to pass through the Bay of Biscay undetected by the Allies, secretly setting up a patrol line in the North Atlantic and then ambushing an Allied westbound convoy. As they joined the patrol line and waited for the convoy, the U-boats were to achieve surprise by remaining submerged as much as possible and maintaining radio silence except for "tactically important or distress signals." If the U-boats could take a convoy by surprise, the theory went, they could then use their increased antiaircraft armament and *zaunkonigs* to overpower the air and surface escorts so that the convoy's merchant ships could be attacked. While concentrating ahead of the convoy, the U-boats were to remain surfaced in the face of Allied air attack, fighting off enemy planes. In the neighborhood of the convoy, the U-boats were to simultaneously engage enemy aircraft and coordinate their air defense. However, unlike Allied escorts, the U-boats were not equipped with high frequency radio telephones. Thus, upon receipt of the radio signal "remain surfaced to engage aircraft," the U-boats were to remain on the surface and repel air attacks with no opportunity for a local commander to make quick, tactical decisions. In the attack on the convoy itself, the U-boats would use *zaunkonigs* to push aside or sink the escorts before attacking the merchant ships.[8]

This scheme was hopelessly naive, for it overestimated the effectiveness of U-boat antiaircraft guns and *zaunkonigs*, and ignored the capabilities of Allied intelligence and the combat power of Allied escorts and aircraft. The Germans were equally naive in believing that they could keep secret the necessary gathering of U-boats in the North Atlantic to resume operations against Allied convoys. As early as 30 July, Commander Rodger Winn, RNVR, the head of the submarine tracking room in the Admiralty, offered this bitingly accurate intelligence analysis of the strategy that the Axis would pursue:

> It is common knowledge both to ourselves and the enemy that the only vital issue in the U-boat war is whether or not we are able to bring to England such supplies of food, oil, and raw material and other necessaries, as will enable us, (a) to survive and (b) to mount a military offensive adequate to crush enemy land resistance. Knowing that this is so, the enemy in withdrawing from the North Atlantic must have intended an ultimate return to this area, so soon as he might be able, by conceiving new measures and devising new techniques, to resist the offensive which we might be able to bring to bear upon him there . . . but it might be the last dying struggle of a caged tiger for the enemy to send back in September or October into the North Western Approaches his main U-boat forces, unless in the meantime, he acquires by sheer luck, or the brilliance of some unknown inventor, the antidote and the panacea to all those well proven weapons which our armory contains. . . . Even if heavy losses of merchant shipping and escort forces on the North Atlantic convoy routes were to be suffered . . . no fear need be felt as to the ultimate outcome.[9]

Thus the element of surprise on which the Germans relied simply never existed. The Allies recognized early that the U-boats would sooner or later return to the North Atlantic convoy routes and waited and watched for this development. Accordingly, it came as no surprise on 13 September when Allied intelligence estimated that there were "about 20 U-boats in the general area of the Azores or further north and it would not be surprised, if a marked renewal of activity occurred in the next week or 10 days." The Germans, though, blithely believed that the Allies were unaware of their intentions to resume operations in the North Atlantic and on 15 September radioed orders to twenty-one U-boats (U-575, U-422, U-341, U-260, U-386, U-338, U-731, U-238, U-305, U-270, U-645, U-402, U-229, U-666, U-42, U-952, U-378, U-377, U-758, U-603) at sea to establish a patrol line, code named *Leuthen*, at 2000A on 20 September. The U-boats of *Leuthen* were to space themselves at 17-mile intervals along the line, the radio orders continued, with the line to run between "POINT (ROMAN) 1 TO POINT (ROMAN) II . . . FROM POINT (ROMAN) 1 POINT 'J' BEARS 082 DEGREES, 185 MILES DISTANT. FROM POINT (ROMAN) II 'H' BEARS 260 DEGREES 70 MILES DISTANT." The locations of points J and H were contained in sealed envelopes given in advance to each U-boat commander. The Allies decoded this order at 0943 on 18 September.[10]

It was amazing to later observers that the BdU had not given the entire order to the U-boat commanders before their vessels left port, for there was no tactical reason to inform the U-boats of the time and place of the new patrol line in a radio message. The BdU had no intelligence on the exact routes or times of Allied convoys in the North Atlantic, and it was "assumed that the enemy [was] again using the shortest route between America and England." Thus the positioning of the *Leuthen* patrol line was done by "dead reckoning" because "the data was scanty."[11]

However, the Germans still believed that their codes were secure and using the radio to issue orders to the *Leuthen* group was easier than giving written ones in advance. Further, the BdU was sure that by super-enciphering the position of the intended patrol line in the radio message, they had added security to their codes. This was also a mistake, for the Allies not only could read the German codes but also quickly broke the super enciphered portions of the text. Indeed, super encipherment almost certainly drew the attention of Allied intelligence officers to the radio message. Allied intelligence quickly figured out the approximate location of the patrol line and on 18 September estimated that it stretched for 340 miles between 56°30′N, 32°00′W and 51°40′N, 27°00′W or, alternatively, 9° to the west.[12]

Unfortunately, the Allies did not detect the location and intentions of the *Leuthen* patrol line soon enough to reroute convoys ONS 18 and ON 202 away from the U-boats. At 0842 on 19 September the BdU informed the *Leuthen* patrol line of the approach of a westbound convoy and ordered the U-boats to "OPERATE AGAINST IT AT MAXIMUM SPEED."[13] The convoy which the Germans thought they were intercepting was the forty-one-merchant-ship ON 202,[14] a westbound convoy which had sailed from Great Britain on 15 September with an escort of six warships of Escort Group C3 (destroyers HMCS *Gatineau* and HMS *Icarus*; corvettes HMCS *Drumheller*, HMCS *Kamloops*, HMS *Polyanthus*; HM Trawler *Lancer*; and the frigate HMS *Lagan* joining on 17 September). However, unknown to the Germans, a second convoy—ONS 18—was ahead of ON 202 and ripe for attack by the *Leuthen* group. The twenty-seven merchant ships of ONS 18 sailed west from Liverpool on 13 September, shepherded by eight warships of Escort Group B3 (destroyers HMS *Keppel* and HMS *Escapade*; corvettes HMS *Narcissus*, HMS *Orchis*, FFS *Roselys*, FFS *Lobelia*, FFS *Renoncule*; HM Trawler *Northern Foam*; with the frigate HMS *Towey* joining later). The merchant aircraft carrier *Empire MacAlpine* also accompanied the convoy. When the Allies realized that ONS 18 and ON 202 would be intercepted by the *Leuthen* patrol line, they sent the five warships of the 9th Escort Group (destroyer HMCS *St. Croix*; frigate HMS *Itchen*; and corvettes HMCS *Chambly*, HMCS *Morden*, and HMCS *Sackville*.) at full steam to catch up with the two threatened convoys. On 18 September both convoys were ordered to alter course to the northward to facilitate air support from Iceland.[15]

In another move designed to strengthen the defense of the two convoys, orders went out at 0645 the morning of 19 September to the 9th Escort Group, then escorting convoy HX 256. The five ships of the group were detached from the westbound convoy to sail to the aid of ONS 18. The group had an eventful twenty-nine-hour journey to its new station. At 2324 on 19 September HMCS *Chambly* obtained a radar contact about 40 miles from ONS 18. The U-boat dived and was attacked by the Canadian warship with ten depth charges. HMS *Itchen* joined HMCS *Chambly* in a futile sonar hunt for the U-boat, while the other three ships of the group continued on their way to ONS 18. Just after midnight, at 0125 on 20 September, HMCS *Chambly* and HMS *Itchen* abandoned the hunt and departed for ONS 18, but at 0142 HMS *Itchen* obtained a radar contact which, when illuminated, proved to be a U-boat which dived at 0152. This may have been the same U-boat which HMCS *Chambly* and HMS *Itchen* had just been hunting only 6 miles away. This U-boat was attacked by HMS *Itchen* with depth charges and a hedgehog. A second depth charge attack was made at 0240, but the attack was abandoned, and the two warships continued steaming for ONS 18 now 50 miles to the westward.[16]

On 19 September air cover was provided to both convoys by three VLR B-24 Liberators, one from RAF 86th Squadron and the other two, part of RCAF 10th (BR) Squadron en route to their base in Newfoundland from Iceland. Both convoys were sighted, and the three planes made repeated sweeps over the area.[17] And at 0857 on 19 September, a day before the Germans intended to intercept a convoy, RCAF aircraft A/10 sighted and attacked the U-341, one of the *Leuthen* group, 120 miles north of ON 202 at a range of 500 miles from Iceland.[18] The Canadian aircraft came in too high on the first pass over the U-boat, but the U-341 stayed on the surface to fight it out. This allowed aircraft A/10 to return for an attack with six depth charges which straddled the U-boat, and, as the U-341 disappeared under the water, the aircraft attacked again with four depth charges which produced "a great eruption of oil and bubbles." Aircraft A/10 then circled the area where the U-341 had been sunk for twenty-five minutes before departing from Newfoundland.[19] At the very beginning of the battle, the BdU's policy of requiring U-boats to fight it out on the surface with aircraft had been tested and found wanting.

During the afternoon of 19 September HMS *Escapade*, a destroyer in ONS 18's escort, picked up a number of HF/DF bearings. However, the escort's commander, Commander M. J. Evans, RN, in HMS *Keppel*, concluded that the radio transmissions from astern of the convoy were probably from ON 202 and the 9th Escort Group. Then, at 2130, HMS *Escapade*'s sonar detected two U-boats attempting to attack the convoy, and the destroyer immediately struck with depth charges followed by three hedgehog attacks. As the destroyer was about to undertake a fourth hedgehog attack, a hedgehog missile accidentally went off on its foredeck, killing and wounding a number of crew members and damaging the destroyer so badly that it had to be sent to the Clyde. The next morning, 20 September, HMCS *St. Croix*, HMCS *Chambly*, and HMCS *Morden* of the 9th Escort Group joined the screen of ONS 18, and at noon the convoy received orders to join ON 202 and form a combined convoy.

Meanwhile, astern of ONS 18, convoy ON 202 was steaming at 12 knots, zigzagging on a mean course of 287°. The visibility was "moderate," and the moon in the second quarter and "obscured." At 0202 on 20 September the convoy's rescue ship *Rathlin* obtained an HF/DF bearing at 210° at an estimated range of 15 miles. This was the U-270 transmitting a sighting report to the BdU. This sighting report was quickly followed by two others from the *Leuthen* group's U-731 and U-238. Upon receipt of these sighting reports, the BdU ordered the patrol group to shadow the convoy during the daylight hours of 20 September and directed grimly: "ALL POSSIBLE BOATS ARE TO GET AT THE CONVOY DURING THE COMING NIGHT." The U-boats were also informed "THAT THE DANGER FROM AIR LOCATION [HAS] BEEN DECREASED BY WEATHER CONDITIONS [WHICH] WILL FAVOUR THE ACHIEVEMENT [OF] SUCCESSFUL SURPRISE DURING THE COMING NIGHT."[20]

HMS *Lagan* was ordered to search down the *Rathlin*'s HF/DF bearing on the U-270. As HMS *Lagan* steamed down this bearing, a radar contact was obtained at a range of 4,800 yards at 0244. At 0300 the contact disappeared from HMS *Lagan*'s radar screen, and it was assumed that the U-boat had submerged. The frigate reduced speed and began a sonar search. At 0303 there was an explosion in the stern of HMS *Lagan* followed by several other bursts as the ship's depth charges exploded. Wreckage from the after part of the frigate was thrown up into the air and rained down on the forward part of the vessel. "Approximately 30 feet" of HMS *Lagan*'s stern had disappeared, blown off by a *zaunkonig* from the U-270. This was the first successful use of a *zaunkonig* against an Allied ship. HMS *Lagan* was dead in the water and could not steam. Twenty-nine crew members were killed, and one was missing as a result of the attack. The frigate, screened by HM Trawler *Lancer* and under the tow of HM Tug *Destiny*, arrived safely at the River Mersey on 24 September.[21]

At 0409 HMS *Polyanthus* obtained a radar contact at a range of 3,400 yards ahead of ON 202. The British corvette ran down the contact, fired a star shell, and saw the contact disappear. HMS *Polyanthus* then conducted two depth charge attacks without result before returning to its position on the screen of the convoy. At 0731 the U-238 torpedoed two American freighters in convoy ON 202: *Theodore Wright Weld* and *Frederick Douglass*.[22] The *Theodore Wright Weld* broke in half, and the stern portion sank immediately, while the *Frederick Douglass*, down by the stern, remained afloat. HMCS *Gatineau* and HMS *Polyanthus* swept through the area dropping depth charges "on doubtful contacts." And the rescue ship *Rathlin* picked up the survivors from the *Theodore Wright Weld* and took the crew off of the *Frederick Douglass*, which was then abandoned.[23]

Although the two convoys had not yet combined by the morning of 20 September, air support for both ONS 18 and ON 202 was carried out by five VLR B-24 Liberators of RAF 120th Squadron from Iceland. At 0945 aircraft X/120 reported to Commander P. W. Burnett, RN, senior officer of ON 202's escort, that there was a U-boat (U-338) about 15 miles north of the convoy. Burnett ordered HMS *Icarus* to the area to hunt for the submarine, and as the destroyer approached, the U-boat dived. Aircraft X/120 then attacked the swirl with depth charges. At 1020 HMS *Icarus* obtained a sonar contact and six minutes later carried out a depth charge attack which was followed by a hedgehog attack nine minutes later. Both of these attacks failed.[24]

Meanwhile, the ships of the 9th Escort Group were closing on ONS 18 and became part of the skirmish. Some 20 miles from that convoy, HMS *Itchen* went to investigate the U-boat sighted and reported by aircraft F/120, while HMCS *Chambly* joined ONS 18. Later in the day HMS *Itchen* also joined the convoy. At 1100 the ships of ON 202 sighted HMS *Itchen* ahead of the convoy, searching for the U-338. The U-boat soon radioed "AM BEING ATTACKED BY A/C" and several minutes later again radioed "AM REMAINING ON SURFACE FOR FLAK DEFENCE."[25] Aircraft F/120 first attacked the U-338 with cannon fire but the U-boat retaliated with antiaircraft guns. Then aircraft F/120 attacked again with four depth charges which "under shot." A third attack was carried out with cannon fire, but the weapon jammed. Then the U-338 was attacked with machine-gun fire. At 1112 the U-boat dived, and aircraft F/120 again attacked the U-boat with a single depth charge. After the U-338 had disappeared below the surface, aircraft F/120 homed HMS *Itchen* in on the area. The frigate conducted a search for the U-boat without result.

Not knowing that the U-338 had been attacked by aircraft, the BdU confidently radioed the U-boats of the *Leuthen* group: "NOW TO REMAIN SURFACED AND PROCEED TO CONVOY AT TOP SPEED." At 1405 aircraft X/120 sighted two U-boats about 6 miles away on the port beam of ON 202 and attacked one with machine-gun fire. When HMCS *Drumheller* sighted this skirmish, the Canadian corvette turned toward the U-boat (probably the U-952) and opened fire at a range of 1,400 yards. Aircraft X/120 then departed, owing to a shortage of fuel, and the U-boat dived. At 1546 a sonar contact was obtained, and a depth charge attack was mounted but then broken off when the contact became "very wooly." HMCS *Drumheller* turned and ran back on a reciprocal course to continue the search for the U-boat and at 1558 an explosion was felt beneath the ship. It was thought that a German magnetic torpedo had exploded deep under the ship. No damage was done. Several minutes later HMCS *Drumheller* was recalled to its station on the screen of the convoy, and the aircraft of RAF 120th Squadron continued to patrol around ONS 18 and ON 202 for the rest of the day, sighting and attacking several more U-boats.[26]

The Admiralty decreed that ONS 18 and ON 202 would join at 1600 on 20 September, forming one combined convoy consisting of sixty-one merchant ships (of the original sixty-one merchant ships which had sailed with the two convoys, two ships had been sunk and several others had turned back for various reasons). In classic British understatement, Commander M. J. Evans, RN, commented: "The junction was not a success." As senior officer of ON 202's escort, Evans received the order calling for the junction of the two convoys in a corrupt state which omitted one position on the route, the course which ON 202 was to steer to effect the junction, and the fact that the commodore of ON 202 was to be the senior commodore of the combined convoy. "As a result," in Evans's words, "the two convoys gyrated majestically round the ocean, never appearing to get much

closer and watched appreciatively by a growing swarm of U-boats."
In the end, ONS 18 was stationed behind ON 202, but the convoys
resembled two groups of ships independently steering more or less
the same course, and they were never fused together into one convoy.[27]

Of course, the junction of the two convoys was made much more
difficult by the presence of U-boats. Distracted by the need to sight
and attack the enemy vessels, the escorts and their commanders
could devote little time to forcing the merchant ships within the two
convoys into alignment. At 1629 HMS *Keppel* obtained a sonar contact and then sighted a U-boat periscope off the starboard beam.
HMS *Keppel* carried out four depth charge attacks before being relieved at 2000 by HMS *Itchen*, HMCS *St. Croix*, and HMS *Narcissus*,
which continued to hunt for the U-boat. At the same time HMCS
Kamloops and HMCS *Gatineau* were attacking a sonar contact off the
port bow of the convoy.[28]

The two convoys were not seriously attacked during the night of
20 to 21 September. At 2350 HMCS *Sackville* illuminated, chased,
and carried out an attack on a U-boat ahead of the convoy. FFS
Roselys attacked a sonar contact at 0122, and at 0445 HMCS *Morden*
also attacked a U-boat. These, however, were the U-boats' only contacts with the main body of ONS 18/ON 202 during the night. Evans
thought that the U-boats were not very "enterprising" and that "the
old rule of 'A submarine detected is an attack averted' still held
good." In the early hours of 21 September, ONS 18/ON 202 altered
course to the southwest to get within range of aircraft based in Newfoundland.[29]

However, during that evening a fierce battle did take place astern
of ONS 18/ON 202. When HMS *Itchen*, HMS *Narcissus*, and HMCS
St. Croix were sent to hunt for the U-boat originally attacked by
HMS *Keppel*, the two convoys had steamed on, leaving the three warships astern to continue the hunt. HMS *Polyanthus* was also astern of
ONS 18/ON 202, escorting the rescue ship *Rathlin* as it steamed to
join the convoy. HMCS *St. Croix* was detached from the hunt to
investigate an aircraft report of another U-boat, and at 1956, just as
HMCS *St. Croix* slowed to begin a sonar search, it was hit on the
port side by a *zaunkonig* fired by the U-305. The Canadian destroyer
began to list, and the cryptic message was sent to HMS *Itchen*: "Am

leaving the office." Shortly afterwards HMCS *St. Croix* was hit in the stern by a second torpedo, which caused the ship to blow up and sink. Three minutes later another *zaunkonig* fired from the U-305 exploded in the wake of HMS *Itchen*, which had been standing by the Canadian destroyer. Then HMS *Polyanthus*, which had arrived on the scene shortly after HMS *Itchen*, obtained a radar contact. As it was hunting down the bearing, it was hit in the stern by a *zaunkonig* fired by the U-952. The corvette sank in a few seconds. HMS *Itchen* was joined by HMS *Narcissus*, and it was decided not to pick up the survivors of the two escorts until daylight. At 0304 the two British warships approached the area of the sinkings and picked up one crew member from HMS *Polyanthus* and eighty-one from HMCS *St. Croix* before rejoining ONS 18/ON 202 at 1100.[30]

As reports of the action against ONS 18/ON 202 flowed into the BdU through 20 September and the early hours of 21 September, the Germans began to sort out intelligence and draw conclusions about the convoys and the action. The Germans estimated that there were at least two Allied aircraft escorting the convoys throughout the daylight hours of 20 September. The BdU also concluded that the convoy was heavily escorted, with the Allies employing remote screens of destroyers. The Germans also knew that the convoy had turned to a southwesterly course and had a speed of 9 knots. Although the U-boat commanders believed that Allied air cover was too strong for them to approach the convoys "without being observed," the BdU disagreed. For instance, when the U-338 signaled that it was remaining on the surface to fight with Allied aircraft, the BdU concluded that all the other U-boats of the *Leuthen* groups should also have remained on the surface to join in combat with Allied planes. This conclusion was a result of the BdU's overestimation of the effectiveness of the U-boat's antiaircraft defensive capabilities. The BdU also drew flattering assessments of the effectiveness of the *zaunkonig* from overly optimistic reports of its first use in combat. The U-boats reported fifteen hits with *zaunkonigs*, claiming seven destroyers as sunk and three other destroyers probably sunk. The BdU accepted these claims at face value and concluded that the combat power of a *zaunkonig* was far greater than was actually the case.[31] The false and premature conclusions about the effectiveness of the

U-boats' antiaircraft armament and the combat power of the *zaun-konig* would haunt the Germans in future operations.

At 2212 on 20 September the BdU ordered the U-boats of the *Leuthen* group to "SEARCH AT TOP SPEED ALONG THE ENEMY'S COURSE BETWEEN 280 AND 240 DEGREES." Eight hours later the U-boats were informed that the convoy's course was 270°. Some two hours afterward, the BdU told the *Leuthen* U-boats that "THE SINKING OF 5 DESTROYERS IS A GREAT SUCCESS. GET INTO CONTACT BY DAYLIGHT TODAY IN ORDER TO SUCCEED IN MASSING AGAINST A/C. MAKE THE MOST OF ANY FURTHER CHANCES AGAINST DESTROYERS BY DAY SO AS TO HAVE THE ENEMY RIPE FOR THE MAIN BLOW AGAINST THE BULK OF THE CONVOY ITSELF BY NIGHT."[32] The BdU confidently expected the U-boats to continue to fight on the surface with Allied aircraft, while picking off escorts during the day before attacking the main body of the convoy at night.

However, bad weather prevented any daylight surface action on 21 September. At dawn ONS 18/ON 202 were blanketed by a fog which lasted until 1430, when it lifted for about an hour. As the fog cleared, the Allies discovered "with considerable surprise" that ONS 18 had moved from a position astern of ON 202 to a station off the starboard beam of that convoy. Neither the convoy's commodore nor Commander Evans ordered such a change of formation. Further, when the fog lifted, the merchant aircraft carrier *Empire MacAlpine* flew off an aircraft only to find herself suddenly shrouded again in fog and forced to recover the aircraft in zero visibility. The frigate HMS *Towey* joined the escort during the day, and at 1530 HMCS *Chambly*, HMCS *Sackville*, and HMCS *Morden* conducted a sweep some 20 miles astern of the convoy and found nothing. At sunset the convoy was again in dense fog and a calm sea with a front of "about 9½ miles" covered by extended and close screens.[33] During the morning three VLR B-24 Liberators from Iceland met the convoy in poor visibility and conducted sweeps but never sighted a German submarine. The U-boats of the *Leuthen* group did not obtain contact with ONS 18/ON 202 during the daylight hours of 21 September.

However, it was the fog and not the Allies that kept the U-boats at bay. Unequipped with search radars, the German submarines were understandably reluctant to be caught on the surface by an escort. Still, the BdU persisted in urging the members of the *Leuthen* group to take the offensive. At 1254 the BdU directed the U-boats to operate on "SOUTHWESTERLY COURSES" and ordered them to use their *wanze* radar detectors, hydrophones, and D/F sets to locate the convoy. At 1417 the U-584 reported the convoy to be in square AK 2949 steering a course of 240°. Less than an hour later, the BdU urged the *Leuthen* group to use the cover of the fog to get ahead of the convoy in order to be in an attacking position when the visibility improved. At 1718, blithely discounting the radar sets on the Allied escorts, the BdU informed the U-boats of the *Leuthen* group that "THE REMOTE ESCORT GIRDLE CAN BE PENETRATED BY U/BOATS IN THE FOG, SO THAT WHEN THE FOG LIFTS THEY CAN ALL BE IN CLOSE PROXIMITY TO THE MAIN BODY OF THE CONVOY."[34]

During the early evening of 21 September a number of HF/DF bearings were obtained by the escorts of ONS 18/ON 202, and it appeared to the commander of the escort that an assault might come from any direction. However, the first attack did not develop until 2100, when FFS *Roselys* on the port bow of the convoy obtained a contact and attacked without result. HMS *Icarus* on the starboard side of the convoy chased another U-boat to the westward until it submerged. Just after midnight, at 0039 on 22 September, HMCS *Chambly* sighted a U-boat ahead of the convoy and took it under gunfire before the U-boat submerged. It was then subjected to a depth charge attack. And at 0134 FFS *Renoncule* obtained a radar contact off the port quarter of the convoy, chasing a U-boat toward the van of ONS 18/ON 202 where FFS *Roselys*'s guns forced the enemy vessel to dive. At 0330 Evans reported a "lull" in U-boat activity and thought that the Allies were "definitely on top of the submarines." Because dawn was near, he did not expect the attacks on the convoy to be resumed. However, at the stern of the convoy's screen, the trawler *Northern Foam* almost ran over a U-boat attempting to close with the convoy from the rear at 0440. The U-boat was taken under gunfire and dived. The British thought that they had holed the enemy vessel, for the U-boat immediately surfaced and escaped, chased by FFS *Renoncule*.[35]

At 0542 HMS *Keppel* obtained an HF/DF reading on the U-229 as it transmitted a hydrophone bearing on the convoy to the BdU. Evans thought that this U-boat was "the contact keeper" which systematically reported the convoy's position. HMS *Keppel* ran down the bearing for thirty minutes and obtained a radar contact at 6,000 yards. At a range of 800 yards the U-boat sighted the destroyer in the thick fog and attempted to turn away, but the British sighted the enemy vessel a few seconds later, "fine on the port bow." Several rounds of gunfire were fired at the U-boat and as the U-229 attempted to dive, HMS *Keppel* rammed it in the "pressure hull just abaft of the conning tower." As the destroyer passed over the enemy vessel, ten depth charges set to explode at 50 feet were dropped. After the ramming and the depth charge attack, a large patch of oil appeared on the surface. The U-229 had been sunk. HMS *Keppel* had almost no damage from the ramming and returned to position in the screen of ONS 18/ON 202. Evans thought that the action was: "A most satisfactory episode, in which H/F D/F, RADAR, plotting, Asdic [sonar], depth charges and ship handling all worked faultlessly to the required conclusion."[36]

This was the last contact between the U-boats and the escorts of ONS 18/ON 202 before daylight on 22 September. Evans credited the failure of the U-boats to attack the convoy successfully during the night to HF/DF fixes. However, Evans shrewdly enhanced this advantage by stationing HMS *Towey*, which was equipped with HF/DF, on the extended screen, thus giving himself "warning of the threatened area in plenty of time before the attack developed." Evans further believed: "The Hun is a most peculiar animal and still likes to make a signal before he starts to attack."[37] Lacking electronic location devices such as radar and HF/DF, the U-boats were at a marked disadvantage compared to the escorts in the fog and darkness.

The BdU thought that the U-boats had sunk enough of ONS 18/ON 202's escorts with *zaunkonigs* to make feasible a mass attack on the main body of the convoy during the night of 21 September, but fog had frustrated this intention. It was now the German strategy for the U-boats to stay in contact with ONS 18/ON 202, hoping that the visibility would increase during the daylight hours of 22 September, thus allowing an attack against the merchant ships of the convoy that night. At 0829 on 22 September the BdU ordered the U-boats of the *Leuthen* group to keep in contact with the convoy "SO THAT WHEN VISIBILITY IMPROVES ALL BOATS ARE ON TO IT AND THE ATTACK ON

THE MAIN BODY CAN BE CARRIED OUT DURING THE COMING NIGHT."[38]

Throughout the morning and afternoon of 22 September, there were only intermittent and inconclusive contacts between the escorts of ONS 18/ON 202 and the U-boats. At dawn HMCS *Sackville,* HMCS *Morden,* and HMCS *Chambly* swept around the flanks and stern of the convoy hunting for U-boats before taking up screening positions astern of the convoy. During the forenoon, the HF/DF sets on the escorts obtained a number of bearings on radio transmissions which were coming mainly from astern of or off the quarters of the convoy. The escorts continuously hunted down each of these bearings, but no sightings resulted. At 1035 the rescue ship *Rathlin* sighted a U-boat in the fog at a range of 100 yards and attempted to ram the enemy vessel as it submerged. At 1150 HMCS *Sackville* took a U-boat under fire astern of the convoy. The U-boat dived and was repeatedly attacked with depth charges, the last producing a "phenomenal explosion followed by a large quantity of oil." It was thought that a U-boat was possibly sunk in this attack and certainly damaged. And at 1508 FFS *Roselys* forced a U-boat to dive off the port bow of the convoy.[39]

When the fog finally cleared at 1520, Evans saw that the merchant ships of the convoy were spread over an area of 30 square miles, with a 4-mile gap between ONS 18 and ON 202. By 1800 the ships of the two convoys had been closed up, steering a course of 210°. Evans intended to turn ONS 18/ON 202 on a course of 250°, but before this turn could be put into effect, the escort's commander received a report of a U-boat bearing 250° at a range of 50 miles. Evans then asked the commodore of the convoy to hold a southerly course until dark, then to turn to a course of 260° to avoid the U-boat. The commodore agreed to make the course change, but then "horrified" Evans by requesting that ONS 18 take station behind ON 202. The commodore did not want to make so drastic a change of course with a combined convoy consisting of eighteen columns. Instead, he suggested that the two convoys carry out the course change as separate units, one behind the other. At this point, in his own words, Evans made "a very grave mistake" by not ordering the course change in daylight and by permitting the two convoys to be formed up one behind the other.[40] Instead he allowed ONS 18/ON 202 to proceed on a narrow front instead of a wide front in the darkness of the North Atlantic. This was a tactical mistake, for the convoy would take much longer to pass a given point, giving the U-boats an increased opportunity to attack the train of merchant ships.

At 1930 FFS *Lobelia* on the convoy's port beam carried out a number of depth charge attacks on a suspected U-boat which produced an "inexplicable explosion" and some wreckage, but did not sink a U-boat. At about the same time, one of the *Empire MacAlpine*'s (a merchant aircraft carrier) Swordfish aircraft sighted and attacked a U-boat, probably the U-238, on the port bow of the convoy. Evans's ship, HMS *Keppel*, followed by HMS *Narcissus*, went to the scene, attempted to gain contact with sonar, and then dropped some "scare" depth charges before returning to the convoy. HMS *Narcissus* continued to hunt this U-boat until the convoy steamed past the position. Just after HMS *Keppel* began to return to the convoy, the warship saw antiaircraft fire some 5 miles away. Evans thought that this was some kind of decoy to draw him away from the convoy, but it was, in fact, another Swordfish aircraft using air-to-surface rockets to attack a U-boat (probably the U-238). No hits were made, and it was dark by the time the aircraft returned to the *Empire MacAlpine*.[41]

The carrier-based planes were reinforced by three VLR B-24 Liberator aircraft of RCAF 10th (BR) Squadron from Newfoundland as soon as the fog cleared during the afternoon of 22 September. In the face of flak, aircraft L/10 attacked the U-270 with four depth charges, which were near misses but put a hole in the vessel's pressure hull, making it impossible for the U-boat to dive. The U-270 was forced to return to base on the surface. Aircraft X/10 used radar to locate the U-377 and attacked with machine-gun fire and four depth charges. Then, as the U-boat was submerging, the aircraft again attacked with two acoustic homing torpedoes. Although this U-boat was not sunk, it was forced out of the battle because the commander had been wounded by gunfire and needed medical assistance. During the attack on the U-277, another U-boat, probably the U-402, was sighted. This U-boat was attacked with machine-gun fire, and it then retreated into a fog bank. And, after sunset 7 miles ahead of the convoy, aircraft N/10 sighted the wake of the U-275 and was taken under the submarine's antiaircraft fire. The plane's commander wanted to drop flares for a night attack, but Evans refused permission as these would light up the ships of the convoy. The U-275 was forced to submerge, and aircraft N/10 made several sweeps around the convoy in the darkness before returning to base.[42]

Even as Allied aircraft conducted sweeps around ONS 18/ON 202 during the afternoon of 22 September, the U-boats of the *Leuthen* group kept contact with the convoy. At 1918 the BdU ordered those U-boats to send radio beacon signals which it hoped other U-boats could use to home in on the convoy. And it also informed the U-boats that "EVERYTHING DEPENDS ON BOATS GETTING TO GRIPS TONIGHT." Even though the beacon signals appear to have been less than successful, a number of U-boats were in position to intercept and attack ONS 18/ON 202.[43]

From HF/DF bearings, Evans estimated that there were some twelve U-boats in attacking positions around the convoy and that the threat came from ahead and from the port side. The commander of the escort also thought that the deployment of the ships of the convoy "was depressing in the extreme," for the change of course had produced a gap of 3 miles between ONS 18 and ON 202, while the combined convoys "had a depth of something like 6 or 7 miles" front to back. "This," Evans recalled gloomily, "was a most unsatisfactory start to a night when a heavy attack was expected."[44]

The first attack was made by the U-952, a U-boat attempting to work its way into the convoy from the stern. This was an unexpected direction, but the U-boat was successfully driven off by the trawler *Northern Foam* and FFS *Renoncule*. What happened next was a confusing melee in the van of the convoy. At 2335 HMCS *Morden* obtained a radar contact ahead of the convoy. When this U-boat was chased, it dived and was then attacked with ten depth charges at 2354. As HMCS *Morden* was turning to run in for another attack, it was forced to turn to starboard to avoid a collision with HMS *Itchen* which had left its station to follow a radar contact off the convoy's port bow. When that enemy vessel disappeared, the *Itchen* immediately followed another radar contact, passing between HMCS *Sackville* and HMS *Narcissus* before almost colliding with HMCS *Morden*.

Just before HMCS *Morden* conducted its depth charge attack, HMCS *Gatineau* obtained a radar contact of a U-boat closing with the convoy on a course of 130°. Followed by HMS *Orchis*, HMCS *Gatineau* turned to starboard in an effort to head off this U-boat. At

2359 HMS *Itchen* illuminated a U-boat with a searchlight at a range of 300 to 400 yards. The British frigate opened fire with a 20mm Oerliken, with HMCS *Morden* firing at the same target.

Fifteen seconds later the searchlight went out, and there was a blinding flash as HMS *Itchen* exploded after being hit by a *zaunkonig* fired by the U-666. At midnight the U-666 fired another *zaunkonig* at HMCS *Morden* which missed. HMS *Itchen* was broken in two by the force of the explosion and sank immediately, killing all but one of its own crew, all but one of the survivors picked up from HMCS *St. Croix*, and all but one rescued from HMS *Polyanthus*. Upon reaching the area of the explosion, HMCS *Gatineau* fired a star shell, but the convoy was bearing down and it returned to its station on the screen. The three survivors from HMS *Itchen* were picked up by the Polish merchant ship *Waleba*.[45]

A minute after HMS *Itchen* blew up, HMCS *Chambly* obtained a radar contact at a range of 3,000 yards on the port beam of the convoy. The Canadian warship chased down the bearing and sighted a U-boat which dived. HMCS *Chambly* then attacked the enemy vessel with depth charges before beginning to return to its station. Two more contacts were obtained by HMCS *Gatineau* and FFS *Lobelia* at 0105 and 0115, respectively, on 23 September. Then HMCS *Chambly*, returning to its station on the port beam of the convoy, obtained a radar contact at a range of 4,900 yards bearing 235°. This was probably the U-260. As the corvette ran in to attack at 0229, a U-boat dived and there was a large explosion as a *zaunkonig* blew up in the warship's wake at 0232. HMCS *Chambly* attacked with ten depth charges at 0240. Then its sonar broke down and, while attempting to repair it, the warship circled the area for twenty minutes before returning to its station.[46]

Meanwhile, the U-238 torpedoed three merchant ships in the starboard outer column of the convoy at 0220. The *Skjelbred* was torpedoed aft on the starboard side and did not sink immediately. The *Oregon Express* was torpedoed in the engine room, broke in half, and sank almost at once, while the *Fort Jemseg* was hit aft on the starboard side and did not sink. The crews of the *Skjelbred* and *Fort Jemseg* abandoned their ships and were picked up by the trawler *Northern Foam* as were the survivors from the *Oregon Express*. Just before the torpedoes hit the three merchant ships, HMS *Icarus* heard their hydrophone effects and obtained radar contact with the U-238 at a range of 2,400 yards at 0221. The British thought that the U-boat had fired the torpedoes from just outside the screen of the convoy and then turned away. HMS *Icarus* pursued the U-238 as the enemy vessel ran from the convoy. Star shells followed by high explosives forced the U-238 to submerge. Sonar contact was obtained on the U-boat a few minutes later, and HMS *Icarus* carried out a depth charge attack without result. After dropping a few more depth charges as "scarers," the British warship resumed its station on the screen of the convoy.[47]

U-boat attacks on ONS 18/ON 202 abated for some four hours until 0650, when the convoy was attacked on the port side. The U-952 fired four torpedoes at the merchant ships of the convoy. While two torpedoes missed, one dud hit the *James Gordon Bennett* and a live torpedo hit the *Steel Voyager*, damaging the vessel. The crew of the *Steel Voyager* abandoned ship but were "induced" to return to their ship by the commander of FFS *Renoncule*. The master of the freighter reported that a bulkhead would not hold and the ship was again given up. Evans later grumbled that the ship should never have been abandoned. Shortly afterwards, HMCS *Chambly* picked up a radar contact on the U-952 and took the U-boat under gunfire. The U-952 then dived, successfully escaping the Canadian ship's subsequent depth charges.[48]

At dawn, HMCS *Sackville* was ordered to search back through the battle area to the point where HMS *Itchen* had been sank, while HMCS *Morden* and HMCS *Chambly* carried out sweeps along the port side and astern of the convoy. The first RCAF VLR B-24 Liberator, P/10, arrived over the convoy from Newfoundland at 0842 and searched the area astern of ONS 18/ON 202, attacking a U-boat 20 miles from the convoy.[49] Later in the mission, aircraft P/10 sighted, attacked, and forced the U-422 to dive. Several hours later, aircraft Y/10 also found and attacked the U-422, again without success.[50]

Evans thought that the Germans owed their success in attacking ONS 18/ON 202 on the night of 22 to 23 September "to a very large extent" to the improper formation of the convoy—ONS 18 sailing astern of ON 202 in a narrow-front formation. During the daylight hours of 23 September, the ships were rearranged into a broad front formation so that ONS 18 was abreast of ON 202. The escorts were refueled and restocked with depth charges. The HF/DF bearings obtained during the daylight hours of 23 September indicated that for the most part the U-boats were dropping astern of ONS 18/ON 202. By nightfall the merchant ships were in close formation proceeding on a board front, and the fifteen warships of the escort were stationed around ONS 18/ON 202 in inner and outer screens. That night the convoy was again engulfed in thick fog. But nothing more than several inconclusive contacts between the escorts of ONS 18/ON 202 and U-boats occurred on the evening of 23 September and the following day. The battle was over, for most of the U-boats had dropped astern of the Allied force.[51]

The withdrawal of the German submarines occurred even though the BdU believed that the U-boats had sunk three destroyers and a merchant ship during the night of 22 to 23 September. At 0830 in the morning of 23 September the BdU ordered the U-boats of the *Leuthen* group to move east and end the operation against ONS 18/ON 202. Only those U-boat ahead of the convoy and in favorable attacking positions were exempted from this order. Later in the day those U-boats still in contact with the convoy were ordered to "MAKE FULL USE OF ATTACKING CHANCES THAT OFFER." In the fleeting contacts between U-boats and ONS 18/ON 202 on 23 September, the BdU mistakenly concluded that a further two destroyers had been sunk and four other ships hit by torpedoes.[52]

The Germans ended the operation against ONS 18/ON 202 after three days for a number of reasons. It was thought that the convoy's escort had been reinforced and that "the escorts are still too strong and that it is not yet possible to make any attack on the ships of the convoy." Further, ONS 18/ON 202 were now approaching "the fog zone" of the Grand Banks of Newfoundland. The U-boats' lack of search radar and the Germans' painful memories of their May 1943 defeat on the Grand Banks in fog during the battle for ONS 5 made the BdU eager to avoid all battles between U-boats and Allied escorts in conditions of fog. Moreover, the operation had been proceeding for three days "under the most difficult weather and defense conditions," and the crews of the U-boats were exhausted. Continuing the operation against ONS 18/ON 202, the BdU feared, "might lead to losses of boats."[53]

In the battle for ONS 18/ON 202, the Allies saw three escorts and six merchant ships sunk and one escort damaged (HMS *Lagan* damaged; HMS *Itchen*, HMS *Polyanthus*, HMS *St. Croix*, and the merchant ships *Theodore Dwight Weld*, *Frederick Douglass*, *Oregon Express*, *Fort Jemseg*, *Skjelbred*, *Steel Voyager*, all sunk). In exchange, the Germans had lost two U-boats (U-341, U-229). These losses were acceptable to the Allies. After the battle, Evans thought that if the U-boats that attacked ONS 18/ON 202 were the German "first team," then it could not "have been a very encouraging result" for the enemy. The British officer thought that the Germans' tactics during the action were "stereotyped," with the U-boats breaking off attacks on "flimsy pretexts" and the enemy showing a general lack of determination "in pressing his attacks." Evans further concluded correctly from the hits in the sterns of ships and from the explosions in their wakes that the Germans were using an acoustic torpedo and judged that "the volume of their Flak appears to have considerably increased." Evans also believed that his biggest mistake in the action was permitting ONS 18 and ON 202 to form up one behind the other on the night of 22 September, complaining that if the formation of the convoy had "been in decent shape we should probably not have lost a single ship after the junction of the convoys."[54]

The analysis made by the anti-U-boat division in the Admiralty basically agreed with the Evans's conclusions. The staff officers concluded that "except for the use of an acoustic homing torpedo fired at closing escorts and the increased gunfire against attacking aircraft, there was no evidence of new tactics or technical developments." Further, the U-boats "seemed more reluctant than previously to press home their attacks and, when once detected, made every effort to escape." It was also concluded that "air cover" and HF/DF were again of great importance to the Allies in blunting and beating back the attacks of the U-boats.[55]

The Germans had totally misjudged the results of their attack on ONS 18/ON 202. The order to the U-boats to stay on the surface and fight it out with Allied aircraft was disastrous from the German point of view. One out of two U-boats lost in the action were sunk by Allied shore-based aircraft.[56] The Germans believed that they had definitely sunk twelve escorts and had probably sunk another three with *zaunkonigs*.[57] Compounding their losses in the engagement, the

Germans convinced themselves that their inaccurate total of Allied losses would have been even greater if fog had not forced the U-boats to break off the action on the second day. What the BdU did not realize was that the U-boats' need to go deep just after firing a *zaunkonig* forced the German submarine commanders to base claims of hits and sinkings on noises of explosions and the like heard through their hydrophones. Lacking visual confirmation, they had inevitably overestimated the number of ships actually sunk. These excessive claims led Karl Doenitz to overestimate greatly the combat power of the *zaunkonig* as a weapon to sink Allied escorts.[58] As a result, the Germans mistakenly thought that the battle for ONS 18/ ON 202 was a great German victory and proclaimed it as such to the U-boats.[59]

Not only did the Germans give the *zaunkonig* undeserved credit for inflicting damage on convoy ONS 18/ON 202, but they were also tragically over-optimistic in assuming their new weapon would play a decisive role in the future. In fact, the Allies were not taken by surprise by the *zaunkonig*. Communications intelligence was largely responsible for warning the Allies that the Germans had developed and tested an acoustic homing torpedo.[60] Further, unknown to the Germans, the Americans had produced an airborne acoustic homing torpedo—the Mark 24 Mine—and used it successfully in combat long before the enemy had introduced the *zaunkonig*.[61] As a result, after the attack on convoys ON 202 and ONS 18, the Allies were quickly able to introduce countermeasures to thwart the *zaunkonig* (a noise maker, known as a Foxer, towed astern of a ship to attract an acoustic torpedo to itself rather than to the towing vessel).

After the battle for ONS 18/ON 202, the overconfident Germans resolved to continue to attack convoys proceeding between North America and Great Britain. On 24 September the BdU ordered nineteen U-boats (U-279, U-436, U-731, U-359, U-666, U-758, U-402, U-584, U-419, U-378, U-592, U-645, U-260, U-603, U-275, U-335, U-610, U-448, U-305) to form a patrol line, code named *Rossbach*, running from 58°N, 33°W to 54°N, 30°W. The U-boats were ordered to "REMAIN AS FAR AS POSSIBLE UNSEEN" and to maintain radio silence "EXCEPT FOR TACTICALLY IMPORTANT REPORTS." The *Rossbach* patrol line was to be in position to intercept ON 203, a westbound convoy by 1600 on 26 September—almost twelve hours after the Allies had decoded the order creating and pinpointing the *Rossbach* line.[62]

By trying to intercept ON 203 southeast of Greenland, the BdU was attempting to outfox the Allies. The standard German procedure after fighting a battle like the one against ON 202 and ONS 18 would have been to set up a patrol line east of Newfoundland to intercept an eastbound SC or HX convoy. The deployment of the *Rossbach* patrol line was an attempt to do the unexpected and was made on the basis of a 23 September decryption that showed part of the stragglers' route for ships belonging to ON 203. In the next several days the Germans obtained additional, if somewhat conflicting, communications intelligence which led them to shift the *Rossbach* group 100 miles to the northwest on 25 September.[63] But ON 203 passed to the northward of the *Rossbach* patrol line without the Germans gaining contact.[64] The Operations Division of the German Naval Staff thought that the failure to intercept ON 203 stemmed from insufficient U-boats to cover all the possible routes which could be taken by a convoy and from the inability of the German air force to provide proper reconnaissance by aircraft.[65]

On 29 September the BdU ordered the *Rossbach* group, now consisting of sixteen U-boats (U-389, U-436, U-642, U-731, U-359, U-666, U-336, U-758, U-584, U-610, U-603, U-375, U-448, U-305, U-631, U-402), to move northeast to a position southwest of Iceland. While the U-boats were moving into position radio silence was to be maintained except for a "TACTICALLY IMPORTANT MESSAGE" and the U-boats were to remain "UNOBSERVED." The new German objective was a pair of westbound convoys, ON 204 and ONS 19, which they expected to intercept on 1 October.[66] The BdU ran a risk by moving the *Rossbach* patrol line northeast because the U-boats were now closer to the Allied air bases in Iceland, but recent intelligence had shown that westbound Allied convoys steered close to Iceland in order to pick up ships from that island, and the hazard seemed unavoidable.[67]

However, the Germans did not realize that they had taken the chance with no possibility of success. While the 29 September order creating the *Rossbach* patrol was not decoded by the Allies until 0731 on 1 October, the security of the U-boats' move was breached much earlier through other means. At 1312 on 29 September the U-631, one of the *Roßbach* group, was ordered to send a weather report. This transmission was no doubt D/F'ed by the Allies. On 30 September another U-boat of the *Roßbach* group was overflown by a "Mitchell" aircraft while still another *Roßbach* submarine was circled by an unarmed Hudson aircraft for about an hour. On 1 October the U-448, U-402, and U-631 were attacked by two VLR B-24 Liberators of 120th Squadron from Iceland which were escorting HX 258, an eastbound convoy.[68]

The aircraft sightings made it clear to the Germans that the Allies knew of the location of the *Roßbach* group. Nevertheless, on 2 October the BdU moved the patrol line further northeast to take station between 63°N, 28°W and 59°N, 27°W.[69] This was done on the basis of new communications intelligence showing that ON 204 and ONS 19 had been routed north of the *Roßbach* patrol line. But by the time this revised order was issued, ONS 19 had passed the *Roßbach* patrol line, and on 3 October ON 204 also slipped around the northern end of the *Roßbach* patrol line.[70] In their quest for ONS 19 and ON 204, the Germans sighted only what were thought to be "the remote escort" of a convoy, and these sightings were reported to the BdU too late to permit pursuit to the westward. The Germans blamed the lack of aircraft reconnaissance and conflicting communications intelligence for their failure to intercept ON 204 and ONS 19.[71]

Worst of all, the Germans had suffered substantial losses while gaining nothing. In their desperate search for the two westbound Allied convoys, they moved the *Roßbach* patrol line within 200 miles of the Allied air bases in Iceland. The dangers of this risk became apparent on 3 October, when the U-610, U-275, and U-952 were attacked by aircraft. Even after the convoys had passed safely through the area, the Allies pressed their advantage. Knowing of the concentration of U-boats southwest of Iceland, the Allies sent ten RAF Hudsons and five US Navy Venturas to sweep over the northern section of the *Roßbach* patrol line on 4 October. In addition, RAF VLR B-24 Liberators flew sorties to provide escort to ON 204 and ONS 19, and these flights produced seven more sightings of U-boats and damage to two. A USN Ventura sank the U-336, but aircraft V/120 was shot down by gunfire from the U-539. The next day Allied aircraft were out again, and a Hudson of 269th Squadron sank the U-389 in a rocket attack.[72] Allied air activity forced the BdU to order the U-boats to move off to the south. Allied aircraft were still active on 5 October for the U-731 was attacked from the air.[73]

On 6 October the BdU ordered sixteen U-boats (U-436, U-641, U-359, U-336, U-448, U-610, U-419, U-279, U-378, U-645, U-260, U-603, U-275, U-631, U-91, U-437) of the *Rossbach* group to move south to form a patrol line between 56°N, 29°W and 53°N, 28°W at 0001 on 8 October. The patrol line was to sweep southwest to intercept the eastbound convoy SC 143. The Allies decoded this order at 1702 on 7 October. In a further set of orders, the *Rossbach* group was told to keep radio silence except for "MESSAGES OF TACTICAL IMPORTANCE."[74] However, the BdU still clung to the belief that their inability to find Allied convoys stemmed from the Allies' use of "THE STRONGEST POSSIBLE AVOIDANCE MOVEMENTS" and the GAF's disinclination to provide reconnaissance over the battle area.[75] Thus the BdU orders to the *Rossbach* vessels explained that, as "THE FINDING OF THE CONVOYS HAS ONCE AGAIN BECOME THE MAIN PROBLEM OF THE U-BOAT WAR," all U-boats were to transmit as quickly as possible to the BdU "THE SLIGHTEST PIECE OF EVIDENCE ABOUT AN EXPECTED CONVOY." To this end, the U-boats of the *Rossbach* group were provided with a special set of short signals with which to make sighting reports.[76]

Their quarry, convoy SC 143, had sailed from Halifax, Nova Scotia, on 28 September. It consisted of twenty-nine merchant ships which were joined at sea two days later by ten more merchant ships from Cape Breton, Nova Scotia. Also sailing with SC 143 was the merchant aircraft carrier *Rapana*. At 1600 on 2 October at 47°05'N, 48°20'W, Escort Group C2—the ocean escort consisting of HMCS *Kamloops*, HMS *Antares*, HMCS *Chambly*, HMCS *Sackville*, HMCS *Morden*, and HMCS *Timmins*—joined SC 143 for the voyage to the United Kingdom. On 3 October HMCS *Drumheller*, which had sailed late from St. John's, Newfoundland, joined the convoy. However, several hours later HMCS *Timmins* was detached on orders from flag officer Newfoundland. On 4 October the escort was reinforced by HM Trawler *Gateshead* and HMS *Icarus*.[77]

As SC 143 proceeded toward the British Isles, the convoy's escort was reinforced yet again. At 1330Z on 4 October HMS *Duckworth* was detached from convoy HX 259 and ordered to join the eastbound group. And the next day the 10th Escort Group—a support group consisting of the destroyers HMS *Musketeer*, HMS *Oribi*, HMS *Orwell*, and ORP *Orkan*—was detached from convoy ONS 19 and sent to join SC143 which it reached at 0850 on 6 October. The Allies not only bolstered the escort of SC 143 because they knew from communications intelligence that the convoy was in danger of being attacked, but they also deliberately altered SC 143's route to pass through or near the *Rossbach* patrol line in order to draw U-boats away from the much less strongly defended convoy HX 259.[78]

At 0955Z on 6 October the destroyers of the 10th Escort Group made sweeps to the depth of 30 to 40 miles to the east and north of SC 143, while HMCS *Sackville*, HMCS *Morden*, and HMS *Icarus* took on oil from a tanker in the convoy. The afternoon was uneventful once HMCS *Chambly* destroyed a drifting British-made mine which was discovered ahead of SC 143 at 1335Z. And during the night, the destroyers of the 10th Escort Group formed an advanced screen ahead of the convoy. HMS *Duckworth* joined SC 143 at 0005Z on 7 October after being homed in by HMS *Icarus* on an HF/DF set. In the course of a sweep by the 10th Escort Group, ORP *Orkan* intercepted "a close enemy [radio] transmission" on its HF/DF set. Two destroyers were sent down the bearing but found nothing. Nevertheless, the Allies thought it likely that the destroyers, but not the convoy, had been sighted.[79]

Electronic warfare came to the German's rescue for once. German shore-based D/F stations obtained a fix on SC 143 during the morning of 7 October.[80] At 1613 the U-731 reported "ONE DESTROYER SQUARE AK 6196, COURSE EAST." Seven minutes later the BdU ordered the U-731 to shadow "AS FAR AS POSSIBLE" and directed nearby U-boats to operate on the U-731's report, while the other U-boats of the *Rossbach* group were commanded to proceed east at cruising speed until "THE SITUATION REGARDING THE CONVOY IS CLARIFIED." And if the U-731 had sighted a convoy then all the U-boats of the *Rossbach* patrol line were to "OPERATE AGAINST IT AT TOP SPEED." In the next several hours the BdU received reports from two other U-boats reporting the sighting of destroyers. By 2145 the BdU had come to the conclusion that a convoy had been intercepted and ordered all the *Rossbach* U-boats to operate against it at top speed because "THERE IS ONLY A SHORT SPACE LEFT TO EASTWARD." The

U-boats were also directed to attack the escorts before pursuing the merchant ships.[81]

At 1900Z, just as the destroyers of the 10th Escort Group were taking up stations for the night, a radio transmission was picked up by HF/DF at a range of between ten to 20 miles on a bearing of 350°. Destroyers conducted a search down this bearing without result. Additional radio transmissions were picked up by the British ships over the next two hours. Even though no bearings were obtained on these transmissions, the Allies deduced that several U-boats were in contact with destroyers of the 10th Escort Group as they conducted sweeps to keep the U-boats away from SC 143.[82]

At 0605Z on 8 October there was an explosion in the wake of ORP *Orkan* some 7 miles astern of SC 143. Thirty seconds later there was a second and larger explosion: several fires were seen around the bridge and funnel of the Polish destroyer, and at 0610 ORP *Orkan* sank stern first. The Polish destroyer had been torpedoed by the U-378. A *zaunkonig* exploded in the destroyer's wake just before it was hit amidships by two other torpedoes. Only one officer and forty-two crew members belonging to ORP *Orkan* were later picked up by HMS *Musketeer*.[83]

By and large, though, the U-boats were clearly finding it extremely difficult to establish contact with the main body of SC 143 because of the wide ranging sweeps conducted by the destroyers of the 10th Escort Group. The U-448 at 0403 radioed the BdU that it had been "REPEATEDLY" located by two destroyers and had not sighted the convoy. And further it thought the "THE DESTROYERS ARE A DECOY GROUP." Twenty minutes later the BdU informed the *Rossbach* U-boats that all the destroyers sighted by various U-boats "MUST BE THE REMOTE ESCORT OF AN EASTBOUND CONVOY. CONTINUE THE SEARCH IN WIDE SWEEPS."[84]

At dawn the *Rapana* flew off a patrol of Swordfish aircraft, and thirty minutes later, at 0730Z, radio contact was made with the first VLR B-24 Liberator to appear over the convoy—the R/86. While carrying out a search near the convoy this aircraft sighted the U-419 about 15 miles off the port beam of SC 143 and dropped four depth charges on the U-boat as it submerged, apparently undamaged. The senior officer of the escort then ordered the aircraft to continue to search around SC 143 for one hour and then to cruise back to the position where the U-419 had dived. At 0954 aircraft R/86 returned to the scene of the first attack on the U-419 and sighted the U-boat again. This time the U-boat did not submerge and was attacked with two depth charges which hit the water alongside its hull. "There was a violent explosion with a white flash and a dirty green cloud," the official account reported, and as aircraft R/86 circled, the U-419 sank by the stern, and 30 feet of its bow "was seen sticking vertically out of the water." HMS *Oribi* saw the final attack the U-419 from a distance of about 5 miles. After the action, it picked up the sole survivor, the commander, Lieutenant Dietrich Giersberg, from "the middle of a large oil patch."[85]

Shortly after leaving the area where the U-419 sank, aircraft R/86 sighted a second U-boat, the U-643, about 30 miles astern of SC 143 at 1010. Having used all its depth charges in sinking the U-419, aircraft R/86 attacked the U-643 with machine-gun fire while homing in another aircraft. Aircraft Z/86 arrived very quickly and attacked the U-643 with four depth charges as the U-boat submerged. The senior officer of the escort then repeated his successful ruse, ordering the aircraft away from the U-boat for one hour. Aircraft R/86 returned to base and aircraft Z/86 resumed patrolling around SC 143. After the departure of the two aircraft, the U-643 surfaced and was sighted and attacked by another VLR B-24 Liberator, G/120. In the first attack, the plane dropped a single depth charge. The U-643 remained on the surface as aircraft G/120 circled and then attacked again with three depth charges before the U-643 submerged. At this point, aircraft T/120 arrived and aircraft G/120 left, having expended its depth charges. At 1305 aircraft T/120 again sighted the U-643 on the surface. A few minutes later, aircraft T/120 attacked with four depth charges in the face of antiaircraft fire from the U-boat. Aircraft Z/86 then returned and immediately attacked the U-643 with two remaining depth charges. Aircraft T/120 resumed attack on the U-643 with four depth charges and machine-gun fire. The depth charges straddled the U-boat and it "slowed down." Both aircraft then showered the U-643 with machine-gun fire until the vessel was seen to take on a list and its crew abandoned ship. Low on fuel, aircraft Z/86 returned to base, while aircraft T/120 continued to circle over the submarine until the U-boat blew up at 1445. Shortly afterwards the destroyers of the 10th Escort Group arrived on the scene, and HMS *Orwell* and HMS *Oribi* picked up twenty-one members of the crew of U-643. The Allied report explained: "It was considered important to pick up survivors for interrogation in view of the recent developments in U-boat weapons."[86]

The Germans were, indeed, playing their strongest hand in supporting the U-boats that day. Throughout the afternoon of 8 October, the convoy escorts' HF/DF sets not only picked up transmissions which indicated that there were a number of U-boats astern of SC143, but also tracked signals that later proved to come from a German BV 222 flying boat which was attempting to home U-boats in on the convoy. At 0523 on 8 October the BdU had informed the *Rossbach* group that this aircraft would appear over SC 143 at noon and attempt to direct the U-boats of the group to the convoy by radio homing signals. The U-boats were directed to watch out for the aircraft's homing signals and to repeat them if no U-boat was shadowing the convoy. The Germans had very few operational BV 222s, and these had seen some service mainly in Russia and the eastern Mediterranean. Even though they had conducted a few reconnaissance missions west of Spain and Ireland, the crews, like most of the GAF, had very little operational experience in working with U-boats in the mid-Atlantic.[87] Thus, while the BV 222 reached SC 143 at 1239, correctly reported the convoy's position, and sent homing signals for fifteen minutes, not a single U-boat heard the homing signals.[88] For some reason, the BdU concluded that the position given for the convoy by the BV 222 was inaccurate "AND UNRELIABLE" and so informed the U-boats of the *Rossbach* group at 1625. As a result, the U-boats on the north end of the patrol line were ordered to search for the convoy to the "NORTHWARD" and those on the southern end, to search to the "SOUTHWARD," while "ALL BOATS ARE TO REMAIN SURFACED IF THEIR FLAK ARMAMENT IS IN ORDER."[89] Thus, the GAF's single attempt to intervene in the U-boat war along the North American-United Kingdom convoy route in October 1943 came to nothing. At the same time German intelligence noted that at least seven Allied aircraft were operating in support of SC 143.[90]

An escort on the starboard quarter of the convoy obtained "a rather indefinite" HF/DF fix at a range of 26 miles at 1826Z. A search of the area resulted in no contact. Four minutes later, however, a Sunderland flying boat from the RCAF's 423rd Squadron sighted the U-610 at a range of 30 miles from the starboard quarter of SC 143. The aircraft flew over the U-boat, raking it with machine-gun fire. The U-610 opened antiaircraft fire. Aircraft J/423 then banked, dropped down to 100 feet, and attacked with three depth charges. When the plumes caused by the explosions had subsided, the U-610 had disappeared and all that could be seen on the surface of the water from the aircraft was about fifteen crew members and a lot of debris floating in the middle of an "oil patch."[91] That was the end of the U-610.

In the evening of 8 October the weather started to deteriorate, and a force seven gale began to blow from the southwest. At 0119 on 9 October, a Leith light (a powerful searchlight fitted to the underside of an antisubmarine aircraft) B-24 Liberator appeared over the convoy and patrolled for over three hours off the starboard quarter of SC 143, the direction from which the escort's senior officer thought an attack would probably come. Between 0510Z and 0600Z the escorts obtained several HF/DF bearings from radio transmissions thought to have come from close astern of the convoy. At 0628Z HMCS *Drumheller* and HMCS *Chambly* reported an explosion. At first this was thought to be depth charges dropped by HMS *Duckworth*, but it proved to be the blast of the U-645's torpedo in the hull of the merchant ship *Yorkmar*. At 0653Z HMCS *Kamloops* discovered the survivors of the *Yorkmar* in the water and picked up fifty-four of them, while HMS *Duckworth* recovered another four. The escort's senior officer thought that the *Yorkmar* had been torpedoed by a U-boat which had somehow managed to close with the starboard side of SC 143 and then fired one or more torpedoes at the convoy at long range.[92] The sinking of the *Yorkmar* was the first and only time that the U-boats gained contact with the main body of SC 143.

In the next three hours the escorts of SC 143 obtained two HF/DF bearings on two distant radio transmissions. These bearings were not run down because they were astern of the convoy, and the destroyers of the 10th Escort Group were running low on fuel and would soon be detached from the convoy.[93] However, this made no difference, for the Germans were about to end the operation. The BdU decided to break off the operation against SC 143 because the U-boats were now moving into "the area of increased activity by land-based aircraft." Further, the sighting of the destroyers had not convinced the Germans that they were in contact with the convoy. To them, it remained a distinct possibility that the destroyers were not part of a convoy screen and that SC 143 might be south of the *Roßbach* patrol line.[94] At 0421 on 9 October the BdU ordered those U-boats which could not get ahead of SC 143 to break off the operation and "MOVE OFF TO THE WESTWARD." Shortly thereafter several U-boats informed the BdU that they were ending the search for SC 143. And at 0745 the BdU officially halted operation against SC 143 and ordered the U-boats of the *Roßbach* group to move to the westward.[95]

The Germans had not accomplished much in the operations against SC 143. The U-boats had only gained contact with the main body of the convoy once and they had sunk only one destroyer and a merchant ship at the cost of three U-boats. The Operations Division of the German Naval Staff thought that the operation "must be considered a failure," and the BdU not only agreed with this assessment but also believed that "nothing in particular was learned from the operation."[96] The senior officer of SC 143's escort believed that the wide ranging sweeps by the destroyers of the 10th Escort Group kept the U-boats at a distance; that aircraft had "contained the U-boats during daylight of the 9th October"; and that "the U-boats had a very healthy fear of being sighted by them." Further, this British officer thought that the U-boats had an "extreme reluctance" to close with SC 143. Allied intelligence thought that the "outstanding feature of this operation [was] the failure to find the actual convoy" and that the "U/boats did not show any eagerness to engage." Allied intelligence further noted that since the Germans had resumed attacks on convoys on the North American-United Kingdom convoy route, they had suffered a very heavy loss rate of those U-boats engaged in the operation.[97]

But the Germans pushed on stubbornly. Fuel shortages forced them to disband the *Roßbach* group. Of the U-boats in that patrol, four were refueled at sea for further operations (U-378, U-410, U-584, U-603) three were refueled at sea before returning to base (U-641, U-731, U-758), and seven (U-539, U-275, U-645, U-305, U-952, U-260, U-666) were sent directly back to base. The remaining six (U-437, U-91, U-309, U-448, U-631, U-672) were sent to an area around 55°N, 35°W where they were to be joined by eight other

U-boats (U-455, U-231, U-470, U-608, U-267, U-413, U-844, U-964) for further operations. On 12 October communications intelligence indicated that Allied convoy ONS 20 would pass through 55°N,25°W on 16 October, and this determined the target of these fourteen submarines. On 13 October these U-boats were formed into the *Schlieffen* group and ordered to form a patrol line by 2400 on 15 October.[98]

The *Schlieffen* group was ordered to form a patrol line west of the point where the convoy was expected.[99] The U-boats were to maintain radio silence until the convoy was sighted, and they were to set up the patrol line unseen by the enemy. Therefore, they were to proceed submerged by day, traveling on the surface at top speed by night. This order was decoded by the Allies at 0143 on 16 October.[100]

In an attempt to increase the probability of intercepting ONS 20, the Germans assigned two U-boats equipped with radio direction finders to the *Schlieffen* group—the U-413 and the U-631. These U-boats were stationed at the northern and southern ends of the patrol line, and it was their task to attempt to discover "any evasion of the line" by an Allied convoy by taking bearings on any Allied radio transmissions and then reporting this information to the BdU and other U-boats in the patrol line.[101] On 14 October the Germans obtained communications intelligence showing that ONS 20 was to pass through 57°N, 20°W on 15 October.[102] Accordingly, the *Schlieffen* patrol was moved to the north. This order was decoded by the Allies at 1017 on 16 October.[103] During the morning of 15 October the Allies obtained a shore-based D/F fix on a transmission made by the U-631.[104]

Fresh intelligence obtained that evening prompted a change of mission for the *Schlieffen* U-boats. At 2117 the U-844, outward-bound from Germany with orders to join the *Schlieffen* group, radioed that it had sighted a destroyer. An hour later the U-844 radioed that it had sighted a westbound convoy steering 270° well north of ONS 20's expected position. The Germans assumed this to be ONS 20, when in fact it was another westbound convoy, ON 206. On receipt of the U-844's sighting report, the BdU ordered that U-boat to keep contact with the convoy while the *Schlieffen* patrol line was shifted 120 miles north to be in position to intercept the newly sighted convoy at 2400 on 16 October. Six outward-bound U-boats (U-964,

U-842, U-281, U-841, U-426) in the vicinity of the U-844 under orders to join the *Schlieffen* group were directed to head for ON 206.[105]

Convoy ON 206, the group of merchant ships misidentified by the BdU as ONS 20, was strongly protected by Escort Group B6 (destroyers HMS *Vanquisher;* frigate HMS *Deveron;* corvettes HNorMS *Rose,* HNorMS *Potentilla,* HNorMS *Eglantine;* and HM Trawler *Grenadier*) and reinforced by Escort Group B7 (destroyers HMS *Duncan,* HMS *Vidette;* corvettes HMS *Pink,* HMS *Sunflower,* HMS *Loosestrife*) which served as a support group. The corvettes of both groups formed a close escort for the convoy, while the destroyers HMS *Duncan,* HMS *Vidette,* and HMS *Vanquisher* served as an extended screen. At 2123 on 15 October HMS *Vanquisher* and HMS *Duncan* began to obtain a series of HF/DF bearings from off the port bow of the convoy. This was the U-844 transmitting its contact report to the BdU. HMS *Vanquisher* immediately began to run down the bearings, and at 2220 the British destroyer obtained a radar contact and turned toward it. Three minutes later the contact disappeared, but at 2255 radar contact was regained. HMS *Vanquisher* turned toward the contact, increased speed to 21 knots, and fired three star shells at a range of 4,400 yards. A U-boat was then sighted which dived before HMS *Vanquisher* could open fire. This was the U-844. The destroyer then turned back toward the convoy and ran down a course of 60° for a mile, turned to 170° and ran down this course for a mile before turning to 225° to close with the estimated position of the U-844. At 2318 HMS *Vanquisher* attacked the estimated position of the U-844 with a pattern of ten depth charges. A calcium flare was also dropped, and HMS *Vanquisher* began circling the area hunting for the U-844 with sonar. Shortly afterwards HMS *Duncan* joined the hunt. At 0006 on 16 October HMS *Duncan* obtained a sonar contact and attacked it with a hedgehog without result. The hunt continued until 0108, when both destroyers were ordered to return to the convoy. Later the captain of the U-844 reported to the BdU that he had been "DRIVEN OFF," lost contact with the convoy, and been hunted for several hours by escorts.[106]

Neither side could count on an element of surprise when dawn broke on 16 October. The Allies not only knew that the Germans had sighted ON 206 but they were also aware of the general location of the *Schlieffen* patrol line, so air cover was arranged for 16 October. The aircraft were to escort not only ON 206, but also ONS 20 which was then about 70 miles to the south and astern of ON 206.[107] On the other hand, the Germans knew that the convoy sighted by the U-844 would probably receive air support at daylight on 16 October and realized only too well that it would be extremely difficult to maintain contact with the convoy if the U-boats had to submerge. A number of officers at the BdU maintained that the U-boats should dive to avoid attack if contacted by Allied aircraft even if this allowed the convoy to evade the U-boats. This was opposed by other officers, among them several experienced U-boat commanders, who maintained that the U-boats should remain surfaced in order to gain and maintain contact with the convoy even in the face of Allied aircraft. Placing a high value on the opinions of his U-boat commanders, Doenitz radioed these orders to the U-boats to "remain surfaced. Shoot your way to the convoy with flak."[108]

The wisdom of these orders would be tested over and over again in the following days. At 0800 on 16 October, ON 206 obtained an HF/DF bearing that indicated that a U-boat was to the "southward of the convoy." Not long afterwards, the first Allied aircraft of the day, L/86, appeared over the convoy. The escort's senior officer ordered the plane to undertake a search around the Allied force. Almost immediately, aircraft L/86 sighted the U-844 about 15 miles on the port beam of the convoy. The plane attacked the U-boat in the face of antiaircraft fire. Two engines were hit, and the aircraft was badly damaged and forced to ditch. The VLR B-24 Liberator crash landed near HMS *Pink*, which picked up its crew, two of them dead. Shortly afterwards, another VLR B-24 Liberator, S/59, appeared over the U-boat and attacked with four depth charges in the face of antiaircraft fire. As the U-844 began to submerge, the aircrew saw "a deep red flash." Four more depth charges were then dropped in the swirl of the submerging U-boat. Aircraft S/59's inner starboard engine had been damaged by gunfire, but the U-844 had been sunk. While returning to base aircraft, S/59 sighted another surfaced U-boat and attacked with machine-gun fire.[109]

Throughout the day and early evening at least two VLR B-24 Liberators remained with ON 206 constantly searching for U-boats ahead of the convoy and along its flanks. At noon on 16 October ON

206 altered course to the southward on orders from the commander
in chief, western approaches. Six hours later, aircraft C/59 sighted
and attacked the U-470 some 30 miles on the port beam of ON 206.
Aircraft C/59 was soon joined by two more VLR B-24 Liberators,
E/120 and Z/120, which took up a joint attack on the U-470 with
depth charges and machine-gun fire. The three aircraft made alter-
nating attacks in the face of continuous antiaircraft fire from the
U-470 until 1830, when they saw the U-470 sinking by the stern as
a number of its crew took to the water. HMS *Duncan* and HMS
Vidette later picked up two members of the U-470's crew.[110]

Just after dark ON 206 altered course further to the southward.
And as HMS *Duncan* and HMS *Vidette* were closing with the port
bow of the convoy, an HF/DF bearing was obtained. Both destroyers
hunted down the bearing, and a radar contact was obtained at 2323.
The U-boat was illuminated with a star shell and dived at 2327. HMS
Duncan then dropped a pattern of depth charges on the estimated
position of the U-boat. The hunt continued. After obtaining a sonar
contact at 0005 on 17 October, HMS *Vidette* attacked, dropping ten
depth charges without result. At 0045 HMS *Duncan* left the region
to rejoin ON 206, and HMS *Vidette* remained in the area for another
two hours continuing the hunt without result. The last direct threat
to ON 206 occurred at 0645 when HMS *Duncan,* 9 miles ahead of
the starboard wing of the convoy, obtained a radar contact on a
U-boat which appeared to be making an attack on the convoy. The
U-boat immediately dived. HMS *Duncan* attacked without result,
and then continued the hunt in company with HMS *Vidette* while the
convoy cleared the area. Later that morning, aircraft D/59, a VLR
B-24 Liberator, sighted and attacked the U-540 as the plane left ON
206 to return to base. Another VLR B-24 Liberator appeared over
the U-boat and attacked with 20mm cannon fire and then made a
second assault with depth charges. A third attack was made with
both 20mm cannon fire and four more depth charges. The aircraft
then saw the U-540 "break in half, the bow and the stern rising out
of the water" just before the U-boat sank."[111]

At 1700 on 17 October it appeared that the U-boats were no
longer in contact with ON 206. Escort Group B7 was detached to
support ONS 20, now under attack about 35 miles to the northeast.
The five ships of the escort group steamed toward ONS 20 on a

course of 44° in a line-abreast formation. At 2135 HMS *Sunflower* obtained a radar contact which disappeared almost immediately as the U-631 dived. Sonar contact was quickly established and the British corvette attacked with depth charges. The U-boat was seen to rise out of the water at a 45 degree angle amidst the depth charge explosions and then disappear. HMS *Sunflower* then made a second depth charge attack, but the contact had disappeared—for the U-631 had been sunk. The ships of Escort Group B7 circled the area for several hours searching for the sunk U-boat before continuing on to join ONS 20.[112]

This westbound convoy, of course, was the original target of the *Schlieffen* group. ONS 20's fifty-seven merchant ships escorted by the 4th Escort Group, consisting of seven frigates and two armed trawlers (frigates HMS *Bentinck*, HMS *Byard*, HMS *Blackwood* HMS *Bezeley*, HMS *Burgess*, HMS *Drury*, HMS *Berry*; and the trawlers *Northern Sky* and *Northern Wave*), had an uneventful voyage for the first six days of its passage. However, on 15 October, when the convoy was some miles astern and to the south of ON 206, a number of HF/DF bearings indicated U-boats in the vicinity. But it was not until late afternoon the following day that the Germans made contact with ONS 20. During the morning of 16 October, VLR B-24 Liberator H/86 escorted ONS 20 until relieved by a Catalina, A/131, which stayed with the convoy until 1500. At 1530 ONS 20 charged course to the northward to pass across the stern of ON 206 and, if possible, to the north of the *Schlieffen* U-boats.[113]

At 1735 that evening Y/86, a VLR B-24 Liberator searching for ON 206, sighted a U-boat some 30 miles from ONS 20 on that convoy's port quarter. Aircraft Y/86 attacked in the face of antiaircraft fire with three depth charges. The U-boat, the U-964, radioed shortly afterwards "AM BEING ATTACKED BY A/C." For the next hour and a half, the aircraft circled the U-964. Each time aircraft Y/86 approached the U-boat, it was met with continuous flak, and repeated attempts by the aircraft to home in on Allied surface forces failed. Just as it was getting dark, the VLR B-24 Liberator attacked again with machine-gun fire and dropped three depth charges. One fell alongside the hull of the U-964. The U-boat began to settle by the bow, and puffs of black smoke began to issue from the afterdeck of the vessel. Some minutes later the U-964 sank, leaving some thirty-five crew members in the water. Four Germans were later picked up by the U-231.[114]

In the early evening of 16 October HF/DF bearings indicated to the escort of ONS 20 that there were a number of U-boats astern of the convoy. At 2110 the merchant ship *Essex Lance* was torpedoed by the U-426 while it straggled about 2 miles behind the convoy because of engine problems. The torpedo hit the ship on the port side between the No. 4 and 5 holds. The crew abandoned the *Essex Lance,* which later sank, and were all picked up by the rescue ship *Accrington.* It was not until 2129 that the escort of ONS 20 realized that the *Essex Lance* had been torpedoed and began a search for the U-boat which had sunk the ship. At 2140 HMS *Bentinck* obtained a radar contact at a range of 6,100 yards on a U-boat moving away from ONS 20. Eight minutes later, the British frigate opened fire, using radar to aim its guns. The U-boat dived, and, after dropping some depth charges on the U-boat's estimated position, HMS *Bentinck* rejoined ONS 20. Throughout the night the escorts of ONS 20 obtained and chased down radar and sonar contacts of U-boats attempting to close with the convoy.[115]

At 0637 the morning of 17 October the commander of the escort radioed the commander in chief, western approaches, that he estimated that "six or more" U-boats were in the vicinity of ONS 20. Strong air support for ONS 20 was carried out that day. Ten Hudsons and five Venturas from Iceland made repeated sweeps over the convoy, while two VLR B-24 Liberators remained over the convoy and five Sunderland flying boats rendered "general support" during the daylight hours. Ten U-boats were sighted, and six were attacked by aircraft. In the course of these attacks a Sunderland, S/422, was so badly damaged by flak that it had to ditch near ONS 20. Three crew members were killed and another seven were picked up by HMS *Drury.*[116]

At 1820 HMS *Byard* of the 4th Escort Group obtained a sonar contact at a range of 1,900 yards. This contact was immediately attacked with depth charges and then a hedgehog. As the frigate was turning to make a third attack, the U-841 surfaced. The U-boat was then taken under gunfire which killed several members of the crew before it sank. Twenty-seven Germans were picked up by HMS *Byard* before the frigate rejoined the convoy at 2033. This was the last serious contact ONS 20 had with the enemy. In the early hours of 18 October, the ships of Escort Group B7 joined the screen of ONS 20, followed by HMS *Vanquisher* on 19 October. During 18 October the escort of ONS 20 obtained several contacts, but by 0440 on 19 October "HF/DF activity [had] receded to the north-eastward."[117]

The BdU must have recognized the degree of its tragic blunder shortly after issuing the 16 October order directing the *Schlieffen* U-boats to remain on the surface and fight back against Allied aircraft. Reports flowed into the BdU from U-boats under attack by Allied aircraft as well as from intercepts of radio messages from the Allied aircraft.[118] The Germans had other problems as well, for the U-boats generally were not gaining contact with the enemy. There was no reconnaissance by German aircraft, and German communications intelligence was at best ineffective. For example, the members of the BdU did not realize for some time that they were dealing with more than one Allied convoy. This in itself was not surprising as not even Allied shore-based D/F stations could "differentiate" between ON 206 and ONS 20 readings because the convoys were so close together.[119] This lack of reliable intelligence, however, forced the BdU to rely largely on U-boat sighting reports for information about the course and positions of ON 206 and ONS 20.

The U-964 sighted ONS 20 at 1252 and then again at 2218 on 16 October. At 1317 that afternoon and at 0341 on the morning of 17 October the U-413 obtained D/F bearings on two Allied radio transmissions showing that the convoy was to the north. However, the BdU chose to disregard the information from the U-413. On the basis of the U-964's sighting reports, the *Schlieffen* U-boats were moved further eastward, and the BdU expected that an Allied convoy would be intercepted on the evening of 16 October. But ONS 20 had, indeed, changed course to the northward, and even though the U-426 sank the straggling *Essex Lance* in midafternoon on 16 October, the convoy as a whole was not brought to battle. At 0117 on 17 October the BdU ordered the U-boats of the *Schlieffen* group to proceed west at 8 knots if a convoy had not been sighted by 0500. But at 0534 the U-309, one of the northernmost U-boats of the *Schlieffen* patrol line, sighted a convoy. The BdU then ordered this group to operate against this convoy "AT TOP SPEED." And it was not until

0935 on 17 October that the BdU saw "A STRONG NORTHWESTERLY TENDENCY ON THE PART OF THE CONVOY."[120]

The whole situation was further confused by the appearance of Allied aircraft in the area that morning. These aircraft not only attacked U-boats on the surface but also forced them to submerge, thus greatly reducing the amount of intelligence they could produce about enemy movements and locations. At 1000 the U-91 deduced from hydrophone bearings that the convoy was on a southwest course, but before this could be followed up, an aircraft forced the U-boat to submerge. At 1750 the U-413 obtained a D/F bearing on a radio transmission at 55° true. And the BdU at 1818 informed the *Schlieffen* group that "THE SOUTHWESTERLY TENDENCY PRESUMED BY HUNGERSHAUSEN [U-91] CANNOT BE ASSUMED" and directed the U-boats to search for the convoy "ALONG ENEMY COURSES OF 270 TO 310." But by 0125 on 18 October the BdU had concluded that the "CONVOY HAS POSSIBLY TURNED AWAY TO THE SOUTHWEST" and directed all the *Schlieffen* U-boats south of 59° to search to the southwest, and those to the north to continue to search in a westerly to northwesterly direction.[121] Even before this order was issued, a number of U-boats were probably operating to the southwest on the U-91's report, and the convoy slipped away from the Germans by making a turn to the southwest after the U-91's report was acted on, passing to the east of the area being searched by the U-boats on the afternoon of 17 October.[122] At 2313 the U-608 sighted ONS 20 on a course of 200° south and east of the area being searched by the other boats of the *Schlieffen* group. By then, however, the operation had already been called off and the U-boats ordered to move westward, submerged by day, to escape from Allied aircraft based in Iceland.[123]

In their operations against ON 206 and ONS 20, the Germans lost six U-boats (U-470, U-844, U-964, U-631, U-540, U-481)—four to aircraft and two to surface escorts—while sinking only the merchant ship *Essex Lance*. In fact, the U-boats barely made contact with the convoys and totally failed to bring them to battle. The Operations Division of the German Naval Staff correctly assigned the reasons for this failure to the lack of German aircraft reconnaissance which made it impossible for the U-boats to locate convoys. This, combined with strong Allied air support of the convoy, prevented the U-boats from approaching near enough to a convoy to attack the Allied ships successfully.[124] Still, even though they had suffered a defeat in the operations against convoys ON 203, ON 204, ON 206, SC 143, ONS 19, and ONS 20, the Germans were not yet ready to call off wolf pack operations along the North American-United Kingdom convoy route.

On the day that operations ended against ON 206 and ONS 20, the BdU ordered still another new patrol line to be set up on 24 October about 500 miles east of Newfoundland. The U-boats were to proceed to their new positions submerged by day, for this "WESTERLY TENDENCY OF PASSAGE MUST NOT BECOME KNOWN TO THE ENEMY." The Allies did not decode this order until 0017 on 28 October. On 20 October, the BdU radioed more specific details, setting the precise time of the patrol's deployment at 1200 on 24 October; and directing that it consist of twenty-three U-boats. Some of these were drawn from the old *Schlieffen* group and the others were U-boats newly arrived in the North Atlantic from their bases. As usual, the U-boats were to maintain radio silence except for "TACTICALLY IMPORTANT REPORTS" and remain submerged during the day. This transmission was not decoded by the Allies until 0712 on 27 October.[125]

The mission of the new "*Siegfried*" group (eventually reduced to eighteen U-boats—U-91, U-842, U-231, *Mahrolz*, U-608, U-969, U-276, U-281, U-413, U-963, U-437, U-426, U-552, *Jaschke*, U-575, U-226, U-373, U-845) was the interception of an eastbound convoy expected by the evening of 24 October. On 22 October the BdU ordered the U-boats of the *Siegfried* group to reach their positions in the patrol line "UNOBSERVED" and to remain submerged by day after arriving as well as to maintain the usual radio silence unless they obtained "ANY CLUE OF THE CONVOY." The Allies did not decode this order until 1226 on 25 October.[126] It was the BdU's intention to surprise a convoy by quickly concentrating all the U-boats of the *Siegfried* group against it and then carrying out a number of simultaneous attacks on the Allied ships.[127] But the BdU failed to anticipated the enormous obstacles created by Allied aircraft and surface escorts—first, when U-boats tried to find a convoy and next, when they tried to bring about a single rapid attack.

The *Siegfried*'s opponents were moving into position as well. At 1800 on 20 October Escort Group B7 was detached from ONS 20 to support convoy ON 207 as it proceeded westward. On 23 October at 0923Z, some 100 miles northwest of ON 207, the ships of Escort Group B7 heard VLR B-24 Liberator Z/224 request by radio that its base inform the warships that it was trying to contact them. Several minutes later, Escort Group B7 heard the aircraft report that it was over a surfaced U-boat. However, for several minutes radio communication between aircraft Z/224 and Escort Group B7 could not be established. While proceeding to escort ON 207, the VLR B-24 Liberator had sighted the U-274, a member of the *Siegfried* group. The VLR B-24 Liberator attacked the U-boat with air to surface rockets, but no damage was done. After the plane finally established radio contact with Escort Group B7 at 0950Z, the aircraft launched depth charges at the U-boat as it was submerging. The position where the U-274 had dived was then marked with a smoke marker.[128]

At 1022Z the ships of Escort Group B7 had steamed far enough to see the aircraft attacking a target over the horizon with depth charges and proceeded toward the area. When HMS *Duncan* and HMS *Vidette* arrived at the smoke marker, the warships began a search with sonar for the U-274. At 1259Z HMS *Duncan* obtained a sonar contact. Speed was reduced to 8 knots as the destroyer ran in on the target to carry out a hedgehog attack. At a range of about 200 yards, the U-274 released a decoy in an attempt to confuse HMS *Duncan*. Nevertheless, the contact was held and a hedgehog attack was carried out without result. During the second attack, the U-274 appeared to be zigzagging about 20° off its mean course at a speed of 2 knots in an attempt to throw HMS *Duncan* off the target, but the British warship held the contact and a second hedgehog attack was made. Sixteen seconds after the projectiles hit the water, there were three explosions. HMS *Vidette*, which also had sonar contact with the U-274, was then ordered to carry out a depth charge attack. After this attack sonar contact could not be regained and at 1335 HMS *Duncan* dropped a Mark X depth charge to ensure the total destruction of the U-724. This attack produced "a large amount of wooden wreckage" on the surface of the sea. After sinking the U-274, Escort Group B7 took up a distant screening position some 60 miles on the port bow of ON 207.[129]

The next two days were uneventful, and by 26 October convoy ON 207 was in range of RCAF aircraft based in Newfoundland. At

1105 a Canadian VLR B-24 Liberator, A/10, sighted the U-420, another member of the *Siegfried* group, about 70 miles off the port quarter of the convoy. The aircraft first attacked the U-boat with several depth charges which failed to explode and then machine gunned the U-420 over and over again for about an hour before the U-boat began to submerge. As the U-420 was diving, the Canadian aircraft attacked again unsuccessfully with a depth charge and then attacked the U-420 again with two acoustic torpedoes which sank the U-boat.[130]

The *Siegfried* group had been deployed in an attempt to intercept eastbound convoys, but poor or nonexistent intelligence led the U-boats into engagements with the escorts of the westbound convoy ON 207—from which the Germans gained nothing at the cost of two U-boats (U-724, U-420). In fact, the U-boats of the *Siegfried* group did not even sight a convoy. On 26 October the U-413 picked up what appeared to be a radio transmission from an escort group. The U-842 heard some propeller noises. And the U-91, U-212, and U-608 were attacked by Allied aircraft screening ON 207.[131] The operation was broken off because of Allied air activity, and the convoy the Germans were attempting to intercept had passed "much further south than assumed."[132]

The Germans remained grimly determined. At 2135 on 26 October the BdU split the *Siegfried* into three groups of seven U-boats each (*Siegfried 1*: U-309, U-212, U-404, U-231, U-608, U-969; *Siegfried 2*: U-267, U-281, U-413, U-963, U-437, U-426, U-552; and *Siegfried 3*: U-842, U-575, U-226, U-373, U-854, U-648, U-705), creating a trio of patrol lines east of Newfoundland. The U-boats were spaced 15 miles apart to intercept another expected eastbound convoy. The U-boats were cautioned: "AT ALL COSTS REMAIN UNSEEN DURING THE APPROACH" by remaining submerged during the day time, and radio silence was to be maintained "EXCEPT FOR TACTICALLY IMPORTANT REPORTS." The Allies decoded this order at 2352 on 27 October.[133]

Although the Germans were apparently attempting to intercept eastbound HX 262, Allied knowledge of the location of the three *Siegfried* patrol lines instead forced the U-boats into engagements with the escort of a westbound group of Allied ships. After sinking the U-274 and refueling from ON 207, the ubiquitous Escort Group

B7 was detached and steamed east northeast to meet the newest west-bound convoy, ON 208. This rendezvous took place at 2300 on 27 October at 51°N, 43°W just before ON 208 entered the U-boat danger area. At 1012 on 28 October the U-256 was attacked by an aircraft ahead of ON 208. At 0612 that morning, when the ships of Escort Group B7 were in line-abreast formation some 15 miles ahead of ON 208, HMS *Vidette* obtained a radar contact at a range of 5,500 yards. Star shells were fired at a range of 4,000 yards, but the U-boat dived before they burst. HMS *Vidette* attacked the estimated position of the U-boat with depth charges and the ships of Escort Group B7 then began to hunt with sonar for U-282. At 0655Z HMS *Duncan* gained sonar contact, and a hedgehog attack was conducted without results five minutes later. The hunt was resumed, and at 0925Z HMS *Sunflower* obtained a sonar contact. While HMS *Duncan* held the U-282 in sonar contact at a range of 1,000 to 1,500 yards, HMS *Sunflower* was directed to the U-boat to deliver a hedgehog attack. At 0953Z, six seconds after the missiles hit the water, there were three explosions. As HMS *Duncan* made the run in for a depth charge attack, explosions and bubbling noises were heard on the destroyer's sonar. HMS *Sunflower* saw wreckage and "human remains" from the U-282 come to the surface. Two days later, Escort Group B7 left ON 208 to screen convoy HX 263 before returning to Britain.[134]

While the *Siegfried* lines did not intercept ON 208, the independently sailing U-405 may have come across HX 262, the designated target of those patrol lines. Convoy HX 262 was covered by the 2nd Escort Group, the escort carrier HMS *Tracker* and five sloops (HMS *Starling*, HMS *Wild Goose*, HMS *Woodcock*, HMS *Magpie*, HMS *Kite*). At 0820 on 29 October the U-405 reported that it had driven off a Swordfish aircraft. Some two hours later the submarine radioed that it had sighted three merchant ships and two escorts and had fired a *zaunkonig* before being "DRIVEN OFF." None of these incidents, however, are recorded in the existing reports of the 2nd Escort Group.[135]

Next, the increasingly desperate BdU disbanded the *Siegfried* groups and formed the *Koerner* and *Jahn* groups consisting of twenty-two U-boats (the *Koerner*: U-714, U-212, *Mueller*, U-309, U-240, U-231, U-969, U-267, U-281, U-413, U-963, U-843; and the *Jahn*: U-437, U-426, U-842, U-575, U-842, U-475, U-226, U-373, U-858,

U-648, U-274) on 30 October. These were to form two patrol lines: one 400 miles northeast and the other 400 miles east southeast of St. John's, Newfoundland. By 1000 on 31 October the U-boats were to take up these positions "UNOBSERVED" to intercept an eastbound convoy, maintaining radio silence and surfacing only at night. This order was read by the Allies at 0501 on 1 November.[136] Nothing was sighted, intercepted, or attacked and at 2319 on 2 November the *Koerner* and *Jahn* groups were disbanded.

The BdU formed the same U-boats into five smaller groups code named *Tirpitz 1* through *Tirpitz 5* (*Tirpitz 1:* U-714, U-240, U-212, U-267; *Tirpitz 2:* U-309, U-413, U-969, U-608; *Tirpitz 3:* U-280, U-281, U-757, U-586; *Tirpitz 4: Mueller, Jaschke,* U-426, U-226; *Tirpitz 5:* U-842, U-373, U-274, U-684). By dividing the U-boats into smaller groups, the Germans hoped to conceal the location and deployment of the whole force from the Allies. The general idea was that if the Allies learned the position of one of the *Tirpitz* groups, they would remain unaware of the existence of the other four groups of U-boats. The *Tirpitz* U-boats were to be stationed in an arc about 450 miles east northeast to east southeast off the southeastern end of Newfoundland, with three U-boats (U-834, U-963, U-552) ahead of the patrol line to serve as advance guards. The objective was to intercept an eastbound convoy expected to arrive during the evening of 5 November. As usual, the U-boats were ordered to take up their stations unobserved, to remain submerged during daylight, and to maintain radio silence. When the U-boats' fuel was down to about thirty-two cubic meters, each was to return to base because refueling at sea was now impossible, for there were no U-boat tankers available. This order was decoded by the Allies at 2112 on 3 November.[137]

Prompt decrypting of the two orders setting up the *Tirpitz* groups enabled the Allies to route merchant convoys away from them while sending the 2nd Escort Group right over *Tirpitz 4* and *5.* After leaving convoy HX 262, this escort group moved off to the southwest to avoid bad weather. Then, on 4 November, the 2nd Escort Group turned northeast and began steaming toward the *Tirpitz* U-boats. On 5 November the U-413 was attacked by one of HMS *Tracker*'s aircraft. At 0200 on 6 November HMS *Kite* obtained a radar contact at a range of 3,800 yards. The contact was illuminated with star shells, and the U-226, a member of *Tirpitz 4,* was seen to submerge. HMS

Kite immediately attacked the estimated position of the U-boat with depth charges. HMS *Tracker*, escorted by HMS *Wild Goose* and HMS *Magpie*, was detached to the westward, while HMS *Starling*, HMS *Kite*, and HMS *Woodcock* began a sonar hunt for the U-226. At 0304 HMS *Starling* obtained a sonar contact on the U-226, which had gone deep. It was then decided to hold the U-boat in sonar contact until daylight and to sink it with a "creeping attack" in order not to risk losing the U-boat in the disturbances caused by regular depth charge attacks. For the next four hours HMS *Starling*, accompanied by HMS *Kite* and HMS *Woodcock*, held the U-226 in sonar contact as the U-boat moved slowly southwest. Then at about 0700, HMS *Woodcock*, directed by HMS *Starling*, began a creeping attack at 44°26'N, 41°21'W. Twenty-six depth charges were dropped on the U-226 by HMS *Woodcock*. Shortly after the attack, HMS *Starling* heard breaking up noises on sonar. Then oil and debris from the U-226 appeared on the surface.[138]

The 2nd Escort Group resumed hunting for U-boats. At 1103, steering a course of 190°, the group's ships obtained an HF/DF bearing at an estimated range of between 20 and 25 miles. An aircraft flew from the *Tracker* and found the U-842, a member of *Tirpitz 5*, on the surface. Once the airplane had forced the U-boat to dive, the sloops HMS *Wild Goose*, HMS *Starling*, and HMS *Magpie* began a sonar search for the submarine at 1239. At 1347 HMS *Wild Goose* obtained a sonar contact, and several minutes later HMS *Starling* gained sonar contact with the same target. HMS *Starling* carried out an attack with ten depth charges without result at 1405. This attack drove the U-842 deep, and it was decided to undertake a creeping attack. At 1502 HMS *Wild Goose*, directed by HMS *Starling*'s sonar contact on the U-842, dropped ten depth charges on the U-boat. HMS *Starling* heard breaking up noises followed by an underwater explosion and shortly thereafter oil and wreckage appeared on the surface.[139]

After the destruction of the U-842, the 2nd Escort Group left the area to provide cover for the eastbound HX 264. But this convoy was not threatened by attack and the 2nd Escort Group headed for Argentia, Newfoundland, after two days. While on route to Argentia, the group was attacked by the U-684 at 1445 on 9 November. The submarine fired a torpedo at HMS *Tracker*, but the missile missed and exploded harmlessly off the port quarter of the escort carrier. A hunt for the U-boat was mounted without result, and the 2nd Escort Group then continued on its way to Argentia, where it arrived on 13 November.[140]

Meanwhile, the BdU had, in fact, tacitly surrendered the mid-Atlantic and withdrawn to the east. On 7 November the U-boats of the *Tirpitz* groups were withdrawn from the North America-United Kingdom convoy routes and deployed in the eastern Atlantic.[141] The Germans abandoned their assaults on these routes because they were suffering heavy losses at the hands of the Allies, without even sighting any convoys much less sinking any ships. Further, owing to the destruction of U-boat tankers by American hunter-killer groups in the central Atlantic, the Germans could no longer refuel U-boats on extended wolf pack operations in the northwest and north central Atlantic.[142] The end of the campaign against the North American-United Kingdom convoy route in the autumn of 1943 marked the end of the German attempts to use U-boat wolf packs to cut Britain's maritime supply lines with North America.

The Germans were totally defeated in the autumn 1943 battles along the North American-Great Britain convoy routes. From 15 September to 7 November, the Germans lost twenty U-boats (U-279, U-336, U-389, U-643, U-610, U-413, U-470, U-844, U-964, U-361, U-540, U-841, U-274, U-420, U-282, U-226, U-892) while the U-boats managed to sink only four Allied warships (ORP *Orkan*, HMCS *St. Croix*, HMS *Polyanthus*, HMS *Itchen*; and the merchant ships *Theodore Dwight Weld*, *Frederick Douglass*, *Oregon Express*, *Fort Jemseg*, *Skjelbred*, *Steel Voyager*, *Yorkmar*, *Essex Lance*). Why were the Germans so totally and absolutely outwitted? There are several reasons. First, the Germans lacked good intelligence on Allied movements and deployments throughout the battle. With the exception of one ineffectual sortie, there was no reconnaissance by German aircraft over the battle area.[143] To locate convoys for attack by U-boats, the Germans had to rely on weak and ineffectual communications intelligence which often just did not supply the information required to deploy their U-boats properly. Then, when the U-boats did manage to find a convoy, outer screens of Allied surface and air escorts usually kept the German vessels at a distance from the main body of the Allied formation, if they did not attack and sink the submarines.

Aside from being capable of sinking U-boats, Allied aircraft also had an inhibiting effect on their operations, for the mere appearance of an enemy plane forced a U-boat to dive, thus greatly reducing its operational capabilities. Further, the BdU decision to operate U-boats within range of Allied aircraft based in Iceland, combined with the order to stay on the surface and fight it out with these planes, was a mistake. Twelve of the twenty U-boats (U-279, U-336, U-389, U-643, U-610, U-470, U-844, U-964, U-540, U-420, U-341) lost during the campaign were sunk by Allied aircraft unassisted by warships. The Germans should have known that a surfaced U-boat in almost every circumstance was no match for a lumbering Sunderland, much less a VLR B-24 Liberator. Ignoring this obvious and painful lesson, the German naval command still talked of strengthening "the antiaircraft defense of submarines by an increase in caliber" as late as 18 October.[144] The Germans clung to the belief that they were on the way to victory with new weapons like the *zaunkonig*, additional antiaircraft armament on U-boats, and new technology such as the *wanze* radar detector and the *aphrodite* radar decoy.[145] But, in fact, they soon found that they had greatly overestimated the effectiveness of heavier antiaircraft armaments and the *zaunkonig*, while the *wanze* and the *aphrodite* just did not function.

Further, the U-boats did not employ any new tactics or stratagems against the Allied escorts. Nor were the U-boats commanded by officers capable of evolving new tactics, for the vessels were increasingly assigned to those with little experience of convoy operations in the North Atlantic.[146] On the other hand, the Allied forces were commanded by officers with considerable tactical experience. For example, the 2nd Escort Group was commanded by Captain F. J. Walker, RN,[147] and Escort Group B7 was commanded by Commander Peter Gretton, RN.[148] Both these officers had a great deal of experience in anti-U-boat and convoy operations.

But in the autumn of 1943 the Allies also had the technology, weapons, tactics, and intelligence to combat wolf packs of U-boats along the North America-United Kingdom convoy route. For some time, the Allies had been able to read German command radio transmissions. The Germans never realized this and still clung to their fantasy of some all-seeing Allied airborne radar location device or an equally mythical technique that enabled the Allies to pinpoint

U-boats through "radiation" given off by those vessels.[149] By the end of the summer the Allies were exploiting this intelligence advantage promptly and consistently, decrypting the BdU's radio orders to the U-boats quickly so that the Allied command knew the location of the patrol lines early enough to route convoys away from areas of danger and to move warships and aircraft to reinforce convoys threatened with attack by U-boats. This supplemented the longstanding use of HF/DF readings to locate a U-boat. The Germans were also tragically ignorant of this device, which enabled the Allies to locate any U-boat making a radio transmission near a convoy with HF/DF equipment.

Further, the Allies had the weapons systems in the form of VLR B-24 Liberators and support groups to beat off and hammer any group of U-boats which threatened a convoy. By the autumn of 1943 there was no area along the North Atlantic-United Kingdom convoy route in which VLR B-24 Liberator aircraft based in Iceland, Newfoundland, and Northern Ireland could not support a convoy threatened with attack by U-boats. The Allies had developed the technology and tactics required to protect convoys with aircraft and support groups. The Germans, to their great cost in the autumn battles along the North American-United Kingdom convoy route, found in defeat that the U-boat wolf pack attack was a tactic whose time had indeed come and passed.

Chapter 7

The Last Wolf Pack Battles in the Atlantic

The Gibraltar Routes, 6 October–7 December 1943

Admitting defeat in submarine warfare in the North Atlantic at the end of October 1943, the Germans chose to move the theater of operations of their U-boats to the only part of that sea where they might be able to overcome the disadvantages under which they labored: the Allied convoy routes between Gibraltar and Great Britain.[1] In other parts of the Atlantic, the wolf packs had become crippled by their inability to refuel their U-boats at sea after the destruction of almost all U-boat tankers at the hands of American hunter-killer groups. French-based U-boats operating against the convoy routes west of Portugal would not require refueling at sea. In the North Atlantic, the U-boats had fought valiantly in the late summer and fall with virtually no reliable intelligence on Allied convoy movements. After the longstanding German advantage in reading Allied codes had vanished in June, the Germans could obtain little more than information on stragglers' routes from code breaking for the North Atlantic, and this was not enough to enable them to intercept Allied convoys on a regular basis. In the U-boats' last campaign against the North America-Great Britain convoy routes in October 1943, the lack of intelligence made it nearly impossible for them even to find Allied convoys to attack.[2] However, in 1943 the region west of Portugal was one of the few areas in the Atlantic where the Germans could still obtain good intelligence on Allied convoy movements. Such details would be available to agents in Spain who could report when convoys left Gibraltar for Great Britain.

Perhaps most important, the Gibraltar-Great Britain convoy

routes were well within range of GAF aircraft based in France. This would solve two problems for the U-boats. In the North Atlantic, Allied aircraft had driven the German vessels underwater in daylight so that they could not compensate for their lack of cryptographic intelligence by conducting surface searches over large areas of ocean for Allied convoys. By the first week of October 1943, the BdU concluded that "the main problem in the U-boat war is the finding of convoys and that this problem will only finally be solved by constant operation of *long range* aircraft."[3] And, without protection from their own air force, the German submarines were often helpless targets for the Allied air-based and carrier-borne planes. Yet, while the Allied air forces took increasing responsibility for protecting their convoys, the GAF remained stubbornly unable or unwilling to provide effective aerial reconnaissance over the mid-Atlantic for the U-boats, much less defend them against enemy planes. Transferring the U-boat operations to seas closer to the GAF's bases on the continent would, it was hoped, inaugurate a period of effective coordination of air and sea forces. West of Portugal, the aircraft of the GAF could provide not only needed information on Allied ship movements but also protection for the U-boats themselves by attacking the ships and planes of the Allied convoys' escorts.[4]

The Germans also knew that this region was well within the range of Allied anti-U-boat aircraft based in Great Britain, Gibraltar, and the Azores. Nevertheless, the Germans concluded that they would have to run the risks posed by Allied aircraft along the Gibraltar convoy routes because the region was the only one in the Atlantic where U-boats had even a remote chance of success.[5] They inaugurated the new campaign while the *Siegfried* and *Tirpitz* patrol groups still struggled in the North Atlantic. On 26 October the BdU ordered a group of eight U-boats (U-466, U-953, U-306, U-211, U-262, U-441, U-707, U-333), code named *Schill,* to form a patrol line running between approximately 42°57'N, 18°45'W and 42°57'N, 16°35'W. These U-boats were to be in position to operate against Gibraltar-Great Britain convoys in conjunction with the GAF by 1900 on 28 October. This order was decoded by the Allies at 2332 on 27 October.[6]

The first convoy to be stalked by the *Schill* group was SL 138/MKS 28, a combined Gibraltar-Freetown convoy proceeding to Britain on a course of 300° at a speed of 8 knots. The convoy consisted of sixty merchant ships escorted by ten warships of the 39th Escort Group (destroyers HMS *Wrestler*, HMS *Whitehall;* sloops HMS *Hastings,* HMS *Rochester,* HMS *Scarborough;* corvettes HMS *Azalea,* HMS *Geranium,* HMS *Balsam;* frigate *Tavy,* and auxiliary antiaircraft cruiser HMS *Alynbank*). On 27 October SL 138/MKS 28 was shadowed by a German BV222 aircraft which circled the ships for about two hours outside antiaircraft gun range, reporting by radio the speed, position, and composition of the convoy. The next day Allied anti-U-boat aircraft appeared over the convoy and escorted it during the daylight hours for the next three days. SL 138/MKS 28 was apparently somewhat further south then the Germans expected, but the BdU radioed the *Schill* group at 2158 on 28 October that a FW 200 aircraft would shadow the convoy during the afternoon of 29 October and home the U-boats in with radio beacon signals. Any U-boat picking up these beacon signals was ordered to report them "IMMEDIATELY" to the BdU. But on 29 October aircraft of the GAF failed to contact the convoy, and the BdU concluded that SL 138/MKS 28 would pass the *Schill* patrol line during the night of 29 October and ordered the U-boats to "KEEP A SMART LOOK OUT" for it.[7]

SL 138/MKS 28 almost got away from the *Schill* group, but at 2200 the U-262 obtained hydrophone bearings on the convoy to the north. The BdU then informed the *Schill* group that the convoy was on a northerly course and ordered the U-boats to attack it. Several hours later the U-boats were ordered to search in a northerly direction for the convoy, sail at top speed on the surface that evening, submerge at dawn, "AND MOVE OFF TO THE WESTWARD."[8] The air commander, Atlantic coast, ordered the GAF to conduct a reconnaissance flight the next day to see "whether the enemy has made any deviations."[9] At daylight on 30 October Allied anti-U-boat aircraft operated over SL 138/MKS 28, but a German FW 200 aircraft still made contact with the convoy and radioed the course, speed, and position before being driven off by an Allied B-24 Liberator aircraft.[10] SL 130/MKS 28 was south of the German "dead-reckoning" position and they thought it "regrettable" that the convoy had not been sighted sooner by GAF reconnaissance aircraft, for "24 valuable hours" had been lost by the *Schill* group.[11] Nevertheless, on the basis of the GAF sighting report, the BdU ordered the U-boats of the *Schill* group to search for the convoy that night on the surface "AT TOP SPEED" and to attack it, for "SOMETHING MUST BE SUNK OUT OF THIS CONVOY TONIGHT, AT 'EM, BRING HONOUR TO YOUR NAME."[12]

At 0609 on 31 October HMS *Scarborough* obtained a radar contact on the starboard side of SL 130/MKS 28. Shortly afterwards a U-boat, probably the U-260, was seen closing with the convoy. The U-boat dived when illuminated with a star shell. HMS *Scarborough,* supported by HMS *Balsam,* then attacked the U-boat with depth charges without result. The escorts continued to hunt this U-boat until the convoy was clear of the area.[13] Shortly after HMS *Scarborough* sighted the U-262, the escort intercepted a radio transmission, probably from the U-707, but an HF/DF bearing could not be obtained. Then an HF/DF bearing was obtained on another radio transmission placing a U-boat, the U-306, about 20 miles ahead of SL 130/MKS 28. HMS *Whitehall* was sent down this bearing, and when a second HF/DF bearing placed the U-boat on the convoy's starboard bow, HMS *Geranium* was sent in support. At 0800 HMS *Whitehall* sighted the U-306 which then dived, and both British warships carried out a series of depth charge and hedgehog attacks which resulted in the destruction of the U-306.[14]

When HMS *Whitehall*'s sighting report was received, the commodore of the convoy ordered SL 138/MKS 28 to make a sharp charge of course to port. As the convoy was altering course at 0832, the merchant ship *Hallfried* was torpedoed by the U-262. The merchant ship sank in about thirty seconds and the escorts conducted a hunt for the submarine. Several depth charge and hedgehog attacks were carried out, but they were without result. There were no further sightings or attacks, for SL 138/MKS was clear, sailing safely north of the *Schill* group.[15]

The BdU still considered the operation against SL 138/MKS 28 worth pursuing. At 0536 on 31 October the *Schill* U-boats were directed to remain surfaced at dawn, to continue to search for the convoy, and to "TAKE ADVANTAGE OF ANY CHANCES TO ATTACK THAT OFFERS." Some fourteen hours later the BdU was still ordering the U-boats of the *Schill* group to attack the convoy that night if they were ahead of SL 138/MKS 28. U-boats behind the convoy were to remain submerged and "MOVE OFF TO THE WESTWARD." The Germans finally ended the operation at 2024 on Halloween, when the

Schill group was ordered to move to the southward, making the passage submerged by day.[16]

Next the BdU planned to have the U-boats attack a southbound convoy in the region of 44°15'N, 18°15'W on the evening of 3 November.[17] On 2 November the eight *Schill* U-boats (U-211, U-333, U-707, U-262, U-446, U-228, U-953, U-358) moved south, searching fruitlessly for their prey.[18] On 5 November the hunt for the southbound convoy was ended, for it was not located by GAF reconnaissance aircraft. The Germans thought that it had been routed beyond the region covered by GAF reconnaissance flights, and the Operations Division of the German Naval Staff concluded "that the enemy is again using a new location method" and that this might be based on "radiation coming from the boats."[19]

On 5 November the BdU informed the *Schill* group, now reduced to seven U-boats (U-211, U-333, U-707, U-262, U-446, U-228, U-358), that an operation was intended for the nights of 8 and 9 November against a northbound Gibraltar-United Kingdom convoy—MKS 29. The U-boats were to head south to 44°N and set up a patrol line between 22°W and 18°W. It would be the task of the GAF to locate MKS 29, then track it, and home in the U-boats on the Allied force by means of radio beacon signals. This order was decoded by the Allies at 1648 on 8 November.[20]

The GAF began searching for MKS 29, but the convoy was not found until 7 November.[21] The BdU expected that MKS 29 would be in 37°40'N, 15°40'W during the night of 8 November, and the *Schill* group, now nearing 40°N, was ordered to operate against the Allied ships at that time. Aircraft of the GAF would shadow the convoy on 8 November and home in U-boats by means of radio beacon signals.[22] But the GAF failed to provide the required aircraft that day when one plane developed engine trouble and another had a radar failure. As a result, there were no reconnaissance flights on 8 November and the U-boats missed contact with MKS 29.[23] However, in the early hours of 9 November the U-262 sighted four red lights and some star shells.[24]

At sunrise the BdU ordered the U-boats of the *Schill* group to dive, but the U-707 did not carry out this order at once.[25] In the half light of dawn, aircraft J/220, a B-17 Fortress flying from the Azores to escort MKS 29, sighted the U-707 on the surface. As the aircraft passed over the U-707, the submarine opened antiaircraft fire and radioed "AM BEING ATTACKED BY A/C."[26] Aircraft J/220 circled and then attacked from the stern of the U-boat with gunfire and four depth charges. The U-boat was seen to be down by the stern, listing 45° to port. Aircraft J/220 again attacked with three depth charges from a height of 30 feet. The U-boat was engulfed by the exploding depth charges, and "a mild glow under water amidships" was seen and the U-707 "disappeared stern first." As aircraft J/220 circled the area, wreckage and an oil patch were seen.[27]

On the morning of 10 November the U-262 and the U-446 each sighted an escort and fired a *zaunkonig* which missed. This was about as close as the U-boats came to MKS 29, for the convoy had been routed west of the patrol line and was now well northwest of the Germans. However, the BdU would not give up and ordered the U-boats of the *Schill* group to chase northward, sailing on the surface if there were no Allied aircraft about, in the hope of gaining contact with the convoy. A FW 200 aircraft did make contact with MKS 29 and shadowed the convoy during the afternoon, transmitting beacon homing signals which the U-boats failed to pick up. The BdU finally ended the operation at midday on 11 November when it ordered the *Schill* U-boats to abandon the chase and prepare for a new operation during the night of 17 November.[28] The BdU blamed the failure of the operation against MKS 29 on the GAF's failure to provide enough aircraft to shadow the convoy properly. This, in turn, resulted in the U-boats' inability to gain contact with the Allied ships.[29]

Group *Schill's* next operation would be an attack on convoy SL 139/MKS 30 in conjunction with the GAF. The Germans knew this would not be an easy campaign, for they had only sunk one merchant ship in their operations against convoys SL 138/MKS 28 and MKS 29 at the cost of two U-boats (U-306, U-707). In both cases, even with the support of GAF, they had obtained at best only fleeting contact with the convoys, and the U-boats had been unable to press home their attacks. To the German naval command the situation was depressing for "the enemy holds all the trump cards." Air power "using location methods that cannot be detected" enabled the Allies to locate the U-boats and to route convoys around patrol lines, the German Naval staff complained. The staff concluded, "We do not have any adequate air reconnaissance up to now." The Germans thought that this situation could be remedied only by improving "our own air reconnaissance and combat of enemy air forces; improvement of our own active and passive methods of location."[30]

To fight the next battle against a Gibraltar-Great Britain convoy, the Germans massed twenty-six U-boats deployed in three patrol lines, one behind the other. The distance between the lines represented about a day's steaming by the convoy. The three U-boat lines were to be supported by GAF reconnaissance of some three flights a day. The strategy behind the plan was simple: if the convoy bypassed or moved through one patrol line, then the next one behind it would be able to intercept the Allied force.[31] On 11 November the BdU ordered six additional U-boats already at sea to reinforce the *Schill* group. This order was decoded by the Allies at 1337 on 14 November.[32]

On 15 November convoy SL 139/MKS 30 was sighted by a GAF reconnaissance aircraft at 35°30'N, 12°30'W. The next day the BdU ordered nine U-boats (U-426, U-608, U-262, U-228, U-515, U-358, U-333, U-211, U-600; the U-426 dropped out of *Schill 1*), code named *Schill 1*, to form a patrol line across the path of SL 139/MKS 30 during the evening of 18 November. When the Allies decoded this order at 2150 on 16 November, they placed the location of the patrol line as running between 40°39'N, 19°42'W and 40°39'N, 16°54'W.[33] SL 139/MKS 30 was again shadowed by a German aircraft for about forty five minutes on 16 November.[34] Decryptions of the Allied convoy's radio transmissions reporting these German reconnaissance aircraft reached the BdU quicker than the GAF reconnaissance reports.[35] On the basis of this intelligence, the BdU ordered *Schill 1* southwest to be ready to intercept SL 139/MKS 30 during the night of 18 November. The U-boats were ordered to remain submerged until 1830, when they were to surface and be ready to receive beacon homing signals from the GAF aircraft shadowing the convoy. This signal was decoded at 0732 on 18 November by the Allies.[36]

Shortly after directing *Schill 1* to move southwest, the BdU on 16 November set up a new nine-boat patrol line (*Weber*, U-969, U-343, U-586, U-648, U-238, U-618, U-86; the U-426 was to have "FREEDOM OF ACTION IN THE AREA"), code named *Schill 2*, north of *Schill 1* and running between 42°39'N, 22°30'W and 42°39'N, 20°06'W. Group *Schill 2* was to be in position by 1800 on 19 November. This order was decoded by the Allies at 0709 on 18 November. On 17 November the U-boats of *Schill 1* were directed to "ENSURE" that they would be able to receive very long wave frequency radio transmissions. This directive was decoded by the Allies at 0655 on 18 November. And on 17 November a German JU 290 aircraft shadowed the convoy at 37°15′N, 18°01′W for about half an hour.[37]

The Allies had ample warning of the German's triple-threat attempt to intercept the convoy. They knew of the impending attack on SL 139/MKS 30 from the GAF overflights of the convoy, from D/F's of radio transmissions made by U-boats, and from decrypts of enemy radio messages. While the convoy initially had an escort of six warships of the 40th Escort Group (frigates HMS *Exe*, HMS *Moyola*; corvettes HMS *Clarkia*, HMS *Petunia*; Sloops HMS *Kistna* and HMS *Milford*; plus the armed merchant cruiser HMS *Ranpura*), there was time to reinforce these vessels by some fourteen additional warships (destroyers HMS *Winchelsea* and HMS *Watchman*; sloops HMS *Crane*, HMS *Pheasant*, HMS *Chanticleer*; frigates HMS *Nene*, HMS *Tweed*; captain class frigates HMS *Foley*, HMS *Essington*, HMS *Garlies*; corvettes HMCS *Lunenburg*, HMCS *Edmundston*, HMCS *Calgary*, HMCS *Snowberry*). At the same time, the Allies also put into effect plans to strengthen the convoy's air escort.

The first contact between SL 139/MKS 30 and the enemy occurred at 0354 on 18 November when an ASV Leigh Light Wellington aircraft (an aircraft equipped with air to surface radar and a powerful search light) sighted and attacked a U-boat on the surface some 270 miles ahead of the convoy. Later in the morning a GAF aircraft shadowed SL 139/MKS 30 for about five hours. The aircraft stayed out of range of the ship's antiaircraft guns and the Allies thought it was "homing" U-boats in on the convoy. Still, the Allies picked up no radio transmissions from aircraft on HF/DF, nor were any U-boat radio transmissions picked up at this time. Throughout the daylight hours of 18 November, Allied aircraft continuously escorted SL 130/MKS 30.[38]

At 1007Z on 18 November HMS *Exe* of the 40th Escort Group obtained a sonar contact at a range of 1,500 yards off the port bow of SL 139/MKS 30. This was the U-333 moving into an attacking position. HMS *Exe* increased speed and steamed forward to strike. Just before the depth charges were to be dropped, a periscope was "sighted fine on the port bow and was abreast the bridge when the order 'fire' was given at 1111." A rating in the engine room of HMS *Exe* heard the periscope of the U-333 scrape down the side of the frigate just before the depth charges exploded. With the explosion of the depth charges, the U-333 was thrust upwards hitting the bottom of the frigate, smashing its conning tower and tearing off its periscopes and deck gun. The U-333 was badly damaged. HMS *Exe* ran out, turned, and attacked a second time with a full pattern of depth charges. The British frigate then regained contact and attacked with a third round of depth charges. At this point the convoy overran the area of attack and HMS *Exe* lost sonar contact as the ships of SL 139/MKS 30 steamed past. Once the convoy had passed HMS *Exe*, now joined by HMS *Petunia*, resumed the hunt for the U-333 and obtained a sonar contact. HMS *Exe* attacked this contact with a hedgehog without result. Believing the U-boat to be destroyed, the two British warships left the area to rejoin the screen of the convoy, but the U-333, though very seriously damaged, was not sunk and managed to return to its base.[39]

SL 139/MKS 30 was reinforced at 1300 that day by HMS *Pheasant*, HMS *Crane*, and HMS *Chanticleer* of the 7th Escort Group. Just after joining the convoy's screen, HMS *Chanticleer* was sent to sweep astern to the limit of visibility in an attempt to find the U-boat which had been attacked by HMS *Exe*. At 1313 HMS *Chanticleer* sighted a U-boat on the surface at a range of 6 miles. This was the U-515, which managed to send off a sighting report before submerging. HMS *Chanticleer* increased speed to 19.5 knots. Two minutes later the U-boat dived, a sonar search was begun, and at 1417 a periscope was seen moving across the bow of the warship from starboard to port. HMS *Chanticleer* ran into attack at a speed of 15 knots intending to drop ten depth charges. At the moment of attack, the warship's commander looked aft and saw the first two depth charges from the throwers go into the air. At that very moment there was a "big explosion" followed by a second blast. HMS *Chanticleer*'s stern was blown off by a *zaunkonig* fired by the U-515. While the British ship did not sink, it was badly damaged and could not steam. Nevertheless, the damaged sloop obtained a sonar contact at a range of 1,500 yards. Being dead in the water, it could not, of course, attack the contact.[40]

Just after HMS *Chanticleer* began its sweep astern of SL 130/MKS

30, HMS *Foley* and HMS *Garlies* joined the escort and HMS *Crane* was detached to join HMS *Chanticleer*. As HMS *Crane* was leaving the convoy, the crew could see the stern of HMS *Chanticleer* explode. HMS *Crane* closed with HMS *Chanticleer*, zigzagging at full speed. Upon receiving HMS *Chanticleer*'s radio report that it had a sonar contact, HMS *Crane*'s A gun opened fire on the spot where the U-boat was thought to be located, hoping to prevent a coup de grace on HMS *Chanticleer*. Then HMS *Crane* obtained a sonar contact at a range of 1,800 yards. Between 1550 and 1751 HMS *Crane* carried out ten depth charge attacks on this sonar contact without result. The search continued, but at 1828 HMS *Chanticleer*, some 4 miles to the south, obtained another sonar contact. HMS *Crane* proceeded to the area, obtained a sonar contact, and attacked it with depth charges at 1846. The contact was regained for a short time and then lost. HMS *Crane* then circled HMS *Chanticleer*, dropping depth charges to serve as "scarers" until the damaged sloop was taken in tow by the salvage tug *Saleda*. HMS *Crane* screened the tug and HMS *Chanticleer* until relieved by HMS *Garlies*. Then HMS *Crane* departed to join SL 139/MKS 30 and HMS *Chanticleer*, under tow, arrived at the Azores two days later.[41]

After receiving the sighting report of the U-515, the BdU came to the conclusion that the convoy had passed the *Schill 1* patrol line and ordered the U-boats to chase to the north.[42] In the early afternoon of 18 November, the BdU informed the U-boats of *Schill 1* that after nightfall a GAF aircraft would drop a marker astern of the convoy, providing a bright white light for several hours. Next, at 1733, the BdU directed the U-boats of *Schill 1* to search for SL139/MKS 30 "AT TOP SPEED." Ninety minutes later, the BdU radioed *Schill 1* "AIR-CRAFT SENDING BEACON SIGNALS," but only the U-262 picked up those beacon signals and two hours later reported sighting a star shell. At 2258 the U-515 radioed "CONVOY ROUGHLY IN CF 2670." The last U-boat of *Schill 1* to sight the ships of SL 139/MKS 30 was the U-262, which spotted "FOUR SILHOUETTES" and two escorts at 0648 on 19 November and later a frigate heading north at "HIGH SPEED AT 0930." The hunt by the U-boats of *Schill 1* during the night of 18 to 19 November was impeded by three ASV Leigh Light Wellington aircraft of 179th Squadron which flew air cover over the convoy during the hours of darkness. At 0345 on 18 to 19 November one of these aircraft, F/179, caught the U-211, obediently following the BdU's order to chase to the north on the surface, and sank the submarine with four depth charges. After the sinking of the U-211, SL 139/MKS 30 changed course 30° to starboard. Another aircraft report that there were U-boats ahead of the convoy caused another altercation at 0738, when SL 139/MKS 30 changed course 20° to port for twenty-eight minutes.[43]

Concluding that SL 139/MKS 30 had passed to the northward of the new patrol line, the BdU called off the operation at 1935 on 19 November. The BdU thought that the failure of *Schill 1* to attack SL 139/MKS 30 successfully stemmed from the inability to pick up the beacon signals sent by the GAF.[44] Further, the BdU reasoned, the GAF beacon signal picked up by the U-262 had not given a good enough bearing to establish the position of the convoy. Beyond this, the BdU complained, the sighting report made by the U-515 before damaging HMS *Chanticleer* was not clear. The U-515 was forced to submerge at that point and did not again report the position of SL 139/MKS 30 until 2258 on 18 November, by which time the convoy had passed *Schill 1* to the north.[45] Perhaps more to the point, *Schill 1* failed to engage SL 139/MKS 30 because the U-boats were deployed in a linear or extended-line formation across the convoy's course. When SL 139/MKS 30 made contact with *Schill 1*, the convoy effectively punched a hole in the formation by attacking and damaging the U-333 and then keeping that U-boat submerged after the U-515 torpedoed HMS *Chanticleer*. SL 139/MKS 30 passed smoothly through this hole in the patrol line while the convoy's air and surface escorts kept the other U-boats of *Schill 1* to the east and west from maneuvering to engage the Allied force as it continued to steam north.

Even as *Schill 1* tried to gain firm contact with SL 139/MKS 30, the BdU was positioning *Schill 2* to intercept the convoy further along its route. Beginning at 1147 on 18 November, the BdU issued a series of orders moving *Schill 2* 60 miles to the north to take station at 1800 the next day. In an order issued at 0022 on 19 November, the U-boats were directed to "KEEP WATCH FOR BEACON SIGNALS" and were also informed that the GAF would provide air reconnaissance during the afternoon and evening of 19 November, dropping flares after sundown to mark the convoy. The U-boats were also told to expect beacon signals from 1800 onwards during the night of 19 November. These radio transmissions were decoded by the Allies at 2051 on 18 November and 0400 on 19 November.[46] *Schill 2*'s successful interception of SL 139/MKS 30 depended in part on luck and in part on the U-boats' ability to pick up the beacon signals of the GAF, for the radio messages ordering *Schill 2* into place had given the Allies advance knowledge of the position of the patrol line.

During the daylight hours of 19 November SL 139/MKS 30 steamed steadily north at a speed of 7 knots. At 0530 HMCS *Calgary* and HMCS *Snowberry* joined the convoy's escort.[47] While these two Canadian warships were steaming to join SL 139/MKS 30, they sighted two U-boats, one probably the U-648, about a hundred miles ahead of the convoy.[48] One U-boat escaped on the surface and the other dived on the approach of the two corvettes. The Canadians conducted a sonar search for the submerged U-boat without result before proceeding to join the convoy. At 0840 the escort was further reinforced by the arrival of the 5th Escort Group consisting of HMS *Nene*, HMS *Tweed*, HMCS *Lunenburg*, and HMCS *Edmundston*, along with HMS *Essington* of the 7th Escort Group. The five ships of the 40th Escort Group, plus HMCS *Calgary*, HMCS *Snowberry*, and HMS *Foley*, were formed into an inner screen, while the ships of the 5th and 7th Escort Groups were stationed on the port and starboard sides of the convoy, respectively, as an extended outer screen.[49]

At 0910 on 19 November a German JU 290 aircraft began circling SL 139/MKS 30 until it was driven off by a B-17 Fortress serving as an air escort. Five-and-a-half hours later, aircraft S/220 sighted a U-boat some 28 miles from the convoy's starboard bow. The U-boat dived before the aircraft could attack. Ships of the 7th Escort Group were sent to the area but could not find the U-boat and rejoined the convoy. At 1740 the escorts began to obtain a series of HF/DF bearings from ahead of the convoy at a range of about 30 miles. The commander of the 40th Escort Group thought that this indicated that a number of U-boats were "concentrating ahead of the convoy's track." HMS *Nene*, HMCS *Calgary*, and HMCS *Snowberry* were ordered to sweep ahead of SL 139/MKS 30. The destroyers HMS *Watchman* and HMS *Winchelsea* joined the convoy at 1915 and became part of the 7th Escort Group on the outer screen. And at the same time, HF/DF bearings obtained to the rear of the convoy prompted the reassignment of HMS *Foley* to a position 8 miles astern.[50]

HMS *Milford* of the inner screen of the convoy obtained a sonar contact off the starboard bow of SL 139/MKS 30 at 2106. This contact was on a bearing of 40° from HMS *Milford* at a range of 2,700 yards. The British warship immediately attacked, holding the contact until it was at a range of 200 yards. Ten depth charges were dropped without result and the contact was lost as the convoy steamed past. Immediately after this attack HMS *Milford* was ordered to rejoin the screen of the convoy. During the night of 19 to 20 November air support to SL 139/MKS 30 was provided by seven ASV Leigh Light Wellington aircraft. No U-boats were sighted by these aircraft, but one U-boat reported being approached three times by an aircraft dropping flares, and the U-608 also reported seeing an aircraft.[51]

While sweeping ahead of SL 139/MKS 30 at 2137, HMS *Nene*, in company with HMCS *Calgary* and HMCS *Snowberry*, obtained a radar contact. At 2145 the British warship fired a star shell which revealed a U-boat steaming at high speed. HMS *Nene* engaged the U-boat with gunfire, forcing it to dive. The British warship then closed with the position where the U-boat had dived and obtained sonar contact at 2229. The position was marked with a flare, and HMCS *Calgary* and HMCS *Snowberry* circled the area while HMS *Nene* conducted an unproductive hedgehog attack. At 2249 HMS *Nene* attacked again with depth charges without result. The contact was then lost and the three Allied warships began to search for the U-boat with sonar. At 2356 HMCS *Snowberry* obtained a sonar contact and attacked with depth charges. HMCS *Snowberry* attacked a second time with ten depth charges, and the Canadians heard three "marked" underwater explosions about three minutes after the attack. The contact was lost and the Allied warships resumed the search until 0052, when HMS *Nene* picked up a sonar contact at a range of 700 yards on what was thought to be a different U-boat. A flare was dropped, and at 0118 HMS *Nene* attacked with depth charges, blowing the U-536 to the surface and forcing the crew to abandon the vessel. HMS *Nene* attempted to put a party on board the U-boat, but it sank before it could be accomplished. The Allied ships then picked up seventeen Germans before returning to the convoys screen.[52]

Meanwhile, beginning at 2020, the escorts in the screen of the convoy obtained a series of HF/DF bearings which indicated that U-boats were moving toward the port bow of SL 139/MKS 30. At 2200 HMCS *Edmundston* on the port bow of the convoy obtained a radar contact at a range of 5,700 yards. HMCS *Edmundston* ran down the bearing. The contact disappeared at 2211, but sonar contact was quickly obtained and then lost owing to equipment failure. A search was begun, and the sonar contact was quickly regained. A deliberate hedgehog attack was conducted against what was later thought to be a decoy set off by the U-boat to mislead the Canadians. HMCS *Edmundston* next launched a depth charge attack which miscarried when only three depth charges were dropped while the others jammed in the rails. HMCS *Edmundston* continued the depth charge attack, but again only three were dropped because the others still could not be freed from the rails. HMS *Tweed*, which had joined the search, then gained sonar contact with the U-boat and began to attack. At the same time HMCS *Edmundston* also regained contact and began to attack the same target. Both warships steamed toward the same point, and at the last minute HMS *Tweed* sheered off, allowing HMCS *Edmundston* to deliver a ten depth charge attack without result. Then HMS *Tweed* turned and attacked with depth charges without result. Sonar contact was not regained, and both escorts returned to the convoy after searching the area for two hours.[53]

At 0240 on 20 November HMS *Pheasant* obtained a radar contact ahead of the convoy at a range of 5,000 yards. The contact disappeared, but sonar contact was quickly obtained at 0245. As HMS *Pheasant* was mounting a depth charge attack, the convoy was bearing down on the position. At 0329 SL 139/MKS 30 made a turn of 45° to starboard to avoid the area as HMS *Pheasant* attacked with depth charges. The attack failed, and at 0430 the convoy returned to its base course and HMS *Pheasant*, having lost contact, rejoined the convoy. Though several HF/DF bearings were obtained showing that there were a number of U-boats ahead of SL 139/MKS 30, this was the last contact with the enemy by the convoy's escort that evening.[54]

Despite another attempt to exploit air support, the U-boats of *Schill 2* failed to engage SL 139/MKS 30 the night of 19 to 20 November. During the afternoon of 19 November, the BdU ordered the U-boats of *Schill 2* to maintain their positions and to stand by to pick up radio bearings after 1800 from a GAF aircraft which would shadow the convoy.[55] The BdU thought that "BEARINGS REPORTS CAN BE DECISIVE FOR THE SUCCESS OF OPERATION."[56] SL 139/MKS 30 was, indeed, located and shadowed from 1800 onwards by a GAF JU 290 aircraft which sent beacon signals, but the U-boats failed to pick up these signals.[57] At 2018 the BdU informed the U-boats of *Schill 2* that "ACCORDING TO DEAD RECKONING AND BEARING CONVOY WILL BE IN (BE) 8780 AT 200A RESUMABLE COURSE NORTH, SPEED 7.5. GO AFTER IT AT TOP SPEED."[58] However, aside from the sinking of the U-536, the only contact the U-boats had with SL 139/MKS 30 was minimal and indecisive. The U-586 sighted three "ILLUMINANT ROCKETS," the U-238 saw a star shell, and the U-608 and the U-714 picked up some hydrophone bearings. The U-238 fired a torpedo at a frigate which missed and the U-boat was run over by the convoy.[59] These were the only contacts that the U-boats of *Schill 2* had with SL 139/MKS 30 that evening.

At 0501 on 20 November the BdU came to the conclusion that the convoy had passed through the *Schill 2* patrol line and ordered the U-boats to chase to the north until daylight and then to dive.[60] The BdU thought that the U-boats of *Schill 2* failed to engage SL 139/MKS 30 because the night was very dark, with the moon in the last quarter, low clouds, and showers—all conditions that prevented or hindered the operations of the U-boats. At the same time the BdU acknowledged that "it is unlikely that the convoy took evasive action." Further, the BdU reasoned, the convoy's surface and air escorts prevented the U-boats from closing with the convoy by constantly forcing the German vessels to dive.[61] However, what truly appears to have happened, is that SL 139/MKS 30's escorts had simply overpowered a part of *Schill 2*'s patrol line, just as they had overwhelmed *Schill 1*, and the convoy then passed through the resulting gap without being attacked.

While the U-boats of *Schill 2* vainly attempted to attack SL 139/MKS 30, the BdU was positioning *Schill 3* to intercept and attack the convoy. At 0356 on 20 November the BdU ordered the U-boats of *Schill 3* to move southward, to surface at 1830, and to be prepared to receive bearings from GAF reconnaissance aircraft. The three reconnaissance aircraft, however, did not materialize on the morning of 20 November, for one was shot down over the Bay of Biscay and another had a faulty radar. The lone aircraft attempting to carry out the evening flights was itself shot down over the Bay of Biscay. The BdU gloomily radioed the U-boats of *Schill 3:* "NO MORE BEACON SIGNALS CAN BE EXPECTED."[62]

As SL 139/MKS 30 steamed north on 20 November, air cover was provided by six B-17 Fortresses from the Azores, and six B-24 Liberators and three Sunderland aircraft from the United Kingdom. At 0900 aircraft P/86 sighted a U-boat some 20 miles in front of the convoy, but the U-boat submerged before the aircraft could attack. HMS *Tweed* and HMCS *Lunenburg* conducted a prolonged search of the area where the U-boat had dived but made no contact with the U-boat and later rejoined the convoy. Later in the day the U-618 shot down a Sunderland aircraft which was attempting to attack the submarine.[63]

At 1226 HMCS *Snowberry* obtained a sonar contact on the port wing of the convoy. HMS *Nene*, supporting HMCS *Snowberry*, also gained sonar contact with the target at 1336 and carried out two depth charge attacks. After the second attack, A gun's crew reported seeing "two periscope standards" break surface of the water. HMS *Nene* turned to starboard and came full speed steering toward the position, but nothing further was seen. Sonar contact could not be regained, and, after searching the area, HMCS *Snowberry* and HMS *Nene* rejoined the convoy at 1700.[64]

SL 139/MKS 30 had altered course 27° to port at 1600, and the escort picked up a number of late-afternoon HF/DF bearings indicating that there were several U-boats astern of the convoy. At 1925 HMS *Essington* on the starboard quarter of the outer screen obtained a sonar contact which was attacked with depth charges. A U-boat was blown to the surface by the explosions and then disappeared. Thirty-six minutes later, while HMS *Essington* and HMS *Winchelsea* searched for this submarine, they heard an underwater explosion, but no trace of the U-boat was found.[65]

From 2000 onwards more HF/DF bearing were obtained which indicated that several U-boats were approaching the port quarter of the convoy from astern and that two others were moving toward the starboard quarter. HMS *Crane*, HMS *Winchelsea*, and HMS *Foley* were sent to sweep astern of the convoy with the ships of the 5th Escort Group. This sweep resulted in a confused series of radar contacts with U-boats which led to depth charge and hedgehog attacks along the sides and astern of SL 139/MKS 30.[66]

Night air support for the convoy was provided by eight ASV Leigh Light B-24 Liberator aircraft of 53rd Squadron from England which constantly flew around SL 139/MKS 30. The aircraft obtained many radar contacts astern of the convoy, and four U-boats were illuminated by Leigh Lights. The U-575 was attacked by aircraft A/53, and the U-648 shot down aircraft N/53. The commander of the 5th Escort Group later complained that the glare of airborne search lights had reduced the chances of surprising a U-boat on the surface.[67]

While conducting a sweep along the port quarter of the convoy, HMS *Foley* obtained a radar contact at 0420. HMS *Crane* also picked it up and fired a star shell which illuminated a U-boat. HMS *Crane* closed as the U-boat dived and then conducted a "scare" attack with one depth charge. At 0502 a deliberate depth charge attack was carried out without result while HMS *Foley*, whose sonar was not working, circled the area carrying out a radar search. Half an hour later, HMS *Crane* attacked again and four minutes later heard an explosion astern which was thought to be a *zaunkonig*. Then HMS *Crane* directed HMS *Foley* as it made a "not very accurate" creeping attack. At 0638 HMS *Crane*, with only sixteen depth charges remaining, carried out a ten depth charge attack. This U-boat, the U-538, began a long series of evasive actions, including firing off decoys, to break contact with HMS *Crane*'s sonar. Finally, at 1005, HMS *Foley* was directed in a "creeping" attack after which oil came to the surface and sonar contact was lost. The U-538 had been sunk. HMS *Winchelsea* and HMS *Watchman* which were joining the hunt came across the wreckage of the U-boat as they approached the scene. At 1225 HMS *Crane* and HMS *Foley* left the region to rejoin SL 139/MKS 30 while the two destroyers searched the area for another two hours before rejoining the convoy.[68]

Just before dawn on 21 November an ASV Leigh Light B-24 Liberator, aircraft B/53, obtained radar contact with a U-boat about 30 miles off the convoy's port quarter, but the U-boat dived before an attack could be undertaken. At dawn the ships of the 5th and 7th Escort Groups conducted line-abreast sweeps along the flanks of SL 139/MKS 30 hunting for U-boats. And at 0918 a GAF aircraft began shadowing the convoy. The aircraft stayed with the convoy for some two hours before departing. At 1300 SL 139/MKS 30 altered course from 27° to 4°.[69]

Schill 3 failed to intercept and attack SL 139/MKS 30. The U-boats saw some star shells, sighted a number of escorts, and were attacked by both aircraft and warships, but never came near the main body of the convoy. At first the BdU thought that *Schill 3* was to the north of the convoy and at 2257 on 20 November ordered the U-boats to steam south at 7 knots if they were not in contact. At 0543 on 21 November the U-boats of *Schill 3* were ordered to dive at 0630 and to "MOVE OFF TO THE SOUTHWARD."[70]

At 1129 on 21 November the BdU signaled the U-boats of the three *Schill* groups that "THE OPERATION IS ENDED." The same orders sent seven U-boats (U-714, U-420, U-226, U-575, U-212, U-967, U-462) back to base while directing the remaining submarines to stay submerged "AS FAR AS POSSIBLE" and wait for the next operation.[71] The BdU believed that *Schill 3*'s operation against SL 139/MKS 30 failed because "the enemy [was] able in this area to take effective action against them [U-boats] very quickly with numerous aircraft and escorting destroyers." Again, as in the case of *Schill 1* and *2*, the U-boats of *Schill 3* found that it was impossible to maneuver on the surface to gain contact and to attack SL 139/MKS 30. Above all, however, the BdU also thought that the operations of the *Schill* U-boats had been hindered by the failure of the GAF to provide enough reconnaissance aircraft and that there had been a general inability to coordinate the operations of the U-boats with those of the GAF reconnaissance aircraft over the battle area.[72]

Less than three and a half hours after the BdU conceded the failure of the *Schill* patrol groups, the German Air Force gave historians of World War II a tantalizing taste of what might have occurred had the GAF acted wholeheartedly in concert with the U-boats. At 1453 on 21 November the 4th Escort Group (captain class frigates HMS *Bentinck*, HMS *Calder*, HMS *Bazely*, HMS *Drury*, HMS *Byard*, HMS *Blackwood*) met SL 139/MKS 30 at 46°15′N, 19°10′W before sweeping south through the battle area looking for U-boats.[73] About an hour later, when the 4th Escort Group was just astern of the convoy, SL 139/MKS 30 was attacked by GAF aircraft with glider bombs (a radio-controlled, rocket-boosted, winged missile carrying 1,000 pounds of explosives with a speed of over 300 miles per hour). The

GAF sent twenty-five He 177 aircraft armed with these weapons against the convoy, the first time these aircraft had operated against a convoy at a range of 800 miles.[74] The German aircraft came in on the convoy from the east at a height of between 2,000 and 5,000 feet, skillfully using the cloud cover. As the aircraft approached the convoy, the ships opened fire with antiaircraft guns. The auxiliary anti-aircraft cruiser HMCS *Prince Robert* zigzagged across the convoy's stern, firing at the enemy aircraft.[75] Straggling some 3 miles astern of the convoy, the merchant ship *Marsa* was attacked by eight aircraft with twelve glider bombs, one of which hit the ship's engine room and sank the vessel. Another glider bomb hit the merchant ship *Delius* in the bridge, killing all but one of the ship's officers. This ship, though damaged, was saved and later made port. At 1657, after launching sixteen glider bombs, the German aircraft ended the attack and turned back to base. Astern of SL 139/MKS 30, the 4th Escort Group was also attacked by several aircraft with glider bombs and suffered no damage.[76]

Although two German aircraft failed to return to base, the German navy considered this air attack to be a "complete success," for it showed the possibilities of cooperation between the GAF and the U-boats in the war against convoys. However, the GAF attack on SL 139/MKS 30 was not only the last German attack on that convoy, but also the first and last GAF attack of the campaign against any Allied convoys west of Portugal, for shortly thereafter the GAF transferred all the He 177 aircraft to the Mediterranean.[77]

Even after the failure of the U-boats' operations against SL 139/MKS 30, the BdU did not give up. Instead, it decided to attack a southbound Great Britain-Gibraltar convoy. On 1644 on 22 November the BdU ordered sixteen U-boats (U-424, U-843, U-618, U-515, U-358, U-542, U-586, U-262, U-764, U-86, U-238, U-648, U-228, U-969, U-538, U-391) of the *Schill* group to form a patrol line running between 43°15'N, 22°05'W and 43°15'N, 22°15'W, while four other U-boats were to "HAVE LIBERTY OF ACTION IMMEDIATELY SOUTH OF THE LINE." Code named *Weddigen*, these U-boats were to be in position by the night of 23 to 24 November. The Allies decoded this order at 0013 on 23 November.[78]

The objective of the *Weddigen* group was convoy OS 59/KMS 33. The GAF attempted to provide reconnaissance for the U-boats, but on 23 November one of the two aircraft dispatched for this purpose returned to base because of engine problems while the other had a radar defect and never located the convoy.[79] Not surprisingly, OS 59/KMS 33 was able to pass safely to the west of the *Weddigen* patrol line on 23 November.[80] At 1935 that evening the U-boats of the *Weddigen* group were ordered to move their patrol line 90 miles southeast at the "HIGHEST POSSIBLE SPEED" and then to dive at daylight. This order was decoded by the Allies at 0851 on 24 November.[81]

As the U-boats of the *Weddigen* group were moving into their patrol line on 22 and 23 November, the area was swept by the 4th Escort Group and Allied aircraft. The U-424 was attacked with depth charges, and the U-714 was hunted for five hours by ships of the 4th Escort Group. On 23 November at 42°40′N, 20°37′W HMS *Bazely*'s radar picked up a U-boat which dived at 0625. Before sonar contact could be obtained, the ship's radar picked up another contact at a range of 5 miles, the U-648. The U-boat dived at 0712. Sonar contact was obtained, and HMS *Bazely*, HMS *Blackwood*, and HMS *Drury* sank the U-648 during the course of a three hour and forty minute series of depth charge and hedgehog attacks.[82]

By the evening of 24 November the BdU realized that OS 59/KMS 33 had passed to the west of the *Weddigen* patrol line. At 2036 seventeen of the *Weddigen* U-boats (U-424, U-618, U-843, U-600, U-542, U-358, U-586, U-262, U-764, U-238, U-86, U-538, U-228, U-391, U-107, U-648, U-969; the BdU did not know of the sinking of the U-648) were ordered to form a new patrol line at 37°N between 17°W and 19°W by the evening of 27 November. The U-boats were to remain submerged by day and to maintain radio silence except for "REPORTS OF TACTICAL IMPORTANCE." This order was decoded by the Allies at 2036 on 25 November.[83]

The new target of the *Weddigen* group was SL 140/MKS 31, a northbound Gibraltar-United Kingdom convoy. As the U-boats moved toward their new patrol line positions, there were a number of contacts with ships of the 4th Escort Group also heading toward SL 140/MKS 31. In the early hours of 25 November the U-262 and the U-843 saw star shells, and at 0128 HMS *Drury* obtained a radar contact bearing 245° at a range of 7.5 miles. While this bearing was being run down, HMS *Bazely* picked up a radar contact on the U-600 on a bearing of 169°. Both HMS *Bazely* and HMS *Blackwood* ran down this bearing at 0154, and the U-600 dived and went deep. HMS *Bazely* immediately conducted four hedgehog attacks in rapid succession, and at 0303, only seconds after the fourth attack, a heavy underwater explosion rocked the ship—the death throes of the U-600. Allied aircraft were also sweeping through the area hunting for U-boats, and both the U-618 and the U-542 were attacked by Allied aircraft during the early hours of 26 November.[84]

At 1848 on 26 November the BdU informed the U-boats of the *Weddigen* group that the GAF would send an aircraft to find the convoy on the morning of 27 November. In the late afternoon, another aircraft would shadow SL 140/MKS 31 and transmit homing signals. The U-boats were to surface at 1830 to pick up these homing signals. Eleven minutes later the BdU sent the *Weddigen* U-boats another directive stating that a GAF reconnaissance aircraft had sighted the convoy, the patrol line was to be moved to the southeast, and be prepared for action at 1800 on 27 November. This order was decoded by the Allies at 0600 on 27 November.[85]

The object of this feverish activity was a convoy of sixty-eight merchant ships escorted by the seven warships of Escort Group B1 (destroyer HMS *Hurricane*; frigate HMS *Glenarn*; corvettes HMS *Oxlip*, HMS *Meadowsweet*, HMS *Borage*, HMS *Dahlia*, and HMS *Honeysuckle*). On 25 November the escort was reinforced by the destroyer HMS *Wanderer*. Further, SL 140/MKS 31 received distant support from a task group built around the American escort carrier USS *Bogue*, known as Task Group 21.13, consisting of the destroyers USS *George E. Badger*, USS *Osmond Ingram*, USS *Clemson*, and USS *Dupont*. The first enemy contact came at 0735 on 27 November, when a German FW 200 aircraft shadowed the convoy for about two hours. After the German aircraft departed, the convoy altered course 20° to the east in order to avoid the U-boats thought to be northwest of the convoy. Shortly after the change of course was made, two PBY Catalina aircraft of the air escort were sent by the senior officer of the convoy's escort to conduct a search for U-boats northwest of SL 140/MKS 31.[86]

When the FW 200 aircraft's report of the position of SL 140/MKS 31 was received by the BdU, it was seen that the convoy was further east than expected. At 0835 on 27 November the *Weddigen* U-boats were ordered to proceed on a course of 45° at a speed of 3 knots.

Later, at 1516, the *Weddigen* U-boats were directed to steam northeast after surfacing at 1830, and at the same time the U-boats were informed that aircraft beacon signals could not be expected before 1930.[87] A German BV 222 aircraft located SL 140/MKS 31 at 39°00′N, 16°30′W and shadowed the convoy for several hours during the evening of 27 November. However, even though some of the beacon signals were picked up by the U-boats, the bearings were too acute for good fixes.[88] In the early evening the U-238 saw three aircraft, the U-391 obtained a hydrophone bearing at 95° true, and the U-262 saw star shells on a bearing of 75° true. At 2120 the BdU informed the *Weddigen* U-boats that aerial reconnaissance and reports from the U-boats indicated that the convoy was north and west of the *Weddigen* group. Therefore, eight U-boats (U-424, U-843, U-618, U-515, U-358, U-542, U-586, U-262) were to operate on courses ranging from 290° to 320°, and another eight U-boats (U-769, U-86, U-238, U-684, U-228, U-969, U-538, U-391) on courses between 320° to 350°. The convoy's speed was 7.5 knots, and the U-boats were further told that "YOU HAVE ONLY TONIGHT LEFT, SO PUT ALL YOU HAVE INTO IT."[89]

SL 140/MKS 31's escort was reinforced still further during 27 November. At 1000 three warships (HMS *Calder*, HMS *Bentinck*, HMS *Byard*) of the 4th Escort Group joined the escort and later in the afternoon HMS *Blackwood* of the 4th Escort Group and four sloops of the 2nd Escort Group (sloops HMS *Starling*, HMS *Wild Goose*, HMS *Kite*, HMS *Magpie*) were added to the convoy's escort. Seven different U-boat radio transmissions bearing from the port beam to the port bow of the convoy were obtained by HF/DF sets on the escorts. The sloops of the 2nd Escort Group were sent down two of these bearings. While searching down one HF/DF bearing, HMS *Starling* and HMS *Kite* sighted some lights and heard gunfire. The commander of the 2nd Escort Group thought that these lights and noise were caused by aircraft belonging to the USS *Bogue* because the British warships had been hearing the radio transmissions of American carrier-borne aircraft all day. But, in fact, it was the U-762 shooting down the British shore-based aircraft O/72. HMS *Wild Goose* and HMS *Magpie* searched down the other HF/DF bearing but found nothing and began to return to the convoy. Then at 2308 about 10 miles from SL 140/MKS 31, HMS *Wild Goose* obtained a radar contact astern. The British sloop turned and fired a star shell illuminating a U-boat which dived as the sloop opened fire with its main armament. A sonar contact was obtained which was considered "not good" and soon lost. At 2330 the crew heard an explosion which they thought might be a *zaunkonig* going off at the end of its run. HMS *Magpie* and HMS *Wild Goose* then searched the area until 0107 on 28 November, when a sonar contact was obtained. HMS *Wild Goose* and HMS *Magpie* tracked this contact for an hour, being joined by HMS *Starling*. At 0246 the U-boat surfaced and was picked up by radar. Taken under gunfire, the submarine promptly submerged. For the next two-and-a-half hours, the three sloops hunted the U-boat, conducting a number of depth charge attacks without result before rejoining the convoy.[90]

While the ships of the 2nd Escort Group were searching for a U-boat, an ASV Leigh Light Wellington aircraft, L/179, attacked and sank the U-542 at 2351 on the port side of the convoy. At the same time HMS *Bentinck* and HMS *Blackwood* ran down an HF/DF bearing for about 30 miles on the convoy's starboard bow. At 2320 HMS *Blackwood* obtained a radar contact at a range of 2,100 yards. This U-boat dived and HMS *Bentinck* attacked with ten depth charges. The contact was lost, and the two British warships searched the area for the U-boat until 0100 by which time the convoy had safely passed. In less than ninety minutes beginning at 2332 on 27 November, the escorts' HF/DF sets picked up eleven radio transmissions from the port side of SL 140/MKS 31. Later U-boat radio transmissions appeared to be coming from off the port quarter and starboard bow of the convoy.[91]

At 0212 on 28 November HMS *Hurricane* obtained an HF/DF bearing some 15 miles ahead of the convoy. HMS *Byard* was sent down the bearing and sighted two U-boats. When one dived, HMS *Byard* attacked with depth charges and then conducted a sonar hunt until the convoy had passed. HMS *Bentinck*, sent to assist HMS *Byard*, chased the second U-boat. At 0328 HMS *Bentinck* obtained a radar contact and then forced the U-boat to dive. Depth charge and hedgehog attacks were mounted before contact was lost. HMS *Bentinck* searched the area with sonar until SL 140/MKS 31 had steamed past.[92]

While HMS *Byard* and HMS *Bentinck* attacked U-boats ahead of

SL 140/MKS 31, HMS *Hurricane* obtained a radar contact about 51/
2 miles astern of the convoy as it moved east. The British destroyer
turned and steamed down through the columns of merchant ships
toward the rear of the convoy. When HMS *Hurricane* was about 3
miles astern of SL 140/MKS 31, the U-boat was still 4 miles from
the convoy and appeared to be moving off to the east. HMS *Hurricane*
gave up the chase so as not to be drawn away from the convoy and
returned to its station in the screen. As HMS *Hurricane* turned away
from the U-boat, the contact disappeared from the radar screen.[93]

On the forward screen of SL 140/MKS 31, HMS *Blackwood* obtained a radar contact at a range of 13 miles at 0338. The frigate went
after the contact, but the U-boat released a radar decoy and then
dived. HMS *Blackwood* dropped a depth charge on the U-boat's estimated position and then hunted for the enemy vessel until 0517 before departing to rejoin the convoy. HMS *Kite* picked up an HF/DF
bearing at a range of 15 miles from the port bow of the convoy at
0401. The sloop ran down this bearing, found nothing, and then returned to its station at 0801. At 0405 HMS *Calder,* on the convoy's
inner screen, obtained a radar contact bearing 70° at a range of 5
miles. HMS *Calder,* joined by HMS *Byard,* hunted down the bearing
for the U-boat. At 0415 the U-boat was seen to turn away from the
convoy at a range of 5,500 yards after firing what appeared to be two
zaunkönigs at HMS *Calder.* The torpedoes missed their mark and the
U-boat dived at 0429. One depth charge attack was conducted without result by HMS *Calder,* and sonar contact with the U-boat was
lost, forcing the British warships to rejoin the screen of the convoy.[94]

Action resumed on the inner starboard screen of SL 140/MKS 31
where HMS *Dahlia* obtained a radar contact between herself and the
main body of the convoy at 0622. This was the U-262, which had
dived under the screen and then surfaced near the starboard side of
SL 140/MKS 31. At first, the contact was thought to be an escort out
of station. Almost at the instant of gaining the radar contact, the HF/
DF sets on three escorts picked up a radio transmission close to the
convoy's starboard side. The U-262 was immediately sighted by
HMS *Dahlia* and dived. Just before submerging, the U-262 fired
four torpedoes which missed and exploded at the end of their runs.[95]
HMS *Blackwood* was sent down the HF/DF bearing in case there had
been a mistake in estimating the range of the U-boat making the

radio transmission, while HMS *Dahlia* proceeded to hunt the U-262 with sonar. Many non-U-boat echoes were picked up as the convoy steamed past, and it was not until 0635 that a sonar contact was obtained. HMS *Dahlia* attacked this contact with depth charges. After this attack no sonar contacts could be obtained and HMS *Dahlia* found patches of oil as it swept through the area. This was the last contact the surface escorts of the convoy had with the U-boats, and no more close HF/DF bearings of U-boat radio transmissions were obtained. At 0800 on 28 November, SL 140/MKS 31's course was altered 20° to starboard to throw off any U-boats attempting to set up daylight submerged attacks. Air searches conducted that morning by escorting aircraft found nothing within 50 miles of the convoy.[96]

From the point of view of the U-boat commanders, the early hours of 28 November had been desperately frustrating. At 2330 on 27 November the BdU informed the U-boats of the *Weddigen* group that the "AIRCRAFT IS STILL WITH THE CONVOY AND TRANSMITTING BEACON SIGNALS." And at 0129 on 28 November the BdU radioed the *Weddigen* U-boats that reports from the GAF reconnaissance aircraft indicated that the convoy was "WITHIN A 10 MILE RADIUS OF NAVAL GRID SQUARE 6347 AT 0100" and the U-boats were to "OPERATE ACCORDINGLY AND SEARCH AT TOP SPEED." The U-107 picked up the beacon signal from the GAF reconnaissance aircraft "VERY LOUD," but the U-boat was almost immediately set upon and attacked with depth charges by the convoy's escort.[97] In addition, and the U-238 obtained a D/F bearing of 92° true on a radio transmission from a ship in the convoy. Nevertheless, the U-boats failed to engage SL 140/MKS 31 successfully during the morning of 28 November. Three U-boats (U-262, U-391, U-618) were attacked in the early hours of 28 November by ASV Leigh Light aircraft. German submarines, like the U-262 which attempted to close with SL 140/MKS 31 before daylight on 28 November, were detected by the escorts and driven away without attacking the convoy successfully. Although they were not able to get close enough to the convoy to attack in the first hours of 28 November, a number of U-boats saw star shells and other lights from the convoy.[98] It was quickly becoming clear to the BdU that the operation was failing, and the U-boats were ordered to submerge at dawn and await further orders. At 1719 the operation was ended and the U-boats of the *Weddigen* group were ordered to

"MOVE AWAY AT ECONOMICAL SPEED IN NORTHWESTERLY DIREC-
TION."[99]

The BdU thought that the operation against SL 140/MKS 31
failed because the *Weddigen* patrol line was "in the wrong place." As
a result, the U-boats were forced to approach the convoy singly and
too late to be effective. This miscalculation had two causes: the D/F
fixes the U-boats obtained from the GAF aircraft's beacon signals
"crossed at an unfavorable angle," and a number of U-boats had been
misled as to the convoy's position by flares set off by the escorts as
decoys. Aside from this, the convoy just had too many air and surface
escorts for the U-boats either to overcome or elude.[100] And, as the
British noted acidly, with the exception of the U-262, there was "a
marked reluctance on the part of the enemy to press home his attacks."[101]

On 29 November, as the U-boats of the *Weddigen* group were moving under orders to the northwest, aircraft from the USS *Bogue* were
sweeping through the region. Fifty miles west of the American Task
Group 21.13, these carrier-borne aircraft caught the U-86 on the
surface and sank her.[102] The next day three American carrier-borne
aircraft found and attacked the U-238, another member of the *Weddigen* group, damaging the vessel and killing two crew members,
while wounding three others including the commanding officer of the
vessel. And the U-764, in the same area, was also attacked by shore-
based aircraft.[103] After these attacks by Allied aircraft, the BdU signaled the U-boats that the tactics used by Allied aircraft in attacking
U-boats were "APPARENTLY STILL BASED ON UNKNOWN PROCE-
DURE."[104]

The BdU intended the *Weddigen* U-boats to operate next against a
southbound convoy, KMS 34.[105] On 30 November the BdU ordered
the eight remaining U-boats (U-618, U-238, U-391, U-107, U-358,
U-228, U-424, U-843; the U-86 was also included in this order, for
the BdU did not know that it had been sunk) of the *Weddigen* group
to form a patrol line running between 41°21′N, 20°38′W and
41°21′N, 17°10′W at 2000 on 1 December. The U-boats were to
remain submerged during the day and steer a course of 310° covering
80 miles per day. This order was decoded by the Allies at 0710 on 1
December.[106] The Germans, however, were hindered in locating
KMS 34 by a shortage of long-range reconnaissance aircraft. The

BdU calculated that the GAF had only five aircraft suitable for such operations over the Atlantic, and only one or two could fly at any given time. By 2 December the BdU had concluded that convoy KMS 34 had passed to the westward of the *Weddigen* U-boats' patrol line without being sighted by aircraft.[107] In the next several days the BdU moved the *Weddigen* patrol from one position to another vainly searching for an Allied convoy.[108] On 7 December the U-424 "fortuitously" sighted a convoy, but none of the U-boats were in position to intercept and attack this convoy without chasing it on the surface during daylight. Because of the threat of Allied aircraft, the BdU rejected the option of daylight surface operations, and with no chance of contact with the convoy, the BdU ordered the *Weddigen* group to break off the operation and disband.[109]

The Allies would be judged the clear victors in the convoy battles west of Portugal in November of 1943 if one used no other criterion than the fact that the vast majority of the ships threatened with attack by the Germans arrived safely at their destinations.[110] In over a month of fighting along the Gibraltar-Great Britain convoy route, the German U-boats managed to sink only one merchantman, the *Hallfried*, and to inflict serious damage on one warship, HMS *Chanticleer*. In an attack by twenty-five German aircraft with glider bombs, the merchant ship *Marsa* was sunk, and the merchant ship *Delius* damaged. This bag of only two ships sunk and two damaged was obtained by the Germans with the deployment of over twenty U-boats and at least thirty aircraft. And it was at the cost of ten U-boats sunk by the Allies (U-306, U-707, U-280, U-211, U-536, U-538, U-648, U-600, U-542, U-86). The question remains: why did the Germans do so badly in these battles?

In the November 1943 battles along the Gibraltar-Great Britain route, the Germans labored under a number of disadvantages. They had great difficulties in locating Allied convoys to attack because their intelligence on the Allied convoy routes ranged from nonexistent to poor. By this time, cryptographic intelligence as a source of information on movements of Allied convoys had almost ceased to exist for the Germans. Indeed, one reason that they undertook the campaign against Gibraltar-Great Britain convoys was the expectation that GAF reconnaissance flights would provide information on the movement of Allied convoys. However, the GAF at best could or would provide only two or three reconnaissance aircraft per day for operations over the Allied convoy routes west of Portugal. Even in the rare instances when GAF aircraft located a convoy, the German aircraft and U-boats found it very difficult if not impossible to coordinate effectively. Compounding the technical problems the U-boats experienced in picking up beacon signals from aircraft, the commanders of the GAF were simply not interested in the U-boat war as shown by the transfer of all the He 177 aircraft to the Mediterranean after the attack on SL 139/MKS 30.

Of course, all the Germans' problems in locating Allied convoys were compounded by the fact that the Allies were reading their command radio transmissions and could often route convoys away from U-boat patrol lines. Unable or unwilling to give serious consideration to the possibility that their radio transmission codes had been compromised, the Germans clung to the notion that the Allies were locating U-boats and patrol lines by means of some kind of unknown "all-seeing" device. The situation continued to baffle the Germans for the duration of the war.[111]

However, by November 1943, the German U-boats had little chance of success even when they managed to contact an Allied convoy. By this time, the Allies' technology, experience, and expertise gave them the ability to fight their way through U-boat concentrations. This became brutally apparent as the ships of SL 139/MKS 30 successfully fought their way through three *Schill* patrol lines. In the course of the November battles over Gibraltar-Great Britain convoys, the Allies deployed an overpowering force of air and surface escorts to protect the convoys. The battle area was well within range of Allied anti-U-boat aircraft based in the Azores and the United Kingdom, and at times as many as three escort groups protected these convoys. However, it was not just brute force that enabled the Allies to overcome U-boat patrol lines but rather tactical superiority and skill. The key to the Allies' tactical success in these convoy battles was their ability to deny the U-boats surface mobility so that a patrol line's U-boats could not concentrate against and attack a convoy. Aircraft sweeping around a convoy by day and night forced U-boats to dive and, thus, to lose mobility. Surface escorts sweeping around a convoy with radar, HF/DF, and sonar on board could detect U-boats at a distance from the convoy and attack them, thus keeping the submarines far from their prey, submerged and unable to pursue Allied merchantmen. The U-boats operated at an overwhelming disadvantage in terms of electronic technology. The submarines were not equipped with radar. Unaware of the existence of HF/DF, they never understood the connection between frequent U-boat radio transmissions and the detection of a U-boat by an escort. When battling a U-boat patrol line, Allied tactics were simple in the extreme: deny the U-boats the opportunity to attack the ships of a convoy by forcing them to forfeit tactical mobility while passing the convoy through the patrol line. Because of the limitations of their technology and the inexperience of their U-boat commanders, the Germans could not and did not develop the tactics needed to overcome the Allies' defenses of their convoys.[112]

In large part, the Germans were defeated in the November 1943 battles over Gibraltar-Great Britain convoys simply because the strategy and tactics of wolf pack attacks on a convoy no longer worked. Advances in Allied intelligence, technology, strategy, and tactics all combined to defeat the German wolf packs. The failure of the attacks on the Gibraltar-Great Britain convoys were more than just a tactical defeat to the Germans, for these battles were the last wolf pack operations conducted by the U-boats in the Atlantic. In the immediate wake of the failure of the *Schill* and *Weddigen* groups, the Germans did establish several new groups and patrol lines, but these formations failed to intercept and attack Allied convoys successfully. The German effort in November 1943 along the Gibraltar-Great Britain convoy route was the last wolf pack operations against Allied Atlantic convoys in World War II. Shortly after these operations the wolf packs were disbanded and the Germans gave up large-scale U-boat operations in the Atlantic west of the British Isles.[113]

Conclusion

The U-boats lost the Battle of the Atlantic in 1943 because they were out thought as well as out fought by the Allies. The U-boat's main objective was to prevent the Allies from sailing merchant ships in the North Atlantic by attacking these ships on the high seas and sinking them. The Allies countered the U-boats with a strategy of convoys. However, just as in World War I, the Germans never developed a strategy which could successfully combat Allies convoys. Convoys presented both the Allies and the Germans with two sets of interlocking problems. The success of any convoy strategy is not measured by battles won or attacking enemy vessels sunk, but rather by the safe and timely arrival of the ships of the convoy at their destinations. If a convoy is not attacked because the attackers are avoided, then the voyage is a strategic success. In the North Atlantic, the Allies attempted to route convoys to avoid the U-boats while the German objective was to deploy U-boats to intercept Allied convoys. Once a convoy was intercepted, the U-boats' ultimate objective was to make a successful attack on the Allied escort force and sink the merchant ships with it. The Allied objective in a convoy battle was, first, to prevent the U-boats from sinking ships and, second, to counterattack and destroy the attacking U-boats in battle. For the Allies the successful defense of a convoy was not measured by U-boats sunk, but rather by the failure of the U-boats to sink the ships within the convoy.

In the course of World War II most Allies convoys sailed the North Atlantic without being contacted by U-boats. The vastness of the sea hindered the convoys' interception by U-boats and assisted in their evasive routing. Intelligence was key both to the interception of a convoy and to the avoidance of U-boats by convoys. From the beginning of the Battle of the North Atlantic, the GAF either could not or would not provide the reconnaissance flights over the North Atlantic which would produce the information the U-boats required to intercept Allied convoys on a regular and effective basis. And the few times when the GAF actually located Allied convoys, the Germans displayed an almost total inability to coordinate the activities of the aircraft with those of the U-boats.

As a result, the Germans obtained most of their intelligence on the movements of Allied convoys from the interception and decryption of Allied coded radio messages. This source of intelligence was invaluable to the Germans, and in the first half of 1943 it enabled them to intercept a number of Allied convoys. But at the beginning of June 1943, poor German communications security gave the Allies the clue they needed to uncover the means by which German naval intelligence was decrypting and reading their radio transmissions. As a result, the Allies changed their codes and the Germans were increasingly denied the intelligence required to track Allied convoys.

For their part, the Allies employed D/F and decryption of German command radio transmissions to gain the information needed to route convoys to avoid concentrations of U-boats. The Germans unknowingly played into the Allied hands by employing a command and control system which required the generation of numerous radio messages between the BdU ashore and U-boats at sea. These radio transmissions provided the Allies with D/F fixes on U-boats. Then, in December 1942, the Allies began to decrypt German command radio transmissions regularly, thus gaining additional details of the activities of the U-boats. Even though the Allies at times encountered delays in decrypting German radio messages, decryption intelligence when combined with D/F fixes increasingly provided the Allies with the information required to direct convoys away from U-boat patrol lines. Such advance notice of the threat of U-boat attack to a convoy also permitted the Allies to dispatch aircraft and surface vessels to reinforce the convoy's escort.

When they encountered increased difficulties in intercepting Allied convoys, the Germans knew that it stemmed in part from their inability to read Allied codes. But, at the same time, the Germans never comprehended the great advantages the Allies gained from communications intelligence in the form of D/F fixes and decryption. Instead of addressing the real and challenging problems, the Germans erroneously attributed the increasing Allied superiority in intelligence not to D/F fixes and decryption, but rather to supposed Allied use of some kind of super all-seeing airborne radar or radiation detector that could locate U-boats in vast areas of ocean. By embracing the theory that the Allies' success lay in some nonexistent super weapons, the Germans neglected a serious investigation of a failure of their own communications security. This doomed the Germans to defeat at the hands of the Allies in the intelligence war at sea.

Even when the German wolf packs did locate and intercept an Allied convoy, they had no guarantee of success. To achieve victory in a convoy battle, the U-boats of a patrol line had to close with the Allied ships and successfully attack and sink the merchant ships within the convoy. At first, the German wolf packs of roving U-boats at sea coordinated by the BdU ashore met with striking success, and it became the task of the Allied air and surface escorts to prevent the U-boats from closing with a convoy and mounting an attack on its merchant ships.

Here the Allies brilliantly countered the German wolf pack tactics by developing weapon systems, electronic devices, and tactics which exploited the weaknesses and shortcomings of the German U-boats, standard radio procedures, and tactics. The U-boats employed by the Germans in World War II were technologically the same craft used in World War I. That is German World War II U-boats were not true submersible craft, like today's nuclear submarines, but ones that could remain underwater for short periods of time, moving at slow speeds over limited distances. While a surfaced U-boat could maneuver efficiently to intercept and attack an Allied convoy, a submerged U-boat could not catch or keep up with the slowest merchant ship in a convoy. The Allies quickly learned that a submerged U-boat could not move quickly enough to attack a convoy and soon lost contact with the Allied formation. Thus it became the tactical objective of the Allied escorts to intercept U-boats as they approached a convoy, force the enemy craft to submerge, and then if possible attack and destroy the U-boat.

Two electronic devices—radar and HF/DF—were the keys to the success of Allied surface escorts. Wolf pack tactics were developed by the Germans before the advent of search radar and called for the

U-boats to penetrate the main body of a convoy undetected by the escorts. Once Allied ships were fitted with radar, an escort could detect a U-boat at a distance as the enemy vessel approached a convoy under cover of fog or darkness. Increasingly the U-boats found it difficult, if not impossible, to make surface attacks or even to approach a convoy on the surface without being intercepted and attacked by an escort. After the battle for convoy ONS 5 in early May 1943, when radar-equipped escorts decisively defeated the U-boats in a confused melee in the darkness and fog on the Grand Banks of Newfoundland, the Germans abandoned for the most part the tactic of night surface attacks on convoys.

HF/DF exploited the habit of U-boats to radio sighting reports and data to the BdU while approaching a convoy. HF/DF enabled an escort to obtain a bearing on a radio transmission made near a convoy. Throughout the war, the Germans never learned of the existence of HF/DF and never figured out the connection between making radio transmissions and the appearance of an escort on the scene. Time and time again, a U-boat that had just made routine radio reports to the BdU found itself surprised by Allied escorts running down a bearing on a radio transmission obtained by HF/DF. The main tactic of Allied escorts was the use of information gained from radar contacts and HF/DF bearings to locate a U-boat in the vicinity of a convoy, force it to dive and lose contact, and then, if possible, attack and sink the enemy vessel.

Because of their great mobility and the ability to search large areas of ocean, aircraft were also decisive in the defense of Allied convoys. It took the Allies a long time to get aircraft over convoys in the mid-Atlantic, but when VLR B-24 Liberator aircraft began operating in conjunction with surface escorts, the U-boats found it extremely difficult to close with a convoy. U-boats on a patrol line were usually deployed in a linear formation extending over many miles across the expected track of a convoy. When a convoy was sighted by one U-boat of a patrol line, the others had to steam for miles on the surface to gain contact with the enemy. Again and again Allied aircraft escorting Atlantic convoys intercepted U-boats steaming on the surface to gain contact with the Allied ships. The planes then attacked, either forcing the submarines to submerge or sinking them. In fact, almost no Allied ships within a convoy protected by both air and surface escorts were sunk during World War II. The Germans learned, at considerable cost to themselves, of the great dangers and difficulties in attacking convoys escorted by both aircraft and surface vessels and would end an operation against a convoy at the mere appearance of an Allied aircraft over the ships.

The Allies also used aircraft carriers to provide air escorts to convoys. At first such carriers were stationed within the main body of a convoy, and the ship's planes provided the formation with close air support. In the summer of 1943 the Americans introduced new tactics when escort groups built around escort carriers began to support convoys by ranging along the convoy routes, using communications intelligence to hunt and attack U-boats at great distances from the Allied convoys. Even though the Germans attempted to counter Allied aircraft by increasing the antiaircraft armament on U-boats, there really was no defense for U-boats against aircraft attack other than remaining submerged. Thus, by the autumn of 1943, U-boats were staying submerged to avoid Allied aircraft even in mid-ocean.

The Germans were totally defeated in the convoy battles of April to December 1943 because of their inability either to overcome the Allied strategy and tactics of convoys or to counter superior Allied technology and intelligence. The U-boats found it increasingly difficult to intercept Allied convoys because of the inability to obtain intelligence on their routes and the Allies use of communications intelligence to route convoys away from U-boat concentrations. And by the last months of 1943, when the U-boats did intercept an Allied convoy, the air and surface escorts of the merchant ships shattered any hopes of a German victory by preventing the U-boats from sinking many merchant ships while at the same time inflicting heavy casualties on the attacking U-boats. From 10 April to 1 December 1943 the U-boats sunk only forty-five ships from mid-ocean North Atlantic convoys, while in the course of these operations sixty-three U-boats were lost in convoy battles or convoy-related battles. At the beginning of December 1943 the Germans finally gave up convoy battles in the mid-Atlantic and retreated to European coastal waters. After 1943 the U-boats could no longer hope to win the war for the Germans by cutting the Allied transatlantic supply lines, but they could maintain a maritime guerrilla war that forced the Allies to deploy hundreds of warships and aircraft to hunt U-boats and escort convoys. The continuation of the U-boat war would prevent the redeployment of these forces against Germany itself. And there was always the hope in the German mind that some new weapon or device would enable the U-boats to turn the tables on the Allies before the total defeat of Germany. So the U-boats fought on—suffering heavy casualties until the end of the war.

The German defeat in the Battle of the North Atlantic had its roots in something beyond the Allies' advantages in terms of personnel and material. More fundamentally, the Allies made better use of their resources. For instance, the German failure to integrate scientific thinking into all levels of their command structure in submarine warfare reflected a flaw epidemic among all German armed forces. The Allies had civilian scientific advisers involved at all levels of anti-U-boat war effort—from the highest reaches of the government down to individual commands at sea. The German armed forces in general, on the other hand, were reluctant if not outright distrustful of outside consultants.

The U-boat service was the victim of a peculiar, idiosyncratic failing: the BdU exemplified over-centralized command and control. Aside from the general inefficiencies such a structure might create, the BdU's insistence on direct control of every aspect of U-boat activities generated endless radio transmissions between the submarines and their shore-based command, transmissions which gave the Allies their enormous technological advantage with HF/DF tracking devices. Indeed, the BdU even exacerbated the problem as the war progressed. When the Germans first realized that the Allies had an uncanny knowledge of the U-boats' movements, the BdU immediately suspected internal espionage. To protect itself against the activities of this nonexistent agent, the BdU reduced its own staff size so that only the most reliable remained. Never did the members of the BdU consider the massive but ultimately effective paper chase by which the Allies identified the codes which the Germans had broken.

Indeed, an overall inability to think in terms of intelligence permeated all branches of the German Armed Forces. Here, too, the Allies proved more open to new ideas than the Germans. Peacetime barristers and academics worked with experienced intelligence officers in the American and British service, while German intelligence showed little openness to new people or new ideas. German intelligence could offer good technical expertise in terms of code breaking, but little or nothing in terms of the imagination and intellectual daring required by the losing side in a naval war. Thus, they quite literally could not imagine that German naval codes had been broken so that the Allies could read BdU radio transmissions. Thus, to the end of the war, the Germans allowed themselves to believe that the Allies had achieved this intelligence victory through mysterious secret weapons, not good, industrious code-breaking.

At an even more basic level, the German U-boat war in the North Atlantic was determined by the nature of the vessel that the Axis sent into battle. The German U-boat of 1939 was no more a fully submersible, modern submarine than its predecessors in World War I. Little more than a seaworthy torpedo boat, the limitations of the U-boat created a situation in which the German naval command was at the mercy of a weapon system so ineffective against modern technology that the BdU, in turn, was severely constrained in its ability to create new tactics.

Thus, the only effective strategy that the Germans devised for confronting the Allied anti-U-boat convoy system throughout World War II was a change in the theater of operations. First the U-boats moved from the British Isles westward into the Atlantic, then to the Western Hemisphere, and then back to the central Atlantic. Then 1943 witnessed desperate shifts of the wolf packs back and forth from the North Atlantic to mid-Atlantic, from convoy routes serving Britain to those serving Gibraltar. But none of these moves had an appreciable affect upon the U-boats' success. Moving the playing field was the only alternative left to them as the U-boat precluded adapting to the new rules by which the Allies were playing this deadly game in the North Atlantic. But by 1943, moving the playing field no longer had any effect on the U-boats' ability to score.

Yet one must ask whether the deeper intellectual problems that crippled the German U-boat command would not have negated important technological improvements. One of the most intriguing unanswered questions of this naval war is what might have occurred had the Germans given priority to building a fleet of Walter U-boats early enough to put these vessels into action to have some affect on the war's outcome. These submarines, with their faster underwater speeds and ability to remain underwater indefinitely, would have made them far more elusive targets for Allied radar and sonar. But without changes in German intelligence and the U-boat command structure, the Walter boats would have remained at the mercy of Allied intelligence, doomed as surely as the archaic U-boats they were designed to supersede.

Appendix A

Allied Ships Sunk in Convoy Battles, 11 April–21 November 1943

Date	Convoy	Ship	U-boat
11 April	ON 176	HMS *Beverley*	U-188
12 April	ON 176	*Lacastrian Prince*	U-404
12 April	HX 232	*Pacific Grove*	U-563
12 April	HX 232	*Fresco City*	U-563/U-706
12 April	HX 232	*Ulysses*	U-563
17 April	HX 233	*Fort Rampart*	U-628
21 April	ON 178	*Ashantian*	U-415
21 April	ON 178	*Wanstead*	U-415
21 April	ON 178	*Scebeli*	U-191
22 April	HX 234	*Amerika*	U-306
23 April	HX 234	*Robert Grey*	U-306
29 April	ONS 5	*Mckeesport*	U-258
4 May	ONS 5	*Lorient*	U-125
5 May	ONS 5	*North Britain*	U-707
5 May	ONS 5	*Harbury*	U-628
5 May	ONS 5	*Harperly*	U-264

Date	Convoy	Ship	U-boat
5 May	ONS 5	*Bristol City*	U-358
5 May	ONS 5	*Wentworth*	U-358
5 May	ONS 5	*Dolius*	U-638
5 May	ONS 5	*West Market*	U-584
5 May	ONS 5	*Selvistan*	U-266
5 May	ONS 5	*Gharinda*	U-266
5 May	ONS 5	*Bonde*	U-266
11 May	SC 129	*Antigone*	U-402
11 May	SC 129	*Grado*	U-402
11 May	HX 237	*Fort Concord*	U-456
12 May	HX 237	*Sandanger*	U-221
12 May	HX 237	*Brand*	U-603
15 May	ONS 5	*West Maximus*	U-264
17 May	ONS 7	*Aymeric*	U-657
22 May	UGS 10	*Lot*	U-572
20 September	ON 202/ONS 18	*Theodore Wright Weld*	U-238
20 September	ON 202/ONS 18	*Frederick Douglass*	U-238
20 September	ON 202/ONS 18	HMCS *St. Croix*	U-305
21 September	ON 202/ONS 18	HMS *Polyanthus*	U-952
22 September	ON 202/ONS 18	HMS *Itchen*	U-666

Date	Convoy	Ship	U-boat
23 September	ON 202/ONS 18	*Fort Jemseg*	U-238
23 September	ON 202/ONS 18	*Oregon Express*	U-238
23 September	ON 202/ONS 18	*Skjelbred*	U-238
23 September	ON 202/ONS 18	*Steel Voyager*	U-952
8 October	SC 143	ORP *Orkan*	U-378
9 October	SC 143	*Yarkmar*	U-645
15 October	ONS 20	*Essex Lance*	U-426
31 October	SL 138/MKS 138	*Hallfried*	U-262
21 November	SL 139/MKS 30	*Marsa*	GAF

Appendix B

U-boats Sunk in Mid-Atlantic Convoy Battles or Convoy-Related Battles, 17 April–29 November 1943

Date	U-Boat	Killer
17 April	U-175	USCGC *Spencer*
23 April	U-189	Aircraft V/120
23 April	U-191	HMS *Hesperus*
25 April	U-203	HMS *Pathfinder*
4 May	U-630	RCAF aircraft
5 May	U-192	HMS *Pink*
5 May	U-638	HMS *Loosestrife*
6 May	U-125	Unknown and HMS *Snowflake*
6 May	U-438	HMS *Pelican*
6 May	U-531	HMS *Oribi*
12 May	U-89	Aircraft from HMS *Biter*, HMS *Broadway*, and HMS *Lagan*
12 May	U-186	HMS *Hesperus*
13 May	U-456	Aircraft B/86
13 May	U-753	Aircraft from HMS *Biter*, HMCS *Drumheller*, and HMS *Lagan*
17 May	U-640	HMS *Swale*

Date	U-Boat	Killer
19 May	U-209	HMS *Jed* and HMS *Sennen*
19 May	U-381	HMS *Duncan* and HMS *Snowflake*
19 May	U-945	Aircraft T/120
20 May	U-258	Aircraft P/120
22 May	U-569	Aircraft from USS *Bogue*
23 May	U-572	Aircraft from HMS *Archer*
5 June	U-217	Aircraft from USS *Bogue*
12 June	U-118	Aircraft from USS *Bogue*
13 July	U-487	Aircraft from USS *Card*
14 July	U-160	Aircraft from USS *Santee*
15 July	U-509	Aircraft from USS *Santee*
16 July	U-67	Aircraft from USS *Core*
23 July	U-527	Aircraft from USS *Bogue*
23 July	U-613	USS *George E. Badger*
30 July	U-43	Aircraft from USS *Santee*
7 August	U-117	Aircraft from USS *Card*
9 August	U-664	Aircraft from USS *Card*
11 August	U-525	Aircraft from USS *Card*
24 August	U-84	Aircraft from USS *Core*
24 August	U-185	Aircraft from USS *Core*

Date	U-Boat	Killer
27 August	U-847	Aircraft from USS *Card*
19 September	U-341	RCAF aircraft
22 September	U-229	HMS *Keppel*
4 October	U-336	USN shore-based aircraft
5 October	U-389	Aircraft F/269
8 October	U-419	Aircraft R/86
8 October	U-610	Aircraft J/423
8 October	U-643	Aircraft Z/86 and T/120
16 October	U-470	Aircraft E/120 and Z/120
16 October	U-844	Aircraft Z/86 and T/120
16 October	U-965	Aircraft Y/86
17 October	U-540	Aircraft H/120
17 October	U-631	HMS *Sunflower*
17 October	U-841	HMS *Byard*
23 October	U-274	HMS *Duncan*, HMS *Vidette*, and aircraft Z/224
26 October	U-420	RCAF aircraft
29 October	U-282	HMS *Duncan*, HMS *Snowflake*, and HMS *Sunflower*
6 November	U-226	HMS *Starling*, HMS *Woodcock*, and HMS *Kite*
6 November	U-842	HMS *Starling* and HMS *Wild Goose*

Date	U-Boat	Killer
9 November	U-707	Aircraft J/220
19 November	U-211	Aircraft F/179
20 November	U-536	HMS *Nene*, HMCS *Snowberry*, and HMCS *Calgary*
21 November	U-538	HMS *Foley* and HMS *Crane*
23 November	U-648	HMS *Bazely*, HMS *Blackwood*, and HMS *Drury*
25 November	U-600	HMS *Bazely* and HMS *Blackwood*
28 November	U-542	Aircraft L/179
29 November	U-86	Aircraft from USS *Bogue*

Appendix C

Convoys and Escorts

Convoy HX 232
  Escort Group B3
    Destroyers

        HMS *Escapade* (HF/DF; E class)
        ORP *Garland* (HF/DF; G class)

    Corvettes

        HMS *Narcissus* (Flower class)
        HMS *Azalea* (Flower class)
        FFS *Roselys* (Flower class)
        FFS *Rononcule* (Flower class)

    Destroyer

        HMS *Witherington* (joined 8 April; V & W
          long range escort class)

  4th Escort Group
    Destroyers

        HMS *Inglefield* (HF/DF; only ship in its class;
          similar to Grenville class)
        HMS *Fury* (F class)
        HMS *Eclipse* (E class)
        HMS *Icarus* (HF/DF; I class)

Convoy HX 233
  Escort Group A3
    Coast Guard Cutters

        USS *Spencer* (HF/DF; Treasury class)
        USS *Duane* (Treasury class)

    Corvettes

        HMS *Dianthus* (Flower class)
        HMS *Bryony* (Flower class)
        HMS *Bergamont* (Flower class)
        HMCS *Wetaskiwin* (Flower class)
        HMCS *Arvida* (Flower class)

  3rd Escort Group
    Destroyers

        HMS *Panther* (P class)
        HMS *Penn* (P class)
        HMS *Impulsive* (I class)
        HMS *Offa* (O class)

Convoy HX 234
  Escort Group B4
    Destroyers   HMS *Highlander* (HF/DF; ex-Brazilian H class)
                                 HMS *Vimy* (joined 21 April; V & W long range escort class)

    Corvettes   HMS *Asphole* (Flower class)
                                 HMS *Anemone* (Flower class)
                                 HMS *Pennywort* (Flower class)
                                 HMS *Clover* (Flower class)
                                 HMCS *Rosthern* (Flower class)

Convoy HX 235
  Escort Group C4
    Destroyers   HMS *Churchill* (Town class)
                                 HMCS *Restigouche* (HF/DF; Fraser class)

    Corvettes   HMCS *Collingwood* (Flower class)
                                 HMCS *Trent* (Flower class)
                                 HMCS *Baddeck* (Flower class)
                                 HMCS *Brandon* (Flower class)

  Task Group 92.3
    Escort Carrier   USS *Bogue* (Bogue class)

    Destroyers   USS *Belknap* (Clemson class)
                                 USS *Greene* (Clemson class)
                                 USS *Osmond Ingram* (Clemson class)
                                 USS *Lea* (Wickes class)

Convoy HX 237
  Escort Group C2
    Destroyer   HMS *Broadway* (HF/DF; Town class)

    Corvettes   HMS *Primrose* (Flower class)
                                 HMCS *Chambly* (Flower class)
                                 HMCS *Morden* (Flower class)
                                 HMCS *Drumheller* (Flower class)

    Trawler   HM Trawler *Vizalma* (purchased from trade)

    Tug   HM Tug *Desterous*

  5th Escort Group
    Escort Carrier   HMS *Biter* (HF/DF; Avenger class)

Destroyers	HMS *Pathfinder* (P class)
	HMS *Obdurate* (O class)
	HMS *Opportune* (O class)

Convoy HX 239
Escort Group B3

Destroyers	HMS *Keppel* (Shakespeare class)
	HMS *Escapade* (HF/DF; E class)
	ORP *Garland* (HF/DF; G class)
Corvettes	HMS *Orchis* (Flower class)
	FFS *Roselys* (Flower class)
	FFS *Lobelia* (Flower class)
	FFS *Renoncule* (Flower class)
Trawler	*Northern Gem* (hired from trade)
HM Tug	*Growler*

4th Escort Group

Escort Carrier	HMS *Archer* (HF/DF; only ship in its class)
Destroyers	HMS *Onslaught* (O class)
	HMS *Impulsive* (I class)
	HMS *Faulknor* (HF/DF; Exmouth class)
Sloop	HMS *Pelican* (Egret class)

Convoy HX 262
2nd Escort Group

Escort Carrier	HMS *Tracker* (HF/DF; attacker class)
Sloops	HMS *Starling* (modified Black Swan class)
	HMS *Wild Goose* (modified Black Swan class)
	HMS *Kite* (modified Black Swan class)
	HMS *Magpie* (modified Black Swan class)

Convoy ON 176
Escort Group B4

Destroyers	HMS *Highlander* (HF/DF; ex-Brazilian H class)
	HMS *Vimy* (V & W long range escort class)
	HMS *Beverley* (Town class)
Corvettes	HMS *Anemone* (Flower class)
	HMS *Asphodel* (Flower class)
	HMS *Pennywort* (Flower class)
	HMS *Clover* (Flower class)

| | HMS *Abelia* (Flower class) |
| Rescue Ship | *Melrose Abby* (HF/DF) |

Convoy ON 178
Escort Group B1

Destroyers	HMS *Hurricane* (ex-Brazilian H class)
	HMS *Rockingham* (Town class)
Frigate	HMS *Kale* (River class)
Corvettes	HMS *Dahlia* (Flower class)
	HMS *Borage* (Flower class)
	HMS *Monkshead* (Flower class)
	HMS *Meadowsweet* (Flower class)
	HMS *Wallflower* (Flower class)

Convoy ON 184
Escort Group C1

Destroyers	HMS *Burwell* (Town class)
	HMS *St. Croix* (Town class)
	HMCS *St. Laurent* (Fraser class)
Frigate	HMS *Itchen* (River class)
Corvettes	HMCS *Sackville* (Flower class)
	HMCS *Woodstock* (Flower class)
	HMCS *Agassiz* (Flower class)

Convoy ON 202
Escort Group C3

Destroyers	HMCS *Gatineau* (E class)
	HMS *Icaris* (HF/DF; I class)
Frigate	HMS *Lagan* (HF/DF; joined 17 September; River class)
Corvettes	HMCS *Drumheller* (Flower class)
	HMCS *Kamloops* (Flower class)
	HMS *Polyanthus* (Flower class)
Trawler	HM Trawler *Lancer* (Military class)
Rescue Ship	*Rathlin* (HF/DF)

9th Escort Group (joined 20 September)

| Destroyer | HMCS *St. Croix* (Town class) |
| Frigate | HMS *Itchen* (River class) |

Corvettes	HMCS *Chambly* (Flower class)
	HMCS *Morden* (Flower class)
	HMCS *Sackville* (Flower class)

Convoy ON 206
  Escort Group B6

Destroyers	HMS *Fame* (HF/DF; F class)
	HMS *Vanquisher* (HF/DF; V & W long range escort class)
Frigate	HMS *Deveron* (River class)
Corvettes	HNorMS *Rose* (Flower class)
	HNorMS *Potentilla* (Flower class)
	HNorMS *Eglantine* (Flower class)
Trawler	HM Trawler *Grenadier* (Military class)

  Escort Group B7

Destroyers	HMS *Duncan* (HF/DF; D class leader)
	HMS *Vidette* (V & W long range escort class)
Corvettes	HMS *Pink* (Flower class)
	HMS *Sunflower* (Flower class)
	HMS *Snowflake* (Flower class)
	HMS *Loosestrife* (Flower class)

Convoy ONS 3
  40th Escort Group

Ex-US Coast Guard Cutters	HMS *Landguard* (Lake class US Coast Guard cutter)
	HMS *Lulworth* (Lake class US Coast Guard cutter)
Sloops	HMS *Bideford* (Shoreham class)
	HMS *Hastings* (Hastings class)
Frigate	HMS *Moyola* (River class)
Trawler	Trawler *Northern Gift* (hired from trade)

Convoy ONS 4
  Escort Group B2

Destroyers	HMS *Hesperus* (HF/DF; ex-Brazilian H class)
	HMS *Whitehall* (V & W long range escort class)
Sloop	HMS *Gentian* (World War I, Flower class)

Corvettes	HMS *Heather* (Flower class)
	HMS *Sweetbriar* (Flower class)
	HMS *Campanula* (Flower class)
	HMS *Clematis* (Flower class)
Trawler	HM Trawler *Cape Argona* (purchased from trade)

5th Escort Group

Escort Carrier	HMS *Biter* (HF/DF; Avenger class)
Destroyers	HMS *Pathfinder* (P class)
	HMS *Opportune* (O class)
	HMS *Obdurate* (O class)

Convoy ONS 5

Escort Group B7

Destroyers	HMS *Duncan* (HF/DF; D class leader)
	HMS *Vidette* (V & W long range escort class)
Frigate	HMS *Tay* (River class)
Corvettes	HMS *Sunflower* (Flower class)
	HMS *Snowflake* (Flower class)
	HMS *Pink* (Flower class)
	HMS *Loosestrife* (Flower class)
Trawlers	*Northern Gem* (hired from trade)
	Northern Spray (hired from trade)

3rd Escort Group

Destroyers	HMS *Oribi* (HF/DF; joined 29 April; O class)
	HMS *Penn* (joined 2 May; P class)
	HMS *Panther* (joined 2 May; P class)
	HMS *Impulsive* (joined 2 May; I class)
	HMS *Offa* (joined 2 May; O class)

1st Escort Group

Ex-US Coast Guard Cutter	HMS *Sennen* (Lake class US Coast Guard cutter)
Frigate	HMS *Wear* (River class)
	HMS *Jed* (River class)
	HMS *Spey* (River class)
Sloop	HMS *Pelican* (Egret class)

Convoy ONS 6

Escort Group B6

Destroyer	HMS *Viscount* (HF/DF; V & W long range escort class)

Corvettes	HNorMS *Acanthus* (Flower class)
	HNorMS *Potentilla* (Flower class)
	HNorMS *Rose* (Flower class)
	HMS *Vervain* (Flower class)
	HMS *Kingcup* (Flower class)
Trawlers	*Northern Pride* (hired from trade)
	Northern Reward (hired from trade)

1st Escort Group

Escort Carrier	HMS *Archer* (HF/DF; only ship of its class)
Destroyers	HMS *Onslaught* (O class)
	HMS *Impulsive* (I class)
	HMS *Faulknor* (HF/DF; Exmouth class)

Convoy ONS 7

Escort Group B5

Frigates	HMS *Nene* (River class)
	HMS *Swale* (River class)
Corvettes	HMS *Buttercup* (Flower class)
	HMS *Pimpernel* (Flower class)
	HMS *Lavender* (Flower class)
	HMS *Godetia* (Flower class)
Trawlers	*Northern Wave* (hired from trade)
	HMS *Stafnes* (purchased from trade)

Task Group 92.3

Escort Carrier	USS *Bogue* (HF/DF; Bogue class)
Destroyers	USS *Belknap* (Clemson class)
	USS *Greene* (Clemson class)
	USS *Osmond Ingram* (Clemson class)
	USS *Lea* (HF/DF; Wickes class)

Convoy ONS 18

Escort Group B3

Destroyers	HMS *Keppel* (HF/DF; Shakespeare class)
	HMS *Escapade* (HF/DF; E class)
Frigate	HMS *Towy* (joined later; River class)
Corvettes	HMS *Narcissus* (Flower class)
	HMS *Orchis* (Flower class)
	FFS *Roselys* (Flower class)
	FFS *Renoncule* (Flower class)

| Trawler | *Northern Foam* (hired from trade) |

| Merchant Aircraft Carrier | *Empire MacAlpine* |

Convoy ONS 20
  4th Escort Group
    Frigates

HMS *Bentinck* (Captain class)
HMS *Blackwood* (Captain class)
HMS *Bazely* (Captain class)
HMS *Drury* (Captain class)
HMS *Berry* (Captain class)
HMS *Burges* (Captain class)

    Trawlers

Northern Sky (hired from trade)
Northern Wave (hired from trade)

    Destroyer

HMS *Vanquisher* (HF/DF; joined 19 October;
    L & W long range escort class)

  Escort Group B7
    Destroyers

HMS *Duncan* (HF/DF; D class leader)
HMS *Vidette* (V & W long range escort class)

    Corvettes

HMS *Pink* (Flower class)
HMS *Sunflower* (Flower class)
HMS *Snowflake* (Flower class)
HMS *Loosestrife* (Flower class)

Convoy SC 129
  Escort Group B2
    Destroyers

HMS *Hesperus* (HF/DF; ex-Brazilian H class)
HMS *Whitehall* (V & W long range escort
    class)

    Corvettes

HMS *Heather* (Flower class)
HMS *Clematis* (Flower class)
HMS *Sweetbriar* (Flower class)
HMS *Campanula* (Flower class)

    Sloop

HMS *Gentian* (World War I, Flower class
    sloop)

    Trawlers

Lady Madeleine (hired from trade)
HMS *Sapper* (Military class)

Convoy SC 130
  Escort Group B7
    Destroyers

HMS *Duncan* (HF/DF; D class leader)
HMS *Vidette* (V & W long range escort class)

Frigate	HMS *Tay* (River class)
Corvettes	HMCS *Kitchener* (attached: Flower class)
	HMS *Snowflake* (Flower class)
	HMS *Sunflower* (Flower class)
	HMS *Loosestrife* (Flower class)
	HMS *Pink* (Flower class)
Trawler	*Northern Spray* (hired from trade)
Rescue Ship	*Zamalek* (HF/DF)

1st Escort Group

Ex-US Coast Guard Cutter	HMS *Sennen* (Lake class US Coast Guard cutter)
Frigates	HMS *Jed* (River class)
	HMS *Wear* (River class)
	HMS *Sprey* (River class)

Convoy SC 143

Escort Group C2

Destroyer	HMS *Icarus* (joined 4 October; I class)
Frigate	HMS *Duckworth* (joined 7 October; Captain class)
Corvettes	HMCS *Kamloops* (Flower class)
	HMCS *Chambly* (Flower class)
	HMCS *Sackville* (Flower class)
	HMCS *Trimins* (detached 3 October; Flower class)
	HMCS *Drumheller* (joined 3 October; Flower class)
Minesweeper	HMS *Antares* (Algerine class)
Trawler	HM Trawler *Gateshead* (purchased from trade)
Merchant Aircraft Carrier	*Rapana*

10th Escort Group (joined 5 October)
    Destroyers   HMS *Musketeer* (L & M class)
                                              HMS *Orwell* (O class)
                                              HMS *Oribi* (HF/DF; O class)
                                              ORP *Orkan* (M class)

Convoy SL 138/MKS 28
  39th Escort Group
    Destroyers   HMS *Wrestler* (V & W long range escort
                                                class)
                                            HMS *Whitehall* (V & W long range escort
                                                class)

    Frigate   HMS *Tavy* (River class)

    Sloops   HMS *Hastings* (Hastings class)
                                              HMS *Rochester* (Shoreham class)
                                            HMS *Scarborough* (Hastings class)

    Corvettes   HMS *Azalea* (Flower class)
                                          HMS *Balsam* (Flower class)

    Auxiliary antiaircraft cruiser   HMS *Alynbank*

Convoy SL 139/MKS 30
  40th Escort Group
    Frigates   HMS *Exe* (River class)
                                            HMS *Moloya* (River class)

    Sloops   HMS *Kistna* (modified Black Swan class)
                                            HMS *Milford* (Shoreham class)

    Corvettes   HMS *Clarkia* (Flower class)
                                          HMS *Petunia* (Flower class)

    Armed merchant cruiser   HMS *Ranpura* (within the convoy and
                                            detached 16 November)

    Auxiliary antiaircraft cruiser   HMCS *Prince Robert* (within the body of the
                                            convoy)

    Destroyers   HMS *Watchman* (joined 19 November; V & W
                                          long range escort class)
                                          HMS *Winchelsea* (V & W long range escort
                                          class)

  5th Escort Group
    Frigates   HMS *Tweed* (River class)
                                          HMS *Nene* (River class)

Corvettes   HMCS *Lunenburg* (Flower class)
                             HMCS *Edmundston* (Flower class)
                             HMCS *Calgary* (Flower class)
                             HMCS *Snowberry* (Flower class)

7th Escort Group
  Frigates   HMS *Foley* (Captain class)
                             HMS *Essington* (Captain class)
                             HMS *Garlines* (Captain class)

  Sloops   HMS *Crane* (modified Black Swan class)
                             HMS *Chanticleer* (modified Black Swan class)
                             HMS *Pheasant* (modified Black Swan class)

4th Escort Group
  Frigates   HMS *Bentinck* (Captain class)
                             HMS *Calder* (Captain class)
                             HMS *Bazely* (Captain class)
                             HMS *Blackwood* (Captain class)
                             HMS *Byard* (Captain class)

Convoy SL 140/MKS 31
  Escort Group B1
    Destroyers   HMS *Hurricane* (ex-Brazilian H class)
                             HMS *Wanderer* (joined 25 November (V & W
                               long range escort class)

    Frigate   HMS *Glenarm* (River class)

    Corvettes   HMS *Oxlip* (Flower class)
                             HMS *Meadowsweet* (Flower class)
                             HMS *Borage* (Flower class)
                             HMS *Dahlia* (Flower class)
                             HMS *Honeysuckle* (Flower class)

Task Group 21.13
  Escort Carrier   USS *Bogue* (HF/DF; Bogue class)

  Destroyers   USS *George E. Badger* (Clemson class)
                             USS *Osmond Ingram* (Clemson class)
                             USS *Dupont* (Wickes class)
                             USS *Clemson* (Clemson class)

4th Escort Group
  Frigates   HMS *Blackwood* (Captain class)
                             HMS *Calder* (Captain class)
                             HMS *Bentinck* (Captain class)
                             HMS *Byard* (Captain class)

2nd Escort Group
  Sloops

                HMS *Starling* (modified Black Swan class)
                HMS *Wild Goose* (modified Black Swan class)
                HMS *Kite* (modified Black Swan class)
                HMS *Magpie* (modified Black Swan class)

UGS and GUS Convoys

Task groups are listed in the order in which they operated.

TG 21.12
  Escort Carrier   USS *Bogue* (HF/DF; Bogue class)

  Destroyers   USS *Clemson* (Clemson class)
                USS *Osmond Ingram* (Clemson class)
                USS *George E. Badger* (Clemson class)
                USS *Greene* (Clemson class)

TG 21.11
  Escort Carrier   USS *Santee* (HF/DF; Sangamon class)

  Destroyers   USS *Bainbridge* (Clemson class)
                USS *Overton* (Clemson class)
                USS *MacLeish* (Clemson class)

TG 21.15
  Escort Carrier   USS *Core* (HF/DF; Bogue class)

  Destroyers   USS *Barker* (Clemson class)
                USS *Bulmer* (Clemson class)
                USS *Badger* (Wickes class)

TG 21.13
  Escort Carrier   USS *Bogue* (HF/DF; Bogue class)

  Destroyers   USS *George E. Badger* (Clemson class)
                USS *Osmond Ingram* (Clemson class)
                USS *Clemson* (Clemson class)

TG 21.14
  Escort Carrier   USS *Card* (HF/DF; Bogue class)

  Destroyers   USS *Barry* (Clemson class)
                USS *Borie* (Clemson class)
                USS *Goff* (Clemson class)

TG 21.15

Escort Carrier   USS *Croatan* (HF/DF; Bogue class)

Destroyers   USS *Belknap* (Clemson class)
                                        USS *Paul Jones* (Clemson class)
                                        USS *Parrott* (Clemson class)

TG 21.12

Escort Carrier   USS *Core* (HF/DF; Bogue class)

Destroyers   USS *Barker* (Clemson class)
                                        USS *Badger* (Wickes class)
                                        USS *Bulmer* (Clemson class)

Notes

PREFACE

1. S. W. Roskill, *The War at Sea 1939–1945* (London, 1956), vol. 2, 470–71, 485.

CHAPTER 1: PREREQUISITES

1. Michael Howard, *Grand Strategy* (London, 1970), vol. 4, 621.
2. Roskill, vol. 1, 615–16; vol. 2, 469–70, 485.
3. Jurgen Rohwer, *The Critical Convoy Battles of March 1943* (Annapolis, 1977).
4. C. B. A. Behrens, *Merchant Shipping and the Demands of War* (London, 1955), 312–35.
5. Maurice Matloff, *Strategic Planning for Coalition Warfare, 1943–1944* (Washington, D.C., 1959), 43–47.
6. Jak P. Mallmann Showell, *The German Navy in World War II* (Annapolis, 1979), 23.
7. Friedrich Ruge, *Der Seekrieg: The German Navy's Story, 1939–1945* (Annapolis, 1955), 51.
8. Roskill, vol. 1, 614; vol. 2, 475.
9. PRO, ADM 223/15, f. 180.
10. Erminio Bagnasco, *Submarines of World War Two* (Annapolis, 1977), 58, 62.
11. Robert C. Stern, *Type VII U-boats* (Annapolis, 1991).
12. Stern, 128–29.
13. J. P. Mallmann Showell, *U-boats Under the Swastika* (New York, 1971), 82–85.
14. Norman Friedman, *Naval Radar* (Annapolis, 1981), 95–96.
15. Cf., BdU War Diary, 31 July 1943.
16. R. V. Jones, *Reflections on Intelligence* (London, 1990), 141–43.
17. Stern, 122–27, 131–33.
18. Cf., Karl Doenitz, *Die U-bootswaffe* (Berlin, 1939).
19. Peter Padfield, *Doenitz: The Last Fuhrer* (London, 1984), 92–151.
20. Arthur J. Marder, *From Dreadnought to Scapa Flow: The Royal Navy in the Fisher Era, 1904–1919* (London, 1964), vol. 4, 63–209.

21. Winston S. Churchill, *The World Crisis* (London, 1929), vol. 4, 347.
22. The world's leading authority on convoys is LCDR W. D. Waters, RN. He has written extensively and authoritatively on every aspect of convoys. The bulk of Waters' writings on the subject are in the Waters Papers in the National Maritime Museum. See especially, National Maritime Museum, WTS/31/1, Notes on the Convoy System of Naval Warfare: Thirteenth to Twentieth Centuries.
23. National Maritime Museum, WTS/32/1, Security with Economy of Force.
24. PRO, PREM 3/414/2, f. 1.
25. Samuel Eliot Morison, *History of United States Naval Operations in World War II* (Boston, 1975), vol. 10, 109–10.
26. Padfield, *Doenitz*, 152–89; Karl Doenitz, *Memoirs: Ten Years and Twenty Days* (New York, 1959), 18–24.
27. Doenitz, 20–22.
28. F. H. Hinsley, et al., *British Intelligence in the Second World War* (London, 1981), vol. 2, 549–51.
29. Doenitz, 142–44.
30. Doenitz, 131–41; [RAF Air Historical Branch], *The Rise and Fall of the German Air Force, 1933–1945* (New York, 1983), 104–13, 115–16, 318–21.
31. Hinsley, vol. 2, 555, 634–37.
32. Carl E. Behrens, *Effects on U-Boat Performance of Intelligence from Decryption of Allied Communications* (Washington, 1954).
33. Willem Hackmann, *Seek & Strike: Sonar, Anti-Submarine Warfare and the Royal Navy, 1914–1954* (London, 1984), 1–123.
34. Roskill, vol. 1, 30, 34–36.
35. Cf., Roland Alfred Bowling, "The Negative Influence of Mahan on the Protection of Shipping in War Time: The Convoy Controversy in the Twentieth Century," Ph.D. dissertation, University of Maine, 1980.
36. Roskill, vol. 1, 35, 44, 46, 106, 615.
37. Ibid., 451–54.
38. Peter Elliott, *Allied Escorts of World War II* (Annapolis, 1977), 14–18, 21–23, 136–47, 171–99.
39. John D. Alden, *Flush Decks & Four Pipes* (Annapolis, 1990); Arnold Hague, *Destroyers for Great Britain* (Annapolis, 1990).
40. Roskill, vol. 1, 581.
41. M. J. Whitley, *Destroyers of World War Two* (Annapolis, 1988), 94–95, 101, 112.
42. Roskill, vol. 2, 366–67.
43. Elliott, 211–24.
44. Friedman, 83–93, 145–53.
45. Anthony Preston, *U-boats* (London, 1973), 113.
46. Friedman, 128–27.
47. Brian Johnson, *The Secret War* (London, 1978), 127–28; Rohwer, *Critical Convoy Battles*, 198–200.

48. PRO, ADM 223/16, 23, 41.

49. Elliott, 517–27, gives a set-by-set account of all the various types of radios, direction finders, and radio telephones used by the Allies.

50. Roskill, vol. 1, 358–60.

51. British and Canadian escort groups, primarily employed to escort convoys in mid-ocean, were designated A1, A3, B1, B2, or C1, C2; while support groups were designated 1st, 2nd, 3rd Escort Groups. At times, support groups were also referred to as 1st, 2nd, 3rd Support Group. However, escort groups were not always deployed according to function. Ocean escort groups, such as B7, were also used at times as support groups and numbered escort groups were often assigned as ocean escorts to convoys. Especially after March 1943, American escorts, regardless of function, were grouped into numbered task groups.

52. Roskill, vol. 2, 201, 366–67.

53. Morison, vol. 1, 17–18.

54. Johnson, 203.

55. Cf., Alfred Price, *Aircraft versus Submarine* (Annapolis, 1973).

56. Admiralty Historical Section, *The Defeat of the Enemy Attack on Shipping, 1939–1945* (London, 1957), vol. 1A, 129.

57. Doenitz, 337–47.

58. PRO, PREM 3/414/3, ff. 3, 5.

59. W. A. B. Douglas, *The Creation of a National Air Force* (Toronto, 1986), 551.

60. PRO, AIR 41/48, Appendix 1, 1, 4, 5.

61. PRO, AIR 20/1065, Minutes by the VCAS, 18 May 1943; ibid., Appendix 1 and 2, to C-in-C Coastal Command, 31 May 1943. This document gives specific details of the modifications.

62. Cf., Douglas, *Creation*, 537–39.

63. Morison, vol. 1, 237–38.

64. PRO, AIR 20/2570, ACC-in-C Coastal Command to RAFDEL, parts 1–2, 19 May 1943.

65. See, e.g., John Slessor, *The Central Blue* (New York, 1957), 464–538.

66. Admiralty Historical Section, *Defeat of the Enemy*, vol. 1A, 24.

67. Roskill, vol. 2, 470–71; vol. 3, part 1, 365–67; Admiralty Historical Section, *Defeat of the Enemy*, vol. 1A, 229.

68. David Syrett and W. A. B. Douglas, "Die Wende in der Schlacht im Atlantik: Die Schliebung des 'Gronland-Luftlochs,' 1942–1943," *Marine-Rundschau* (1986), vol. 83, 2–11, 70–73, 147–49.

69. Roskill, vol. 1, 477–79.

70. R. C. Bayne, "Merchant Ship Aircraft Carriers," *Journal of the Royal United Service Institution* (November 1947), vol. 92, 548–53.

71. William Y'Blood, *Hunter-Killer: U.S. Escort Carriers in the Battle of the Atlantic* (Annapolis, 1983), 35–36.

72. Roskill, vol. 2, 201.

73. Roskill, vol. 2, 464–66.

74. Stefan Terzibaschitsch, *Escort Carriers and Aviation Support Ships of the US Navy* (Annapolis, 1981), 32–35, 38, 40–50, 52–53, 55, 61–67, 193–94.
75. Morison, vol. 10, 39n.
76. Ibid., 19–20.
77. W. G. D. Lund, "The Royal Canadian Navy's Quest for Autonomy in the North Atlantic: 1941–43," *The RCN in Retrospect*, 1910–1968, James A. Boutilier, ed. (Vancouver, 1982), 138–57.
78. NA, SRH-367, Battle of the Atlantic, A Preliminary Analysis of the Role of Decryption Intelligence in the Operational Phase of the, OEG Report #66, 8/20/51, 012.
79. Morrison, vol. 1, 226–28.
80. Hinsley, vol. 1, 12–13.
81. Patrick Beesly, *Very Special Intelligence: The Story of the Admiralty's Operational Intelligence Centre, 1939–1945* (London, 1977).
82. Mac Milner, *The North Atlantic Run: The Royal Canadian Navy and the Battle of the Convoys* (Annapolis, 1985), 189; Wesley K. Wark, "The Evolution of Military Intelligence in Canada," *Armed Forces & Society* (Fall, 1989), vol. 16, 83–85.
83. Beesly, 108–10; Morison, vol. 10, 24.
84. See, e.g., PRO, ADM 1/12663, [COMINCH] to Edelston, 28 October 1943.
85. Beesly, 169–70.
86. The boarding of the U-110 was not made public until 1959. S. W. Roskill, *The Secret Capture* (London, 1959). The capture of an enigma code machine was not known by the public until the 1970s.
87. Hinsley, vol. 1, 163, 336–39.
88. Ibid., vol. 2, 178–79, 223, 548, 551–52, 747–52.
89. Beesly, 98, 169–70; Hinsley, vol. 2, 551n.
90. David Kahn, *Seizing the Enigma: The Race to Break the German U-boat Codes* (Boston, 1991), 237–44; NA, SRMN-035, Admiralty COMINCH Ultra Message Exchange, 25 June 1942–17 October 1944; NA, SRMN-038, Functions of the "Secret Room" (F-211) of Cominch Combat Intelligence, Atlantic Section Anti-Submarine Warfare WW II (undated); NA, SRH-208, US Navy Sub Warfare MSG Reports COMINCH to Admiralty, 3 June 1942–9 June 1943; NA, SRH-236, Submarine Warfare Message Reports Admiralty to COMINCH; Hinsley, vol. 2, 57.
91. NA, SRGN, ff. 1–49668.
92. David Syrett, "The Sinking of HMS *Firedrake* and the Battle for Convoy ON 153," *American Neptune* (Spring, 1991), vol. 51, 105–6.
93. PRO, DEFE 3/717, intercepted 1230/3/5/43 decoded 1431/5/5/43.
94. Roskill, vol. 1, 599–600, 615–16; vol. 2, 467–70, 485.
95. Admiralty Historical Section, *Defeat of the Enemy*, vol. 1A, 1–86.

CHAPTER 2: THE BATTLE OF THE ATLANTIC IN THE BALANCE

1. Ministry of Defense (Navy), *The U-Boat War in the Atlantic* (London, 1989). vol. 2, 95.

2. Roskill, vol. 2, 486.
3. Rohwer, *Critical Convoy Battles.*
4. NA, SRMN-037, COMINCH File of U-Boat Intelligence Summaries, January 1943–May 1945, f. 28. See also Sir Peter Gretten, *Crisis Convoy: The Story of HX 231* (Annapolis, 1974).
5. Roskill, vol. 2, 469–70.
6. NA, SRMN-036, COMINCH File of U-Boat Situation Estimates, 15 January 1942–21 May 1945, f. 47.
7. PRO, ADM 219/35, Past and Future in Anti-Submarine Warfare, 2 April 1943.
8. BdU War Diary, 1 April 1943.
9. Ministry of Defense (Navy), *U-Boat War,* vol. 2, 100.
10. Ibid., 102–3.
11. PRO, DEFE 3/175, intercepted 1748/5/4/43 decoded 2126/6/4/43.
12. NA, SRGN 1541. In the American decrypts the decoded super-enciphered positions are in plain text.
13. BdU War Diary, 5 April 1943.
14. PRO, ADM 223/17, U-Boat Trend replacing report dated 5.4.43; PRO, ADM 199/580, f. 118.
15. BdU War Diary, 7, 8 April 1943.
16. PRO, ADM 199/2101, f. 233.
17. PRO, ADM 237/98, Commanding Officer HMS *Highlander* to Commodore Commanding Londonderry Escort Forces, 23 April 1943.
18. Ibid., Commander Task Unit 24.1.8 to Commander Task Force 24, 15 April 1943; PRO, DEFE 3/715, intercepted 1219/10/4/43 decoded 0653/11/4/43, intercepted 1345/10/4/43 decoded 0655/11/4/43.
19. PRO, DEFE 3/715, intercepted 1313/10/4/43 decoded 0653/11/4/43.
20. BdU War Diary, 10 April 1943.
21. NA, SRMN-034, COMINCH, Rough Notes on Daily U-boat Positions and Activities 1943–1945, f. 0151.
22. PRO, ADM 237/98, Commander Task Unit 24.1.8 to Commander Task Force 24, 15 April 1943.
23. Ibid.
24. PRO, DEFE 3/715, intercepted 1743/10/4/43 decoded 0759/11/4/43; ibid., intercepted 0326/11/4/43 decoded 0858/11/4/43.
25. PRO, ADM 237/98, Commander Task Unit 24.1.8 to Commander Task Force 24, 15 April 1943; Report of Attack on U-boat, in position 52°37′N, 39°28′W, by HMS *Clover* at 0352Z to 0408Z, 11th April 1943, on occasion of torpedoing of HMS *Beverley;* Jurgen Rohwer, *Axis Submarine Successes* (Annapolis, 1983), 162.
26. PRO, ADM 237/98, Commander Task Unit 24.1.8 to Commander Task Force 24, 15 April 1943; ibid., Chart No. 1, Convoy ON 176 Ocean Track.
27. PRO, DEFE 3/715, intercepted 1721/11/4/43 decoded 0539/16/4/43; ibid., intercepted 2049/11/4/43 decoded 0259/16/4/43; idib., intercepted 1745/11/4/43 decoded 0510/16/4/43.

28. NA, SRGN 15496; NA, SRH-367, Battle of the Atlantic, A Preliminary Analysis of the Role of Decryption Intelligence in the Operational Phase of the, OEG Report #66 20/8/51, f. 012.

29. PRO, ADM 237/98, Commander Task Unit 24.1.8 to Commander Task Force 24, 15 April 1943; ibid., Voyage Report No. 7, ON 176, SS *Melrose Abbey*.

30. PRO, ADM 237/98, Commander Task Unit 24.1.8 to Commander Task Force 24, 15 April 1943.

31. NA, SRGN 15564, 15586, and 15592.

32. PRO, DEFE 3/715, intercepted 2022/12/4/43 decoded 0318/15/4/43; BdU War Diary, 12 April 1943. 33. PRO, ADM 237/98, Commander Task Unit 24.1.8 to Commander Task Force 24, 15 April 1943; BdU War Diary, 12 April 1943.

35. PRO, ADM 199/576, f. 364, 454; PRO, ADM 199/575, f. 397.

36. PRO, ADM 199/575, f. 365, 370.

37. PRO, ADM 199/575, f. 370.

38. PRO, ADM 199/575, ff. 365, 370; PRO, ADM 199/376, f. 454; PRO, DEFE 3/715, intercepted 0929/11/4/43 decoded 1455/11/4/43.

39. BdU War Diary, 11 April 1943.

40. PRO, DEFE 3/715, intercepted 1405/10/4/43 decoded 0733/11/4/43; ibid., intercepted 0935/11/4/43 decoded 1456/11/4/43.

41. Ibid., intercepted 1010/11/4/43 decoded 1545/11/4/43; PRO, ADM 199/575, ff. 365–66.

42. PRO, ADM 199/575, f. 366, 382–83.

43. Ibid., f. 388.

44. Ibid., ff. 366, 395–96, 399–400; Rohwer, *Axis Submarine Successes*, 162–63.

45. PRO, ADM 199/575, ff. 366–67.

46. Ibid., f. 367; PRO, AIR 27/708, 12 April 1943; PRO, AIR 27/911 12 April 1943.

47. NA, SRGN 15567.

48. PRO, DEFE 3/715, intercepted 1701/12/4/43 decoded 0253/15/4/43.

49. NA, SRGN 15679; PRO, AIR 27/708, 12 April 1943.

50. PRO, ADM 199/575, f. 367, 368.

51. PRO, DEFE 3/715, intercepted 1548/12/4/43 decoded 0545/15/4/43; ibid., intercepted 2021/12/4/43 decoded 0318/14/4/43.

52. NA, SRGN 15664.

53. BdU War Diary, 12–13 April 1943.

54. PRO, DEFE 3/715, intercepted 1146/11/4/43 decoded 0501/16/4/43; ibid., intercepted 1146/11/4/43 decoded 0502/16/4/43; ibid., intercepted 1015/12/4/43 decoded 0848/16/4/43.

55. BdU War Diary, 12 April 1943.

56. NA, SRMN-034, COMINCH: Rough Notes on Daily U-Boats Positions and Activities 1943–1945, f. 0151.

57. PRO, ADM 223/17, U-Boat Trend, Period 12/4–19/4; PRO, ADM 199/583, ff. 377–378; PRO, ADM 199/2101, f. 235.

58. PRO, ADM 199/580, f. 129; PRO, ADM 199/2101, f. 21.

59. PRO, DEFE 3/715, intercepted 1519/13/4/43 decoded 1415/16/4/43; PRO, DEFE 3/716, intercepted 1619/14/4/43 decoded 0658/19/4/43.

60. BdU War Diary, 14 April 1943.

61. NA, SRGN 15806, 15825.

62. PRO, DEFE 3/716, intercepted 0729/15/4/43 decoded 0830/10/4/43, intercepted 1822/15/4/43 decoded 0304/19/4/43.

63. For an account of the U-262's mission to the Gulf of St. Lawrence, see Michael L. Hadley, *U-Boats against Canada: German Submarines in Canadian Waters* (Kingston and Montreal, 1985), 168–75.

64. BdU War Diary, 15 April 1943.

65. A forward firing weapon which launched a number of small rockets which fell into the water ahead of the attacking ship and exploded on contact with a submerged U-boat's hull. This weapon is similar to a hedgehog in concept. However, the missiles fired by a mousetrap are much smaller than those of a hedgehog.

66. NHC, Action Report: Commander Task Unit 24.1.3, 21 April 1943.

67. NA, SRGN 15892.

68. NA, SRGN 15912, 15924, 15927, 15928, 15930, 15933.

69. NHC, Action Report: Commander Task Unit 24.1.3, 21 April 1943.

70. Ibid.

71. Ibid.

72. PRO, ADM 199/575, ff. 403–08, 410–14, 416, 418–19; PRO, AIR 41/48, 53.

73. NHC, Action Report: Commander Task Unit 24.1.3, 21 April 1943.

74. PRO, DEFE 3/716, intercepted 0024/18/4/43 decoded 2252/18/4/43; BdU War Diary, 18 April 1943.

75. PRO, ADM 199/579, f. 289.

76. BdU War Diary, 16, 17 April 1943.

77. PRO, ADM 199/580, f. 129.

78. PRO, DEFE 3/716, intercepted 1958/16/4/43 decoded 2038/18/4/43.

79. NA, SRGN 15945, 15949.

80. BdU War Diary, 18 April 1943; NA, SRGN 15999.

81. NA, SRGN 15863.

82. PRO, ADM 223/15, ff. 187–88.

83. PRO, ADM 223/17, U-Boat trend, period 12/4–19/4.

84. BdU War Diary, 20 April 1943.

85. PRO, DEFE 3/716, intercepted 1620/20/4/43 decoded 1435/22/4/43; NA, SRGN 16067.

86. PRO, ADM 237/111, Report of the proceeding by the Commodore of the convoy which sailed from Liverpool at 1000 BST on Monday 6th April 1943.

87. PRO, DEFE 3/716, intercepted 0201/21/4/43 decoded 2210/22/4/43; PRO, ADM 237/111, Section 1: Attack on Convoy. Ons 3. Narrative; PRO, DEFE 3/716, intercepted 0431/21/4/43 decoded 1205/11/4/43; PRO, ADM 237/111, Report of an interview with the master—Captain W. B. Johnston SS

Wanstead; ibid., Report of an interview with the Chief Officer — Mr. F. Imaz SS *Ashantian.*

88. PRO, ADM 237/111. Section 1: Attack on Convoy. Ons 3. Narrative.
89. PRO, DEFE 3/716, intercepted 1031/21/4/43 decoded 1400/22/4/43; ibid., intercepted 092821/4/43 decoded 0840/22/4/43; ibid., intercepted 1127/21/4/43 decoded 1135/21/4/43.
90. PRO, ADM 199/2101, f. 22; PRO, ADM 199/575, f. 436.
91. PRO, DEFE 3/716, intercepted 0928/21/4/43 decoded 0840/22/4/43, intercepted 1229/21/4/43 decoded 0945/22/4/43; PRO, ADM 199/575, ff. 436, 448.
92. PRO, DEFE 3/716, intercepted 0920/21/4/43 decoded 11/25/21/4/43, intercepted 1127/21/4/43 decoded 1135/21/4/43; ibid., intercepted 0401/22/4/43 decoded 1112/22/4/43.
93. Ibid., intercepted 1350/21/4/43 decoded 0950/22/4/43, intercepted 1751/21/4/43 decoded 0803/22/4/43; ibid., intercepted 1839/21/4/43 decoded 1142/22/4/43, intercepted 2152/21/4/43 decoded 1321/22/4/43.
94. PRO, ADM 199/583, ff. 390–92; PRO, ADM 199/2101, f. 237.
95. PRO, ADM 237/99, E. C. Bayldon to Commodore Commanding Londonderry Escort Force, 26 April 1943.
96. PRO, DEFE 3/716, intercepted 1534/21/4/43 decoded 0720/22/4/43; Rohwer, *Axis Submarine Successes,* 163.
97. PRO, ADM 237/99, E. C. Bayldon to Commodore Commanding Londonderry Escort Force, 26 April 1943.
98. Ibid.
99. PRO, ADM 199/575, f. 437; PRO, AIR 4/48, 55.
100. A *python* is a square search conducted at a distance from a convoy. Directorate of History, National Defense Hdqtrs., Ottawa, Eastern Air Command Operational Instructions B. R. Operations. All other information on British and Canadian air searches by aircraft serving as air escorts to convoys are drawn from this source.
101. PRO, DEFE 3/716, intercepted 2046/21/4/43 decoded 0802/22/4/43; PRO, AIR 27/911, 21 April 1943; PRO, ADM 199/575, f. 442.
102. PRO, ADM 199/575, ff. 437, 442.
103. Rohwer, *Axis Submarine Successes,* 163.
104. PRO, AIR 27/911, 22 April 1943; PRO, ADM 199/575, f. 437.
105. PRO, DEFE 3/716, intercepted 1024/22/4/43 decoded 0358/24/4/43; ibid., intercepted 2235/22/4/43 decoded 0624 24/4/43; ibid., intercepted 0915/23/4/43 decoded 0156/24/4/43.
106. NA, SRGN 16309.
107. PRO, ADM 199/575, ff. 437–38.
108. Ibid., ff. 438, 443–44.
109. Ibid., f. 446.
110. PRO, AIR 27/911, 23 April 1943.
111. PRO, DEFE 3/716, intercepted 0630/23/4/43 decoded 0631/24/4/43; ibid.,

intercepted 1110/23/4/43 decoded 0156/24/4/43, intercepted 2257/23/4/43
decoded 0216/24/4/43; ibid., intercepted 1519/23/4/43 decoded 0946/24/4/43;
ibid., intercepted 0040/24/4/43 decoded 0932/24/4/43; ibid., intercepted 0449/
24/4/43 decoded 1058/24/4/43; PRO, ADM 199/575, ff. 439, 448.

112. BdU War Diary, 23 April 1943.
113. PRO, ADM 199/575, f. 439.
114. PRO, AIR 41/48, 56; PRO, ADM 199/575, f. 439; PRO, DEFE 3/716,
     intercepted 1205/24/4/43 decoded 1427/25/4/43; ibid., intercepted 1219/24/
     43 decoded 1331/25/4/43; ibid., intercepted 1351/24/4/43 decoded 1620/25/4/
     43; ibid., intercepted 1443/24/4/43 decoded 1514/25/4/43. See also PRO,
     DEFE 3/716, intercepted 2047/24/4/43 decoded 1605/25/4/43.
115. BdU War Diary, 24 April 1943.
116. PRO, DEFE 3/716, intercepted 2330/24/4/43 decoded 1439/125/4/43; ibid.,
     intercepted 0920/25/4/43 decoded 1524/25/4/43.
117. BdU War Diary, 25 April 1943.
118. PRO, DEFE 3/716, intercepted 1312/24/4/43 decoded 0403/24/4/43.
119. BdU War Diary, 23 April 1943.
120. PRO, DEFE 3/716, intercepted 1540/23/4/43 decoded 0431/24/4/43; ibid.,
     intercepted 1717/23/4/43 decoded 0408/24/4/43.
121. PRO, ADM 199/2101, f. 323; PRO, ADM 237/112, Convoy ONS 4
     Positions at 0800 (D.B.S.T.); ibid., Commander, Escort Group B2 to Captain
     (D), Liverpool, 30 April 1943.
122. PRO, ADM 237/112, Commander, Escort Group B2 to Captain (D),
     Liverpool, 30 April 1943; ibid., Remarks on the operation of air support
     groups. Appendix 1, to "Biter" letter No. 2511/021 dated 3rd May 1943;
     ibid., Daily summary of flying. Appendix 4 to "Biter" Letter No. 2511/021
     dated 3rd May 1943.
124. NA, SRGN 16364.
125. A Mark X depth charge consisted on 1,000 pounds of explosives and was 16
     feet 2 inches long. This weapon was only carried by destroyers and fired from
     a torpedo tube.
126. PRO, ADM 237/112, Appendix 1. Narrative of Operations against U-boat
     on 23 April 1943; ibid., Commanding officer HMS *Clematis* to Commander,
     B2 Escort Group, 30 April 1943.
127. PRO, ADM 237/112, Appendix 1. Narrative of Operations against U-boat
     on 23 April 1943; ibid., Appendix 2. Co-operation with 5th escort group.
128. PRO, ADM 237/112, Commander, Escort Group B2 to Captain (D),
     Liverpool, 30 April 1943; Daily summary of flying. Appendix 4 to "Biter"
     Letter No. 2511/021 dated 3rd May 1943; PRO, ADM 199/2101, f. 323;
     PRO, ADM 237/112, Commanding officer HMS *Biter* to Commander-in-
     Chief Western Approaches, 3rd May 1943; PRO, DEFE 3/716, intercepted
     0717/25/4/43 decoded 1325/4/43.
129. NA, SRGN 16570, 16587.
130. PRO, DEFE 3/716, intercepted 2150/25/4/43 decoded 1245/26/4/43.

131. Cf., PRO, ADM 237/112, Commanding officer HMS *Biter* to Commander-in-Chief Western Approaches, 3rd May 1943.
132. Ministry of Defense (Navy), *U-Boat War*, vol. 2, 103.
133. PRO, ADM 237/112, Commander, Escort Group B2 to Captain (D) Liverpool, 30 April 1943; ibid., Commanding officer HMS *Biter* to Commander-in-Chief Western Approaches, 3rd May 1943.
134. PRO, ADM 237/112, Commander HMS *Pathfinder* to Commanding officer HMS *Biter*, 1 May 1943; ibid., Appendix 2 information gained from Prisoners.
135. PRO, ADM 199/2101, f. 323; PRO, ADM 237/112, Convoy ONS 4 Positions at 0800 (D.B.S.T.); NA, SRGN 16360.
136. PRO, 237/112, Commander, Escort Group B2 to Captain (D), Liverpool, 30 April 1943; ibid., Senior Officer, 1st Supporting Group to Commander-in-Chief, Western Approaches, 2 May 1943.
137. PRO, ADM 237/112, Commander, Escort Group B2 to Captain (D), Liverpool, 30 April 1943.
138. BdU War Diary, 25 April 1943.
139. PRO, ADM 199/580, ff. 135, 136; PRO, ADM 199/2101, f. 116; NA SRGN 16092.
140. NA, SRGN 16067; BdU War Diary, 21 April 1943.
141. PRO, DEFE 3/716, intercepted 0924/23/4/43 decoded 0524/24/4/43; PRO, ADM 199/580, f. 136.
142. NA, SRGN 16252, 16313, 16360.
143. BdU War Diary, 23 April 1943.
144. PRO, ADM 199/580, f. 136.
145. BdU War Diary, 24 April 1943; PRO, ADM 199/580, f. 136; PRO, ADM 199/2101, f. 116.
146. NA, SRGN 16577; PRO, ADM 199/580, f. 138; PRO, ADM 199/2101, f. 116.
147. PRO, ADM 199/583, ff. 399, 402; PRO, ADM 199/2101, f. 239; NA, SRGN 16252.
148. NA, SRMN-030, COMINCH File of Biweekly Messages on U-Boat Trends, 1 September 1942–1 May 1945, f. 022.
149. PRO, ADM 199/575, ff. 479, 490, 496; PRO, ADM 199/2101, f. 24.
150. NHC, USS *Bogue*, Escort of Convoy HX-235. Report of Air Coverage and ASW Patrol from Convoy from Argentina to British Isles 24–30 April 1943.
151. PRO, ADM 199/577, ff. 6–12; PRO, ADM 199/578, ff. 31, 47–49; PRO, ADM 199/2102, ff. 25, 26.
152. BdU War Diary, 27 April 1943.
153. Cf., Kahn, *Seizing the Enigma*, 278–80.
154. NA, SRMN-030, COMINCH File of Biweekly Messages on U-Boat Trends, 1 September 1942–1 May 1945, ff. 021–022.
155. Ibid., f. 021; NA, SRMN-048, Reports on U-Boat Dispositions and Status, December 1942–2 May 1945, f. 024.

CHAPTER 3: THE BATTLE FOR CONVOY ONS 5

1. PRO, ADM 223/88, f. 270; PRO, DEFE 3/716/717; NA SRGN 16587-16659; Hinsley vol. 2, 569; PRO, ADM 223/15, f. 192; PRO, ADM 223/17, U/Boat trend, period 3/5–10/5/43.
2. BdU War Diary, 27 April 1943.
3. PRO, ADM 199/2101, f. 111; PRO, ADM 237/202, Convoy SC 128, Daily Positions 0800 BST.
4. NA, SRH-08, Battle of the Atlantic, vol. 2, U-Boat Operations, 69.
5. PRO, ADM 199/2101, f. 111; PRO, ADM 199/583, ff. 335–37.
6. PRO, ADM 199/583, ff. 410–13; PRO, ADM 199/2101, f. 241.
7. NA, SRH-08, Battle of the Atlantic, vol. 2, U-boat Operations, 69.
8. PRO, ADM 199/2101, f. 395; PRO, ADM 237/113, Convoy ONS 5, Report of proceeding, Senior officer in HMS *Duncan.*
9. Cf., Sir Peter Gretton, *Convoy Escort Commander* (London, 1964).
10. PRO, ADM 237/113, Convoy ONS 5, 8 A.M. Positions British Double Summer Time; PRO, ADM 223/88, f. 270.
11. Gretton, 134–35.
12. Gretton, 135; PRO, ADM 237/113, Convoy ONS 5; ibid., Report on Collision between "Bornholm" and "Berkel"
13. PRO, ADM 237/113, Convoy ONS 5, Report of Proceedings, Senior officer in HMS *Duncan.*
14. Gretton, 135.
15. PRO, ADM 237/113 Convoy ONS 5, Report of Proceedings, Senior officer in HMS *Duncan.*
16. BdU War Diary, 27 April 1943.
17. Ministry of Defense (Navy), *U-Boat War,* vol. 2, 104.
18. BdU War Diary, 1 May 1943.
19. PRO, ADM 237/113, Convoy ONS 5, Report of Proceedings, Senior Officer in HMS *Duncan.*
20. Ibid.
21. Ibid.
22. Ibid., HMS *Sunflower,* Report of Proceedings with Convoy ONS 5.
23. Ibid., Convoy ONS 5, Report of Proceedings, Senior Officer in HMS *Duncan.*
24. Ibid., HMS *Snowflake,* Narrative of Events during passage of Convoy ONS 5; ibid., Convoy ONS 5, Report of Proceedings, Senior Officer in HMS *Duncan.*
25. Ibid., Convoy ONS 5, Report of Proceedings, Senior Officer in HMS *Duncan;* ibid., HMS *Vidette* Report of Proceedings on ONS 5.
26. Rohwer, *Axis Submarine Successes,* 164.
27. PRO, ADM 237/113, Convoy ONS 5, Report of Proceedings, Senior Officer in HMS *Duncan;* ibid., HMS *Snowflake,* Narrative of Events during passage of Convoy ONS 5.

28. Ibid., Convoy ONS 5, Report of Proceedings, Senior Officer in HMS *Duncan.*
29. Ibid.; ibid., HMS *Sunflower,* Report of Proceedings with Convoy ONS 5.
30. PRO, AIR 41/48, 58; PRO, AIR 27/911, 30 April 1943.
31. PRO, ADM 237/113, Convoy ONS 5, Report of Proceedings, Senior Officer in HMS *Duncan;* ibid., HMS *Snowflake,* Narrative of Events during passage of Convoy ONS 5.
32. PRO, ADM 237/113, Convoy ONS 5, Report of Proceedings, Senior Officer in HMS *Duncan;* PRO, AIR 27/911, 1 May 1943.
33. NA, SRGN 1665.
34. BdU War Diary, 1 May 1943.
35. Ibid.
36. NA, SRGN 16709, 16715, 16731, 16739, 16750, 16753.
37. BdU War Diary, 2 May 1943.
38. PRO, DEFE 3/718, intercepted 1029/3/5/43 decoded 0125/15/5/43; PRO, DEFE 3/717, intercepted 1625/3/5/43 decoded 1529/5/5/43; PRO, ADM 237/113, Convoy SC 128, Daily Positions 0800 BST.
39. PRO, DEFE 3/717, intercepted 1646/3/5/43 decoded 1443/5/5/43.
40. BdU War Diary, 3 May 1943.
41. NA, SRGN 16914, 16915, 16919, 16920, 16922, 16931, 16932, 16949, 16960, 16968.
42. PRO, DEFE 3/717, intercepted 1637/4/5/43 decoded 1158/5/5/43; ibid., intercepted 1720/4/5/43 decoded 1241/5/5/43.
43. PRO, ADM 237/113, Convoy ONS 5, Report of Proceedings, Senior Officer in HMS *Duncan;* ibid., Commanding Officer HMS *Offa* to Senior Officer, 3rd Escort Group, 8 May 1943.
44. PRO, ADM 237/113, Convoy ONS 5, Report of Proceedings, Senior Officer in HMS *Duncan;* ibid., Copy of Naval Messages, Enclosures to HMS *Duncan*'s Report of Proceedings With Convoy ONS 5; ibid., Convoy ONS 5, Continuation of Report by Commanding officer HMS *Tay.*
45. PRO, ADM 237/113, LCDR J. C. A. Ingram to Senior Officer 3rd Escort Group, 8 May 1943.
46. PRO, DEFE 3/717, intercepted 1925/4/5/43 decoded 1220/5/5/43.
47. NA, SRGN 16993.
48. Douglas, *Creation,* 552–53.
49. PRO, ADM 237/113, Convoy ONS 5, Continuation of Report by Commanding Officer HMS *Tay;* ibid., Copy of Naval Messages HMS *Tay* ONS 5.
50. PRO, ADM 237/113, Convoy ONS 5, Continuation of Report by Commanding Officer HMS *Tay.*
51. Rohwer, *Axis Submarine Successes,* 165.
52. PRO, ADM 237/113, Report of Survivors From ONS 5.
53. Ibid., HMS *Vidette,* Report of Proceedings on ONS 5, Vide Four & Five.
54. Ibid., Vide One & Two.

55. Ibid., Report of Survivors From ONS 5, Report of an Interview with the Master, Captain J. E. Turgoose, SS *Harperley;* ibid., Report of an Interview with the Master Captain W. E. Cook, SS *Harbury.*

56. Ibid., Commanding Officer, HMS *Snowflake* to Senior Officer B7 Escort Group, HMS *Duncan,* 8 May 1943.

57. Ibid., Commanding Officer, HMS *Snowflake* to Senior Officer B7 Escort Group, HMS *Duncan,* 8 May 1943; ibid., LCDR J. C. A. Ingram to Senior Officer, 3rd Escort Group, 8 May 1943.

58. Rohwer, *Axis Submarine Successes,* 165.

59. PRO, ADM, 237/113, Report of an Interview with the Master, Captain A. L. Webb, SS *Bristol City;* ibid., Report of an Interview with the Master, Captain R. G. Phillips, SS *Wentworth.*

60. Rohwer, *Axis Submarine Successes,* 165.

61. PRO, ADM 237/113, Commanding Officer HMS *Loosestrife* to Senior Officer B7 Escort Group; ibid., Convoy ONS 5, Continuation of Report by Commanding Officer, HMS *Tay.*

62. PRO, ADM 237/113, Convoy ONS 5, Continuation of Report by Commanding Officer HMS *Tay;* ibid., LCDR J. C. A. Ingram to Senior Officer, 3rd Escort Group, 8 May 1943.

63. PRO, ADM 237/113, Commanding Officer HMS *Offa* to the Senior Officer, 3rd Escort Group, 8 May 1943.

64. Rohwer, *Axis Submarine Successes,* 165.

65. PRO, ADM 237/113, Report of an Interview with the Master Captain G. R. Cheetham M. V. Dolius; ibid., Convoy ONS 5, Continuation of Report by Commanding Officer HMS *Tay;* ibid., HMS *Sunflower,* Report of Proceedings with Convoy ONS 5.

66. PRO, ADM 237/113, HMS *Pink,* Report of Proceedings For ONS 5 (Straggler Portion), Narrative of Attack by HMS *Pink* on a U-boat, 5 May 1943.

67. Rohwer, *Axis Submarine Successes,* 165.

68. PRO, ADM 237/113, HMS *Pink,* Report of Proceedings For ONS 5 (Straggler Portion), Statement of H. Schoeder, Master of "ex" SS *West Market* Concerning Torpedoing of Vessel on 5 May 1943.

69. Ibid., HMS *Pink,* Report of Proceedings For ONS 5 (Straggler Portion).

70. PRO, ADM 223/16, f. 91; NA, SRGN 17053, 17048, 17067, 17079, 17058, 17085, 17146, 17161, 17186, 17189.

71. Rohwer, *Axis Submarine Successes,* 166.

72. PRO, ADM 237/113, Commanding Officer HMS *Offa* to Senior Officer 3rd Escort Group, 8 May 1943; ibid., Report of an Interview with the First Officer, Mr. C. D. Head, SS *Selvistan;* ibid., Report of an Interview with the Master, Captain R. Stone, SS *Ghanida.*

73. PRO, AIR 27/911, 5 May 1943.

74. PRO, ADM 237/113, Convoy ONS 5, Continuation of Report by Commanding Officer HMS *Tay;* ibid., Commanding Officer HMS *Offa* to

Senior Officer 3rd Escort Group; ibid., LTCD J. C. A. Ingram to Senior Officer, 3rd Escort Group, 8 May 1943.

75. PRO, ADM 237/113, Convoy ONS 5, Continuation of Report by Commanding Officer HMS *Tay.*

76. Ibid., HMS *Sunflower,* Report of Proceedings with Convoy ONS 5.

77. Ibid., Commanding Officer, HMS *Snowflake* to Senior Officer B7 Escort Group, HMS *Duncan,* 8 May 1943.

78. PRO, ADM 237/113, HMS *Sunflower,* Report of Proceedings with Convoy ONS 5.

79. PRO, ADM 237/113, Commanding Officer HMS *Loosestrife* to Senior Officer B7 Escort Group.

80. PRO, ADM 237/113, HMS *Vidette,* Report of Proceedings, ONS 5; Vide Six & Seven; Roskill, vol. 2, 374, states that HMS *Vidette* sank the U-125 in this action. However, there is no evidence that the U-boat attacked by HMS *Vidette* was the U-125 or that the destroyer actually sank a U-boat in this action.

81. PRO, ADM 237/113, LTCD J. C. A. Ingram to Senior Officer, 3rd Escort Group, 8 May 1943.

82. PRO, ADM 237/113, Commanding Officer, HMS *Snowflake* to Senior Officer B7 Escort Group, HMS *Duncan,* 8 May 1943.

83. Ibid.

84. NA, SRGN 17231.

85. PRO, ADM 237/113, Commanding Officer, HMS *Snowflake* to Senior Officer B7 Escort Group, HMS *Duncan,* 8 May 1943.

86. NA, SRGN 17270; PRO, ADM, 237/113, HMS *Sunflower,* Report of Proceedings with Convoy ONS 5.

87. PRO, ADM 237/113, LTCD J. C. A. Ingram to Senior Officer, 3rd Escort Group, 8 May 1943.

88. PRO, ADM 237/113, Commanding Officer HMS *Loosestrife* to Senior Officer B7 Escort Group; Commanding Officer, HMS *Snowflake* to Senior Officer B7 Escort Group, HMS *Duncan,* 8 May 1943.

89. PRO, ADM 237/113, Senior Officer 1st Support Group to Commander in Chief, Western Approaches, 12 May 1943; ibid., LTCD F. H. Thorton to Commanding Officer HMS *Pelican,* 9 May 1943.

90. PRO, ADM 237/113, Senior Officer 1st Support Group to Commander in Chief, Western Approaches, 12 May 1943.

91. PRO, ADM 237/113, HMS *Pelican:* Report of an Attack on U-Boat, 6 May 1943.

92. PRO, ADM 237/113, HMS *Spey:* Report of Attack on U-Boat, 6 May 1943.

93. NA, SRGN 17195, 17227, 17228, 17270, 17273, 17274, 17261, 17291, 17310.

94. PRO, ADM 223/16, 89, f. 85, 88–89.

95. PRO, ADM 237/113, Convoy ONS 5, Continuation of Report by Commanding Officer HMS *Tay.*

96. BdU War Diary, 6 May 1943; PRO, DEFE 3/717, intercepted 0920/7/5/43 decoded 1747/9/5/43.
97. Doenitz, 339.
98. BdU War Diary, 6 May 1943.

CHAPTER 4: THE FIRST DEFEAT OF THE WOLF PACKS

1. PRO, ADM 199/2101, f. 327; PRO, ADM 237/114, Acting Commander J. V. Waterhouse to Captain (D) Liverpool, 14 May 1943.
2. PRO, ADM 237/114, Convoy ONS 6, 0800 BST Positions; ibid., Acting Commander J. V. Waterhouse to Captain (D) Liverpool, 14 May 1943; PRO, AIR 41/48, 70; BdU War Diary 7, 8 May 1943.
3. PRO, ADM 199/2101, f. 327; PRO, ADM 237/114, Commanding Officer HMS *Archer* to Commander in Chief Western Approaches, 17 May 1943; ibid., Convoy ONS 6, 0800 BST Positions.
4. NA, SRGN 17270; PRO, ADM 223/15, f. 194; PRO, ADM 199/583, ff. 421–424; PRO, ADM 199/2101, f. 243.
5. PRO, ADM 199/577, ff. 38, 41; PRO, ADM 199/2020, 3.
6. PRO, ADM 199/577, ff. 38, 41, 73–74, 87, 94.
7. BdU War Diary, 7 May 1943.
8. PRO, DEFE 3/717, intercepted 1015/7/5/43 decoded 1555/9/5/43; PRO, DEFE 3/718, intercepted 1048/7/5/43 decoded 1902/21/5/43; PRO, DEFE 3/717, intercepted 1124/7/5/43 decoded 0651/21/5/43.
9. BdU War Diary, 7 May 1943.
10. NA, SRGN 17448, 17445.
11. BdU War Diary, 7 May 1943.
12. Ibid., 8 May 1943.
13. PRO, DEFE 3/718, intercepted 1950/8/5/43 decoded 0909/21/5/43.
14. BdU War Diary, 8 May 1943.
15. PRO, DEFE 3/718, intercepted 2130/8/5/43 decoded 0905/21/5/43.
16. Ibid., intercepted 2304/8/5/43 decoded 1515/22/5/43. The American text of this decrypted order reads: "THE EXPECTED CONVOY, ACCORDING TO SURE REPORT, IS FURTHER SOUTH AND FURTHER AHEAD THAN ASSUMED." NA, SRGN 17553; ibid., 17631.
17. PRO, DEFE 3/718, intercepted 2248/8/5/43 decoded 0855/21/5/43, intercepted 2228/8/5/43 decoded 0355/22/5/43.
18. BdU War Diary, 8 May 1943.
19. BdU War Diary, 8 May 1943.
20. NA, SRMN-037, COMINCH File of U-Boat Intelligence Summaries January 1943–May 1945, f. 042.
21. PRO, ADM 223/15, f. 195.
22. PRO, ADM 199/577, f. 95, 127–.128.
23. PRO, ADM 199/577, ff. 38–39, 42–43, 95-96.

24. Ibid., f. 43; PRO, DEFE 3/718, intercepted 1306/9/5/43 decoded 0818/21/5/ 43; NA, SRGN 17592.

25. PRO, ADM 199/577, ff. 61–62.

26. Ibid., ff. 43–44.

27. BdU War Diary, 9 May 1943; PRO, DEFE 3/718, intercepted 1224/9/5/43 decoded 1555/21/5/43; ibid., intercepted 1730/9/5/43 decoded 0549/21/5/43, intercepted 1850/9/5/43 decoded 0532/21/5/43, intercepted 2143/9/5/43 decoded 0835/21/5/43.

28. BdU War Diary, 9 May 1943; PRO, DEFE 3/718, intercepted 1524/9/5/43 decoded 0529/21/5/43.

29. PRO, ADM 199/577, f. 44, 96.

30. PRO, ADM 199/577, f. 45.

31. PRO, DEFE 3/718, intercepted 2311/10/5/43 decoded 2144/16/5/43. See also PRO, DEFE 3/718, intercepted 1429/10/5/43 decoded 2139/16/5/43, intercepted 1841/10/5/43 decoded 1915/10/5/43.

32. BdU War Diary, 10 May 1943; PRO, DEFE 3/718, intercepted 1745/19/5/43 decoded 1841/16/5/43, intercepted 1919/10/5/43 decoded 1923/16/5/43; OD War Diary, 10 May 1943.

33. PRO, ADM 199/577, ff. 45, 109, 125–126. 37. Ibid., f. 45.

35. BdU War Diary, 11 May 1943.

36. OD War Diary, 11 May 1943.

37. PRO, ADM 199/577, f. 46, 109.

38. PRO, DEFE 3/718, intercepted 2003/11/5/43 decoded 0340/16/5/43, intercepted 2208/11/5/43 decoded 2050/15/5/43, intercepted 2028/11/5/43 decoded 0647/16/5/43; PRO, DEFE 3/717, intercepted 2003/11/5/43 decoded 2050/15/5/43, intercepted 2028/11/5/43 decoded 0647/16/5/43. Rohwer, *Axis Submarine Successes*, 166, states that there is a possibility that the U-456 sank this ship. Rohwer also thinks that the *Fort Concord* and not the *Sandanger* was sunk at this time. But, the *Fort Concord's* life boats were found too far to the east, and therefore it must have been the *Sandanger*.

39. PRO, DEFE 3/717, intercepted 0503/13/5/43 decoded 1337/14/5/43; PRO, ADM 199/577, ff. 46, 97–98, 109; PRO, DEFE 3/718, intercepted 0744/12/ 8/43 decoded 0541/16/5/43; PRO, DEFE 3/717, intercepted 0744/12/5/43 decoded 0541/16/5/43; ibid., intercepted 1833/12/5/43 decoded 1125/14/5/43. For an account of being hunted, hounded, and bombed by aircraft near convoy HX 237, see Herbert A. Werner, *Iron Coffins* (New York, 1969), 118– 26.

40. This weapon was known as a Mark 24 Mine for security reasons. This was the first time that Allies used an airborne acoustic homing torpedo in combat. PRO, AIR 41/48, 63.

41. PRO, AIR 27/708, 12 May 1943; PRO, ADM 199/577, f. 46, 48; PRO, DEFE 3/717, intercepted 1151/12/5/43 decoded 1000/14/5/43; ibid., intercepted 1201/12/5/43 decoded 1052/14/5/43; ibid., intercepted 1248/12/5/ 43 decoded 1002/14/5/43; ibid., intercepted 1252/12/5/43 decoded 1015/14/5/

43; ibid., intercepted 1428/12/5/43 decoded 1032/14/5/43; ibid., intercepted 1635/12/5/43 decoded 1102/14/5/43; ibid., intercepted 1926/12/5/43 decoded 1408/14/5/43.

42. BdU War Diary, 12 May 1943. Postwar assessments credited the sinking of the U-456 to HMCS *Drumheller*, HMS *Lagan*, and an aircraft from RCAF 423rd Squadron on 13 May. See, e.g., Roskill, vol. 2, 471. But it seems certain from radio intercepts and Allied after action reports that the U-456 was sunk as a result of damage inflicted by aircraft B/86 on 12 May 1943. R. M. Coppock of the Ministry of Defense, Naval Staff Duties (Foreign Documents Section), who is conducting reassessment of the Battle of the Atlantic, has concluded that aircraft B/86 sank the U-456. R. M. Coppock to David Syrett, 28 February 1990, enclosing "Loss of U-89, U-456 and U-753 in May 1943."

43. PRO, ADM 1299/577, ff. 46–48, 55–56.

44. PRO, ADM 199/577, ff. 48–49, 66–67. See also note 38.

45. Ibid., ff. 48–49.

46. PRO, ADM 199/577, ff. 49, 63; PRO, DEFE 3/717, intercepted 2229/12/5/43 decoded 1349/14/5/43.

47. PRO, DEFE 3/717, intercepted 2229/12/5/43 decoded 1203/14/5/43; ibid., intercepted 0051/13/5/43 decoded 1132/14/5/43; ibid., intercepted 0108/13/5/43 decoded 1313/14/5/43; ibid., intercepted 0316/13/5/43 decoded 1312/14/5/43; ibid., intercepted 0536/13/5/43 decoded 1337/14/5/43; BdU War Diary, 12 May 1943; PRO, AIR 27/708, 12 May 1943; PRO, DEFE 3/717, intercepted 0228/13/5/43 decoded 1428/14/5/43; ibid., intercepted 0925/13/5/43 decoded 1318/14/5/43.

48. PRO, AIR 27/1832, 13 May 1943.

49. PRO, ADM 199/577, ff. 49, 99. A number of authorities think that the U-456 was sunk in this action when, in fact, it was most likely sunk on 12 May. These same authorities list the U-573 as being lost on 15 May to unknown causes. However, OD War Diary, 16 May 1943, lists the U-573 as being sunk by an escort of HX 237 on 13 May 1943. See also note 43.

50. PRO, ADM 199/577, f. 50, 99; PRO, DEFE 3/717, intercepted 1722/13/5/43 decoded 1645/14/5/43.

51. PRO, ADM 199/579, f. 380; PRO, ADM 199/580, f. 160.

52. BdU War Diary, 8 May 1943; PRO, DEFE 3/718, intercepted 1524/10/5/43 decoded 0529/21/5/43; BdU War Diary, 10 May 1943; PRO, DEFE 3/718, intercepted 1524/9/5/43 decoded 0529/21/5/43.

53. PRO, ADM 199/579, ff. 380–381; Rohwer, *Axis Submarine Successes*, 166.

54. Macintyre, in his after action report of the battle (PRO, ADM 199/579, ff. 381, 384–385) states that there were two U-boats. In his account of the battle written after the war, *U-Boat Killer* (New York, 1956), 165–173, Macintyre says that HMS *Hesperus* only engaged one U-boat, the U-223, which was depth charged, hedgehogged, rammed, and damaged in the action. There was in fact only one U-boat, the U-223. This is confirmed by R. M. Coppock to David Syrett, 28 February 1990.

55. BdU War Diary, 11 May 1943; PRO, ADM 199/579, f. 381.
56. PRO, DEFE 3/717, intercepted 1320/12/5/43 decoded 1016/14/5/43; PRO, DEFE 3/718, intercepted 1021/12/5/43 decoded 2248/15/5/43.
57. PRO, DEFE 3/717, intercepted 1031/12/5/43 decoded 1002/14/5/43; e.g., PRO, DEFE 3/717, intercepted 1206/12/5/43 decoded 0954/14/5/43, intercepted 1249/12/5/43 decoded 0830/14/5/43, intercepted 1013/12/5/43 decoded 1410/14/5/43, intercepted 1521/12/5/43 decoded 0825/14/5/43, intercepted 1710/12/5/43 decoded 1132/14/5/43, intercepted 1720/12/5/43 decoded 1137/14/5/43, intercepted 1751/12/5/43 decoded 1147/14/5/43; PRO, DEFE 3/717 intercepted 2211/12/5/43 decoded 1344/14/5/43; PRO, ADM 199/579, ff. 381, 386; Macintyre, *U-Boat Killer*, 173–74.
58. PRO, ADM 199/579, ff. 381, 392–393.
59. PRO, ADM 199/579, f. 382, 383, 387, 393.
60. PRO, ADM 199/579, ff. 383, 388; PRO, DEFE 3/717, intercepted 1835/12/5/43 decoded 1135/14/5/43; ibid., intercepted 2355/12/5/43 decoded 1208/14/5/43; ibid., intercepted 0108/13/5/43 decoded 1313/14/5/43; BdU War Diary, 12 May 1943.
61. PRO, DEFE 3/717, intercepted 0156/13/5/43 decoded 1153/14/5/43; PRO, AIR 27/708, 13 May 1943; PRO, DEFE 3/717, intercepted 2305/13/5/43 decoded 1830/14/5/43; ibid., intercepted 2317/13/5/43 decoded 1853/14/5/43; ibid., intercepted 1424/13/5/43 decoded 1706/14/5/43; ibid., intercepted 1546/13/5/43 decoded 1727/14/5/43.
62. BdU War Diary, 13 May 1943; OD War Diary, 13 May 1943.
63. PRO, ADM 199/579, ff. 382–383; PRO, DEFE 3/718, intercepted 1751/14/5/43 decoded 0846/17/5/43; Rohwer, *Axis submarine Successes*, 167; e.g., PRO, DEFE 3/718, intercepted 1751/14/5/43 decoded 0846/17/5/43, intercepted 2255/14/5/43 decoded 0839/17/5/43; PRO, DEFE 3/718, intercepted 1138/14/5/43 decoded 0544/17/5/43.
64. NA, SRH-008, Battle of the Atlantic: vol. 2, U-boat Operations, 2: 72.
65. NA, SRH-009, Battle of the Atlantic: vol. 1, Allied Communications Intelligence, December 42–May 45, 80–90; NA, SRGN 17547, 17553, 17781; NA, SRMN-054, OP-20-G1 Special Studies relating to U-boat Activity 1943–1945, 132–35.
66. BdU War Diary, 10–11 May 1943.
67. BdU War Diary, 10, 11, 12 May 1943; NA, SRGN 17925; PRO, DEFE 3/718, intercepted 1431/11/5/43 decoded 2120/15/5/43, intercepted 2248/11/5/43 decoded 2201/15/5/43, intercepted 1405/12/5/43 decoded 0958/14/5/43; PRO, ADM 199/583, ff. 430–34; PRO, ADM 199/2101, f. 245.
68. PRO, ADM 199/2101, f. 329; PRO, ADM 237/115, Report of Proceedings by Commodore of Convoy which sailed from Oban at 0158 on 8th May 1943; ONS 7 Positions at 0800 BST; PRO, DEFE 3/718, intercepted 0034/13/5/43 decoded 1207/14/5/43.
69. BdU War Diary, 12 May 1943.
70. NA, SRGN 18098, 18145, 18161, 18162; e.g., NA, SRGN 18138, 18212.

71. PRO, ADM 237/115, Report of Proceedings ONS 7, 22 May 1943; PRO, DEFE 3/718, intercepted 1812/13/5/43 decoded 1848/14/5/43; PRO, AIR 41/48, 73; PRO, DEFE 3/718, intercepted 0110/14/5/43 decoded 1747/15/5/43.

72. PRO, AIR 41/48, 73; PRO, ADM 237/115, Report of Proceedings ONS 7, 22 May 1943; ONS 7 Positions at 0800 BST.

73. NA, SRGN 18271; PRO, ADM 237/115, Report of Proceedings ONS 7, 22 May 1943, ONS 7 Positions at 0800 BST.

74. Rohwer, *Axis Submarine Successes*, 167.

75. PRO, ADM 237/115, Report of an Interview with the Master, Captain S. Morris, SS *Aymeric*, 24 June 1943; ibid., Report of Proceedings ONS 7, 22 May 1943; ibid., W. J. Hartley to Director of Sea Transport, 28 May 1943; PRO, ADM 199/2101, f. 329.

76. PRO, ADM 199/587, f. 21; PRO, ADM 199/2101, f. 29, 247; PRO, ADM 199/583; ff. 450–55.

77. Sir Peter Gretton, *Convoy Escort Commander* (London, 1964), 152, 209.

78. PRO, ADM 199/2020, 1; PRO, ADM 199/1336, f. 10.

79. PRO, ADM 199/580, f. 183; PRO, ADM 199/1336, f. 15.

80. PRO, ADM 199/1336, f. 10; PRO, ADM 237/203, Remarks on Aircraft Co-operation.

81. BdU War Diary, 17 May 1943; Minister of Defense (Navy), *U-Boat War* 2:88–89.

82. NA, SRGN 18355, 18363, 18365; PRO, ADM 199/1336, f. 10; PRO, ADM 237/203, HMS *Vidette*, Report of Proceedings during passage of Convoy SC 130; PRO, DEFE 3/718, intercepted 0040/19/5/43 decoded 1925/19/5/43.

83. PRO, ADM 237/203, Remarks by Commodore (D), Western Approaches, Convoy SC 130.

84. PRO, ADM 223/15, f. 98.

85. PRO, ADM 199/1336, f. 46.

86. PRO, ADM 199/1336, f. 10; BdU War Diary, 18 May 1943; NA, SRGN 18563; PRO, DEFE 3/718, intercepted 0040/19/5/43 decoded 1925/19/5/43.

87. PRO, ADM 199/1336, f. 11; PRO, ADM 237/203, Log of Shadowing and Attacks; PRO, AIR 27/911, 19 May 1943; PRO, DEFE 3/718, intercepted 0917/19/5/43 decoded 1612/20/5/43.

88. PRO, ADM 199/1336, f. 11; PRO, AIR 27/911, 19 May 1943.

89. PRO, AIR 27/911, 19 May 1943; PRO, ADM 237/203, HMS *Vidette*, Report of Proceedings during passage of Convoy SC 130; PRO, ADM 199/1336, f. 11; PRO, ADM 237/203, Log of Shadowing and Attacks.

90. PRO, ADM 199/1336, f. 11; PRO, ADM 237/203, HMS *Sunflower*, Narrative from 14 May with SC 130; PRO, AIR 27/911, 19 May 1943; PRO, ADM 237/203, Remarks on Aircraft Cooperation.

91. PRO, ADM 199/1336, f. 11; PRO, ADM 199/2020, 2; Gretton, *Convoy Escort Commander*, 155–56.

92. PRO, ADM 199/1336, f. 11.

93. Rohwer, *Axis Submarine Successes*, 167.

94. PRO, DEFE 3/718, intercepted 1129/19/5/43 decoded 2045/20/5/43; ibid.,

intercepted 1234/19/5/43 decoded 2109/19/5/43; ibid., intercepted 0836/19/5/43 decoded 0111/20/5/43.

95. PRO, ADM 199/1336, f. 11.
96. PRO, AIR 27/911, 19 May 1943.
97. PRO, ADM 199/1336, ff. 46–47.
98. PRO, ADM 199/1336, ff. 45, 47, 50–56.
99. PRO, ADM 199/1336, ff. 47, 50.
100. PRO, ADM 237/203, Report of U-boat transmissions received by HMS *Tay* . . . between 14th 1943; PRO, ADM 199/1336, f. 12; PRO, AIR 27/911, 19 May 1943.
101. PRO, ADM 199/1336, f. 12; PRO, DEFE 3/718, intercepted 2033/10/5/43 decoded 1951/20/5/43.
102. PRO, ADM 199/1336, f. 12; PRO, AIR 27/911, 19 May 1943.
103. PRO, DEFE 3/718, intercepted 1637/19/5/43 decoded 1717/20/5/43; ibid., intercepted 0223/10/5/43 decoded 1851/20/5/43; ibid., intercepted 2018/19/5/43 decoded 1957/20/5/43; ibid., intercepted 1637/19/5/43 decoded 1824/20/5/43; ibid., intercepted 1449/19/5/43 decoded 1850/20/5/43; ibid., intercepted 1746/19/5/43 decoded 1419/22/5/43.
104. Ibid., intercepted 2300/19/5/43 decoded 1834/20/5/43; PRO, ADM 237/203, HMS *Sunflower*, Narrative from 14 May with SC 130; PRO, ADM 199/1336, f. 12; PRO, ADM 237/203, Signals In, 10374/19/5/43; ibid., Signals Continued.
105. PRO, AIR 27/911, 20 May 1943.
106. PRO, ADM 199/1336, f. 12.
107. PRO, AIR 27/911, 20 May 1943; PRO, ADM 199/1336, f. 12; PRO, AIR 27/911, 20 May 1943.
108. PRO, DEFE 3/718, intercepted 0337/20/5/43 decoded 1916/20/5/43; ibid., intercepted 0930/20/5/43 decoded 1945/20/5/43; ibid., intercepted 1945/20/5/43 decoded 1330/22/5/43; ibid., intercepted 2314/20/5/43 decoded 1030/22/5/43.
109. PRO, ADM 199/1336, f. 13; PRO, DEFE 3/718, intercepted 1942/20/5/43 decoded 0905/22/5/43.
110. Gretton, *Convoy Escort Commander*, 157.
111. BdU War Diary, 20 May 1943.
112. PRO, ADM 199/2101, f. 30; PRO, ADM 237/4, M. J. Evans to [Commander in Chief, Western Approaches], 29 May 1943.
113. BdU War Diary, 19 May 1943.
114. NA, SRGN 18514; PRO, ADM 237/4, Convoy HS 239: Positions at 0800 May, BST.
115. BdU War Diary, 21 May 1943.
116. NA, SRGN 18659, 18625, 18678, 18695, 18746.
117. NA, SRGN 18625, 18746.
118. NA, SRMN-054, Op-20-GI Special Studies Relating to U-boat Activities, 1943–1945, 143–47.

119. PRO, ADM 199/2101, f. 247; PRO, ADM 237/100, Positions for Convoy ON 184 at 0800 BST
120. NHC, Report of Proceedings, USS *Bogue* Escorting Convoy ON 184.
121. NHC, Report of Proceedings, USS *Bogue* Escorting Convoy ON 184; LTCR Drane, USN, Attack on 21 May 1943.
122. PRO, ADM 199/577, f. 151.
123. PRO, ADM 237/4, M. J. Evans to [Commander in Chief, Western Approaches], 29 May 1943; PRO, ADM 199/577, ff. 151–52.
124. PRO, DEFE 3/719, intercepted 1324/22/5/43 decoded 2218/23/5/43.
125. PRO, DEFE 3/719, intercepted 1126/22/5/43 decoded 2054/23/5/43; NA, SRGN 18744; PRO, DEFE 3/719, intercepted 1726/22/5/43 decoded 2152/23/5/43; ibid., intercepted 1923/22/5/43 decoded 2119/23/5/43.
126. NHC, Report of Proceedings, USS *Bogue* Escorting Convoy ON 184; ibid., Chronicle of Flight Operations, USS *Bogue* 15 May–26 May 1943; ibid., Lt(jg) R. C. Kuhn, USNR, Attack on 22 May 1943; ibid., Ensign S. E. Doty, USNR, Attack on 22 May 1943; ibid., Lt(jg) R. L. Stearns, USNR, Attack on 22 May 1943. Lt. W. F. Chamberlain, USNR, Attack on May 22, 1943; ibid., Lt. H. S. Roberts, USNR, Attack on May 22, 1943; PRO, ADM 237/100, Commanding Officer, HMCS *St. Laurent:* Report of Proceeding, ON 184, 27 May 1943.
127. PRO, ADM 237/100, Senior Officer C1 Group in HMS *Itchen* to Captain (D), Newfoundland, 1 June 1943; NHC, Report of Proceedings, USS *Bogue* Escorting Convoy ON 184; ibid., Chronicle of Flight Operations, USS *Bogue* 15 May–26 May 1943.
128. BdU War Diary, 22 May 1943.
129. PRO, ADM 199/577, f. 152; PRO, ADM 237/4, M. J. Evans to [Commander in Chief, Western Approaches], 29 May 1943; PRO, AIR 27/708, 23 May 1943.
130. PRO, ADM 199/577, f. 153-154; NA, SRGN 18825, 18837.
131. PRO, ADM 237/4, M. J. Evans to [Commander in Chief, Western Approaches], 29 May 1943; NA, SRGN 18793.
132. E.g., NA, SRGN 18734, 18751, 18763, 18777, 18780, 18784, 18790, 18795.
133. BdU War Diary, 23 May 1943.
134. PRO, ADM 237/4, M. J. Evans to [Commander in Chief, Western Approaches], 29 May 1943.
135. BdU War Diary, 24 May 1943.
136. BdU War Diary. This document can be found after the 31 May 1943 entry.
137. Doenitz, 341.
138. BdU War Diary, 24, 31 May 1943.
139. Cf., Kahn, *Seizing the Enigma*, 278–80.
140. Doenitz, 235–37, 253.
141. BdU War Diary, 24 May 1943.

CHAPTER 5: ESCORT CARRIERS AND U-BOATS

1. Doenitz, 406–07.
2. Ministry of Defense (Navy), *U-Boat War*, vol. 3, 7–9.

3. NA, SRGN 18877.
4. Morison, vol. 10, 110–11.
5. Patrick Beesly, *Very Special Intelligence* (London, 1977), 189–90.
6. NA, SRMN-037, COMINCH File of U-boat Intelligence Summaries, January 1943–May 1945, 066; NA, SRGN 18555.
7. NA, SRMN-054, OP-20-GI Special Studies Relating to U-boat Activities, 1943–1945, 148–49, 150–51, 155–56; NA, SRGN 18952.
8. NA, SRH-009, Battle of the Atlantic: vol. 1, Allied Communication Intelligence, 88.
9. For the British side of this story see, Hinsley vol. 2, 553–55, 635–38.
10. NA, SRH-367, Battle of the Atlantic, A Preliminary Analysis of the Role of Decryption Intelligence in the Operational Phase of the, OEG Report #66 20 August 1951.
11. NA, SRGN 18897, 19053, 19054, 19215, 19223; NA, SRMN-054, OP-20-GI Special Studies Relating to U-boat Activities, 1943–1945, 157–59.
12. NHC, Report of Proceedings CTG 21.12 Operations for the Period 31 May–20 June 1943.
13. NA, SRGN 18877.
14. NHC, Report of Proceedings CTG 21.12 Operations for the Period 31 May–20 June 1943.
15. NA, SRH-08, Battle of the Atlantic, vol. 2, U-boat Operations, 105.
16. NHC, Report of Proceedings CTG 21.12 Operations for the Period 31 May–20 June 1943.
17. NHC, Flight Operations, USS *Bogue*, 4 June 1943.
18. PRO, ADM 199/1408, ff. 75–76.
19. Ibid., ff. 93–94.
20. PRO, ADM 199/1408, ff. 106–08.
21. NHC, Report of Proceedings CTG 21.12 Operations for the Period 31 May–20 June 1943.
22. BdU War Diary, 4 June 1943.
23. NHC, Flight Operations, USS *Bogue*, 5 June 1943.
24. PRO, ADM 199/1408, ff. 123–25.
25. NHC, Report of Proceedings CTG 21.12 Operations for the Period 31 May–20 June 1943.
26. NA, SRMN-054, OP-20-GI Special Studies Relating to U-boat Activity, 1943–1945, 157–59.
27. NA, SRH-08, Battle of the Atlantic: vol. 2, U-boat Operations, 105, E1.
28. BdU War Diary, 5 June 1943.
29. NA, SRGN 19340, 19342, 19363.
30. NHC, Report of Proceedings CTG 21.12 Operations for the Period 31 May–20 June 1943.
31. NHC, Flight Operations, USS *Bogue*, 8 June 1943.
32. NA, SRH-08, Battle of the Atlantic: vol. 2, U-boat Operations, 134.
33. PRO, ADM 199/1408, ff. 134–36.

34. PRO, ADM 199/1408, ff. 141–44.

35. NA, SRGN 19509.

36. NHC, Report of Proceedings CTG 21.12 Operations for the Period 31 May–20 June 1943.

37. BdU War Diary, 8 June 1943.

38. Cf., NA, SRGN 19545.

39. NHC, Report of Proceedings CTG 21.12 Operations for the Period 31 May–20 June 1943.

40. NA, SRH-08, Battle of the Atlantic, vol. 2, U-boat Operations, 136; NA, SRGN, 19510, 19512.

41. NA, SRH-08, Battle of the Atlantic, vol. 2, U-boat Operations, 136; NA, SRGN 19533, 19544, 19555, 19606, 19655, 19571, 19572.

42. NA, SRH-08, Battle of the Atlantic, vol. 2, U-boat Operations, 137.

43. NHC, Flight Operations, USS *Bogue*, 12 June 1943.

44. PRO, ADM 199/1408, ff. 162–64.

45. NA, SRGN 19751, 19768.

46. NA, SRH-08, Battle of the Atlantic: vol. 2, U-boat Operations, 140–43.

47. Ibid.; NA, SRGN 19676.

48. NHC, Report of Proceedings CTG 21.12 Operations for the Period 31 May–20 June 1943.

49. NA, SRGN 19676.

50. Rohwer, *Axis Submarine Successes*, 168.

51. NHC, Task Group 21.11, Operations of (13 June–6 August 1943).

52. NA, SRGN 20073.

53. BdU War Diary, 21 June 1943.

54. Hinsley, vol. 2, 636–39.

55. David Kahn, *Hitler's Spies: German Military Intelligence in World War II* (New York, 1978), 218–19.

56. NA, SRGN 20315.

57. BdU War Diary, 26 June 1943.

58. Ibid.

59. NA, SRGN 20362, 20416, 20417, 20453, 20454.

60. BdU War Diary, 11 July 1943.

61. Ibid.

62. NHC, 10th Fleet Convoy and Routing Files, Box 154, UGS-11.

63. NHC, Task Group 21.11, Operations of (13 June–6 August 1943).

64. Y'Blood, 70.

65. Ministry of Defense (Navy), *U-Boat War*, vol. 3, 16–17.

66. NA, SRGN 21020; NA, SRH-08, Battle of the Atlantic, vol. 2, U-boat Operations, 377.

67. Y'Blood, 72–73.

68. BdU War Diary, 18 July 1943.

69. NA, SRGN 21272.

70. NA, SRGN 20991; PRO, ADM 199/1408, ff. 498–501.

71. Y'Blood, 77.
72. NHC, Task Group 21.11, Operations of (13 June–6 August 1943); NA, SRGN 21020, 21440; NA, SRH-08, Battle of the Atlantic, vol. 2, U-boat Operations, 149–50.
73. NHC, Task Group 21.11, Operations of (13 June–6 August 1943).
74. BdU War Diary, 15 July 1943.
75. NHC, Task Group 21.11, Operations of (13 June–6 August 1943).
76. NA, SRGN 21141.
77. NHC, Task Group 21.11, Operations of (13 June–6 August 1943).
78. BdU War Diary, 15 July 1943.
79. NHC, Task Group 21.11, Operations of (13 June–6 August 1943).
80. NA, SRGN 21665.
81. BdU War Diary, 15 July 1943.
82. NHC, Task Group 2.11, Operations of (13 June–6 August 1943).
83. NHC, Report of Proceedings, CTG 21.13 Operations for the period 12 July–1 August 1943.
84. Ibid.
85. NA, SRGN 20911, 21052.
86. PRO, ADM 199/1408, ff. 192–95.
87. NHC, Report of Proceedings, CTG 21.13 Operations for the period 12 July–1 August 1943.
88. NA, SRGN 21-15; NA, SRGN 21214, 21272, 21426; NA, SRH-08, Battle of the Atlantic, vol. 2, U-boat Operations, 11–14.
89. PRO, ADM 199/1408, ff. 200–2.
90. NHC, Report of Proceedings, CTG 21.13 Operations for the period 12 July–1 August 1943.
91. NA, SRGN 21434, 21435, 21426.
92. NHC, Report of 21.14 Anti-Submarine Operations, 27 July–10 September 1943.
93. NA, SRGN 21640, 21816, 21997 (2204), 22059, 22077, 22100, 22154.
94. NHC, Report of 21.14 Anti-Submarine Operations, 27 July–10 September 1943; Y'Blood, 83.
95. BdU War Diary, 3 August 1943.
96. NA, SRGN 22272, 22280, 22285, 22288.
97. NHC, Report of 21.14 Anti-Submarine Operations, 27 July–10 September 1943.
98. PRO, ADM 199/1408, ff. 288–93.
99. NA, SRGN 22331.
100. NHC, Report of 21.14 Anti-Submarine Operations, 27 July 10–10 September 1943.
101. PRO, ADM 199/1408, ff. 307–17.
102. NA, SRGN 22357.
103. BdU War Diary, 9 August 1943.
104. Ibid., 11 August 1943; ibid., 13 August 1943; ibid., 14 August 1943.

105. NA, SRGN 22523, 22525, 22537, 22540.

106. NHC, Report of 21.14 Anti-Submarine Operations, 27 July–10 September 1943.

107. NA, SRGN 22213, 22277.

108. NHC, Report of 21.14 Anti-Submarine Operations, 27 July–10 September 1943; Y'Blood, 87–88.

109. NHC, Report of 21.14 Anti-Submarine Operations, 27 July–10 September 1943.

110. PRO, ADM 199/1408, ff. 341–98; NHC, Report of 21.14 Anti-Submarine Operations, 27 July–10 September 1943.

111. NHC, Report of 21.14 Anti-Submarine Operations, 27 July–10 September 1943.

112. Morison, vol. 10, 124; NA, SRGN 22409; NA, SRH-08, Battle of the Atlantic, vol. 2, U-boat Operations, op. 155.

113. PRO, ADM 199/1408, ff. 399–407.

114. NHC, Report of 21.14 Anti-Submarine Operations, 27 July–10 September 1943.

115. BdU War Diary, 18 August 1943.

116. NA, SRH-08, Battle of the Atlantic, vol. 2, U-boat Operations, 156.

117. NA, SRGN 22394, 22433; NHC, Report of Operations of Task Group 21.15 from 6 August–22 September 1943.

118. NHC, Report of Operations of Task Group 21.15 from 6 August–22 September 1943; NHC, USS Croatan (CVE-25): From Pre-Commissioning to 25 April 1945, 7.

119. NA, SRGN 22537; Morison, vol. 10, 125.

120. NHC, Report of Operations of Task Group 21.15 from 6 August–22 September 1943; USS Croatan (CVE-25): From Pre-Commissioning to 25 April 1945, 8–9.

121. NHC, 10th Fleet Convoy and Routing Files, Box 155, UGS-15; Y'Blood, 92.

122. NA, SRGN 22518, 22523, 22603, 22623, 22632, 22680.

123. PRO, ADM 199/1408, ff. 517–22.

124. Y'Blood, 94–96.

125. NHC, Report of 21.14 Anti-Submarine Operations, 27 July–10 September 1943. 126. Y'Blood, 98–99; NHC, Report of 21.14 Anti-Submarine Operations, 27 July–10 September 1943.

127. NHC, Report of 21.14 Anti-Submarine Operations, 27 July–10 September 1943; NHC, Report of Operations of Task Group 21.15 from 6 August–22 September 1943.

128. Cf. BdU War Diary, 22 August 1943

CHAPTER 6: MORE BATTLES ALONG THE NORTH AMERICAN-UNITED KINGDOM CONVOY ROUTE

1. Cf., PRO, ADM 223/16, f. 21; Roskill, vol. 2, 377.

2. Doenitz, 416–18.

3. Hinsley, vol. 2 (1981), 548–51, 554–55, 635–39.

4. Ministry of Defense (Navy), *U-Boat War*, vol. 3, 27–28.

5. PRO, ADM 199/2060, f. 301.

6. Douglas, *Creation*, 550–51.

7. Ministry of Defense (Navy), *U-Boat War*, vol. 3, 23–24

8. Ibid., vol. 3, 24; BdU War Diary, 6, 13, 15, 16 September 1943.

9. Jurgen Rohwer and W. A. B. Douglas, "Canada and the Wolf Packs, September 1943," *The RCN in Transition, 1910–1985*, ed. W. A. B. Douglas (Vancouver, 1988), 163.

10. PRO, ADM 223/20, f. 132; PRO, DEFE 3/724, intercepted 1727/15/9/43.

11. BdU War Diary, 15 September 1943.

12. PRO, ADM, 223/184, Rodger Winn to C. in CWA, 18 September 1943.

13. PRO, DEFE, 3/722, intercepted 0842/19/9/43 decoded 0010/21//9/43.

14. BdU War Diary, 19 September 1943.

15. PRO, ADM 199/2022, Analysis of U-boat operations in the vicinity of Convoys ONS 18 and ON 202 19–24 September 1943.

16. PRO, ADM 199/353, ff. 531–32.

17. Pro, ADM 199/2022, Analysis of U-boat operations in the vicinity of Convoys ONS 18 and ON 202 19–24 September 1943.

18. Ministry of Defense (Navy), *U-Boat War*, vol. 3, 25.

19. Douglas, *Creation*, 562.

20. PRO, ADM 199/353, f. 570; PRO, DEFE 3/724, intercepted 0406/20/9/43 decoded 1318/25/9/43, intercepted 0846/20/9/43 decoded 1129/25/9/43; ibid., intercepted 0805/20/9/43 decoded 1419/25/9/43.

21. PRO, ADM 199/353, ff. 570–72; PRO, DEFE 3/722, intercepted 1544/20/9/43 decoded 1500/25/9/43.

22. Rohwer, *Axis Submarine Successes*, 171.

23. PRO, ADM 199/353, ff. 551–52.

24. PRO, AIR 27/911, 20 September 1943; PRO, ADM 199/2022, Analysis of U-boat in the vicinity of Convoys ONS 18 and ON 202 19–24 September 1943.

25. PRO, ADM 199/353, ff. 531–32; PRO, DEFE 3/722, intercepted 1708/20/9/43 decoded 1317/25/9/43, intercepted 1713/20/9/43 decoded 1436/25/9/43.

26. PRO, DEFE 3/722, intercepted 1632/20/9/43 decoded 1437/25/9/43; PRO, ADM 199/353, f. 555, 556; PRO, AIR 27/911, 20 September 1943.

27. PRO, ADM 199/353, ff. 507–08.

28. PRO, ADM 199/2022, Analysis of U-boat operations in the vicinity of Convoys ONS 18 and ON 202 19–24 September 1943.

29. PRO, ADM 199/353, f. 508; PRO, ADM 199/2022, Analysis of U-boat operations in the vicinity of Convoys ONS 18 and ON 202 19–24 September 1943.

30. It is extremely difficult, if not impossible, to reconstruct just what happened in this action because there are no after action reports from HMCS *St. Croix*, HMS *Polyanthus*, and HMS *Itchen*: only three members of the crews of these

ships survived the battle for convoys ONS 18 and ON 202. PRO, ADM 199/
2022, Analysis of U-boat approaches in the vicinity of Convoys ONS 18 and
ON 202 19–24 September 1943; PRO, DEFE 3/722, intercepted 040/21/9/4s
decoded 1846/25/9/43, intercepted 0436/21/9/43 decoded 1505/25/9/43;
Joseph Schull, *Far Distant Ships: An Official Account of Canadian Naval
Operations* (Toronto, 1987), 179; Rohwer and Douglas, "Canada and the Wolf
Packs," 173–74.

31. BdU War Diary, 20 September 1943

32. PRO, DEFE 3/722, intercepted 2121/20/9/43 decoded 1503/25/9/43; ibid.,
    intercepted 0836/21/9/43 decoded 1505/25/9/43; ibid., intercepted 1254/21/9/
    43 decoded 1756/24/9/43.

33. PRO, ADM 199/353, ff. 508–09, 588.

34. PRO, DEFE 3/722, intercepted 1417/24/43 decoded 1741/24/9/43,
    intercepted 1718/21/9/43 decoded 1617/24/9/43, intercepted 1512/21/9/43
    decoded 193/24/9/43, intercepted 1527/21/9/43 decoded 1937/9/43.

35. PRO, ADM 199/353, f. 509.

36. PRO, DEFE 3/722, intercepted 1305/22/9/43 decoded 2155/24/9/43; PRO,
    ADM 199/353, f. 509–10.

37. PRO, ADM 199/353, f. 510.

38. Ibid.; PRO, DEFE 3/722, intercepted 0829/22/9/43 decoded 1613/24/9/43.

39. PRO, ADM 199/353, f. 510.

40. Ibid., ff. 510–11.

41. PRO, ADM 199/353, f. 511, 589–90; PRO, DEFE 3/722, intercepted 2044/
    22/9/43 decoded 2233/24/9/43, intercepted 2212/22/9/43 decoded 2100/24/9/
    43.

42. Douglas, *Creation*, 565–65.

43. PRO, DEFE 3/722, intercepted 1918/22/9/43 decoded 2052/24/9/43; ibid.,
    intercepted 2259/22/9/43 decoded 2337/24/9/43.

44. PRO, ADM 199/353, f. 512.

45. PRO, ADM 199/2022, Analysis of U-boat operations in the Vicinity of
    Convoys ONS 18 and ON 202 19–24 September 1943.

46. PRO, ADM 199/353, f. 512, 533.

47. PRO, ADM 199/2022, Analysis of U-boat operations in the Vicinity of
    Convoys ONS 18 and ON 202 19–24 September 1943.

48. PRO, ADM 199/353, ff. 513, 533; Rohwer, *Axis Submarine Successes*, 172.

49. PRO, ADM 199/2022, Analysis of U-boat operations in the Vicinity of
    Convoys ONS 18 and ON 202 19–24 September 1943.

50. Douglas, *Creation*, 565.

51. PRO, ADM 199/353, f. 514–15.

52. BdU War Diary, 22–23 September 1943; PRO, DEFE 3/722, intercepted
    0830/23/9/43 decoded 2038/24/9/43; ibid., intercepted 1356/23/9/43 decoded
    0344/26/43.

53. BdU War Diary, 22–23 September 1943.

54. PRO, ADM 199/353, f. 516.

55. PRO, ADM 199/2022, Analysis of U-boat operations in the Vicinity of Convoys ONS 18 and ON 202 19–24 September 1943.
56. Roskill, vol. 3, part 1, 38–39, the U-341.
57. NA, SRGN 2358.
58. Ministry of Defense (Navy), *U-Boat War*, vol. 3, 25–27.
59. E.g., NA SRGN 23577, 23578.
60. Hinsley, vol. 3, part 1, 223.
61. Montgomery C. Meigs, *Slide Rules and Submarines* (Washington, D.C., 1989), 106, 123, 130–31.
62. PRO, DEFE 3/722, intercepted 1543/24/43 decoded 0446/26/9/43, intercepted 1559/24/9/43 decoded 0529/26/9/43, intercepted 1806/24/9/43 decoded 0445/26/9/43.
63. Ministry of Defense (Navy), *U-Boat War*, vol. 3, 28.
64. PRO, ADM 199/583, ff. 646–52.
65. OD, War Diary, 29 September 1943.
66. PRO, DEFE 3/722, intercepted 2023/29/9/43 decoded 0731/1/10/43.
67. Ministry of Defense (Navy), *U-Boat War*, vol. 3, 29.
68. PRO, DEFE 3/722, intercepted 1312/29/9/43 decoded 0731/1/10/43; ibid., intercepted 1532/30/9/43 decoded 2120/1/10/43; ibid., intercepted 1532/30/9/43 decoded 2120/1/10/43; ibid., intercepted 0524/1/10/43 decoded 2122/1/10/43.
69. Ibid., intercepted 2112/2/10/43 decoded 1531/5/10/43.
70. Ministry of Defense (Navy), *U-Boat War*, vol. 3, 29
71. OD War Diary, 4 October 1943.
72. PRO, AIR 41/48, 182.
73. NA, SRGN 23953, 23954, 23959; 24040.
74. PRO, DEFE 3/722, intercepted 1232/6/10/43 decoded 1702/7/10/43; ibid., intercepted 1942/6/10/43 decoded 1757/7/10/43.
75. NA, SRGN 24084.
76. PRO, DEFE 3/722, intercepted 1024/6/10/43 decoded 1918/7/10/43.
77. PRO, ADM 237/208, Mercantile Convoy No. SC 143; PRO, ADM 199/1337, f. 16.
78. PRO, ADM 237/208, Commanding Officer HMS *Duckworth* to Senior Officer Group C2, 11 October 1943; ibid., Report of the Proceedings of the 10th Escort Group from 2330 on 28 September to 1500 on 10 October 1943; PRO, ADM 223/18, ff. 60, 64; Hinsley, vol. 3, part 1, 224.
79. PRO, ADM 199/1336, f. 170, 171.
80. NA, SRGN 24194.
81. PRO, DEFE 3/722, intercepted 1613/7/10/43 decoded 0209/9/10/43; ibid., intercepted 1620/7/10/43 decoded 0111/9/10/43; ibid., intercepted 2100/7/10/43 decoded 0208/9/10/43, intercepted 2158/7/10/43 decoded 0200/9/10/43, intercepted 2212/7/10/43 decoded 0224/9/10/43; ibid., intercepted 2145/7/10/43 decoded 0335/9/10/43.
82. PRO, ADM 199/1336, Report of the Proceedings of the 10th Escort Group from 2330 on 28 September to 1500 on 10 October 1943.

83. PRO, DEFE 3/722, intercepted 1254/8/10/43 decoded 0156/8/10/43; PRO, ADM 237/208, Report of the Proceedings of the 10th Escort Group from 2330 on 28 September to 1500 on 10 October 1943.

84. PRO, DEFE 3/722, intercepted 0403/8/10/43 decoded 0231/9/10/43; ibid., intercepted 0425/8/10/43 decoded 0124/9/10/43.

85. PRO, ADM 199/1337, f. 17, 172; PRO, AIR 27/708, 8 October 1943; PRO, ADM 237/208, Commanding Officer HMS *Oribi* to Senior Officer 10th Escort Group, 10 October 1943.

86. PRO, AIR 27/708, 8 October 1943; PRO, AIR 27/911, 8 October 1943; PRO, ADM 237/208, Report of the Proceedings of the 10th Escort Group from 2330 on 28 September to 1500 on 10 October 1943.

87. PRO, ADM 199/1337, f. 18; PRO, ADM 223/4, Summary of BV 222 Operations in the Western Area, 10 November 1943.

88. NA, SRGN 14331.

89. PRO, AIR 41/48, 183; PRO, DEFE 3/722, intercepted 1626/8/10/43 decoded 0606/9/10/43.

90. OD War Diary, 8 October 1943.

91. PRO, ADM 199/1336, f. 172; PRO, AIR 27/1832, 8 October 1943.

92. PRO, ADM 199/1336, f. 173.

93. Ibid., f. 173.

94. BdU War Diary, 8 October 1943.

95. PRO, DEFE 3/722, intercepted 0421/9/10/43 decoded 0645/9/10/43; ibid., intercepted 0449/9/10/43 decoded 0655/9/10/43, intercepted 0632/9/10/43 decoded 0906/9/10/43, intercepted 0713/9/10/43 decoded 1034/9/10/43; ibid., intercepted 0745/9/10/43 decoded 1035/9/10/43.

96. OD War Diary, 9 October 1943; BdU War Diary, 9 October 1943.

97. PRO, ADM 199/1336, ff. 175, 178; PRO, ADM 223/8, Convoy SC 143; PRO, ADM 223/19, f. 60.

98. NA, SRGN 24794, 24880.

99. Ministry of Defense (Navy), *U-Boat War,* vol. 3, 30.

100. PRO, DEFE 3/722, intercepted 2247/13/10/43 decoded 0143/16/10/43.

101. BdU War Diary, 13 October 1943.

102. Ministry of Defense (Navy), *U-Boat War,* vol. 3, 31.

103. PRO, DEFE 3/722, intercepted 1127/14/10/43 decoded 1017/16/43.

104. NA, SRGN 25006.

105. PRO, DEFE 3/722, intercepted 2117/15/10/43 decoded 0932/17/10/43; ibid., intercepted 2221/15/10/43 decoded 0931/17/10/43, intercepted 2326/15/10/43 decoded 0933/17/10/43; ibid., intercepted 2203/14/10/43 decoded 1717/16/10/43; BdU War Diary, 15 October 1943.

106. PRO, ADM 237/106, Narrative of Events (A), Convoy 206; ibid., Commanding Officers HMS *Vanquisher* to Senior Officer B6 Group, 23 October 1943; PRO, DEFE 3/723, intercepted 0310/16/10/43 decoded 1936/17/10/43.

107. PRO, AIR 41/48, 186.

108. Ministry of Defense (Navy), *U-Boat War*, vol. 3, 31
109. PRO, ADM 237/106, HMS *Fame*, Report of Proceedings, Section 1, Narrative of Events; PRO, AIR 27/708, 16 October 1943; PRO, ADM 237/106, Commanding Officer HMS *Pink* to Commodore D, 18 December 1943; PRO, AIR 27/555, 16 October 1943.
110. PRO, AIR 41/48, 187; PRO, AIR 27/555, 16 October 1943; PRO, AIR 27/911, 16 October 1943; PRO, DEFE 3/722, intercepted 1739/16/10/43 decoded 1122/17/10/43.
111. PRO, ADM 199/2024, 3; PRO, AIR 27/555, 17 October 1943; PRO, AIR 27/911, 17 October 1943.
112. PRO, ADM 199/2024, 3; PRO, ADM 237/106, Narrative of Attack on U-boat by HMS *Sunflower*, 17 October 1943.
113. PRO, ADM 199/1706, Convoy ONS 20; PRO, AIR 41/48, 187.
114. PRO, DEFE 3/722, intercepted 1739/16/10/43 decoded 1122/17/10/43; PRO, AIR 27/708, 16 October 1943; PRO, DEFE 3/722, intercepted 2245/16/10/43 decoded 1024/17/10/43.
115. PRO, ADM 237/117, Report of Proceedings, Convoy ONS 20; PRO, DEFE 3/722, intercepted 0400/17/10/43 decoded 0953/17/10/43; PRO, ADM 237/117, Report of an Interview with the Master, Captain A. H. Dean, SS *Essex Lance*, 26 January 1944.
116. PRO, ADM 199/1760, SO Escort Group to C. in C., WA, 17 October 1943; PRO, AIR 41/48, 187.
117. PRO, ADM 237/117, Report of Proceedings, Convoy ONS 20; PRO, ADM 199/204, 3–4; PRO, ADM 237/117, Commanding Officer HMS *Vanquisher* to Senior Officer, EG 4, 27 October 1943.
118. E.g., PRO, DEFE 3/722, intercepted 1120/16/10/43 decoded 0934/17/10/43; intercepted 1739/16/10/43 decoded 1122/17/10/43, intercepted 1916/16/10/43 decoded 1125/17/10/43 and DEFE 3/723, intercepted 1928/16/10/43 decoded 0645/19/10/43; Ministry of Defense (Navy), *U-Boat War*, vol. 3, 31.
119. PRO, ADM 199/1706, Admiralty to COMINCH, 16 October 1943.
120. PRO, DEFE 3/722, intercepted 1252/16/10/43 decoded 0915/17/10/43; ibid., intercepted 1317/16/10/43 decoded 1036/17/10/43, intercepted 0341/17/10/43 decoded 1118/17/10/43; ibid., intercepted 1305/16/10/43 decoded 1124/17/10/43, intercepted 1824/16/10/43 decoded 1025/17/10/43, intercepted 202516/10/43 decoded 0953/17/10/43; ibid., intercepted 0117/17/10/43 decoded 1050/17/10/43; ibid., intercepted 0534/17/10/43 decoded 1040/17/10/43; ibid., intercepted 0515/17/10/43 decoded 0954/17/10/43; ibid., intercepted 0935/17/10/43 decoded 1204/17/10/43.
121. E.g., PRO, DEFE 3/723, intercepted 1109/17/10/43 decoded 1533/17/10/43, intercepted 1247/17/10/43 decoded 1004/18/10/43, intercepted 2147/17/10/43 decoded 1013/18/10/43, intercepted 1506/17/10/43 decoded 1044/18/10/43; ibid., intercepted 1521/17/10/43 decoded 1002/18/10/43; ibid., intercepted 1730/17/10/43 decoded 1030/18/10/43; ibid., intercepted 1818/17/10/43 decoded 1103/18/10/43; ibid., intercepted 0125/18/10/43 decoded 0955/18/10/43.

122. Ministry of Defense (Navy), *U-Boat War*, vol. 3, 32.

123. PRO, DEFE 3/723, intercepted 2313/18/10/43 decoded 1000/24/10/43; ibid., intercepted 1435/18/10/43 decoded 1000/24/10/43.

124. OD War Diary, 17, 18 October 1943.

125. PRO, DEFE 3/723, intercepted 2154/18/10/43 decoded 0017/27/10/43; ibid., intercepted 1755/20/10/43 decoded 0712/27/10/43.

126. PRO, DEFE 3/723, intercepted 1142/20/10/43 decoded 1525/25/10/43; ibid., intercepted 1502/22/10/43 decoded 1226/25/10/43.

127. NA, SRGN 25415.

128. PRO, ADM 199/2024, 4; PRO, ADM 237/106, Narrative of Events Convoy 207; PRO, AIR 27/1388, 23 October 1943.

129. PRO, ADM 237/106, Narrative of Events Convoy 207; ibid., Narrative of Attack on U-boat by HMS *Duncan*; PRO, ADM 199/2024, f. 5.

130. PRO, AIR 41/48, 188.

131. PRO, DEFE 3/723, intercepted 0816/26/10/43 decoded 1158/26/10/43, intercepted 1109/26/10/43 decoded 1340/26/10/43; ibid., intercepted 1215/26/10/43 decoded 0017/28/10/43, intercepted 1610/26/10/43 decoded 0017/28/10/43, intercepted 1653/26/10/43 decoded 0011/28/10/43.

132. OD War Diary, 25–26 October 1943.

133. PRO, DEFE 3/723, intercepted 2135/26/10/43 decoded 2352/27/10/43.

134. PRO, ADM 199/2060, f. 384, 394; PRO, DEFE 3/723, intercepted 1012/28/10/43 decoded 1225/28/10/43; PRO, ADM 237/106, Narrative of Attack on U-boat by HMS *Duncan*; PRO, ADM 199/2024, 7.

135. PRO, DEFE 3/723, intercepted 0802/29/10/43 decoded 1959/30/10/43, intercepted 1000/30/10/43 decoded 1251/30/10/43, intercepted 1012/30/10/43 decoded 1306/30/10/43; PRO, ADM 199/2024, 1–2.

136. PRO, DEFE 3/723, intercepted 1455/30/10/43 decoded 0501/1/11/43.

137. PRO, DEFE 3/723, intercepted 2319/2/11/43 decoded 2112/3/11/43.

138. Ibid., intercepted 2320/5/11/43 decoded 1801/8/11/43; PRO, ADM 199/2024, 3–4.

139. PRO, ADM 199/2024, 4, 5; PRO, DEFE 3/723, intercepted 1401/6/11/43 decoded 1228/8/11/43.

140. PRO, DEFE 3/724, intercepted 0402/9/11/43 decoded 0419/11/11/43; PRO, ADM 199/2024, 5.

141. PRO, DEFE 3/723, intercepted 2125/6/11/43 decoded 1411/8/11/43.

142. Ministry of Defense (Navy), *U-Boat War*, vol. 3, 32–33.

143. Cf., BdU War Diary, 2 November 1943.

144. OD War Diary, 18 October 1943.

145. BdU War Diary, 24 September 1943.

146. PRO ADM 223/18, Amount of Experience of U-boat Commanding Officers now in operations, 1 November 1943.

147. D. E. G. Wemyss, *Walker's Groups in the Northern Approaches* (Liverpool, 1948).

148. Sir Peter Gretton, *Convoy Escort Commander* (London, 1964).

149. BdU War Diary, 5 November 1943. The notion that the Allies were locating

U-boats by means of radiation emitted may have come about through an Allied deceptive stratagem. See R. V. Jones *Reflections on Intelligence* (London, 1990), 141–43.

CHAPTER 7: THE LAST WOLF PACK BATTLES IN THE ATLANTIC: THE GIBRALTAR ROUTES

1. BdU War Diary, 2 October 1943.
2. Ministry of Defense (Navy), *U-Boat War*, vol. 3, 23–24, 32–33, 36.
3. Ibid., 27–28.
4. OD War Diary, 29 September 1943.
5. BdU War Diary, 2 November 1943.
6. NA, SRGN 25559; PRO, DEFE 3/723, intercepted 2238/26/10/43 decoded 2338/27/1043.
7. PRO, ADM 199/2024, 1–2; PRO, ADM 199/585, Convoy MKS 28, Narrative; PRO, ADM 199/966, Report of Proceedings for Convoys SL 138/MKS 28; PRO, AIR 41/48, 189; PRO, DEFE 3/724, intercepted 2158/28/10/43 decoded 1440/29/10/43; PRO, DEFE 3/723, intercepted 1935/29/10/43 decoded 2221/29/10/43.
8. PRO, DEFE 3/723, intercepted 2209/29/10/43 decoded 0103/30/10/43; ibid., intercepted 2243/29/10/43 decoded 0135/30/10/43, intercepted 2347/29/10/43 decoded 0345/30/10/43; ibid., intercepted 0540/30/10/43 decoded 0805/30/10/43.
9. OD War Diary 29 October 1943.
10. PRO, AIR 27/1388, 30 October 1943.
11. OD War Diary, 30 October 1943.
12. PRO, DEFE 3/723, intercepted 1620/30/10/43 decoded 0512/1/11/43.
13. PRO, ADM 199/2024, 1; PRO, ADM 199/966, Report of Proceedings for Convoy SL 138/MKS 28.
14. Roskill, vol. 3, part 1, 368.
15. PRO, DEFE 3/723, intercepted 2049/31/10/43 decoded 0150/1/11/43; PRO, ADM 199/2024, 1–4.
16. PRO, DEFE 3/723, intercepted 0536/31/10/43 decoded 0431/1/11/43; ibid., intercepted 1946/31/10/43 decoded 1317/1/11/43; ibid., intercepted 2024/1/11/43 decoded 1733/3/11/43.
17. NA, SRGN 2579.
18. PRO, DEFE 3/723, intercepted 1924/3/11/43 decoded 0323/7/11/43.
19. OD War Diary, 4–5 October 1943, 2–5 November 1943.
20. PRO, DEFE 3/723, intercepted 1919/5/11/43 decoded 1649/8/11/43.
21. BdU War Diary, 7 October 1943.
22. PRO, DEFE 3/724, intercepted 1542/7/11/43 decoded 0836/11/11/43.
23. Ministry of Defense (Navy), *U-Boat War*, vol. 3, 38.
24. NA, SRGN 26098, 26100.
25. PRO, DEFE 3/724, intercepted 0817/9/11/43 decoded 0430/11/11/43.

26. NA, SRGN 26102.
27. PRO, AIR 27/336, 9 November 1943.
28. PRO, DEFE 3/724, intercepted 2039/9/11/43 decoded 2109/10/11/43, intercepted 0003/10/11/43 decoded 1821/10/11/43; ibid., intercepted 1214/9/11/43, decoded 1810/10/11/43; ibid., intercepted 1907/9/11/43, decoded 1810/10/11/43; ibid., intercepted 1421/11/11/43, decoded 1405/14/11/43.
29. BdU War Diary, 10 November 1943.
30. OD War Diary, 12 November 1943.
31. Ministry of Defense (Navy), *U-Boat War*, vol. 3, 38.
32. PRO, DEFE 3/724, intercepted 1304/11/11/43, decoded 1337/14/11/43.
33. PRO, AIR 41/48, 197; PRO, DEFE 3/724, intercepted 1632/16/11/43, decoded 2150/16/11/43; NA, SRGN 26368.
34. PRO, ADM 199/966, Senior Officer, 40th Escort Group to Captain (D) Greenock, 26 November 1943.
35. Ministry of Defense (Navy), *U-Boat War*, vol. 3, 38.
36. PRO, DEFE 3/724, intercepted 1922/17/11/43, decoded 0732/18/11/43.
37. PRO, DEFE 3/724, intercepted 1923/17/11/45, decoded 0709/18/11/43; ibid., intercepted 2012/17/11/43, decoded 0655/18/11/43; PRO, ADM 199/966, Senior Officer, 40th Escort Group to Captain (D) Greenock, 26 November 1943.
38. PRO, ADM 199/966, Senior Officer, 40th Escort Group to Captain (D) Greenock, 26 November 1943; PRO, AIR 41/48, 199.
39. PRO, ADM 199/966, Attack on Submarine by HMS *Exe;* ibid., Precis of Attack by HMS *Exe.* For an account by the commander of the U-333, see Peter Cremer, *U-Boat Commander: A Periscope View of the Battle of the Atlantic* (Annapolis, 1985), 154–59.
40. PRO, ADM 199/2026, 2; PRO, AIR 41/48, 199; PRO, DEFE 3/724, intercepted 0742/19/11/43 decoded 1132/19/11/43; ibid., intercepted 0742/19/11/43 decoded 1132/19/11/43; PRO, ADM 199/966, Commanding officer HMS *Chanticleer* to C in C Western Approach 11 December 1943.
41. PRO, ADM 237/243, Commanding officer HMS *Crane* to Senior officer 7th Escort Group, 21 November 1943.
42. Ministry of Defense (Navy), *U-Boat War*, vol. 3, 39; PRO, DEFE 3/724, intercepted 2340/18/11/43 decoded 0333/19/11/43.
43. PRO, DEFE 3/724, intercepted 1315/18/1143 decoded 2105/18/11/43; ibid., intercepted 1733/18/11/43 decoded 2135/18/11/43; ibid., intercepted 1941/18/11/43 decoded 2153/18/11/43; ibid., intercepted 2105/18/11/43 decoded 0006/19/11/43; ibid., intercepted 2258/18/11/43 decoded 0125/19/11/43; ibid., intercepted 2025/19/11/43 decoded 1027/20/11/43; PRO, AIR 41/48, f. 199; PRO, AIR 27/1127, 18 November 1943; PRO, ADM 199/2026, 4.
44. PRO, DEFE 3/724, intercepted 1935/19/11/43 decoded 1046/20/11/43; ibid., intercepted 0058/19/11/43 decoded 0425/19/11/43.
45. BdU War Diary, 18 November 1943.
46. PRO, DEFE 3/724, intercepted 1147/18/11/43 decoded 2051/18/11/43; ibid., intercepted 0022/19/11/43 decoded 0400/19/11/43.

47. PRO, ADM 199/2026, 4.
48. NA, SRGN 26488.
49. PRO, ADM 199/966, Commanding officer HMCS *Calgary* to commanding officer HMS *Nene*, 23 November 1943; PRO, ADM 199/2026, 4.
50. PRO, ADM 199/2026, 4–5; PRO, AIR 27/366, 19 November 1943; PRO, ADM 199/966, Senior officer, 40th Escort Group to Captain (D) Greenock, 19 November 1943.
51. PRO, ADM 199/966, Precis of attack by HMS *Milford*, 10 January 1944; PRO, AIR 41/48, 200; PRO, DEFE 3/724, intercepted 2137/19/11/43 decoded 1148/20/11/43; ibid., intercepted 0237/20/11/43 decoded 1227/20/11/43.
52. PRO, ADM 199/966, Senior officer 5th Escort Group, Report of Proceedings, 25 November 1943; ibid., Commanding officer HMCS *Snowberry* to Commanding officer HMS *Nene*, 24 November 1943.
53. PRO, ADM 199/966, Senior officer, 40th Escort Group to Captain (D) Greenock, 26 November 1943; ibid., HMCS *Edmundston*, Narrative of attack on U-boat on the night of 19–20 November 1943.
54. PRO, ADM 199/966, Senior officer, 40th Escort Group to Captain (D) Greenock, 26 November 1943; PRO, ADM 199/2026, 7.
55. PRO, DEFE, 724, intercepted 1247/19/11/43 decoded 1400/20/11/43, intercepted 1530/19/11/43 decoded 1022/20/11/43, intercepted 1848/19/11/43 decoded 1044/20/11/43.
56. NA, SRGN 26512.
57. Ministry of Defense (Navy), *U-Boat War*, vol. 3, 39.
58. NA, SRGN 26531.
59. PRO, DEFE 3/724, intercepted 2100/19/11/43 decoded 1145/19/11/43; ibid., intercepted 2115/19/11/43 decoded 1447/20/11/43; ibid., intercepted 2128/19/11/43 decoded 1140/20/11/43, intercepted 0237/20/11/43 decoded 1227/20/11/43; ibid., intercepted 1229/20/11/43 decoded 1609/20/11/43.
60. PRO, DEFE 3/724, intercepted 0501/20/11/43 decoded 1120/20/11/43.
61. BdU War Diary, 19 November 1943.
62. PRO, DEFE 3/724, intercepted 0356/20/11/43 decoded 1040/20/11/43; ibid., intercepted 1941/20/11/43 decoded 0140/21/11/43; Ministry of Defense (Navy), *U-Boat War*, vol. 3, 39.
63. PRO, AIR 41/48, 200; PRO, AIR 27/708, 20 November 1943; PRO, ADM 199/2026, 7; PRO, DEFE 3/724, intercepted 1915/20/11/43 decoded 1517/21/11/43.
64. PRO, ADM 199/966, Senior officer, 5th Escort Group, Report of Proceedings, 25 November 1943.
65. PRO, ADM 199/2026, 7; PRO, ADM 199/966, Report of Proceedings for the 7th Escort Group between 8–26 November 1943.
66. PRO, ADM 199/2026, 7–8; PRO, ADM 199/966, Report of Proceedings for the 7th Escort Group between 8–26 November 1943; ibid., Senior Officer, 40th Escort Group to Captain (D) Greenock, 26 November 1943; ibid.,

Senior Officer, 5th Escort Group, Report of Proceedings, 25 November 1943.

67. PRO, AIR 41/48, 200; PRO, AIR 27/505, 21–22 November 1943; PRO, ADM 199/966, Senior Officer, 5th Escort Group, Report of Proceedings, 25 November 1943.

68. PRO, ADM 199/2026, 9.

69. PRO, AIR 27/505, 21 November 1943; PRO, ADM 199/2026, 9.

70. E.g., PRO, DEFE 3/724, intercepted 2041/20/11/43 decoded 0212/21/11/43, intercepted 0008/21/11/43 decoded 0317/21/11/43, intercepted 0112/21/11/43 decoded 0512/21/11/43, intercepted 0314/21/11/43 decoded 0526/21/11/43; e.g., ibid., intercepted 0044/21/11/43 decoded 0345/21/11/43, intercepted 0421/21/11/43 decoded 0533/21/11/43; e.g., ibid., intercepted 2134/20/11/43 decoded 0117/21/11/43, intercepted 2355/20/11/43 decoded 0315/21/11/43, intercepted 0134/21/11/43 decoded 0517/21/11/43; ibid., intercepted 2257/20/11/43 decoded 0510/21/11/43; ibid., intercepted 0543/21/11/43 decoded 0845/21/11/43.

71. PRO, DEFE 3/724, intercepted 1129/21/11/43 decoded 0704/22/11/43.

72. BdU War Diary, 21 November 1943.

73. PRO, ADM 237/242, An Analysis of the Operations of the Fourth Escort Group, 20 November–2 December 1943.

74. OD War Diary, 21 November 1943.

75. Cf., Fraser M. McKee, "Princes Three: Canada's Use of Armed Merchant Cruisers during World War II," *RCN in Retrospect, 1910–1968,* James A. Boutilier, ed. (Vancouver, 1982), 116–31.

76. PRO, ADM 199/2026, 10; PRO, ADM 199/1316, Convoy SL 139 & MKS 30 Report on A/C Attack; PRO, ADM 237/9, Report of an interview with Captain T. H. Buckle S SS *Marsa;* ibid., Report of an Interview with the Chief Officer Gordon Marshall MV *Delius;* PRO, ADM 237/242, Analysis of the Operations of the 4th Escort Group, 20 November–2 December 1943.

77. Ministry of Defense (Navy), *U-Boat War,* vol. 3, 39.

78. PRO, DEFE 3/724, intercepted 1644/22/11/43 decoded 0013/23/11/43; SRGN 26708.

79. NA, SRGN 26749.

80. Ministry of Defense (Navy), *U-Boat War,* vol. 3, 40.

81. PRO, DEFE 3/724, intercepted 1935/23/11/43 decoded 0851/24/11/43.

82. Ibid., intercepted 2216/22/1143 decoded 0543/24/11/43, intercepted 2007/23/11/43 decoded 0853/24/11/43; PRO, ADM 237/242, Analysis of the Operations of the 4th Escort Group, 20 November–2 December 1943.

83. PRO, DEFE 3/724, intercepted 2036/24/11/43 decoded 1154/25/11/43.

84. Ibid., intercepted 0240/25/11/43 decoded 0601/25/11/43, intercepted 0306/25/11/43 decoded 0608/25/11/43; ibid., intercepted 015/26/11/43 decoded 0426/26/11/43, intercepted 0522/26/11/43 decoded 0730/26/11/43; PRO, ADM 237/242, Analysis of the Operations of the 4th Escort Group, 20 November–2 December 1943.

85. PRO, DEFE 3/724, intercepted 1859/26/11/43 decoded 0608/27/11/43; ibid., intercepted 1859/26/11/43 decoded 0600/27/11/43.
86. PRO, ADM 199/2026, Analysis of Anti-U-Boat Operations in the vicinity of Convoy SL 140/MKS 31, 27–28 November 1943.
87. PRO, DEFE 3/724, intercepted 0855/27/11/43 decoded 1145/27/11/43; ibid., intercepted 1515/27/11/43 decoded 1031/28/11/43.
88. Ministry of Defense (Navy), *U-Boat War*, vol. 3, 40.
89. PRO, DEFE 3/724, intercepted 1810/27/11/43 decoded 1048/28/11/43, intercepted 1824/27/11/43 decoded 1115/28/11/43; ibid., intercepted 2019/27/11/43 decoded 1045/28/11/43; ibid., intercepted 2046/27/11/43 decoded 1112/28/11/43; ibid., intercepted 2120/27/11/43 decoded 1110/28/11/43.
90. PRO, ADM 199/2026, Analysis of Anti-U-Boat Operations in the vicinity of Convoy SL 140/MKS 31, 27–28 November 1943; PRO, ADM 199/966, HMS *Wild Goose*, The Report of Proceedings during the night of 27–28 November 1943; ibid., Report of Proceedings 2nd Support Group, 22 November–5 December 1943.
91. PRO, AIR 27/1127, 27 November 1943; PRO, ADM 199/2026, An Analysis of the Operation of the 4th Escort Group, 20 November–2 December 1943; PRO, ADM 199/2026, Analysis of Anti-U-Boat Operations in the vicinity of Convoy SL/MKS 31, 27–28 November 1943.
92. PRO, ADM 199/2026, An Analysis of the Operations of the 4th Escort Group. 20 November–2 December 1943.
93. PRO, ADM 237/10, Commander HMS *Hurricane*, 5 December 1943.
94. PRO, ADM 199/966, Report of Proceedings 2nd Support Group 22 November–5 December 1943.
95. NA, SRGN 26983.
96. PRO, ADM 199/966, Report of Proceedings 2nd Support Group 22 November–5 December 1943; PRO, ADM 199/2026, An Analysis of Anti-U-Boat operations in the vicinity of Convoy SL 140/MKS 31, 27–28 November 1943.
97. PRO, DEFE 3/724, intercepted 2330/27/11/43 decoded 1102/28/11/43; ibid., intercepted 0129/28/11/43 decoded 1100/28/11/43; ibid., intercepted 0221/28/11/43 decoded 1225/28/11/43.
98. PRO, DEFE 3/724, intercepted 0110/28/11/43 decoded 1000/28/11/43, intercepted 0353/28/11/43 decoded 1035/28/11/43, intercepted 0645/28/11/43 decoded 1152/28/11/43; NA, SRGN 26924–26928, 26930, 26933, 26935, 26939.
99. PRO, DEFE 3/724, intercepted 0730/28/11/43 decoded 1104/28/11/43, intercepted 1719/28/11/43 decoded 1137/29/11/43.
100. BdU War Diary, 28 November 1943.
101. PRO, ADM 199/2026, Analysis of Anti-U-Boat Operations in the Vicinity of Convoy SL 140/MKS 31 27–28 November 1943.
102. Y'Blood, 120.
103. PRO, DEFE 3/724, intercepted 2344/30/11/43 decoded 0736/1/12/43; ibid., intercepted 0129/1/12/43 decoded 0744/1/12/43.

104. NA, SRGN 17103.
105. PRO, DEFE 3/724, intercepted 2158/29/11/43 decoded 1135/1/12/43; BdU War Diary, 30 November 1943.
106. PRO, DEFE 3/724, intercepted 1850/30/11/43 decoded 27103.
107. BdU War Diary, 2 December 1943.
108. PRO, DEFE 3/724, intercepted 1720/4/12/43 decoded 2154/4/12/43, intercepted 1432/6/12/43 decoded 0425/7/12/43, intercepted 2059/6/12/43 decoded 0505/7/12/43.
109. BdU War Diary, 7 December 1943.
110. For the strategy of convoys, see Admiralty Historical Section, *Defeat of the Enemy* and Roland Alfred Bowling, "The Negative Influence of Mahan on the Protection of Shipping in War Time: The Convoy Controversy in the Twentieth Century," Ph.D. diss., University of Maine, 1980.
111. Cf., OD War Diary, 12 November 1943.
112. Cf., PRO, ADM 223/18, Amount of Experience of U-Boat Commanding Officers now in operations, 1 November 1943.
113. Ministry of Defense (Navy), *U-Boat War*, vol. 3, 41.

Bibliography

MANUSCRIPTS

Befehlshaber der Unterseeboote (BdU) War Diary of the German U-Boat Command, 1939–1945. Microfilm edition of the English translation of this source; original at the Naval Historical Center, Washington, D.C.

Operations Division, German Naval Staff (OD) War Diary. Microfilm edition of the English translation of this source; original at the Naval Historical Center, Washington, D.C.

Directorate of History, National Defense Headquarters, Ottawa

Eastern Air Command, Operational Instructions, B.R. Operations.

National Archives, Washington, D.C. (Record Group 457)

SRGN 1-494668, German Navy/U-Boat Message Translations and Summaries, 1941–1942.

SRH-08, Battle of the Atlantic, vol. 2, U-Boat Operations.

SRH-09, Battle of the Atlantic, vol. 1, Allied Communication Intelligence. December 1941–May 1945.

SRH-25, Battle of the Atlantic, vol. 4, Technical Intelligence from Allied C.I.

SRH-208, US Navy Sub Warfare MSG Reports COMINCH, 3 June 1942–45.

SRH-236, Submarine Message Reports Admiralty COMINCH.

SRH-367, Battle of the Atlantic, A Preliminary Analysis of the Role of Decryption Intelligence in the Operational Phase, OEG Report #66, 20 August 1951.

SRMN-030, COMINCH, File of Biweekly Messages on U-Boat Trends, 1 September 1942–1 May 1945.

SRMN-034, COMINCH, Rough Notes on Daily U-Boat Positions and Activities, 1943–1945.

SRMN-035, Admiralty, COMINCH Ultra Message Exchange, 25 June 1942–17 October 1944.

SRMN-036, COMINCH, File of U-Boat Situation Estimates, 15 June 1942–21 May 1945.

SRMN-037, COMINCH, File of U-Boat Intelligence Summaries, January 1943– May 1945.

SRMN-038, Functions of the 'Secret Room' F211 of COMINCH Combat Intelligence, Atlantic Section Anti-Submarine Warfare, WW II.

SRMN-048, Reports on U-Boat Disposition and Status, December 1942–2 May 1945.

SRMN-054, OP20GI, Special Studies Relating to U-Boat Activity, 1943–1945.

National Maritime Museum, London

The Waters Papers.

Naval Historical Center (NHC), Washington, D.C.

Action Report: Commander Task Unit 24.1.3, 21 April 1943.

USS *Bogue*, Escort of Convoy HX 235. Report of Air Coverage and ASW Patrol from Convoy from Argentina to British Isles, 24–30 April 1943.

Report of Proceedings—USS *Bogue* Escorting Convoy ON 184 including Chronicle of Flight Operations USS *Bogue* 15 May to 26 May 1943; LTCR Drane, USN—Attack on 21 May 1943; Lt. (jg) R. C. Kuhn, USNR—Attack on 22 May 1943; Ensign S. E. Doty, USNR—Attack on 22 May 1943; Lt. (jg) R. L. Stearns, USNR—Attack on 22 May 1943; Lt. W. F. Chamberlain, USNR—Attack on 22 May 1943; Lt. H. S. Roberts, USNR—Attack on 22 May 1943.

Task Group 21.11—Operations of (13 June 1943 to 6 August 1943).

Report of Proceedings—CTG 21.12 Operations for the period 31 May–20 June 1943; Flight Operations—USS *Bogue*, 4, 5, 8, 12 June 1943.

Report of Proceedings—CTG 21.13 Operations for the period 12 July–1 August 1943.

Report of 21.14 Anti-Submarine Operations 27 July to 10 September 1943.

Report of Operations Task Group 21.15 from 6 August to 22 September 1943.

S.S.S. *Coratan* (CVE-25): From Pre-Commissioning to 25 April 1945.

10th Fleet convoy and routing files, boxes 154, 155.

Public Record Office (PRO), London

ADM 1/12663. General subject files.

ADM 199/208, 353, 575, 576, 577, 578, 579, 580, 583, 585, 587, 966. Convoy files and after action reports.

ADM 199/1408. Reports of attacks on U-boats by US carrier aircraft.

ADM 199/1316, 1336, 2020, 2022, 2024, 2026, 2060, 2101, 2102. Convoy papers.

ADM 219/35. Naval operational studies files.

ADM 223/4, 8, 15, 16, 17, 18, 19, 20, 88, 99, 113, 184. Intelligence appreciations and situation reports.

ADM 237/4, 9, 98, 100, 106, 110, 111, 112, 113, 114, 115, 117, 202, 203, 208, 242, 243. Convoy after action reports.

AIR 27/336, 505, 555, 708, 911, 1125, 1127, 1388, 1832. Squadron logs.

AIR 41/418. Staff history.

DEFE 3/715, 716, 717, 718, 719, 720, 721, 722, 723. Intercepted German radio messages.

PREM 3/414/2. Prime Minister's papers.

SECONDARY WORKS

Admiralty Historical Section. *The Defeat of the Enemy Attack on Shipping, 1939–1945.* London: Admiralty, 1957.

Alden, John D. *Flush Decks & Four Pipes.* Annapolis, Md.: US Naval Institute Press, 1990.

Bagnasco, Erminio. *Submarines of World War Two.* Annapolis, Md.: US Naval Institute Press, 1977.

Bayne, R. C. "Merchant Ship Aircraft Carriers." *Journal of the Royal United Service Institution* 92 (Nov. 1947): 548–53.

Beesley, Patrick. *Very Special Intelligence: The Story of the Admiralty's Operational Intelligence Centre, 1939–1945.* London: Hamish Hamilton, 1977.

Behrens, C. B. A. *Merchant Shipping and the Demands of War.* London: Her Majesty's Stationery Office, 1955.

Behrens, Carl E. *Effects on U-Boat Performance of Intelligence from Decryption of Allied Communications.* Washington, D.C.: Department of the Navy, 1954.

Bowling, Roland Alfred. "The Negative Influence of Mahan on the Protection of Shipping in War Time: The Convoy Controversy in the Twentieth Century." Ph.D. diss., University of Maine, 1980.

Churchill, Winston S. *The World Crisis.* London: Thornton Butterworth, 1923–1931.

Cremer, Peter. *U-Boat Commander: A Periscope View of the Battle of the Atlantic.* Annapolis, Md.: US Naval Institute Press, 1985.

Doenitz, Karl. *Die U-bootswaffe.* Berlin: Mittler, 1939.

———. *Memoirs: Ten Years and Twenty Days.* New York: World Publishing Company, 1959.

Douglas, W. A. B. *The Creation of a National Air Force.* Toronto: University of Toronto Press, 1986.

Elliott, Peter. *Allied Escort Ships of World War II.* Annapolis, Md.: US Naval Institute Press, 1977.

Friedman, Norman. *Naval Radar.* Annapolis, Md.: US Naval Institute Press, 1981.

Gretton, Sir Peter. *Convoy Escort Commander.* London: Cassel, 1964.

———. *Crisis Convoy: The Story of HX 231.* Annapolis, Md.: US Naval Institute Press, 1974.

Hackmann, William. *Seek & Strike: Sonar, Anti-submarine Warfare and the Royal Navy, 1914–54*. London: Her Majesty's Stationery Office, 1984.

Hadley, Michael L. *U-Boats Against Canada: German Submarines in Canadian Waters*. Kingston and Montreal: McGill-Queen's University Press, 1985.

Hague, Arnold. *Destroyers for Great Britain*. Annapolis, Md.: US Naval Institute Press, 1990.

Hinsley, F. H., et al. *British Intelligence in the Second World War*. London: Her Majesty's Stationery Office, 1979–1990.

Howard, Michael. *Grand Strategy*. London: Her Majesty's Stationery Office, 1970.

Johnson, Brian. *The Secret War*. London: British Broadcasting Corporation, 1978.

Jones, R. V. *Reflections on Intelligence*. London: Mandarin, 1990.

Kahn, David. *Hitler's Spies: German Military Intelligence in World War II*. New York: Macmillan Publishing Co., Inc., 1978.

———. *Seizing the Enigma: The Race to Break the German U-Boat Codes*. Boston: Houghton Mifflin Company, 1991.

Lund, W. G. D. "The Royal Canadian Navy's Quest for Autonomy in the North West Atlantic: 1941–43." In *The RCN in Retrospect, 1910–1968*, edited by James A. Boutilier. Vancouver: University of British Columbia Press, 1982.

Macintyre, Donald. *U-Boat Killer*. New York: Norton, 1956.

Marder, Arthur J. *From Dreadnought to Scapa Flow: The Royal Navy in the Fisher Era, 1904–1919*. London: Oxford University Press, 1961–1970.

Matloff, Maurice. *Strategic Planning for Coalition Warfare, 1943–1944*. Washington, D.C.: Office of the Chief of Military History, Department of the Army, 1959.

McKee, Fraser M. "Prince Three: Canada's Use of Armed Merchant Cruisers during World War II." In *The RCN Retrospect, 1910–1968*, edited by James A. Boutilier. Vancouver: University of British Columbia Press, 1982.

Meigs, Montgomery C. *Slide Rules and Submarines*. Washington, D.C.: National Defense University Press, 1989.

Milner, Mac. *The North Atlantic Run: The Royal Canadian Navy and the Battle of the Convoys*. Annapolis, Md.: US Naval Institute Press, 1985.

Ministry of Defense (Navy). *The U-Boat War in the Atlantic, 1939–1945*. London: Her Majesty's Stationery Office, 1989.

Morison, Samuel Eliot. *History of United States Naval Operations in World War II*. Boston: Little, Brown and Company, 1975.

Padfield, Peter. *Doenitz: The Last Fuhrer*. London: Victor Gollancz, 1984.

Preston, Anthony. *U-Boats*. London: Excalibur Books, 1973.

Price, Alfred. *Aircraft versus Submarine*. Annapolis, Md.: US Naval Institute Press, 1973.

[RAF, Historical Branch]. *The Rise and Fall of the German Air Force, 1933–1945*. New York: St. Martin's Press, 1983.

Rohwer, Jurgen. *The Critical Convoy Battles of March 1943*. Annapolis, Md.: US Naval Institute Press, 1977.

———. *Axis Submarine Successes, 1939–1945*. Annapolis, Md.: US Naval Institute Press, 1983.

————, and W. A. B. Douglas. "Canada and the Wolf Packs, September 1943." *The RCN in Transition, 1910–1985*, edited by W. A. B. Douglas. Vancouver: University of British Columbia Press, 1988.

Roskill, S. W. *The Secret Capture*. London: Collins, 1959.

————. *War at Sea, 1939–1945*. London: Her Majesty's Stationery Office, 1954–1961.

Ruge, Friedrick. *Der Seekrieg: The German Navy's Story, 1939–1945*. Annapolis, Md.: US Naval Institute Press, 1957.

Schull, Joseph. *Far Distant Ships: An Official Account of Canadian Naval Operations*. Toronto: Stoddart Publishing Co. Limited, 1987.

Showell, J. P. Mallmann. *U-boats Under the Swastika*. New York: Arco Publishing Company, Inc., 1971.

————. *The German Navy in World War II*. Annapolis, Md.: US Naval Institute Press, 1979.

Sleesor, John. *The Central Blue*. New York: Praeger, 1957.

Stern, Robert. *Type VII U-Boats*. Annapolis, Md.: US Naval Institute Press, 1991.

Syrett, David. "The Safe and Timely Arrival of Convoy SC 130, 15–25 May 1943." *American Neptune* 50 (Summer, 1990): 219–27.

————. "The Sinking of HMS *Firedrake* and the Battle for Convoy ON 153." *American Neptune* 51 (Spring, 1991): 105–11.

————, and W. A. B. Douglas. "Die Wende in der Schlacht im Atlantik: Die Schiebung des 'Gronland-Luftlochs,' 1942–1943." *Marine-Rundschau* 83 (1986): 2–11, 70–73, 147–49.

Terzibaschitsch, Stefan. *Escort Carriers and Aviation Support Ships of the US Navy*. Annapolis, Md.: US Naval Institute Press, 1981.

Wark, Wesley K. "The Evolution of Military Intelligence in Canada." *Armed Forces & Society* 16 (Fall, 1989): 77–98.

Wemyss, D. E. G. *Walker's Group in the Western Approaches*. Liverpool: Liverpool Daily Post & Echo, 1948.

Werner, Herbert A. *Iron Coffins*. New York: Holt, Rinehard and Winston, 1969.

Whitley, M. J. *Destroyers of World War Two*. Annapolis, Md.: US Naval Institute Press, 1988.

Y'Blood, William T. *Hunter-Killer: U.S. Escort Carriers in Battle of the Atlantic*. Annapolis, Md.: US Naval Institute Press, 1983.

Index